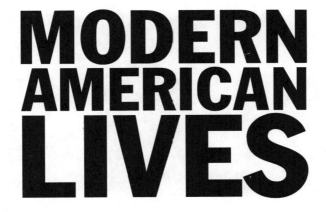

MODERN AMERICAN LIVES

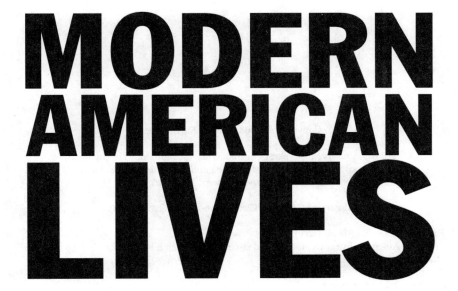

MODERN AMERICAN LIVES

Individuals and Issues in American History Since 1945

Blaine T. Browne and Robert C. Cottrell

M.E.Sharpe
Armonk, New York
London, England

Library of Congress Cataloging-in-Publication Data

Browne, Blaine T. (Blaine Terry)
  Modern American lives : individuals and issues in American history since 1945 /
Blaine T. Browne, Robert C. Cottrell.
      p. cm.
  Includes bibliographical references.
  ISBN 978-0-7656-2222-8 (cloth : alk. paper)—ISBN 978-0-7656-2223-5 (pbk. : alk. paper)
1. United States—History—1945—Biography. 2. United States—Social conditions—1945–
3. United States—Politics and government—1945–1989. 4. United States—Politics and
government—1989– 5. Popular culture—United States—History—20th century. 6. Popular
culture—United States—History—21st century. I. Cottrell, Robert C., 1950– II. Title.

E747.B87 2008
973.91—dc22   2007025422

For

My father, Lt. Ted J. Browne (USN, Ret.), one of the "greatest generation" of
World War II to whom we all owe an immense debt of gratitude
—Blaine T. Browne

and

My mother, Lt. Sylvia Light Cottrell (U.S. Army, Ret.), and other U.S. veterans
of World War II who liberated the prisoners at the Nazi concentration camps
—Robert C. Cottrell

Contents

Preface

A glance at any dictionary of quotations will confirm that many prominent thinkers and writers have acknowledged the importance of biography to history. Perhaps most famously, the nineteenth-century American essayist Ralph Waldo Emerson asserted, "There is properly no history—only biography." An eminent historian of the same century, Thomas Carlyle, phrased the thought somewhat differently: "History is the essence of innumerable biographies." This text has grown out of the authors' conviction that the history of contemporary America can be more thoroughly comprehended, and students more fully engaged, through an examination of the lives of those individuals who decisively shaped the course of events in the decades following World War II.

Primary texts on American history since 1945 rarely accord sufficient coverage to individual lives, most often because of editorial constraints. At best, students might be offered capsule biographies, often relegated to a box on the page that isolates the subject from the text and invites less committed students to ignore the material. Likewise, primary texts designed to survey broad expanses of time cannot always offer detailed examinations of all issues; some topics of considerable interest and importance are granted only superficial coverage. *Modern American Lives* seeks not only to fill the biographical void, thereby acquainting students with the lives of a variety of influential Americans, but also to provide a comprehensive examination, through those lives, of the critical issues that determined the course of modern American history.

The individuals presented in these narrative biographies had a significant and sometimes decisive impact on contemporary American life in a wide range of areas: national politics, foreign policy, social and political activism, popular and literary culture, sports, and business. Their origins are as diverse as the society that produced them; some came from privileged backgrounds, some from that broad stratum identified as the middle class, and others from what can only be described as oppressed groups. Clearly, Carlyle's dictum that "the history of the world is but the biography of great men" cannot be literally applied to the course of postwar American history unless one grants a broad meaning to the terms "great" and "men." Those American men and women whose activities and ideas were crucial to shaping the second half of what Henry Luce deemed the "American Century" were not all great in the sense of wielding considerable authority and power. Their importance came from their willingness to engage the central issues of the period and their influence on the thoughts, habits, and practices of their fellow Americans.

This text is divided into three broad chronological periods; a brief statement prefaces each section, introducing the major themes covered therein. Each chapter focuses on two individuals and a key issue, development, or era that they helped to define. The twenty-six individuals included were selected after careful deliberation. We have sought to identify men and women who, through their thoughts and deeds, helped define the key issues and developments of the postwar era. We have intentionally excluded presidents from this reader since most core texts offer adequate coverage of important chief executives. These pages, we believe, are better dedicated to introducing students to significant Americans who too often receive only cursory examination in core texts. Readers should note that *Modern American Lives* was not designed to offer a strictly "point-counterpoint" approach to historical biography. To be sure, some chapters explore a specific issue through the lives of individuals who represent opposite sides of that issue. In other chapters, however, two individuals who represent different aspects of a common theme or era are considered comparatively and in a complementary fashion. This approach reflects our desire to examine as many cogent issues as possible within a text of reasonable length. Each chapter begins with a brief introduction of the two subjects and an explanation of their relationship to the issue under consideration. The biographies, the core of each chapter, present the subjects' lives and contributions in the broad context of relevant events in order to illustrate the connections between individuals and issues. Each chapter concludes with a short summary, followed by study questions and a selected bibliography.

Observant readers will no doubt discern that this text begins and concludes with chapters focusing on debates over America's role in the world. Just as the transformative events of World War II prompted Americans to reassess their international role in the years after 1945, the dramatic events of September 11, 2001, compelled a similar reevaluation as the nation faced the uncertainties of the twenty-first century. The organization of this text reflects that reality.

Introduction

In the more than six decades since the end of World War II, the United States has undergone tremendous transformations in many areas of public and private life. The war, which demanded unity and common sacrifice, was the crucible out of which modern America emerged. One of the conflict's most significant consequences was the forging of a new national consensus, a general agreement as to the validity of American ideals and institutions. For the next two decades, this consensus was a strong cohesive force, providing a sense of national purpose and bolstering confidence in the future. The war also established the nation as an international superpower with new global obligations. As the world's first nuclear power, the United States wrestled with numerous challenges and responsibilities, made all the more daunting by the advent of the Cold War. That lengthy ideological struggle decisively shaped many areas of American life, affecting both foreign policy and domestic politics. The United States also emerged from World War II as the dominant global economic power, and for nearly two decades Americans enjoyed an unprecedented prosperity that determined material conditions while shaping American politics, society, and culture.

Nevertheless, during the early postwar era, Americans confronted a number of serious threats to their way of life and even, as many believed, to their very existence. International communism, widely perceived as a Soviet-supervised global conspiracy, seemed poised to challenge American interests around the world. Domestic subversives, alleged to pervade major American institutions, purportedly threatened the nation from within. Yet the same era saw many Americans enjoying the benefits of an abundant society that promised a future of material plenty and social harmony. In the 1950s, a generally stable and affluent society proved receptive to new directions in popular culture, which produced not only a debate over social and cultural standards but also a new emphasis on celebrity. The flaws in the abundant society were too evident to be ignored, however, and even this generally conservative decade produced individuals willing to challenge American prejudices and conformity. Ironically, despite the material improvements in national life by the end of the decade, Americans had a growing if ambiguous sense of a higher national purpose that remained undefined.

The 1960s dawned as an era of great expectations, encouraged by the confident rhetoric of a young, dynamic president and by a general perception that the nation's full potential remained unrealized. Spurred by a belief that many critical issues could no longer be ignored, Americans from all walks of life made the decision to engage a diverse array of issues, including civil rights, social justice, and politics. In some areas, such as civil rights, great progress was made, often only because of the courage of committed individuals. The very force of heightened expectations, however, produced demands for more thoroughgoing and rapid change; a backlash ensued by mid-decade, driven by the inevitable fears accompanying major social transformations. Even as a coalescing conservative movement sought to define and give voice to growing public concerns about the rapidity and direction of change, radicals questioned the legitimacy of the political system itself, arguing that it was incapable of providing social, economic, or political justice. The great revelations for those radicals stemmed from the nation's glaring racial inequities and the war in Vietnam. Though the most egregious forms of racial discrimination were addressed through federal legislation at mid-decade, race relations continued to deteriorate, creating, as the Kerner Commission—a presidential body convened to examine U.S. race relations, warned—"two societies, separate and unequal." Many radicals concluded that the sources of racial injustice were too fundamental to be resolved within the system. The American war in Vietnam, escalating rapidly after 1965, likewise became a metaphor for what some saw as the fatal corruption of American ideals and institutions. At the same time, Middle America, already alarmed by growing racial strife and political radicalism, was further goaded by the excesses of the counterculture, whose advocates dismissed many traditional values as obstacles to self-realization. By the late 1960s, American society appeared on the verge of coming apart under the stresses of war, racial strife, and domestic turmoil.

As the decade came to an end, the results were evident. The radical left and the counterculture all but self-destructed; more ominously, the consensus that had assured national cohesion since 1945 was shattered, leaving behind a badly divided country.

The final three decades of the century brought more shocks to the nation's confidence. In the 1970s, the economic vitality of earlier years gave way to new uncertainties, born out of the transition to a postindustrial economy and a growing energy crisis. Even as Americans struggled to come to grips with the meaning of the lost war in Vietnam, trust in the nation's leadership and political system was severely undermined in the course of two failed presidencies, one devastated by scandal, the other seemingly dissipated by indirection and ineptness. Festering social and political divisions grew more evident in the 1970s as a popular and increasingly potent conservative movement challenged liberalism and the new values that social activists of the 1960s had propounded. Concerned over the apparent decline of traditional values, social conservatives organized to challenge the basic premises of feminism and other social protest movements of the 1960s. The conservative impulse drew additional strength from the heightened political activism of evangelical Christians, many of whom felt that liberalism, together with libertine counterculture values, threatened the nation's social and moral fabric.

The 1980s were ushered in with stinging electoral rebukes to liberalism as conservatives won newfound power and influence in the nation's capital and elsewhere. In the early years of the decade, Ronald Reagan's presidency gave promise of founding a new national consensus based on conservative ideas, which were widely applied in both foreign and domestic policy. The stumbling economy gained new momentum, provided in part by the rising strength of high-technology industries, which would play a growing role in the national economy in subsequent years. Despite its initial dynamism, however, the conservative wave ebbed by the end of the decade, having failed to establish a clear direction for the nation. With the Cold War ended, popular disaffection due to new economic doldrums and political inertia in the nation's capital characterized the early 1990s. Facing unresolved public ills related to race, crime, poverty, the national debt, and health care, the nation appeared starkly unprepared to embrace the next millennium. Bill Clinton, elected as president in 1992, initially gave promise of defining a renewed national covenant and ending the deep public cynicism about politics, but such hopes soon foundered in the midst of increasingly bitter political partisanship and scandals reaching into the White House. Even as the American people celebrated the new millennium, deep divisions over political, economic, social, and cultural issues were evident. The extent of the polarization was evident in the 2000 presidential election, which showed the American electorate almost evenly divided in its political allegiance. The new president, George W. Bush, failed to win a popular majority and struggled to advance a conservative agenda prior to the shattering events of September 11, 2001. Though the terrorist attacks temporarily united the public, disagreements soon arose over Bush's determination to invade Iraq as part of the overall "war on terror." Although Bush won reelection in 2004, his popularity plummeted in subsequent years due to divisions over the Republican domestic agenda, apparent government ineptitude, and the seemingly endless carnage in Iraq. As of 2007, the possibility of uniting Americans around a consensus as enduring as that which came out of World War II seemed extremely unlikely in the short term. The American people were compelled to confront the unprecedented challenges of the twenty-first century as a nation divided, fundamentally at odds over the most basic questions that a people might face.

The following chapters trace the lives and legacies of some of those individuals who, in the past six decades, defined the crucial issues that determined the course of modern American history. Some achieved great fame through their achievements; others gained only modest or passing recognition, but nonetheless significantly influenced American national life. Many experienced, in varying degrees, both triumph and tragedy; a fortunate few gained their objectives knowing only success and adulation. In common, their lives illustrate the power of individuals to significantly affect the resolution of critical issues and the direction of a nation.

Part I

The Years of Consensus, 1945–1960

The American people emerged from World War II with their confidence in the nation's institutions and ideals greatly strengthened. This newborn consensus, along with unprecedented material abundance, greatly enhanced the nation's internal cohesion during a time of perceived peril. As the world's first nuclear superpower, the United States embraced new international obligations as the ideological confrontation with the Soviet Union unfolded in the postwar years.

This Cold War produced new challenges, and Americans sometimes disagreed as to how the nation's enemies, at home and abroad, could be overcome. The great majority of Americans, accepting the prevailing thesis that the Cold War was the consequence of Soviet aggression, endorsed the "containment" of communism. Some high-level civilian and military officials argued that an aggressive nuclear strategy, including the willingness to wage nuclear war, was a necessity in the face of such an implacable foe. A dissident few, however, contending that apparent Soviet belligerence was a product of fear rather than an indication of unlimited ambition, advocated a less confrontational approach in foreign policy as a means of reducing tensions. The Cold War also had a significant domestic impact, perhaps most conspicuously in the contentious debate over how national security needs might be balanced against constitutionally protected civil liberties. The era of the Second Red Scare often pitted advocates of expanded government investigative and prosecutorial powers against those who argued that dissent was not necessarily subversion.

Despite the anxieties generated by the Cold War during this period, the new prosperity and relative social stability were conducive to new directions in popular culture and entertainment, leading, among other things, to a revolution in popular music. Abundance and domestic tranquility likewise allowed for a tentative questioning of core social values. While many Americans unquestioningly embraced the pleasures and material comforts of the postwar era, other individuals were estranged from mainstream society. Some minorities, excluded because of their race, struggled valiantly for acceptance; others rejected the basic premises of the abundant society and offered alternative definitions of a meaningful existence. Thus, even during an era of broad national consensus, American society still produced the rebellious few. A broader impulse for significant social and cultural change would not emerge until the 1960s, but the mass social movements of that era have obvious predecessors in the previous decade.

1

Defining the Cold War

The Cold War dominated both the international arena and American politics for nearly a half-century following the end of World War II. Pitting wartime partners, the United States and the Soviet Union, against each other, this conflict involved allies, surrogates, and seemingly neutral countries in military, paramilitary, economic, cultural, and ideological battles. Although not leading directly to a martial clash involving American and Russian soldiers, the costs of the Cold War were enormous, nevertheless, in terms of lives lost, resources expended, and opportunities missed. Soviet-American hostilities resulted in a massive arms race and dramatically affected emerging nations across the globe. In the United States, a domestic version of the Cold War led to a militarization of American foreign policy, the expansion of a national security state, the restriction of civil liberties, and a failure to address social and economic problems. During its early phases, a few perceptive individuals foresaw how expensive, financially and otherwise, the Cold War would become.

George F. Kennan and Henry A. Wallace, two of the most astute observers of the Cold War, eventually challenged the activities of their own nation, seeking to shape U.S. policies, albeit in decidedly different fashions. Indeed, operating in the midst of humankind's greatest conflagration, Kennan and Wallace articulated contrasting visions of the future, representing, however imperfectly, the so-called realist and idealist schools of foreign policy strategists. At the height of U.S. involvement in World War II, Kennan served as a little-known adviser in the State Department, while Wallace held the second-highest elective office in the land. The impact of both men proved enduring. Kennan became associated with the doctrine of containment, which called for the United States to meet the threat posed by the Soviet Union on the European continent. Eventually, that doctrine came to define American postwar foreign policy on a global basis, a development that troubled its architect, ironically enough. Nor was Kennan pleased with this country's increasing reliance on military solutions, rather than political or economic ones. At the same time, he advocated the use of covert operations against pro-Soviet regimes throughout Eastern Europe and in the Soviet Union itself, a policy he later attempted to downplay.

Wallace, for his part, offered a different perspective, envisioning a "People's Century" unfolding in both the United States and elsewhere once the guns of war were silenced. Unlike Kennan, Wallace hoped to retain the wartime alliance with the Soviet Union, seeking to draw the leaders of the Politburo into the world community, rather than isolate them as pariahs with little vested interest in amicable relationships. Had it not been for the insistence of Democratic Party bosses at the 1944 Democratic National Comvention that Wallace be replaced as vice president, he would have become president upon Franklin Delano Roosevelt's death in April 1945. Instead, the succession fell to Harry S Truman. The new American president viewed the Soviet Union in a more jaundiced manner and eventually adopted a more hardline approach than Wallace favored. During Truman's administration, the Cold War tore apart the wartime Grand Alliance that allowed the United States, Great Britain, and the Soviet Union to thwart the Axis powers. It also tilted the United States away from the liberalism that had characterized the country during the New Deal era and even throughout much of the war. This shift troubled Wallace considerably more than Kennan, who was generally less concerned about domestic developments than the former vice president.

GEORGE F. KENNAN
Architect of Containment

At 9:00 PM on February 22, 1946, George Kennan, a forty-four-year-old seasoned diplomat residing in Moscow, fired off a warning to Secretary of State James F. Byrnes. His message, which came to be referred to as the Long Telegram, articulated the need for the United States to contain the Soviet Union. At this defining moment in the Cold War, Kennan, drawing on his familiarity with Russian history, underscored how "urgent" it was to predict postwar Soviet policy and devise an appropriate, realistic American response. According to Kennan, Soviet leaders feared "antagonistic 'capitalist encirclement,'" believed that "no permanent peaceful coexistence" was possible, possessed a "neurotic view" of world events, and "sacrificed every single ethical value in their methods and tactics." The "neurotic" Politburo, exhibiting a "traditional and instinctive Russian sense of insecurity" and aided by "an elaborate and far flung apparatus" unprecedented in scope, boasted "a police regime par excellence" and stood "committed fanatically" to the disruption of American society and the destruction of "our traditional way of life." The Soviet threat posed the gravest problem American diplomats had ever encountered, Kennan acknowledged, but one that could be confronted without resort to war, in part because the Soviet Union, unlike Nazi Germany, was "neither schematic nor adventuristic" and was "highly sensitive to [the] logic of force."

7

Thus, Kennan remained convinced that the "capitalist' world" could indeed live "at peace with itself and Russia" if the "forces of intolerance and subversion" were held in check. Although this new brand of Russian nationalism, drawing on international Marxism, was "more dangerous and insidious than ever before," the U.S. government needed to educate the American people about the great communist state, thereby dampening "hysterical anti-Sovietism" in the process. Ultimately, Kennan argued, "much depends on [the] health and vigor of our own society," for "world communism is like [a] malignant parasite which feeds only on diseased tissue." In fact, the greatest peril confronting the American people "is that we shall allow ourselves to become like those with whom we are coping."

Kennan's Long Telegram provided a blueprint for postwar U.S. foreign policy by warning that Soviet expansionism could not go unchecked. Yet it also insisted that the Politburo hardly had a plan for worldwide dominance; thus, peace was possible and hysteria must be avoided. In the period ahead, too few U.S. policy makers heeded Kennan's words regarding the limited nature of Soviet goals and the need to ensure that the United States remain an authentic beacon of liberty and freedom. They also failed to appreciate how conflicted Kennan was in interpreting the moves and designs of the USSR, how he lacked the certainty that both Sovietphiles and Sovietphobes possessed in abundance.

The intensely driven, insecure but ambitious man who became known as the father of containment was a product of the early twentieth-century American Midwest, a not altogether happy elite education, and lengthy training as a diplomat with a particular expertise in Russian history, culture, and ideology. Born in frigid Milwaukee, Wisconsin, on February 16, 1904, George Frost Kennan boasted Scotch-Irish and English ancestors, some of whose ties to the North American continent could be traced back to early colonial times. Overcoming a hardscrabble background, his father, Kossuth Kennan, became both a lawyer and an engineer before settling in Milwaukee, where he established a reputation as a leading tax attorney. Kossuth, whose second wife died shortly after giving birth to George, had three other children with his third wife. The family lived in a comfortable, three-story, Victorian-style house. Kennan's father demonstrated a fondness for languages and an elegant writing style, as would his son; Kossuth also possessed an emotional reserve and a demanding nature that made for a difficult relationship with his oldest child. George Kennan undertook his initial trip abroad at the age of eight, joining his father in traveling to Germany, where he met a cousin of his grandfather. That gentleman, also named George Kennan, was the renowned author of *Siberia and the Exile System*, which condemned penal life under the czar. Considering his "moody, self-centered, neurotic" son in need of discipline, Kossuth sent George off to St. John's Military Academy in Delafield, Wisconsin, and then to Princeton University. The Ivy League's snobbery hardly suited the ill-prepared Kennan, who later self-effacingly suggested, "I may have been the most undistinguished student Princeton ever had."

Not wishing to return to Milwaukee, Kennan—tall, thin, and sporting already rapidly thinning hair—took the examination for the U.S. Foreign Service. His early diplomatic career took him overseas where, while studying Russian at the University of Berlin, he met a Norwegian woman, Annelise Soerensen, whom he married in September 1931. After a brief stint in Washington, DC, with the State Department's Division of Eastern European Affairs, Kennan returned overseas in late 1933, assisting Ambassador William Bullitt in Moscow. From October 1937 through August 1938, Kennan joined the Soviet desk for the State Department in Washington, DC. Next, stationed as second secretary and consul in Prague, Czechoslovakia, Kennan exhibited certain disturbing attitudes, noting at one point that "benevolent despotism," not democracy, possessed "greater possibilities for good," an astonishing pronouncement in an era when dictators imperiled democracy's very existence. Equally troubling, he demonstrated a disconcerting reluctance to assist those pleading for assistance in escaping from Nazi-controlled territory. The entrance of the United States into World War II while Kennan was serving in the American consulate led to a five-month internment at Bad Nauheim, Germany. Following his release in June 1942, Kennan returned to the State Department, before heading overseas to take up posts in Lisbon, London, and Moscow. In February 1946, now stationed as chargé d'affaires in Moscow, he received a request from the U.S. Treasury Department to produce a report on the Soviet Union.

Prior to drafting the Long Telegram, Kennan had achieved a growing recognition as a Soviet expert highly critical of the Stalinist regime. Kennan's analysis of the Soviet Union drew from his sense of history, rather than from ideological considerations alone. While serving in Tallinn, Estonia, and Riga, Latvia, in the early 1930s, Kennan and other young diplomats had operated under the tutelage of Robert Kelley, who served in the East European Affairs division of the State Department and opposed U.S. recognition of the Soviet Union. Although the Roosevelt administration discarded the policy of nonrecognition, Kennan remained skeptical about the Soviet Union, having tracked the Soviet purge trials that resulted in the murder of Old Bolsheviks and many others, communists and noncommunists alike. While viewing the

Germans as "the final despair of Western European civilization," Kennan, unlike many liberals and radicals in the West, never deemed the Soviet Union "a fit ally or associate, actual or potential" for the United States. Although recognizing that financial assistance for the Soviets might be necessary to further "our own self-interest," Kennan warned against identifying the United States with Soviet depredations by welcoming the USSR "as an associate in the defense of democracy."

President Roosevelt and British prime minister Winston Churchill determined that the Red Army must be aided in its battle against German invaders. Following the Japanese attack on Pearl Harbor and subsequent declarations of war against each other by Germany and the United States, the Grand Alliance emerged as a kind of antifascist front. Kennan, however, remained scathingly critical of America's new Soviet ally. Meanwhile, both liberals and conservatives, ranging from Vice President Henry Wallace to Henry Luce, editor and publisher of *Time*, *Fortune*, and *Life*, portrayed the Soviet Union and its leader, Joseph Stalin, in a glorified, simplistic light, which led to unrealistic expectations and, ultimately, dashed hopes. It also resulted in many Americans undertaking the kind of dramatic ideological shift that was foreign to Kennan.

Shortly after his return to Moscow in 1944, Kennan produced a lengthy essay, "Russia—Seven Years Later," which he considered more finely honed than a more celebrated paper he would draft three years later; this document displayed his characteristically ambivalent analysis of the communist state. Though the purges were "enormously destructive in human values," he commended the Russian people, who had endured the loss of between 25 and 30 million citizens, for "their own extraordinary capacity for heroism and endurance"—yet warned that it would be foolish to downplay the "potential—for good or for evil" of the 200 million people under Soviet dominion. As the war in Europe ended, Kennan produced another paper exploring the Soviet Union's stance, seeking to contest "the Rooseveltian dream"—shared by Henry Wallace—of cordial relations with that powerful state, which held "conquered provinces in submission." Again, Kennan insisted it was not ideology but rather an "age-old sense of insecurity" that drove the Politburo to act as it did. While the communist movement seemed "unrivaled . . . in energy, initiative, unity, discipline, and ruthlessness," Russian control involved "the inevitable drawbacks of foreign rule." In addition, the communist leaders had "lost moral dominion over the Russian people" because "the fire of revolutionary Marxism has definitely died out." Kennan concluded his observations by indicating that no Russian leader believed that the West could quash Soviet demands, a sensibility that he became convinced, shortly after the war, had to be refuted.

By January 1946, Stalin apparently questioned whether communist and capitalist states could coexist. Kennan, serving as chargé d'affaires in Moscow, responded to a request from the United States Treasury for an evaluation of recent Soviet actions, including demands for certain portions of northern Iran. Believing that the timing was ripe, Kennan issued the Long Telegram: "They had asked for it. Now, by God, they would have it." Although some chroniclers later disputed the impact of Kennan's missive, Clark Clifford, then serving as a presidential assistant, termed it "probably the most important and influential message ever sent to Washington by an American diplomat." Propitiously, President Truman himself was in attendance in Fulton, Missouri, on March 5, 1946, when Winston Churchill delivered his "iron curtain" address. Churchill indicated that the Soviets, in taking control of countries throughout Eastern Europe, had divided the continent between free and enslaved peoples. His speech seemed to underscore Kennan's argument that the Soviets had to be viewed realistically, not through utopian-shaded lens.

For Kennan personally, the impact of the Long Telegram, which Secretary of State Byrnes tagged a "splendid analysis," was considerable. As he later recorded, the document "changed my life. My name was now known in Washington." With the backing of Secretary of the Navy James Forrestal, Kennan joined the National War College, where he served as deputy for foreign affairs. For once, Kennan seemed pleased about returning to the States, where he hoped to help "restrain the hot-heads and panic-mongers and keep policy on a firm and even keel." Thus, in the very period when he was urging that unrealistic expectations about Soviet intentions—including the kind now associated with Wallace—should not influence U.S. policy making, he worried about another impulse—a type of blind anticommunism—that threatened to become at least equally dangerous. It took considerable fortitude to deliver the kind of speech Kennan did at the University of Virginia in late 1946, when he asserted that while no communist himself, he recognized that communist theory, although "not the practice," contained "certain elements which . . . are probably . . . the ideas of the future." He worried that his own country, if blinded by ideological concerns, might "reject the good with the bad" and land "on the wrong side of history." Thus, he urged "greater coolness, greater sophistication, greater maturity and self-confidence in our approach to this whole problem of Russia and communism." On another occasion, Kennan deemed it "unrealistic" that the Soviet Union would establish a global "communist sphere of influence."

Nevertheless, speaking at the War College, Kennan asked why the United States could not "contain the Russians indefinitely by confronting them firmly and politely with superior strength at every turn." In January 1947, at Forrestal's behest, Kennan wrote an essay clarifying the "psychological background of Soviet foreign policy" while elaborating on the theory of containment. He called for a policy "designed to confront the Russians with unalterable counter-force everywhere" they imperiled "the interests of a peaceful and stable world." In a speech delivered to members of the Council of Foreign Relations, in Manhattan, Kennan questioned the effectiveness of a "get-tough-policy" while also insisting that the Soviets should not be dealt with in the fashion that Henry Wallace supposedly favored: "on a personal basis, by the glad hand and the winning smile."

The next few months witnessed a heightening of both Cold War rhetoric and Kennan's standing in top government circles. Notwithstanding Kennan's objections, President Truman delivered a strident address to Congress to garner support for assistance to the beleaguered, but authoritarian governments of Greece and Turkey. Kennan favored the granting of such aid, but was troubled by the rhetoric of the Truman Doctrine, which declared, "the United States would support free peoples who were resisting subjugation by armed minorities or by outside pressures." This pronouncement provided an ideological blueprint for much of U.S. foreign policy throughout the Cold War era. At the end of April, Secretary of State George Marshall asked Kennan to help establish a State Department policy planning staff, which would shape the Marshall Plan for reconstructing Western Europe. The Communist Party in France and Italy could sweep to power, Kennan warned, if economic conditions in those two countries failed to improve. He also emphasized the need to economically rebuild both Germany and Austria, arguing that the United States should provide assistance for a European recovery program. Somewhat cynically, he also favored offering such assistance to the USSR and to Soviet-dominated Eastern European states, recognizing that requirements of openness would not enable them to participate.

Nevertheless, Kennan, as head of the policy planning staff, worried that the Truman Doctrine would be considered a blank check promising economic and military support wherever communism threatened. In July, the article Kennan had drafted for Forrestal appeared in the distinguished journal *Foreign Affairs*, published by the Council on Foreign Relations. Appearing under the pseudonym Mr. X, the essay became, for many readers, the clearest articulation of the containment doctrine. To the dismay of George Marshall, who believed that "planners don't talk," Arthur Krock, the Washington columnist of the *New York Times*, unveiled the article's authorship. Still, its publication furthered Kennan's reputation and pinpointed the need to restrain the Soviet Union. Indeed, Kennan insisted that American policy regarding the USSR demanded "long-term, patient but firm and vigilant containment of Russian expansive tendencies." At the same time, he stressed that a containment policy required no "outward histrionics . . . threats or blustering or superfluous gestures of outward 'toughness,'" but rather "the adroit and vigilant application of counter-force as a series of constantly shifting geographical and political points, corresponding to the shifts and maneuvers of Soviet policy." The Soviet Union itself remained an economically vulnerable state with a "physically and spiritually tired" population. Significantly, the Soviet state possibly contained "within it the seeds of its own decay . . . the sprouting of these seeds is well advanced."

Later, Kennan suggested deficiencies in his analysis. He pointed to his failure to highlight, as he had previously, the difficulties the Soviet Union would encounter in retaining control of Eastern Europe. He also had not stressed the importance of "political containment of a political threat" or indicated that the policy of containment should be applied only to Western Europe and Japan. Such "errors," Kennan believed, led to caustic condemnations by America's leading print journalist, Walter Lippmann, a friend of his. In a dozen columns and in his book, *The Cold War: A Study in U.S. Foreign Policy*, Lippmann blasted Kennan for suggesting the need for worldwide military containment, terming it a "strategic monstrosity" that would overextend the United States. In spite of such criticisms, fairly delivered or not, Kennan remained a highly influential figure in top government circles at this crucial juncture in the emerging Cold War dividing East from West. He supported moves to prop up the governments in both Greece and Italy, which continued to face challenges, whether of a guerrilla or political cast, from communist forces. He went so far as to champion plans to send combat troops to either country if conditions worsened and even suggested the outlawing of the Italian Communist Party.

As 1947 neared its close, Kennan's support of another controversial program, involving U.S. covert operations in the Soviet bloc, even more markedly demonstrated his ambivalent attitude about the communist behemoth. He predicted the 1948 communist coup in Czechoslovakia, which would be designed to prevent the "entry of really democratic forces into Eastern Europe in general." Following the lead of State Department adviser John Davies, Kennan favored calling on the large number of political refugees who could purportedly make political control more troublesome for Stalinist regimes. Like his insistence that

Soviet machinations be thwarted at every turn, Kennan's backing of Western covert activities beyond the Iron Curtain emboldened uncompromising policy makers. In May 1948, Kennan joined with staff members and State Department representatives in examining his memorandum to initiate "organized political warfare." Kennan urged establishment of a "directorate" for "overt and covert political warfare," which would later be referred to as the Department of Dirty Tricks. This proposal was passed on to the National Security Council, resulting in approval of NSC 10/2, "a directive authorizing a dramatic increase in the range of covert operations directed against the Soviet Union, including political warfare, economic warfare, and paramilitary activities." By mid-1948, the Truman administration backed Kennan's call for paramilitary operations in Eastern Europe and the Soviet Union, a program that the Joint Chiefs of Staff considered reckless. Operation Rollback, as the program came to be known, proved to be largely a disaster, with Kennan later acknowledging that the activities "were unnecessarily dangerous and provocative" and failed to shake the stranglehold of existing regimes. More successful were other political operations for Eastern Europe that Kennan championed, including Radio Free Europe and Radio Liberation, which transmitted a Western slant on global and national events. Both Kennan and Davies envisioned the emergence of communist figures in Eastern Europe, like Josip Tito in Yugoslavia, who would refuse Soviet dictates. Kennan helped convince U.S. policy makers to support Tito's breakaway from the Soviet sphere.

While Kennan later deemed his sponsorship of covert operations "the greatest mistake I ever made," he more immediately opposed the establishment of the North Atlantic Treaty Organization (NATO), designed as a military alliance against the Soviet Union. In a paper prepared for George Marshall in November 1948, Kennan warned against fixating on military matters, prophesying that such an approach would not affect Soviet policies. One colleague suggested that Kennan probably refused to back NATO "because he had neglected to invent it." Kennan's discarding of his earlier plea for German dismemberment and his support for German unification and neutralization, as the Americans instituted an airlift to defeat a Soviet-run blockade of West Berlin, also put him at odds with the Truman administration. His growing estrangement only intensified when Dean Acheson replaced Marshall as secretary of state and Kennan's access to the nation's chief of foreign policy diminished. Kennan's refusal to back the administration's plan to develop thermonuclear weapons, his support for international control of such weapons, and his proposal that the United States adopt a no-first-strike policy undoubtedly influenced Acheson's decision to "gradually exclude" him from top policy-making decisions.

Kennan, for his part, began to view himself as something of "a court jester, expected to enliven discussion, privileged to say shocking things, valued as an intellectual gadfly on the hides of slower colleagues, but not to be taken fully seriously when it came to the final, responsible decisions of policy." Referring to Kennan in a speech before the War College, Acheson stated, "I have rarely met a man the depth of whose thought, the sweetness of whose nature combined to bring a real understanding of the problems of modern life." But as Kennan continued to emphasize the need to rein in nuclear weapons, Acheson bristled, suggesting that his friend might depart the Foreign Service and "go out and preach your Quaker gospel." Kennan's disdain for NSC-68, a National Security Council statement calling for a massive increase in military spending, further riled the Secretary of State.

Increasingly, the State Department focused on events in Asia, heeding Kennan's advice in various instances and ignoring it in others. Kennan and the policy planning staff had pressed General Douglas MacArthur, who headed the occupation forces in Japan, to ward off communist activities by promoting political and economic stability for that key Asian state. Worrying that economic anarchy and coerced "socialization" might result, Kennan opposed moves to break up the *zaibatsu*, the great Japanese corporations, a policy that MacArthur initially favored. Along with John Davies, Kennan argued against propping up Chiang Kai-shek's corrupt, despotic regime in China, insisting that its collapse "would be deplorable" but probably not calamitous for the U.S. position there. After the communists took control of the mainland, Kennan urged recognition of the People's Republic of China and normalization of diplomatic relations. With the outbreak of the Korean War in the summer of 1950, Kennan supported the expulsion of North Korean forces from South Korea but condemned carrying the war across the thirty-eighth parallel dividing the Korean peninsula. Both Davies and Kennan insisted on Southeast Asia's strategic importance. The policy planning staff reasoned that resisting Stalinism demanded meeting the needs of "militant nationalism," an astute analysis but one that U.S. diplomats and politicians freely disregarded. Before departing from the State Department in late 1950, Kennan attempted to convince Acheson of the perils of following the Pentagon's lead in Southeast Asia. Prophetically, Kennan warned that U.S. support for the French in Indochina was problematic, involving "an undertaking which neither they nor we, nor both of us together, can win."

While continuing to serve as an adviser to the Truman administration, Kennan began to carve out a new, academically based career. Due to his stellar reputation as a policy analyst, he received feelers from Columbia, Dartmouth,

Harvard, and MIT, among other institutions. Eventually, he decided to accept an offer by his friend Robert Oppenheimer to join Princeton's Institute for Advanced Study. In 1951, Kennan published *American Diplomacy, 1900–1950*, the first in a series of highly acclaimed books. In December 1951, Kennan agreed to serve as U.S. ambassador to the Soviet Union. "It was a task for which my whole career had prepared me, if it had prepared me for anything at all," Kennan later reported, but the assignment proved something of a fiasco. The Soviets declared Kennan persona non grata after he carelessly likened Soviet government operatives to the Nazis and informed a Western journalist that American diplomats were treated terribly in Moscow. The new Eisenhower administration and Secretary of State John Foster Dulles viewed Kennan as a political liability, resulting in his resignation from the Foreign Service in 1953.

In several instances during this period, Kennan spoke on behalf of Foreign Service officers and old friends like Oppenheimer whose loyalty was called into question as the domestic Red Scare escalated. In mass-circulation publications like *Look* and the *New York Times Magazine*, Kennan condemned Senator Joseph McCarthy's antics. After Oppenheimer was grilled by the Atomic Energy Commission he once headed, Kennan penned an article in the *Atlantic Monthly* with the following warning: "We have seen . . . the faith of our people in great and distinguished fellow citizens systematically undermined; useful and deserving men hounded thanklessly out of honorable careers of public service; the most subtle sort of damage done to our intellectual life."

More and more, Kennan, perhaps finally able to reconcile his own contradictory positions concerning communist states, devoted himself to academic pursuits, although he briefly served as U.S. ambassador to Yugoslavia during the Kennedy administration; that tenure ended following Kennan's opposition to Captive Nations Week, which called for the ouster of all Eastern Europe governments. Kennan's two-volume study *Soviet-American Relations, 1917–1920* (1956, 1958) was well regarded—the first volume garnered the Pulitzer Prize for History in 1957—as were other works, such as *Russia and the West under Lenin and Stalin* (1960) and *Soviet Foreign Policy, 1917–1941* (1960). Holding the Eastman Visiting Professorship at Oxford College in 1957 and 1958, Kennan presented the BBC's Reith Lectures; to the dismay of many old friends and former State Department colleagues, including an outraged Dean Acheson, Kennan favored the demilitarization and unification of Germany and the removal of nuclear weapons from the European continent. In subsequent years, Kennan lectured at Princeton, Harvard, and Oxford while continuing to produce acclaimed books. The first volume of his *Memoirs: 1925–1950* (1967) won him a second Pulitzer Prize—this time for the field of biography or autobiography—in 1968.

As U.S. involvement in Vietnam escalated, top government officials and academics alike revisited Kennan's earlier warnings against the United States' serving as a kind of international policing agent. At the request of J. William Fulbright, Kennan testified before the Senate Foreign Relations Committee in 1966, questioning whether the fate of Vietnam would dramatically impact American security interests. Due to ongoing strife between China and Russia, Kennan suggested, a united Vietnamese state, even one ruled by Ho Chi Minh, would likely chart its own course. Although dismayed by the antics of many student protesters, Kennan backed the bid of Minnesota senator Eugene McCarthy to capture the 1968 Democratic Party presidential nomination, which largely revolved around opposition to the war.

Increasingly, Kennan focused on the danger posed by nuclear weapons, blasting President Ronald Reagan's call for a Strategic Defense Initiative that seemingly threatened to carry the nuclear arms race into space. Kennan worried that the United States was involved "in a state of undeclared war—an undeclared war pursued in anticipation of an outright one now regarded as inevitable." The recipient of the 1981 Einstein Peace Prize, Kennan championed the nuclear freeze movement that swept across Western Europe during the early 1980s. Very early, he recognized that Mikhail Gorbachev, who appeared willing to consider genuine reductions of nuclear weapons, promised to be a new kind of leader for the Soviet Union. Still, by 1989, Kennan recognized that "we are seeing today . . . the final overcoming and disappearance of the Russian Revolution of 1917."

As the twentieth century neared an end, Kennan reflected on the tragedies that spanned his lifetime, while insisting that "a return to Soviet communism . . . [was] completely impossible." The most serious issues confronting his own country, he informed an interviewer, were the global environmental crisis, involving overpopulation, urban problems, and the depletion of resources, and the existence of weapons of mass destruction; he advocated "their total abolition." On March 18, 2005, Kennan died in Princeton, New Jersey, at the age of 101. Historian Ronald Steele termed him "the nearest thing to a legend that this country's diplomatic service has ever produced." Another leading historian, John Gaddis, contended that Kennan's policy of containment "held up awfully well." Its architect remained unique in recognizing the need to contest both Soviet aggression and the dogmatic application of his own theory of containment.

HENRY A. WALLACE
Champion of the Common Man and Cooperation

Determined to help frame the rationale for which World War II was being fought, Vice President Henry A. Wallace delivered a thirty-minute address titled "The Price of Free World Victory," in Manhattan on May 8, 1942. The speech came to be known for its most striking phrase, "the century of the common man." Wallace emphatically declared, "This is a fight between a slave world and a free world." In typical fashion, Wallace noted that "the idea of freedom" was "derived from the Bible with its extraordinary emphasis on the dignity of the individual." Now, "a long-drawn-out people's revolution," ready to safeguard "the rights of the common man" with "the ferocity of a

18

she-bear who has lost a cub," battled against the "Nazi counter-revolution," which seemingly made use of Satan in an effort to plunge the common man "back into slavery and darkness." Believing in "the dignity that is in every human soul," the people viewed "as their credo the Four Freedoms" heralded by Franklin Roosevelt in January 1941. Those freedoms—of speech, of worship, from want, and from fear—stood at "the very core of the revolution" associated with the United Nations.

Striving for an "American Century"—the goal of conservative publishing magnate Henry Luce—made no sense to Wallace. By contrast, he foresaw the coming era as "the century of the common man." Perhaps, Wallace declared, the United States could serve as a beacon of liberty and responsibility. Still, no state in the new world order would possess "the God-given right to exploit other nations," and the American people were "no more a master race than the Nazis." Then, like a Biblical prophet, Wallace closed his address by proclaiming, "The people's revolution is on the march, and the devil and all his angels can not prevail against it . . . for on the side of the people is the Lord." Thus, Wallace envisioned utopian possibilities while offering an astute evaluation of world events and his own nation.

A product of the American heartland, Henry Agard Wallace was a member of a family of Scottish and Irish ancestry, noted for its celebration of the agrarian life, the American farmer, and democracy. His grandfather, Henry Wallace, and his father, Henry "Harry" Cantwell Wallace, edited their own journal, *Wallaces' Farmer*, known as the "Wallaces' gold mine." The journal enabled Harry Wallace, who had left his position as professor of agriculture at Iowa State, to build a $50,000 mansion in Des Moines's finest neighborhood. Henry Agard Wallace was born in 1888 and graduated from Iowa State College in 1910, determined to work for the family newspaper. In 1913, he married a fellow Iowan, Ilo Browne. Henry and Ilo purchased a forty-acre farm close to Johnston, Iowa, and rented an additional forty-seven-acre plot of land from his father. In 1916, Harry and Henry began serving as coeditors of *Wallaces' Farmer*. Having received a wartime occupational deferment for his work with "a necessary agricultural enterprise," Henry insisted on the need to stabilize farm commodity markets and prices, a perspective that led to publication of his first book, *Agricultural Prices* (1920), which condemned classical, laissez-faire economics.

The election of Warren G. Harding to the presidency resulted in Harry Wallace's appointment as secretary of agriculture, the very position his own father had declined to accept a generation earlier. Now the lone editor of *Wallaces' Farmer*, Henry Wallace dealt with the death of his father in 1924, the year his discontent with the Republican Party led Wallace to back Wisconsin Senator Robert M. La Follette's third-party presidential bid. Wallace continued his search for new, improved means to increase agricultural productivity, becoming something of a proselytizer for hybrid corn; his Hi-Bred Corn Company eventually made a small fortune for Henry and Ilo Wallace. Responding to the Great Depression, which ravaged American farms and tore through urban centers as well, Wallace indicated the "cure for hard times . . . is simply that a greater percentage of the income of the nation be turned back to the mass of the people." In 1932, Wallace backed New York governor Franklin Delano Roosevelt's candidacy for the presidency; later, the president-elect chose Wallace to fill the same cabinet post Harry Wallace had occupied.

Over the next eight years, Wallace became arguably the nation's finest secretary of agriculture. At the same time, any number of his programs and several of his appointees proved controversial, in their own fashion. His tenure opened with Rexford Tugwell, one of the New Deal Brain-Trusters, serving as an assistant secretary, and Jerome Frank, operating as general counsel. The Wallace team crafted an expansive farm bill establishing the Agricultural Adjustment Administration (AAA), which sought to control production levels. A Republican legislator condemned the agency as "the most revolutionary proposal" ever associated with the U.S. government. However, Wallace's unpretentious nature, ruffled appearance, and unrelenting work ethic garnered favorable journalistic treatment, with Walter Lippmann declaring in May 1934, "You have been doing one of the finest bits of public education that I have seen done by anybody in a very long time." For a time, the Department of Agriculture attracted the brightest, most ambitious individuals, including young attorneys Abe Fortas and Adlai Stevenson, who sought to help Roosevelt transform the national economy. Criticism soon arose, however, over Wallace's plan to kill "six million baby pigs" and plow under millions of acres of cotton in the midst of the Great Depression. Soon Wallace confronted problems within his own department. Chester Davis, who headed the AAA, opposed the plans of Jerome Frank and the members of his legal division to provide greater protection for sharecroppers and tenant farmers, rather than prop up corporations and planters. In early 1935, under pressure from Davis, Wallace conducted a "purge of the liberals," resulting in the ouster of Frank, Lee Pressman, assistant general counsel of the AAA, and Gardner Jackson, assistant consumers' counsel of the AAA, among others.

Increasingly, there was talk of a possible run by Wallace, who had registered as a Democrat shortly before the previous presidential campaign, for the nation's highest elective office in 1940. In the meantime, he strongly backed

Roosevelt's call for international collective security in the face of aggression by Japan and Nazi Germany. In a public address on May 29, 1940, Wallace asserted, "This is an hour of trial for the entire world. . . . The ideas of the madmen run beyond all imagination. They respect force and force alone." Thus, Wallace said, the United States must be adequately armed and increase its economic preparedness. Opting for a third-term bid, President Roosevelt insisted that Wallace replace John Nance Garner as his running mate, notwithstanding considerable opposition within his own party. Roosevelt angrily dismissed accusations that Wallace was a mystic, bristling that he was "a philosopher. He's got ideas. He thinks right. He'll help the people think." Although the press lauded Wallace's intellectual makeup and drive, his candidacy was almost derailed by the threatened release of correspondence he had earlier engaged in with the mystic Nicolas Roerich, revered by theosophists who believed that knowledge of God could be attained through revelation or intuition. The letters were not published following the counterthreat that the press, in turn, would receive information about an affair involving Wendell Willkie, the Republican presidential nominee.

After the Democratic triumph in November, Roosevelt named Vice President Wallace chair of the Economic Defense Board, which was to oversee the international financial affairs of the United States. With Roosevelt's blessing, Wallace articulated a progressive vision of the postwar world, seemingly similar to that of the president, who had long championed Wilsonian ideals involving the spread of democracy and economic liberalism. Wallace argued that World War II afforded a "second opportunity to make the world safe for democracy." Predictably invoking religious imagery, he called for young Americans to appreciate that "the essence of democracy is belief in the fatherhood of God, the brotherhood of man and the dignity of the individual soul."

After the official entry of the United States into the war following the Japanese attack on Pearl Harbor on December 7, 1941, Wallace's power only seemed to grow. He was privy to information about the atomic bomb project, served as chair of the Supply Priorities and Allocations Board, and headed the Board of Economic Warfare. James Reston of the *New York Times* referred to Wallace as the administration's "defense chief, economic boss and No. 1 postwar planner. He is not only Vice President, but 'Assistant President.'" But Wallace's stature within the Roosevelt administration would soon be curtailed by bureaucratic battles, particularly with Secretary of Commerce Jesse Jones. Through it all, Wallace maintained his efforts to imbue American war efforts with a moral purpose, as in his "century of the common man" address in May 1942. Although warmly applauded, the speech proved troubling to key figures like Adolf Berle Jr. of the State Department, who was displeased with its missionary quality. The *Wall Street Journal* also questioned whether Wallace was promising more than the United States could deliver to poor nations, while Henry Luce took affront at the seeming challenge to his own championing of American preeminence. The criticism foreshadowed the later, often highly partisan domestic clash over postwar U.S. foreign policy, regarding which interests the great democracy should represent. It also portended a divide among foreign policy strategists, who viewed themselves as fitting within either a realist or an idealist camp.

In November 1942, Wallace, at Roosevelt's bidding, spoke before the Congress of American-Soviet Friendship. In the fashion of Popular Front liberals of the 1930s, Wallace delivered a "Tribute to Russia," declaring that the American and Russian people had much in common. "A practical balance between economic and political democracy," he contended, was needed. The task of the present generation, he exclaimed on December 28, was "to organize human affairs" so that "no Adolf Hitler, no power-hungry war mongers whatever their nationality, can ever again plunge the whole world into war and bloodshed." A "worldwide new democracy," rooted in American ideals of "Liberty and Unity," Wallace insisted, must result from the present conflagration. His concluding remarks, a speech delivered on March 8, 1943, warning of the likelihood of a third world war should the United States "double-cross Russia," produced another firestorm of criticism.

His outspokenness and clashes with rivals like Jesse Jones ultimately led to a campaign to dump Wallace from the Democratic Party's 1944 presidential ticket. Shortly after his removal in mid-1943 as head of the Board of Economic Warfare, Wallace affirmed at a labor conclave in Detroit that Roosevelt "always puts human rights first" and that "our choice is between democracy for everybody or for the few." Although first lady Eleanor Roosevelt remained supportive, top presidential advisers Harry Hopkins and James Byrnes, along with party bosses, urged that Wallace be dropped from the presidential ticket. Speaking at a Jackson Dinner on January 22, 1944, Wallace defiantly declared, "The New Deal has yet to attain its full strength." In an address before the American Palestine Committee in Washington, DC, on March 9, he cried out, "This is a people's war. The peace must be a people's peace—for all the peoples and races of mankind." To the chagrin of the *New York Times*, he also began to loosely characterize anti-Semites, Catholic-phobes, and racists as "fascists." Such reliance on charged language would return to haunt forces on the American left and liberals too, when the nation's political atmosphere shifted rightward.

As the 1944 Democratic Party national convention unfolded, Wallace desperately battled to hold onto his job. On July 20 in Chicago Stadium, he delivered a remarkable talk before the crowd of 30,000. The Democrats' strength, he claimed, "has always been the people—plain people . . . ordinary folks, farmers, workers, and business men along Main Street." Now, "the greatest liberal in the history of the United States" headed that party. The nation's priorities, Wallace continued, had to involve both winning the war and conducting a peace, in a manner that would enable "New World liberalism" to prevail. As for the future, Wallace declared, it "belongs to those who go down the line unswervingly for the liberal principles of both political democracy and economic democracy regardless of race, color or religion." With a lengthy ovation forthcoming, Florida senator Claude Pepper, among others, sought to kick off an early nomination for the vice presidential spot. The crowd roared, "WE WANT WALLACE! WE WANT WALLACE!" but National Committee chair Robert Hannegan refused to allow Pepper to speak or the nomination to be conducted. The following day, Wallace fell one hundred votes short of the necessary total on the second ballot and his strength soon waned, leading to Harry Truman's selection as Roosevelt's running mate.

During the fall campaign, Wallace stood behind Roosevelt, declaring that the peace to come "must be a people's peace." Having promised Wallace any cabinet post other than that of secretary of state, which was still manned by an ailing Cordell Hull, Roosevelt appointed his soon-to-be former vice president as secretary of commerce, providing the delicious irony, from Wallace's vantage point, of displacing his ardent foe, Jesse Jones. But first Wallace faced a tough confirmation battle in the U.S. Senate, which he won by the relatively close vote of 56–32. Recognizing how infirm the president was, Wallace, like so many Americans, mourned Roosevelt's death on April 12, 1945.

Within a matter of weeks, Wallace expressed fears that "it begins to look like the psychology is favorable toward our getting into war with Russia," a conflict he believed would enable "world communism" to triumph. In August, Wallace wrote in his diary that "the cornerstone of the peace of the future consists in strengthening our ties of friendship with Russia," but he worried that the attitude of Truman and the new secretary of state, James F. Byrnes, "will make for war eventually." Outspoken and opposed to the administration's increasingly hard-line, anti-Soviet posture, Wallace, the only holdover from Roosevelt's cabinet, unhappily listened as rhetoric heated up between East and West. At a dinner party thrown by Undersecretary of State Dean Acheson, Wallace, like George Kennan, expressed dismay at Churchill's "iron curtain" address, which he saw as containing "war-like words." Speaking at a dinner hosted by the American Society for Russian Relief two weeks after Churchill's speech, Wallace—who had cleared his talk with Truman—declared his own country's large indebtedness to Russia, whose citizens had "paid a heavier price for our joint victory over fascism than any other people." Rather than relying on nuclear weapons, far-flung military bases, and vast defense appropriations, Wallace said, "the only way to defeat communism in the world is to do a better and smoother job of maximum production and optimum distribution." His reading of international tensions suggested both a desire, perhaps quixotic, to hold onto the wartime alliance and a more hardheaded analysis of the costly nature of an expansive, anticommunist U.S. foreign policy.

Political allies like C.B. "Beanie" Baldwin, who had worked with Wallace in the Department of Agriculture and later headed the Farm Security Administration before working for the Congress of Industrial Organizations' Political Action Committee; Henry Morgenthau Jr., former Secretary of the Treasury; and Harold Ickes, the ex-Secretary of the Interior, urged Wallace to resign his cabinet post and challenge Truman for the 1948 Democratic Party presidential nomination. Instead, Wallace maintained his efforts to influence both Truman and a national audience. Again having vetted a speech with Truman, Wallace spoke on "The Way to Peace" at Madison Square Garden on September 12, 1946, proclaiming, "I am neither anti-British nor pro-British—neither anti-Russian nor pro-Russian." Like Kennan, Wallace urged that the American people closely examine "how the Russian character was formed" through repeated invasions, czarist rule, Allied intervention after World War I, geography, and the strength of the Russian soil. Marxist-Leninist tenets also afforded "tremendous emotional power" to the Soviet leaders. Seemingly accepting the notion of spheres of influence, at least temporarily, Wallace indicated that the Russians had no more right to goad "native communists to political activity in western Europe, Latin America, and the United States than we have interfering in the politics of eastern Europe and Russia."

Considerable criticism of Wallace's address appeared in both the mainstream press and the Communist Party's *Daily Worker*, while Secretary of State Byrnes expressed anger about Wallace's foray into the sphere of foreign policy. Despite mounting pressure, Wallace refused to retract his statements, leading Truman to write in his diary that the secretary of commerce was "a pacifist one hundred percent" and the kind of "dreamer" he could not fathom. Indeed, Truman somewhat hysterically recorded, "The German-American Bund under Fritz Kuhn was not half so dangerous. The Reds, phonies and the 'parlor pinks' seem to be banded together and are becoming a national danger." Wallace was forced to resign on September 20, 1946, promising, "I shall continue to fight for peace." FBI agents now tailed him and closely followed his activities. At the same time, kudos came his way too, with Albert Einstein offering, "Your courageous intervention deserves the gratitude of all of us who observe the present attitude of our government with grave concern."

A new forum became available to Wallace when Michael Straight, publisher of the *New Republic*, named him editor of the journal. Wallace informed his readers on October 21, 1946, that he sought to convince "the liberally minded people of the whole world" of the "need of stopping this dangerous armament race." He also intended, as he indicated two months later, "to help organize a progressive America." Pressure continued for Wallace to cast his lot with various left-leaning organizations, particularly the newly formed Progressive Citizens of America (PCA), which welcomed any member, including communists, in the very period when political litmus tests were becoming the norm in labor, academic, and government circles. Talking before a group of liberals gathered in New York City at the Hotel Commodore on December 29, Wallace affirmed, "Those who put hatred of Russia first in all their feelings and actions do not believe in peace."

Shortly thereafter, anticommunist liberals fired back in their own fashion, forming Americans for Democratic Action (ADA). Prominent ADA figures included Eleanor Roosevelt, fan .ed theologian Reinhold Niebuhr, labor chieftain Walter Reuther, Walter White of the National Association for the Advancement of Colored People (NAACP), and Minneapolis mayor Hubert H. Humphrey. In contrast to the PCA, the ADA condemned any linkage "with Communism or sympathizers with Communism in the United States as completely as we reject any association with Fascists or their sympathizers." Appearing on *Meet the Press*, Wallace dismissed concerns about communist involvement in the PCA: "If you allow that little thing to dominate your mind, it means that you have become a red-baiter, a person who wants to sic the FBI onto your neighbor; it interferes with everything you want to do."

The divide pitting liberals against progressives of various sorts widened as Cold War tensions escalated. The promulgation of the Truman Doctrine and its seeming support for repressive governments distressed Wallace. Responding to Truman's apparent articulation of the containment theory, Wallace spoke on NBC radio on March 13, 1947, declaring that there was no "Greek crisis that we face, it is an American crisis. . . . a crisis of the American spirit." Truman's determination to deliver massive military assistance to Greece and Turkey, Wallace charged, amounted to "a down payment on an unlimited expenditure aimed at opposing communist expansion." Wallace went on to declare, "There is no regime too reactionary for us provided it stands in Russia's expansionist path. There is no country too remote to serve as the scene of a contest which may widen until it becomes a world war." Wallace also worried about the domestic implications of a rigid foreign policy, fearing that civil liberties would be curtailed and economic costs increased. Eight days later, President Truman initiated a federal loyalty oath.

Notwithstanding the nation's obviously altered political atmosphere, Wallace refused to back down, adopting instead a still more strident tone that infuriated his opponents. Touring Western Europe, he continued to criticize Truman's approach, worrying that "the American century of power politics" would supplant his hoped-for "century of the common man." Senator James Eastland of Mississippi accused Wallace of conspiring "with foreign peoples . . . to undermine and . . . weaken the hand of his country." Firing back, Wallace blasted the "witch hunt" that he saw as "part of a larger drive to destroy the belief, which I share, that capitalism and communism can resolve their conflicts without resort to war." Senator Arthur Vandenberg of Michigan claimed that Wallace was voicing "treasonable utterances." Members of the House Un-American Activities Committee sought to have Wallace indicted under the eighteenth-century Logan Act, which precluded nongovernment figures from seeking to "influence the measures or conduct of any foreign government" regarding disputes involving the United States.

The damage to Wallace's political reputation was considerable. As indicated by a Gallup poll, his standing with the American public sank precipitously, never to regain the lofty stature he had earlier attained. Nevertheless, Wallace remained determined to contest American policy making. Back home, he undertook an extensive tour, during which he blasted the Truman Doctrine as "a doctrine of unlimited aid to anti-Soviet governments," a by-product of fear that fed "hatred and hysteria." While thousands of citizens turned out to support the former vice president, others attempted to silence him. Opponents ridiculed him by sarcastically waving the flag of the USSR or playing the Communist "Internationale." At various venues, including a number of academic institutions, officials refused to allow him to speak. He responded with orations like the one delivered to a crowd of 30,000 at Gilmore Stadium in Los Angeles, where he warned, "Today an ugly fear is spread across America—the fear of communism." Defiantly, he exclaimed, "I say those who fear communism lack faith in democracy. I am not afraid of communism."

Michael Straight, Wallace's publisher at the *New Republic* and a man who had earlier idealized the Soviet Union, now expressed concern about the involvement of communists in Progressive Citizens of America, which provided a necessary forum for his editor. Wallace, who saw himself as a religiously based "progressive capitalist," dismissed Straight's worries, offering that the communists "get out the crowds." By mid-1947, Beanie Baldwin of the PCA was urging Wallace to consider a third-party presidential bid. At this point, Wallace was pleased by the announcement of the Marshall Plan to reconstruct war-torn Europe, but viewed the program less charitably when it became clear that the Soviet Union and Eastern European states would not participate. On December 29, 1947, Wallace confirmed on the Mutual Broadcasting System that he was running for the presidency. Claiming, "The people are on the march," Wallace declared, "We have assembled a Gideon's Army, small in number, powerful in conviction, ready for action," and he prophesied, "the people's peace will usher in the century of the common man." His movement stood "for old-fashioned Americanism," civil liberties, strong unions, economic security, and racial integration, while he himself opposed any form "of imperialism or expansion" associated with England, the Soviet Union, or the United States.

More bitter condemnations of Wallace resulted. The Wallace crusade, journalist Stewart Alsop declared, "has been indecently exposed for what it is: an instrument of Soviet foreign policy. . . . The bones revealed are communist bones." With Senator Glen H. Taylor of Idaho agreeing to stand as his running mate, Wallace continued his impracticable quest. But the charges of communist entrapment, fed by Democratic and Republican Party operatives, doomed the Wallace candidacy. So too did a series of pronouncements and missteps on Wallace's part. As a communist coup occurred in Czechoslovakia, Wallace suggested, "that a 'get tough' policy only provokes a 'get tougher' policy." The *New York Times* charged that Wallace's presidential bid was providing support for "the ideology of International Communism." Following George Kennan's lead, investigators at the State Department sought to determine whether Wallace had broken federal law in drafting an open letter to Stalin. Attorney General Tom Clark pushed the FBI to again determine if Wallace had violated the Logan Act.

As the Progressive Party—as the organization backing Wallace came to be called—gathered in Philadelphia in July 1948 to nominate him for the presidency, his poll numbers continued to drop. Michael Straight, opposed to the third-party effort, fired Wallace from the *New Republic*. Passages from "the guru letters" that Roosevelt had prevented from being released in 1940 now appeared in Westbrook Pegler's syndicated column in the Hearst newspaper chain. Yet Wallace spoke confidently to the Progressive Party delegates in Shibe Park, home of both Philadelphia major league teams, the Athletics and the Phillies: "The future belongs to those who go down the line unswervingly for all the liberal principles of political democracy regardless of race, color or religion."

Wallace's campaign swing through the South inspired Beanie Baldwin's comment that he had never witnessed a political figure display such "sheer physical courage." Deliberately challenging Jim Crow ordinances, Wallace encountered vicious campaign signs, including one urging him to "Peddle Your Junk in Moscow," hotels refusing admission, threats of violence, hostile epithets, and both eggs and tomatoes. This display of "human hate in the raw" led him to tell a huge crowd in Yankee Stadium in New York City, "Fascism has become an ugly reality." Although demonstrating considerable fortitude on his part, Wallace's continued campaigning cemented the unpopularity of many of the ideals associated with him. In the November election, the American people resoundingly rejected Wallace's message. As Truman surprisingly defeated the Republican candidate, Thomas Dewey, Wallace came in a distant fourth, receiving fewer votes than Strom Thurmond, the Dixiecrat candidate running on a segregationist platform. Despite his poor showing, Wallace vowed to continue the struggle, claiming, "to save the peace of the world the Progressive Party is more needed than ever before."

Still determined to stand as a public figure, Wallace viewed with displeasure the formation of NATO, worrying that it would intensify the arms race. But he also displeased many Progressive Party representatives when he charged, "The United States and Russia stand out today as the two big brutes of the world." After the North Korean invasion of South Korea in June 1950, Wallace broke with that organization altogether in backing the military campaign by American and United Nations forces. Still, Wallace presciently warned, "The United States will fight a losing battle in Asia as long as she stands behind feudal regimes based on exorbitant charges of land lords and money lords."

Wallace soon headed into political oblivion, retiring to his farm in Iowa. He defended his record when attacks came his way, unaware that the FBI continued to tail him. He traveled widely, often dealing with agricultural concerns, while occasionally delivering talks heralding liberal ideals and liberalism in general. He supported the concept of world government, the abolition of nuclear weapons, and extensive economic ties across the globe. Wallace's reputation rebounded somewhat during the Kennedy and Johnson administrations, with President John F. Kennedy inviting Wallace to the inaugural ceremony and Curtis D. MacDougall producing the three-volume *Gideon's Army* on Wallace's 1948 presidential bid, published in 1965. Suffering from amyotrophic lateral sclerosis, the same disease that felled baseball great Lou Gehrig, Wallace died on November 18, 1965, leading President Johnson to applaud him as "an original American voice." Secretary of Agriculture Orville Freeman suggested, "No single individual has contributed more to the abundance of freedom we enjoy."

Conclusion

At the peak of their influence in the late 1940s, George Kennan and Henry Wallace appeared to approach world events from wholly different perspectives. Kennan, who articulated the theory of containment, seemed to be situated in the realist camp, which argued that the West, and particularly the United States, must be prepared to stand up against the Soviet Union. Wallace came across as an idealist, extolling the ideal of a people's century, but also suggesting that the USSR possessed legitimate security concerns about its borders. Eventually, both men ended up criticizing large portions of U.S. postwar foreign policy. Worrying that his containment theory had been oversimplified and misapplied on a global scale, Kennan became critical of American operations in Southeast Asia and U.S. nuclear strategy. Distressed that the Progressive Party he had represented had adopted a doctrinaire stance on the Korean War, Wallace again became a lonely voice protesting the country's Cold War policies. Notwithstanding real differences, the critical perspectives offered by both figures appeared increasingly aligned, providing a useful counterweight to triumphalist perspectives pertaining to U.S. dealings with other nations in the postwar period.

For a time, their challenge to American international policy, albeit derived from different sources and delivered in contrasting fashions, cast both men out of the foreign policy establishment. This estrangement undoubtedly prevented both from reaching the diplomatic or political summit, but neither had demonstrated a readiness to compromise or equivocate in a manner that might have made that possible. Kennan was welcomed back into the ambassadorial ranks, but failed to shape U.S. foreign policy as he once had, while Wallace suffered through political ignominy. Yet the Vietnam War and the continued battle raging between East and West eventually led many scholars and political figures to acknowledge the prophetic nature of the warnings that Kennan and Wallace had once delivered.

Study Questions

1. Discuss the containment policy that characterized U.S. foreign policy throughout the Cold War.

2. Analyze how George Kennan became disenchanted with the containment policy that he helped define.
3. Discuss Henry Wallace's estrangement from the Truman administration and the latter's policies regarding the Soviet Union.
4. Explain how liberals and conservatives responded to the formation of the Progressive Party, which supported Wallace's third-party presidential bid in 1948.
5. Compare the realist and idealist schools of foreign policy strategy.

Selected Bibliography

Blum, John Morton, ed. *The Price of Vision: The Diary of Henry A. Wallace, 1942–46.* Boston: Houghton Mifflin, 1973.

Culver, John C., and John Hyde. *American Dreamer: A Life of Henry A. Wallace.* New York: W.W. Norton, 2000.

Harper, John Lamberton. *American Visions of Europe: Franklin D. Roosevelt, George F. Kennan, and Dean G. Acheson.* New York: Cambridge University Press, 1994.

Isaacson, Walter, and Evan Thomas. *The Wise Men: Six Friends and the World They Made.* New York: Simon and Schuster, 1987.

Kennan, George F. *At a Century's Ending: Reflections, 1982–1995.* New York: W.W. Norton, 1996.

———. *Memoirs, 1925–1950.* Boston: Little, Brown, 1967.

———. *Memoirs, 1950–1963.* Boston: Little, Brown, 1972.

Kleinman, Mark L. *A World of Hope, a World of Fear: Henry A. Wallace, Reinhold Niebuhr, and American Liberalism.* Columbus: Ohio State University Press, 2000.

Leebaert, Derek. *The Fifty-Year Wound: How America's Cold War Victory Shapes Our World.* Boston: Back Bay Books, 2002.

LuKacs, John. *George Kennan: A Study of Character.* New Haven: Yale University Press, 2007.

MacDougall, Curtis D. *Gideon's Army.* 3 vols. New York: Marzani and Munsell, 1965.

Markowitz, Norman D. *The Rise and Fall of the People's Century: Henry A. Wallace and American Liberalism, 1941–1948.* New York: Free Press, 1973.

Wallace, Henry A. *The American Choice.* New York: Reynal and Hitchcock, 1940.

———. *The Century of the Common Man.* New York: Reynal and Hitchcock, 1943.

———. *Democracy Reborn.* New York: Reynal and Hitchcock, 1944.

Walton, Richard J. *Henry Wallace, Harry Truman and the Cold War.* New York: Viking, 1976.

Weiner, Tim, and Barbara Crossette. "George F. Kennan, Leading U.S. Strategist of the Cold War, Dies at 101." *New York Times*, March 19, 2004.

2

Fighting the Cold War at Home

They stood on opposite sides of many of the controversial issues that arose at the height of the Red Scare that beset America, as the Cold War emerged and then intensified during the early postwar period. In print, congressional hearings, and public addresses, (radical journalist I.F. "Izzy" Stone) and (J. Edgar Hoover,) the director of the Federal Bureau of Investigation (FBI), presented contrasting perspectives on the Communist Party of the United States (CPUSA), Alger Hiss, the Rosenbergs, and other hotly debated topics. One condemned the readiness to tag individuals and groups as "subversive," while the other insisted on the need to do exactly that, both in public and within the inner recesses of the federal agency he headed.

The two men viewed each other as despised adversaries. Stone condemned "our lawless G-men" and asked whether Hoover aspired to become "an American Himmler." Dismayed by what he considered the FBI's apparent disdain for the rule of law, Stone likened the organization to Hitler's Gestapo or the OGPU, Stalin's secret police. He particularly feared that the FBI remained the bastion of rabid anti-New Dealers who might someday perform "a sinister role" in the United States. Evidently stung by Stone's criticism, Hoover had his agents maintain a close watch on the journalist, eventually compiling a massive dossier of 2,600 pages. One report to Hoover, dated July 29, 1941, indicated, "Stone is not his correct name. He is of Jewish descent and . . . is very arrogant, very loud spoken . . . and is most obnoxious personally." Hoover responded by asking, "What is his name? What have we on him?" After yet another critical piece by Stone appeared in the *Nation*, a leading progressive journal, Hoover informed his top assistants, "I would like a prompt analysis . . . of this article." An infuriated Hoover subsequently claimed that Stone was seeking "to create distrust, lack of confidence in and hatred for the F.B.I." Repeatedly, Hoover and his agents suggested that Stone was fabricating information about the bureau and doing everything possible to besmirch its operations. Although most impassioned during this period, the battle between Stone and Hoover would continue throughout the director's tenure at the FBI, which concluded only with his death in 1972.

I.F. STONE
Dissenter in an Age of Conformity

The note from the Senate Internal Security Subcommittee arrived at the home of I.F. Stone and his wife, Esther, in the northwest sector of Washington, DC, on Friday, December 1, 1955. The note contained a request for a subscription to the four-page newsletter *I.F. Stone's Weekly*. The request and the accompanying five-dollar voucher enraged the tempestuous Stone. On Sunday, he typed out a note to Senator James Eastland, the prosegregationist chair of the subcommittee, insisting that public funds could not be expended for surveillance of the press. On Monday, Stone filed suit in U.S. District Court in the nation's capital, resulting in the delivery of summonses to the subcommittee members and their staff. On being informed of the lawsuit, an irate Senator Eastland blurted out, "It's bunk," and indeed the suit would soon be dismissed.

Stone explained to his readers why he had filed the lawsuit. (American journalists, he feared, were about to suffer "intimidation, slander, and guilt-by-association," as had government employees during the postwar Red Scare. Publishers, he insisted, had to demand the right to remain free from "ideological inquiry.") Despite the brief tussle with Eastland and the Senate subcommittee—an important instrument in the postwar witch-hunt and a frequent recipient of materials from the FBI—Stone never suffered a congressional inquest himself. This immunity was surprising, for Stone was one of the few well-known representatives of the American Old Left who continued to voice radical ideas throughout the late 1940s and the 1950s. However, because he was acknowledged as a "goddamned red," Stone reasoned, investigators could garner little mileage by investigating him. In addition, thanks to the newsletter, he was his own boss. Still, the Eastland subcommittee did name Stone as "one of the eighty-two most active and typical sponsors of Communist-front organizations."

The early Cold War years had proved both taxing and energizing for Izzy Stone, a man who often thrived on contention. As the era opened, he stood as Washington editor of the *Nation* magazine and a columnist for *PM*, an experimental, adless, left-wing newspaper based in Manhattan. By 1952, the shutting down of the *New York Daily Compass,* the second in a line of *PM*'s successors, left Stone unemployed; earlier, he had cut his ties with the *Nation*. Given the country's rightward drift, Stone believed he stood little chance of being hired by any reputable newspaper or magazine. His apparent fate seemed to parallel that of the American Left, which had suffered from the early onset of the Cold War and Vice President Henry Wallace's disastrous third-party presidential bid in 1948 and was now at a nadir, with McCarthyism flourishing and left-wing ideas considered suspect at best.

Born in Philadelphia on December 24, 1907, Stone was the son of Russian-Jewish immigrants, Bernard and Katherine Feinstein, who maintained a kosher home. Bernard Feinstein, a peddler and shopkeeper, eventually opened a dry goods store in Camden, New Jersey. The two-story building provided comfortable living space for the family, soon to include four children, including Isidor, or Izzy, the eldest. Like many first-generation Jews of that era, Stone—who always believed he "was sort of born a radical"—was drawn to left-of-center ideas, early viewing himself as an anarchocommunist. Along with a small band of friends at the University of Pennsylvania, he championed the cause of immigrant anarchists Nicola Sacco and Bartolomeo Vanzetti and read John Reed's classic, *Ten Days That Shook the World*, which spawned "day dreams about the great new world of the Kremlin."

By the end of the 1920s, Stone, who had briefly joined the Socialist Party, dropped out of Penn to pursue a career in journalism. In 1929, the short, stocky, bespectacled young journalist married Esther Roisman, whom he had "met on a blind date and a borrowed dollar." Within two years, he joined the staff of the *Philadelphia Record*, owned by newspaper magnate J. David Stern, who soon moved Stone over to another of his publications, the *New York Post*. Both the *Record* and the *Post* espoused a liberal editorial slant, presented by Stone and Sam Grafton, the papers' top columnists, applauding President Franklin Delano Roosevelt and his New Deal. Early during Roosevelt's tenure, however, Stone, writing under a pseudonym, also contributed articles to the *Modern Monthly*, run by the independent radical V.F. Calverton. In "Roosevelt Moves Toward Fascism," Stone contended that heading toward "a Soviet America" offered "the one way out that could make a real difference to the working classes." Less strident articles by the ambitious Stone soon appeared in the top left-liberal journals of the era, the *New Republic* and the *Nation*.

Throughout the decade, Stone remained intimately associated with the band of radicals—many connected to the Communist Party—later referred to as the Old Left. The Old Left was caught up in the swirl of ideological currents that included a belief in some version of socialism, disdain for fascism, and fascination with the world's lone "socialist" state. Stone, unlike numerous other Old Leftists during the 1930s, opted not to join the CPUSA and expressed ambivalence about the Soviet Union, which he believed exhibited "cruel and bloody ruthlessness" but remained a great socialist experiment. Revolutions, Stone recognized, "do not take place according to Emily Post" as "the birth of a new social order . . . is a painful process." Stone was particularly pleased when, in the middle of the decade, the Communist International, or Comintern, supported the Popular Front, an antifascist alliance of left-of-center forces. From that point forth, Stone remained a confirmed Popular Fronter and viewed Roosevelt's New Deal as "history in the making" that must not be allowed "to go down the drain." Nevertheless, still fearing that fascism might envelop America, he opted, in 1937, to change his name to I.F. Stone, as his boss had suggested so that the *Post* would not appear so Jewish. His relationship with Stern deteriorated, however, after the *Post* condemned the very idea of a united front.

The world of the Popular Fronters, along with many of the dreams of the Old Left, was shaken by the announcement on August 23, 1939, that the Soviet Union and Nazi Germany had signed a nonaggression pact. Journalist Richard Rovere recalled that "no one from that period" was "more outraged by that outrageous document" than Stone. Writing to his friend Michael Blankfort, the screenwriter, novelist, and playwright, Stone declared, "I'm off the Moscow axis." The Soviet Union's willingness to join with Germany in assaulting Eastern Europe, he exclaimed, "turned my stomach." Over the next several months, Stone walked something of a tightrope, refusing to fully adopt either an interventionist viewpoint or the isolationist stance that the American Communist Party, like America Firsters, had come to champion.

As the nation readied for war, Stone, in the pages of both the *Nation* and *PM*, condemned the "peculiar kind of Americanism" exhibited by both J. Edgar Hoover's FBI and the House Un-American Activities Committee (HUAC), which, he charged, was "smearing, terrorizing and pillorying" its foes. Adopting a lonely and prophetic stance, he condemned legal action—which the CPUSA cheered—undertaken against the Trotskyist Socialist Workers Party. The prosecution relied on the Alien Registration Act or Smith Act of 1940, which criminalized advocacy of the violent overthrow of any government. Stone warned, "You cannot kill an idea by putting its spokesmen in jail." And yet there was a blind side to Stone's reading of wartime civil liberties. In May 1942, notwithstanding the herding of tens of thousands of Japanese Americans and Japanese aliens into relocation centers, which he failed to mention at this point, Stone proclaimed that only the case involving the Trotskyites "haunt(ed) our speeches about free government." In addition, Stone followed the lead of Freda Kirchwey, editor of the *Nation,* in demanding that American fascists face legal restraints.

Though Stone saw "the Red Army, like an avenging juggernaut," ushering in the final days of Hitler and the Third Reich, he seemed to overlook the Soviet Union's designs on Eastern Europe. Thus, after a cerebral hemorrhage felled Franklin Roosevelt in April 1945, Stone unhappily watched the new administration of Harry S Truman adopt a harsher anti-Soviet line. When Winston Churchill claimed in early 1946 that an "iron curtain" separated free and unfree peoples on the European continent, Stone, like Henry Wallace, feared that an anti-Soviet alliance was emerging. Acknowledging that "unlimited expansionist demands" by the Soviets could not be permitted, Stone reasoned that the United States had to determine whether such demands were "unlimited, and where we draw the line."

Developments on the home front appeared equally troublesome to Stone. In 1946, the Chamber of Commerce issued a report calling for a crusade against communist influence in America, with particular emphasis on education, the media, entertainment, and government service. Wielding the club of anticommunism, the Republican Party regained control of the legislative branch in the 1946 congressional elections. Responding to the political debacle suffered by the Democratic Party, President Truman required that federal employees take a loyalty oath, while Attorney General Tom Clark devised a list of purportedly subversive organizations. Over Truman's veto, Congress passed the Taft-Hartley Act, which compelled union officials to sign an affidavit declaring that they were not affiliated with subversive groups. Both congressional and state committees began grilling individuals about their reputed involvement with such organizations, with blacklists becoming all too common.

Stone viewed such developments, along with the nation's rightward shift, with trepidation. As early as October 1946, he pointedly questioned just what J. Edgar Hoover, in delivering an address on the "Red menace" to an American Legion convention, desired. Why had the FBI boss not spoken out on "the menace of racism, or anti-Semitism, or anti-Negro feeling"? Why was Hoover attempting to turn the CPUSA, "which can't elect a dog-catcher outside New York City, into Public Enemy No. 1'"? Stone wondered if "even the palest pinks" were about to be viewed as suspect. But as talk of communist-sponsored espionage proliferated, Stone acknowledged, "The Russians cannot have the cake of conspiracy and the penny of cooperation at the same time. That is an issue the Kremlin must face." In the United States, he warned, "the conspiratorial habits" of a small number of communists might soon result in the most sweeping Red Scare yet.

Increasingly, Stone worried that his own nation was becoming "the citadel of world reaction." In March 1947, the Truman Doctrine proclaimed that the United States would back "free people" who battled against "outside pressures" or "armed revolts." Congress supported Truman's call to provide $400 million in aid to the tottering, right-wing regimes in Greece and Turkey. Sadly, Stone wrote, "we seem to have opened a military shopping service for dictators, guns for the asking to anti-democratic regimes from Iran to Turkey to Brazil and Argentina, guns for use against their own people, guns marked U.S.A., not the best kind of advertising."

During this early phase of the Cold War, Stone, in contrast to many people on both the right and the left, also championed an expansive civil libertarian perspective. He decried those who urged the silencing of the anti-Semitic Christian Front and a right-wing, Jew-baiting priest named Arthur W. Terminiello. Such "screwballs," he insisted, must be allowed to speak. It was, he reminded his readers, "as easy as rolling off a log to uphold basic rights when our own side is involved. The test of the quality of our thinking and the quality of our faith comes when it's the other fellow's right to speak that's at stake." Insisting that freedom of thought possessed as much "absolute value as anything in this finite world," Stone contended that socialist states must adopt Lockean and Jeffersonian precepts or deteriorate into Nazism's "facile falsehoods."

But as the campaign to root out supposed subversives from government operations intensified, Stone reported in mid-1947 that the nation's capital appeared to be "under the shadow of a terror." Legitimate security concerns existed, but "the kernel of fact" was being submerged by a groundswell of ludicrous charges and "purges for opinion." HUAC was accomplishing precisely what it had envisioned: feeding the mounting paranoia with the suspicion that communists lurked everywhere, the committee was destroying people's reputations and livelihoods through a kind "of plot-and-persecution system akin to paranoid obsession and like paranoia impervious to correction by rational government."

Shortly after the Soviets began a blockade of West Berlin, Stone, in the summer of 1948, angrily called for a plague to befall both superpowers. Fortunately, he noted, less powerful states in both the East and West appeared increasingly disenchanted with the "arrogance . . . egotism and . . . boundless fears" of both the Soviet Union and the United States. Displeased by Cold War antics, Stone backed the third-party presidential effort of Henry Wallace, notwithstanding concerns about Wallace's "naïve ventures into Soviet zone politics." Admitting that he was not fond of either "yogis" or "commissars," Stone chortled that "when Socialism comes I'll fight for the right to spit in the nearest bureaucrat's eye." If the American comrades swept into power, he acknowledged, "I'd soon find myself eating cold *kasha* in a concentration camp in Kansas."

Wallace's campaign foundered badly, and Truman won a little anticipated victory over Republican nominee Thomas Dewey, the governor of New York. Truman's 1949 inaugural address greatly disturbed Stone, who considered it a belligerent exhortation for the American people to "set ourselves up to police the world." Like both Wallace and George Kennan, he was no happier when the United States joined with eleven other nations to create the North Atlantic Treaty Organization (NATO). Stone likened NATO to "a new Holy Alliance" intended to stifle the forces of change. It was true that the "Russian Revolution, the biggest event of our time," had generated "brutalities, fanaticisms, cruelties and stupidities," but the advance of socialism would continue, he predicted. Still less astute was Stone's characterization of Chinese communists as agrarian reformers seeking "a rural New Deal rather than Sovietism."

Stone's condemnation of Cold War practices in both the East and the West earned him criticism from both left and right. Or, as Stone pointed out, in Washington he was considered "a dirty red," while in New York City's Union Square—where left-wing protests still took place—he was viewed as "a dirty counter-revolutionary." After a tough line of questioning from Stone on *Meet the Press*, Major General Patrick Hurley, former ambassador to Nationalist China, blurted out, "I know you. You are noted because you are not for the United States. You are for Russia. . . . You just give us your old party-line and it's red." Eventually, Stone wondered aloud what purpose was served by his appearance as "the 'Hot' radical" on a program like *Meet the Press*. Such an intemperate declaration ensured that he would not appear on a nationally syndicated radio or television program for almost two full decades.

In 1949, Cold War tensions heightened in the United States following the takeover of China by the communists and the Soviets' detonation of an atomic bomb. Stone urged that U.S. policy makers treat China, the "newly awakened giant," soberly and graciously. He worried that Secretary of State Dean Acheson subscribed to "the bogeyman theory of history," which contended that revolutionary doctrine was a type of bacteria, and change, the product of conspiracy alone. Such paranoid delusions, Stone insisted, had long papered over "the pseudopolitics of stupid rulers and ruling classes." On February 24, 1950, a mere two days after Senator Joseph McCarthy began claiming communist infiltration of the U.S. government, Stone criticized the refusal of a cowed State Department to recognize the government of Ho Chi Minh in Vietnam. The U.S. government, Stone prophesied, was about to embark on a "costly failure." As he saw it, "the more politically antiseptic the State Dept. becomes, the bigger a help it is to the Kremlin."

Cold War fever soared again after North Korean forces moved across the thirty-eighth parallel, beginning on June 25, 1950, in an attempt to take control of the entire peninsula. As the United States acted to shield South Korea and its dictator, Syngman Rhee, Stone wondered why his country cast its lot with "the unpopular side in Asia." In a highly controversial book, *The Hidden History of the Korean War*, Stone charged Rhee; Chiang Kai-shek, former ruler of China, now residing on the island of Taiwan; American commander Douglas MacArthur; and President Truman with conspiring to bring about the North Korean attack. The start of the Korean War convinced Stone to accept an assignment as the *Daily Compass*'s European correspondent, and in August

1950, he and his wife, Esther, took their three children to live in France. He was unable to "stand America any longer" because of its "Mad Hatter quality" and apparent movement "toward Fascism and folly."

With the *Compass* experiencing financial difficulties, Stone soon returned to Washington, where he declared that "the land of the brave and the home of the free" appeared increasingly like "the land of the belly-crawler and the home of the fearful." As members of the CPUSA continued criticizing him, Stone bristled that "the possessors of the One True Faith" always dismissively viewed "erring heathen like me." The persistent red-baiting of the Old Left, already weakened by the sectarianism that divided it, eventually doomed the *Compass*, which stopped publishing in late 1952. Its demise left the forty-four-year-old Stone, now viewed with still greater suspicion by the FBI, which opened "Espionage" and "Security" files on him, without work. the *Nation* turned down his request for his old job in Washington, the editor recalling Stone's petulant dealings with colleagues and egomaniacal manner. Consequently, Stone decided to establish his own brand of "independent liberal journalism." In a letter to friends and subscribers of a series of leftist publications, Stone indicated that he had been allowed to operate in America without "dictation, personal or political." While the socialism they believed in was inevitable, Stone declared, so too was "the libertarian ideal" they favored, though authoritarians of both the left and the right imperiled it.

On January 17, 1953, the initial edition of *I.F. Stone's Weekly*—produced out of Izzy's basement in Washington, DC—appeared, mere days before Dwight David Eisenhower's inauguration as president of the United States. Stone quickly amassed 5,300 charter subscribers, including such old friends and fans as Albert Einstein, the world's most renowned scientist; Bertrand Russell, the Welsh philosopher, mathematician, writer, social activist, and recent recipient of the Nobel Prize for Literature; and Eleanor Roosevelt willing to pay the five-dollar annual rate for the four-page newsletter. Of considerable help was the second-class mailing rate afforded by the U.S. Postal Service, which made it possible to ship each copy for only one-eighth of a cent. Izzy determinedly served as publisher, editor, reporter, proofreader, and layout artist in an often pressure-packed situation, while Esther handled financial affairs. Stone envisioned a paper that was radical in content but conservative in appearance, featuring documentation culled from the records of official hearings, other public transcripts, and government records, as well as "the significant trifle" overlooked by other journalists.

Less than two months later, when Joseph Stalin died on March 5, 1953, Stone acknowledged the self-styled "Man of Steel" as one of the modern era's "giant figures." Yet the early issues of the *Weekly* displayed Stone's continuing concern about "the gloomy thought controls" characterizing Soviet-style communism and about the Soviet Union's "indifference to mass suffering and individual injustice, a sycophancy and an iron-clad conformity" that "disgraced the socialist ideal." When riots protesting labor conditions broke out later that year in East Germany, Stone, in the fashion of many on the left, was initially dumbfounded but had to acknowledge that the riots were "all too real." When Nikita Khrushchev won the power struggle in the Soviet Union, Stone hoped that the Russians were finally learning to unloosen the "unpleasant draconian . . . stooge rule" they had held over much of Eastern Europe. But again like many Old Leftists, he was stunned when, at the Soviet Communist Party's Twentieth Congress in February 1956, Khrushchev denounced Stalin as a paranoid, maniacal butcher whose purges and slave labor camps had disgraced the communist state. On March 26, Stone referred to Khrushchev's speech as "communism's self-exposure," which demonstrated that the Soviet Union, "backward" as it had proven to be, was no fit role model. The communists themselves were revealed "as prize idiots abroad and prize cowards within Russia." It was time, Stone declared, for the Left to acknowledge that the communist movement was finished.

He considered it essential now to visit the Soviet bloc, a trip he had previously avoided making. To ensure that his latest passport was approved, he had to submit a handwritten note to the U.S. Passport Office declaring that he was "not and never . . . (had) been a member of the Communist Party." Now, no matter the consequences, he felt compelled to tell the truth as he saw it. The Soviet Union "*is not a good society,*" he charged, "*and it is not led by good men.* No society is good in which men fear to think—much less speak—freely." For the independent thinker, the intellectual, or anyone concerned about humanistic values, the Soviet Union remained "a hermetically sealed prison, stifling in its atmosphere of complete, rigid and low-level thought control" that had spawned an entire generation of bootlickers.

When Russian tanks rolled into the streets of Budapest in October 1956, quashing the Hungarian freedom fighters who sought to discard Soviet control and usher in democracy, Stone's disillusionment deepened. Even before the Politburo acted, Stone acknowledged that it was unsettling "for those of us who all our lives regarded socialism as our ideal" to witness the depth of the workers' discontent with the workers' state. Now heading the revolt in Hungary, like the one that had recently occurred in Poland, were the very groups—workers, students, and intellectuals—that had been most drawn to the socialist banner during the lifetime of Karl Marx, the nineteenth-century philosopher and political economist who became a founding father of communism. They might be doing the same in Czechoslovakia and Russia in the not-too-distant future, he suggested. Thus, for Stone, the Hungarian Revolution had vanquished "the last illusions of an era." More was at stake, he warned, than the image of the Soviet Union. Socialism's good name had been marred by communist rule, which was unfortunate because socialism was needed to uplift "underdeveloped" countries.

In his own country, Stone hoped that a reconstituted Left could appear. He affirmed that the CPUSA boasted "good, devoted and heroic people," but also a small cadre of "submissive and obsequious fanatics" who blindly accepted party directives. In late October 1957, Stone noted his favorite quotation, penned by the great French writer Albert Camus: "Every revolutionary ends by becoming either an oppressor or a heretic." Such pronouncements hardly delighted all Stone's subscribers, but many were pleased by his determination to aid "the search for peace," as he put it. They applauded the *Weekly*'s revelation in 1958 that the Atomic Energy Commission had been disingenuous regarding its ability to track nuclear tests, as required for the creation of a test-ban treaty. A good number of his readers also appreciated Stone's warning that Cuba, taken over by a group of young revolutionaries headed by Fidel Castro, not be transformed into "our Latin American Hungary." Stone praised Castro as a modern hero who had successfully battled against "the Colossus of the North." Once again, Stone proved susceptible to utopian visions of romantic revolutionaries ushering in the good society, albeit in other lands.

Such a propensity hardly endeared Stone to government officials, who were already little disposed to think well of him. On January 27, 1959, Francis E. Walter, head of the HUAC denounced Stone as having "publicly the worst front record of anybody that I know." Nevertheless, Stone's star rose as the 1960s unfolded. His consistent support for the civil rights movement, praise for the early New Left, and prophetic warnings about American operations in Southeast Asia caused the *Weekly*'s subscription figures to soar. While Stone had previously called for an American Gandhi to head a civil rights crusade, he appreciated the frustrations and anger that led many African Americans to identify with the militant stance of Malcolm X and black power advocates. He applauded the formation of the Student Non-Violent Coordinating Committee (SNCC) and Students for a Democratic Society (SDS), organizations that promised to avoid the ideological straitjacket that had crippled the Old Left. Members of the New Left, in turn, devotedly read the *Weekly*; many, like SDS leaders Tom Hayden and Todd Gitlin, considered Stone an iconic figure who was one of the few able to bridge the chasm between the new, young radicals and the Old Left.

To the delight of New Leftists, the journalist warned that in the swamps of Vietnam, "swarming gnats can devour a giant," and he condemned "the Steve Canyon comic strip mentality" that appeared to guide U.S. policy regarding Southeast Asia. Elegantly, Stone suggested that military theorists at the Pentagon failed to take into account "the injured racial feelings, the misery, the rankling slights, the hatred, the devotion, the inspiration and the desperation" of guerrilla fighters. Consequently, those strategists proved unable to understand what compelled those men "to take to the bush and live gun in hand like a hunted animal." Stone dismissed counterinsurgency as "the dazzling latest military toothpaste for social decay" and condemned the U.S. military for "the uprooting of the rural population and its incarceration in stockaded villages, the spraying of poisons from the air on crops and cattle in violation of the Geneva Convention, the use of napalm for attack on villages suspected of harboring rebels." He worried that the American government seemed to subscribe to the doctrine that "pure 'might' is right" and to view Vietnam as "a training ground for the Legions of the Pax Americana." ♦

But Stone also condemned hate-filled rhetoric and Leninist tactics that, by the late 1960s, replaced SNCC's call for the "beloved community" and SDS's affirmation of participatory democracy. He was particularly troubled by the playing-at-revolution antics of groups like the Black Panthers and the Weathermen—which included his niece, Kathy Boudin. And he pointedly wrote, "We are not going to sell peace by spreading hate and hysteria." In addition, he warned, "You cannot beat men into angels, nor make them better by calling them 'pigs.'" His Vietnam analyses were perhaps his most poignant and undoubtedly his most popular articles, enabling the *Weekly*'s subscription totals to surpass the 70,000 mark by 1971. Stone presciently warned that the longer the war went on, the more difficult the peace process would become.

Due to deteriorating health, Stone shut down the newsletter in December 1971. He continued to write for the influential *New York Review of Books*—to which he had first contributed essays in 1964—and other leading publications around the country. With the closing of the *Weekly*, the *Washington Post* acclaimed Stone as possibly "the only Marxist ever to make good as a capitalist in the fiercely competitive jungle of American free enterprise journalism." Columnist Nicholas von Hoffman noted that Stone's "skeptical way of working" had required insider information, making Izzy "the top investigative reporter of his era." In the period of his semi-retirement, Stone wrote a best seller, *The Trial of Socrates*, and appeared at countless universities in the United States and abroad. In the process, a prediction he had made long ago came to fruition; increasingly, he was no longer viewed as "a pariah" or simply "a character" but rather as something of "a national institution." Perhaps this was so because Stone's reportage had lost its dramatic flair, and the journalistic lion, despite the occasional roar, seemed somewhat defanged. He died at Boston's Brigham and Women's Hospital on May 21, 1989.

The controversies that had always swirled about him never entirely abated. After his death, the *National Review* dismissed him as "a conformist, a lock-step leftist." More disturbing still were charges that Stone had been paid for delivering information to Soviet agents. Although these charges were never substantiated, they renewed decades-long battles regarding the very nature of the American Old Left. At the same time, in journalism schools and throughout the journalistic trade, I.F. Stone remained highly esteemed for his principled stands and the quality of his investigative work and for having inspired a generation of journalists. **)**

J. EDGAR HOOVER
Fighter Against the Red Menace

As chief of the General Intelligence Division (GID) of the Department of Justice, J. Edgar Hoover initially made his mark shortly after World War I by devising a card file index to monitor radicals in the United States. Covering radical individuals, groups, and publications throughout the country, the GID also singled out such liberal figures as Senator Robert M. La Follette, social worker Jane Addams, and federal judge George Anderson. Within a matter of months, the collection contained some 150,000 names, a figure that tripled by 1921. In 1919 and 1920, federal agents relied on Hoover's list to carry out the Palmer raids, a series of actions against radical aliens, under the auspices of Attorney General A. Mitchell Palmer. Over the next half-century, Hoover proved instrumental in ensuring that the U.S. government and the American people viewed radicals in a suspicious light. Through both legal and extralegal means, he targeted a procession of left-of-center individuals and organizations, particularly those tied to the American Communist Party but also other leading representatives of the Old Left, such as I.F. Stone, notwithstanding the distance he maintained from the Communist Party. Hoover's early involvement with the World War I–era Red Scare only convinced him that all radicals were suspect and should be closely followed by government agents.

John Edgar Hoover was born on January 1, 1895, into a middle-class family that resided in a Victorian house in the southeastern sector of the nation's capital. He was the last of four children raised by Dickerson Naylor Hoover, who boasted English and German origins, and Annie Marie Scheitlin, whose Swiss ancestors immigrated to the United States in the early nineteenth century. Distinguished relatives on Annie's side included her grandfather and great-uncle, both of whom served as Swiss consul to the United States; a federal judge; and U.S. Supreme Court justice Harold Burton. Dickerson, like his own father, had a job with the U.S. Coast and Geodetic Survey, working as a plate maker before heading the printing division. His son, Dickerson Jr., several years older than John Edgar, eventually was named inspector general of the U.S. Steamboat Inspection Service.

The family disciplinarian, Annie particularly influenced her youngest, John Edgar, fostering both belief in time-honored virtues and an ambitious nature. Nevertheless, he discarded his mother's Lutheranism to attend the renowned Old First Presbyterian Church, whose members included many top government officials. Drawn to Old First's young minister, Donald Campbell MacLeon, Hoover was soon teaching in the Sunday school, which championed traditional American values. Attending segregated Central High, one of Washington's finest schools, Hoover excelled on the debate team, served as one of three captains of the Central High School Cadet Corps, and became class valedictorian. Although aspiring to become an attorney, rather than a preacher as some friends had anticipated, Hoover retained a belief, as historian

Richard Gid Powers noted, "in progressive America's white Christian vision of good and evil."

During Hoover's senior year, his father suffered a nervous breakdown. Declining a scholarship to the University of Virginia, Hoover chose to remain in the family home and to accept a position as junior messenger for the Library of Congress, while enrolling in evening classes at George Washington University. Within three years, Hoover moved up the ranks at the Library of Congress, becoming first a cataloger and then a clerk. He joined the Kappa Alpha fraternity at George Washington, excelled in the classroom, and proved adept at moot court proceedings. In 1916, he completed his bachelor of law degree; the following year, he took a master's in law. In late July 1917, three months after the United States entered World War I, Hoover joined the Department of Justice as an intelligence clerk, receiving an exemption from military service. Within a year, he was promoted to the position of attorney, which virtually doubled his pay to $1,800 a year.

Hoover's ascent within the Justice Department proved meteoric. The young attorney clearly stood out, dressing well, exhibiting an extraordinary attention to detail, and seeking more responsibility, all of which apparently impressed his superiors. The new special assistant to the attorney general for war work, John Lord O'Brian, named Hoover to head a branch of the Enemy Alien Registration Section. The Justice Department, which included the Bureau of Investigation, was involved in a campaign against German spies, saboteurs, and traitors; aliens were particularly viewed as suspect. The administration of Woodrow Wilson, allied to the progressive movement that flourished during the first decade-and-a-half of the twentieth century, sought to ameliorate the worst aspects of industrial capitalism. Yet there was another side to progressivism, a near-hysterical obsession with immigration restriction, prohibition of alcohol, and the restriction of civil liberties. Although Hoover favored attempts by progressives to modernize corporate or government practices, he exuded both a stern sense of Victorian moralism and a marked parochialism.

After the war, Hoover, now special assistant to the attorney general, largely instigated the Palmer Raids of 1919 and 1920, resulting in the arrest and deportation of thousands of alien radicals. It was Hoover, rather than Attorney General Palmer, who devised the card index system in Justice's Radical Division, soon renamed the General Intelligence Division, and selected the individuals and groups to be rounded up. Quick to recognize the publicity value of singling out key individuals for prosecution, Hoover went after anarchist leaders Emma Goldman and Alexander Berkman, among the 249 aliens deported to communist Russia on the "Red Ark." As the Red Scare continued,

Hoover evidently convinced Palmer to employ charged phrases like "moral rats," "scum of the earth," and "pale pink parlor Bolsheviks." He also edited a newsletter, the *Bureau of Investigation General Intelligence Bulletin*, which castigated leading figures on the left and condemned critics of the bureau's anticommunist drive, such as Assistant Secretary of Labor Louis B. Post and journalist Walter Lippmann. In addition, Hoover initiated an investigation of Marcus Garvey, the Jamaican immigrant and black nationalist, the first of his campaigns against black leaders.

Hoover successively was appointed assistant director, acting director, and finally, on December 19, 1924, permanent director of the Bureau of Investigation. Attorney General Harlan F. Stone wanted Hoover to clean up the bureau, which had acquired an unsavory reputation for politically motivated investigations under director William J. Burns. Having dissolved the GID, Stone ordered Hoover to investigate only "violations of law," not political beliefs or activities. Hoover agreed to this condition, but continued to covertly tail a series of individuals, along with various organizations. Later, the administration of Herbert Hoover demanded political intelligence from the bureau. In 1930, its director willingly appeared before the Fish Committee, headed by Representative Hamilton Fish III, which sought to investigate communist activities in the United States.

Determined to reshape the bureau's image, Hoover underscored its professionalism, ensuring, for example, that the agency became renowned for its fingerprinting expertise and compiling of crime statistics. During the Great Depression of the 1930s, Hoover and the bureau achieved great fame battling a crime wave sweeping over the country. Hoover cracked a series of cases involving notorious gangsters like Pretty Boy Floyd and John Dillinger. Hollywood films, such as *G-Men*, starring James Cagney, extolled the FBI. Hoover became a trusted ally of President Franklin Delano Roosevelt, and the bureau appeared to be integrally tied to the New Deal reforms. In 1935, Hoover established a National Police Academy, linking the bureau and local police forces. Aided by top assistants like Clyde Tolson, who had become Hoover's lifelong companion, he maintained strong-arm control of the agency, renamed the Federal Bureau of Investigation in 1936. Perhaps most important of all, Roosevelt removed any shackles that dated back to Harlan F. Stone's tenure. Hoover consequently increased the bureau's domestic intelligence work, trailing "Nazi groups." Then, on August 24, 1936, Roosevelt called for intelligence information on "subversive activities in the United States, particularly Fascism and Communism."

To provide such information, Hoover devised a new General Intelligence

Section within the FBI. At the same time, he relied on an index of 2,500 individuals purportedly "engaged in activities of Communism, Nazism and various forms of foreign espionage." He leaked information to the HUAC, which was formed in 1938, so that leftists in particular could be assailed. Hoover also initiated the Custodial Detention Program, which targeted individuals to be incarcerated during a national emergency. He cultivated relationships with organizations across the American political and cultural landscape, including the American Legion, the American Bar Association, and the U.S. Chamber of Commerce, and established a network of informers designed to ferret out "subversive activities" throughout the nation.

In addition, Hoover allowed FBI agents to wiretap without court orders, to open mail, and to conduct break-ins of those considered subversive or engaged in espionage. Even after America entered the war in 1941, the FBI continued to follow Soviets officials and American communists more closely than it did Axis agents and their supporters in the United States. Nevertheless, the FBI long failed to identify Soviet espionage operations or to build a case to prosecute either Soviet operatives or their American accomplices. Criticisms of FBI practices, such as those offered by I.F. Stone, occurred from time to time. After the attack on Pearl Harbor, for example, critics, including Senator Harry S Truman, questioned why Hoover had not detected the presence of so-called fifth columnists in Hawaii. Characteristically, Hoover dismissed such queries as part of a concerted smear campaign by communists and their "propagandists."

Throughout this period, Hoover remained a trusted lieutenant of President Roosevelt, who allowed him to help orchestrate censorship of news accounts as the nation headed for war. The president also authorized the establishment of a Special Intelligence Service within the FBI to ferret out information about Axis operations in South America. Hoover successfully warded off a bid by William Donovan's Office of Strategic Services to conduct domestic intelligence operations in the United States. Consequently, at the end of World War II, the FBI's preeminence in the field of domestic security was assured. In addition, Hoover had painstakingly carved out alliances with key media and congressional figures, generally of a decidedly conservative cast. Beginning in mid-April 1945, a pleased Hoover could listen to a new radio serial, *This Is Your FBI*, which the bureau promoted.

However, Hoover's relations with Roosevelt's successor, President Truman, proved troubled, just as a new international crisis brewed. Truman, after all, had attacked the FBI's failure to ward off the attack on Pearl Harbor. On hearing that Roosevelt had died, Hoover ordered one of his top assistants to

47

bring him any files on Truman. As suggested by a note Truman wrote to his wife, Bess, the FBI director had good reason to be concerned. Declaring that he was determined to prevent an "NKVD or Gestapo in this country," Truman wrote, "Edgar Hoover's organization would make a good start toward a citizen spy system. Not for me." Still, the advent of the Cold War was timely for Hoover, an inveterate anticommunist who had initially made his reputation in government circles by assailing alien radicals. Hoover warned that American communists were again adopting a militant posture. Over the next several years, in public addresses, in congressional hearings, and in print, he assailed the CPUSA and its members as subversives who were determined to harm the United States and provide comfort to its enemies. In the process, he helped create the virulent Red Scare of the early postwar years.

Unleashing FBI agents to conduct political surveillance, Hoover increasingly fed information to the White House, Congress, and friendly media sources regarding the purported subversive activities of various individuals. He quickly came to believe that the Truman administration was little inclined to heed such warnings involving government officials like John Stewart Service and Alger Hiss. Service, a leading China expert in the State Department, was accused of delivering classified documents to *Amerasia*, a radical publication that focused on international affairs. Hiss, who had steadily moved up the ranks at State, had reportedly passed on crucial government papers to communist spies during the 1930s. Much of the information the FBI received came from ex-communists who themselves had been involved in espionage but had soured on the Soviet Dream. Two of the most important of these figures were Elizabeth Bentley, the "blond spy queen," and Whittaker Chambers, who singled out Hiss for his supposed communist ties and espionage operations.

In these and other noteworthy cases, the FBI seemingly failed to turn up damning evidence. Its agents declined to reveal the discovery of highly sensitive documents in the *Amerasia* offices, signs of espionage, and indications that additional classified documents would be leaked. The bureau's investigation of Hiss, which included wiretapping, produced nothing incriminating; even if it had, evidence obtained through break-ins and unauthorized wiretaps could not be used in a court of law. Ironically, the FBI's own heavy-handed practices imperiled the prosecution of a number of celebrated cases, such as the one involving Judith Coplon, a Justice Department employee accused of delivering FBI documents to a Soviet official. Hoover informed Attorney General Tom Clark that if the defense team were allowed access to FBI materials, "the future not only of the Bureau but of the Department and its effectiveness to discharge its responsibilities in the more important field of national security" would be endangered. FBI documents pertaining to Coplon had been garnered through wiretaps, while some of the records had been destroyed.

Although the FBI failed to prove it, the Soviet Union was indeed conducting espionage operations in the United States, relying on a small group of Communist Party members or sympathizers willing to provide information because of ideological commitment or for a price. Military intelligence, rather than the FBI, carried out the Venona Project, which proved that actual cases of espionage were occurring. President Truman remained unaware of Venona at the time. Once again, thanks to publicity campaigns Hoover orchestrated, he managed to mute criticism of the FBI, which more than ever was viewed as the embodiment of moral rectitude and American ideals.

At the same time, Hoover stood ready to condemn those he viewed as remiss in attacking the enemy. Hoover considered Truman's response to the loyalty dilemma inadequate, as demonstrated in the FBI director's appearance before HUAC on March 26, 1947. He charged that the CPUSA sought the violent overthrow of the American government. The party members, he declared, subscribed to "the one cardinal rule . . . that the support of Soviet Russia is the duty of Communists of all nations." Ominously, while one communist could be found among every 2,277 individuals in prerevolutionary Russia, "in the United States today there is one Communist for every 1814 persons in the country." Hoover offered his full support for HUAC's determination to root out "Communists and sympathizers" from government service. At the same time, he feared "for the liberals and progressives . . . hoodwinked and duped into joining hands with the Communists."

All the while, the FBI engaged in a crusade of its own against countless individuals and numerous groups, including those unfortunate enough to be placed on the attorney general's list of supposedly subversive organizations in November 1947. As it had since early in the war, the bureau examined purported communist influence in Hollywood. Repeatedly, agents broke into the headquarters of the Communist Party in Los Angeles to garner the names of those who would soon be grilled by investigative committees. In similar fashion, the FBI attempted to find out who in government service might be homosexual. Such individuals, the reasoning went, could be subjected to blackmail. Indeed, the FBI had been collecting such information since 1937. Later, the FBI established a Sex Deviate program that allowed allegations of homosexual activity to be delivered to government officials. Cards in Hoover's Official and Confidential File referred to Democratic Party leader Adlai Stevenson, among others. Given rumors about Hoover's own ambiguous sexual orientation, the homophobic cast of the FBI proved hypocritical at best.

In March 1948, President Truman issued an executive order foreclosing the release of FBI files to Congress. Notwithstanding the presidential directive, Hoover continued to leak information to key allies in the legislative branch, such as Senator Pat McCarran of Nevada, who chaired the Senate Internal Security Subcommittee, and to other conservatives. Although his relationship with Truman remained uneasy, Hoover strongly backed the Justice Department's decision to use the 1940 Smith Act, which criminalized advocating the violent overthrow of the U.S. government, to prosecute top leaders of the Communist Party. The first trial saw Herbert Philbrick, reputedly a party official, deliver gripping testimony as an FBI informant. This trial and others that followed drove many communists underground and all but fatally weakened the party.

When Senator Joseph McCarthy of Wisconsin became a leading red-baiter in 1950, he possessed a willing ally in Hoover, whose bureau passed him confidential information. Without Hoover's assistance, McCarthyism would not have flourished as it did. Indeed, the entire postwar Red Scare, like the one that followed World War I, owed much to Hoover's machinations. Both campaigns garnered great attention for Hoover, support for his crusades, and, ultimately, heightened power for the FBI and its predecessor. During the zenith of the domestic Red Scare, Hoover remained fixated on the political activities and beliefs of those who were stationed on the left side of the ideological spectrum, including Albert Einstein; Charlie Chaplin, the great Hollywood actor; and Paul Robeson, also a film actor, who was one of the nation's foremost theatrical performers, and a social activist increasingly viewed as pro-Soviet.

However, following Dwight Eisenhower's election to the presidency, McCarthy's attacks became still more outlandish, and Hoover's friendship cooled. Hoover, in a concerted effort to ensure Eisenhower's defeat of Adlai Stevenson, had fed information to McCarthy and to Eisenhower's running mate, Richard M. Nixon, about Stevenson's alleged homosexual escapades. Now, Hoover had another ally in the White House, who, like the FBI chief, favored a go-slow approach regarding civil rights. Hoover's refusal to allow more materials to be funneled to McCarthy proved damaging to the senator when his tactics were challenged by CBS newsman Edward R. Murrow, Republican senators Margaret Chase Smith and Ralph Flanders, and, to a certain extent, the Eisenhower administration, which came to consider McCarthy out of control. Hoover's readiness to withdraw support from McCarthy did not surprise one former assistant who later recalled, "He used him when he was useful and then, later, dumped him when he wasn't."

By contrast, the FBI continued to provide information—when it could not be traced back to the bureau—to investigative committees and friendly media that attacked both radicals and liberals. Moreover, Hoover was called on by the administration to dig up dirt against its antagonists. In public forums, such as his annual sessions with the House Appropriations Committee, Hoover was received warmly, with plaudits generously offered. One reason for such favorable treatment was the batch of FBI files, replete with all sorts of innuendoes and scuttlebutt, which Hoover held on both political figures and journalists. These were the same kinds of documents he had gathered on liberal and radical figures four decades earlier.

During the Eisenhower era, Hoover's power reached its height. Both President Eisenhower and Vice President Nixon maintained friendly relations with Hoover, as did their staffs, enabling him to help determine government policy. His influence also extended to his cronies in Congress, many situated in key committee posts, and throughout the State Department, including its Passport Division. At Hoover's behest, countless well-known individuals suffered indignities, including the denial or revocation of passports. A number were placed on a watch list, which allowed FBI agents to track the overseas travel of figures ranging from author John Steinbeck to U.S. Supreme Court justice William O. Douglas. The nation's top court was itself shaped, at least in part, by Hoover, whose bureau carried out full field investigations of potential nominees.

One issue—organized crime—did threaten to cause tensions between the FBI and the Eisenhower administration. The attorney general, William Rogers, believed that organized crime should be pursued. Hoover continued to insist, as he had all along, that the very idea of a national crime network was "baloney." Earlier, Hoover had refused to provide assistance to Senator Estes Kefauver, the head of the Senate Special Committee to Investigate Organized Crime in Interstate Commerce. Kefauver had been forced to rely on Harry Anslinger of the Federal Bureau of Narcotics, whom Hoover despised, along with the chiefs of crime commissions across the country. The FBI proved unwilling even to help shield witnesses from hit men. Then, after two of his witnesses had been murdered, Kefauver had to listen to Hoover say, "I regret to advise the Federal Bureau of Investigation is not empowered to perform guard duties." However, the discovery by New York state police in November 1957 of a meeting of top Mafia bosses in Apalachin, New York, finally compelled Hoover to make an effort to target organized crime.

He never did so with the kind of determination he demonstrated with regard to the threat supposedly presented by domestic radicals. By 1957, the U.S.

Supreme Court, headed by Chief Justice Earl Warren, appeared increasingly ill-disposed to support the infringements on the civil liberties of dissidents that investigative committees and police agencies had long undertaken. Perhaps the Court was able to render such decisions because the CPUSA, battered by disturbing revelations of Stalinist horrors by Soviet premier Nikita Khrushchev, appeared weaker than ever. In the very period when the CPUSA's membership had plummeted and its moral standing, even among longtime party faithful, seemed more tenuous than ever, Hoover chose to institute a new, aggressive campaign against radicals. His Counter Intelligence Program, or COINTELPRO, was designed to further weaken the CPUSA by engaging in dirty tricks among the party faithful. (The program relied on false rumors and innuendoes, but also break-ins and wiretaps not approved by the courts.) These methods made perfect sense to Hoover, who continued to view the American communist as "Public Enemy No. 1." His worldview was expressed in the ghost-written, best-selling book *Masters of Deceit,* which was released in 1958 by the Henry Holt publishing company, owned by Clint Murchison, a right-wing Texas oilman who was a good friend of Hoover's. The small size of the CPUSA, the book claimed, made little difference because the Soviet Union continued to steer the international communist movement: "Night after night, week after week, these men and women are plotting against America, working out smears, seeking to discredit free government, and planning for revolution. They form the base of a gigantic pyramid of treason, stretching from the little gray house with green shutters to the towers of the Kremlin."

As the tumultuous 1960s unfolded, Hoover's standing waxed and waned. His relationship with President John F. Kennedy and especially Attorney General Robert F. Kennedy proved troubled. Hoover, long ago having discarded any progressive pretenses, cared little for the reform agenda of the Kennedy administration. He was particularly displeased with Robert Kennedy's determination to rein in organized crime and his support, however belated, for the civil rights campaign then flourishing in the American South. Hoover was appalled by the attorney general's style, disheveled appearance, and readiness to pop into FBI headquarters uninvited. The Kennedys received reports from some of their top advisers about hysterical rants on the part of the FBI director. Not surprisingly, Hoover maintained an extensive file on both Kennedys, focusing heavily on the president's extramarital affairs.

While especially reluctant to devote the energies of the FBI to assisting the Justice Department in protecting civil rights activists, Hoover expanded the operations of COINTELPRO. Over the next several years, the FBI targeted the Socialist Workers Party, the civil rights movement, and antiwar forces, (sometimes using illegal wiretapping, break-ins, and dirty tricks) The FBI also singled out individuals like Martin Luther King Jr. for surveillance. Seeking cover, Hoover obtained authorization for bugging King from the attorney general, who was worried about possible communist influence on the civil rights leader and the damage the Kennedy administration would suffer if news of that connection were released to the general public.

In contrast to President Kennedy, his successor, Lyndon Baines Johnson, developed a much warmer relationship with the FBI director. Johnson, like Hoover, apparently relished exploring the personal lives of various individuals. (He also called on Hoover to provide damaging information about administration foes.) Johnson particularly sought derogatory reports regarding antiwar critics. So did Johnson's successor, Richard Nixon. An earlier beneficiary of FBI largesse and the recipient of political advice from Hoover after his defeat in the 1960 presidential race, Nixon finally entered the Oval Office in 1969. Early in his administration, Hoover's support appeared indispensable as the FBI boss provided apparently damning information about sitting Supreme Court justices Abe Fortas and William O. Douglas. Nixon wanted to transform the High Court by replacing liberal jurists with more conservative ones. Hoover also offered information that Vice President Spiro T. Agnew wielded against campus activists, the Black Panthers, and antiwar protesters. At the behest of the Nixon administration, the FBI agreed to wiretap Washington journalists, White House staffers, and employees of the National Security Council, the State Department, and the Department of Defense. Still, the bureau, like the Central Intelligence Agency, never found the proof sought by Nixon, like Johnson before him, that the antiwar movement was orchestrated from abroad.

Nixon's support for Hoover waned dramatically when the FBI director refused to support a full-scale campaign by the White House to widen the scope of domestic security operations. Hoover's opposition hardly rested on principle, as his agents had repeatedly engaged in illegal wiretappings, buggings, and break-ins. Rather, he feared the political fallout that might occur if the new campaign came under public scrutiny. His resistance ensured that the Nixon administration would begin to view Hoover as a liability and consider removing him from his post. Refusing to resign, Hoover held onto his job until his death on May 2, 1972. Within a matter of weeks, the dirty tricks carried out by the Nixon administration culminated in the break-in at the Democratic Party's national headquarters at the Watergate complex in Washington, DC. The discovery of that felony and the ensuing cover-up, along with the unveiling of other purported violations of the law by the Nixon administration eventually led to impeachment proceedings in Congress and, ultimately, the president's resignation.

In the mid-1970s, congressional hearings documented some of the abuses that the FBI had undertaken under Hoover's stewardship. In early 1976, Attorney General Edward Levi, appointed by President Gerald R. Ford, crafted new directives regarding domestic security investigations by the FBI. Some critics urged that the J. Edgar Hoover Building in Washington, where the headquarters of the FBI was situated, be renamed. As the United States began conducting a so-called war against terrorism in the early twenty-first century, the administration of George W. Bush lifted the earlier restrictions on the FBI.

Conclusion

I.F. Stone and J. Edgar Hoover stood on opposite sides of a political divide separating strong-willed Americans in the first three-quarters of the twentieth century. Over the course of his lifetime, Stone engaged in an odyssey through the sectarian-ravaged thicket of American radicalism, delving into or skating around the edges of liberalism, progressivism, socialism, and communism. During the early stages of his lengthy career, Hoover also was part of the progressive movement that then dominated American life, favoring its modern-looking approach to order and efficiency but also exhibiting its sometimes darker, moralistic side. Hoover became a leading figure in devising antiradical crusades, which he considered necessary to sustain sacrosanct American values. The two men operated in different fashions, with the loner Stone, alternately grumpy and gregarious, ever determined to carve out his own path, even if that required him to criticize ideological kin, and the consummate government bureaucrat Hoover constructing his own empire at the FBI that even presidents proved loath to challenge.

Study Questions

1. The American Left proved enormously controversial. What factors led to the perception that the Left was "un-American"?
2. I.F. Stone is considered a journalistic gadfly who questioned American domestic and foreign policies. Why did he adopt this posture?
3. J. Edgar Hoover carved out a bureaucratic empire at the highest levels of American government. What ideas guided Hoover as he became such a powerful figure?

4. What role did Hoover play in the emergence of the postwar Red Scare?

5. Compare and contrast Stone's and Hoover's visions of the American nation.

Selected Bibliography

Ackerman, Kenneth D. Young, J. Edgar Hoover, *The Red Scare, and the Assault on Civil Liberties*. New York: Carroll & Graf, 2007.

Braudy, Susan. *Family Circle: The Boudins and the Aristocracy of the Left*. New York: Knopf, 2003.

Cottrell, Robert C. *Izzy: A Biography of I.F. Stone*. New Brunswick: Rutgers University Press, 1992.

Gentry, Curt. *J. Edgar Hoover: The Man and the Secrets*. New York: W.W. Norton, 1991.

Hersh, Burton. *Bobby and J. Edgar: The Historic Face-Off Between the Kennedys and J. Edgar Hoover that Transformed America*. New York: Carroll & Graf, 2007.

Hoover, J. Edgar. *Masters of Deceit: The Story of Communism in America and How to Fight It*. New York: Henry Holt, 1994.

Keller, William W. *The Liberals and J. Edgar Hoover: Rise and Fall of a Domestic Intelligence State*. Princeton: Princeton University Press, 1989.

MacPherson, Myra. *"All Governments Lie": The Life and Times of Rebel Journalist I. F. Stone*. New York: Scribner, 2006.

O'Reilly, Kenneth. *Hoover and the Un-Americans: The FBI, HUAC, and the Red Menace*. Philadelphia: Temple University Press, 1983.

Powers, Richard Gid. *Secrecy and Power: The Life of J. Edgar Hoover*. New York: Free Press, 1987.

Stone, I.F. *I.F. Stone's Weekly*, 1953–1971.

———. *In a Time of Torment, 1961–1967*. New York: Random House, 1967.

———. *Polemics and Prophecies, 1967–1970*. New York: Random House, 1970.

———. *The Truman Era, 1945–1952*. New York: Monthly Review Press, 1953.

———. *The War Years, 1939–1945*. Boston: Little, Brown, 1988.

Summers, Anthony. *Official and Confidential: The Secret Life of J. Edgar Hoover*. New York: G.P. Putnam, 1993.

Theoharis, Athan G., ed. *From the Secret Files of J. Edgar Hoover*. Chicago: Ivan R. Dee, 1993.

———. *J. Edgar Hoover, Sex, and Crime: An Historical Antidote*. Chicago: Ivan R. Dee, 1995.

Theoharis, Athan G., and John Stuart Cox. *The Boss: J. Edgar Hoover and the Great American Inquisition*. Philadelphia: Temple University Press, 1988.

3

The Transformation
of Popular Culture

In many ways, the 1950s were especially conducive to an unusually vibrant American popular culture. American society was considerably more stable than in past decades, undergirded by unprecedented material abundance, and few social problems seemed urgent. More leisure time and spendable income meant greater opportunities to enjoy films, sports, theater, books, magazines, radio, television, and recorded music. While these circumstances produced a great variety of celebrities in multiple areas, few captured the public's attention as did Marilyn Monroe and Elvis Presley.

During the 1950s, Marilyn Monroe was widely celebrated as America's sex goddess, but her undeniable sexual allure was only part of her appeal. A compelling innocence and modesty, combined with significant dramatic and musical abilities, also fueled her meteoric rise to stardom. Monroe's preeminence as a pop icon coincided with an era in which Americans began a tentative reevaluation of sexual mores. Fears about the erosion of morality drove many people to a defense of traditional values and conventional attitudes about female sexuality. Others, rejecting the hypocritical values of the past, embraced a more open, healthy sexuality; their voices presaged a building sexual revolution that erupted in full force in the following decade. Monroe, the virtual embodiment of sensuality in a society that remained predominantly conservative in its sexual attitudes, was at best an ambiguous symbol. Her personal tragedy stemmed from her inability to transcend the persona that had brought her fame.

Elvis Presley was an unlikely avatar of the music revolution that he sparked. The Mississippi-born teen was shy, unassuming, and initially unsure of his musical identity. Nevertheless, the fusion of musical traditions that he represented not only gave definition to Presley's unique style, but also laid the foundations for the rock and roll revolution. Presley's arrival on the scene in the mid-1950s marked the end of a musical era dominated by bland, unchallenging "adult" music. Henceforth, American youth had their own music, and it was one of many things that increasingly differentiated them from their elders. It was sensual, raw, loud, and, equally threatening, performed by musicians like Presley, whose suggestive physical movements provoked shockingly emotional responses from screaming fans. An overnight celebrity, Presley showcased his music on television and in film as well as on records, achieving worldwide fame by the late 1950s. His most innovative music came from these years; by the 1960s, his career slumped as he devoted more time to films and innocuous pop ballads. After a surprising comeback in 1968, Presley rapidly fell victim to success and celebrity. His early death from drugs and self-indulgence was testimony to the many stresses and inner conflicts that overwhelmed him. Nevertheless, legions of rock musicians have testified to Presley's influence on them and his centrality to the pop music revolution.

MARILYN MONROE
Symbol of the New Sexuality

On a cold, gray day in mid-February 1954, some 13,000 men of the First Marine Division assembled at their isolated, mountainous base camp in the northern reaches of South Korea. Shivering in the cold, they eagerly awaited the arrival of a visitor whose appearance promised some relief from long months of tedious duty. Eventually, an Army helicopter swooped in for a low pass along the mountainside above the gathering. The aircraft's side door slid open to reveal a vision that must have seemed unreal to the hard-bitten Marines. Marilyn Monroe, safely secured by two soldiers who sat on her feet as she lay on her stomach, hung out the door laughing and blowing kisses to the awed troops, whose cheering increased in volume with each of the four passes that the helicopter made. By the time the craft set down, the crowd was delirious with excitement.

The twenty-eight-year-old actress, only recently married to baseball legend Joe DiMaggio, was already a cultural phenomenon, and her fame extended to the multitude of military outposts that had spread across the globe with the advance of the Cold War. Her popularity as a pinup girl, judged by the photos displayed in GI barracks, was unrivaled. She received more fan letters from military personnel than any other Hollywood star. Her appeal was in part sensuous; blonde, blue-eyed, five–foot–five in height, and boasting measurements of 37–23–36, Monroe projected a smoldering sexuality. The complement to this, however, was a modest demeanor that conveyed vulnerability and even loneliness. In her USO-sponsored performance, she gave the Marines the show they were expecting. Discarding her khaki pants and windbreaker for a low-cut, sequined sheath dress, Monroe gamely rendered an upbeat version of "Diamonds Are a Girl's Best Friend," a showstopper from her film *Gentlemen Prefer Blondes*. She followed up with "Do It Again," a selection that brought howls of delight from the now nearly berserk audience. The USO tour took her to nine more sites over four days, during which she entertained over 100,000 GIs. Her Korean tour was a turning point in her life. Long insecure and dependent on the advice and approval of a succession of husbands, directors, and acting coaches, Monroe discovered that she could succeed on her own. "Standing in the snowfall facing these yelling soldiers," she recounted to writer Ben Hecht, "I felt for the first time in my life no fear of anything. I felt only happy."

Her happiness proved fleeting. In later years, Monroe was persistently haunted by feelings of inadequacy. Seeking to move beyond the limitations of the sex-kitten persona that had won her renown, she encountered numerous obstacles and stresses that gradually overwhelmed her. Her celebrity career paralleled an era during which American social and cultural values were in subtle flux, reshaped by a multitude of postwar dynamics. Her public image was built around a carefree celebration of sensuality, a concept that contravened stubbornly conventional prevailing values in the 1950s. As the decade wore on, a series of developments portended a coming revolution in sexual mores and behavior, but Marilyn Monroe would not live to see its culmination.

The woman that the world came to know as Marilyn Monroe was born on June 1, 1926, in Los Angeles. Though she carried the name Norma Jean Mortenson, she never knew with certainty who was her father. Her mother, Gladys Mortensen, garnered a bewildering array of surnames (including Monroe) in the course of an erratic personal life. A film cutter at RKO Studios, Gladys proved ill suited to motherhood and suffered extended episodes of mental instability. Consequently, friends Albert and Ida Bolender took in Norma Jean as a foster child only days after her birth. Thus began a childhood filled with loss, uncertainty, and jarring shifts in direction. In 1933, Gladys, accompanied by friend Grace McKee, appeared at the Bolender home to reclaim her daughter, and the two moved into a home near the Hollywood Bowl. During these childhood years, Norma Jean was introduced to the cinematic world of alluring actresses like Mae West, Katharine Hepburn, and, most significantly, the famous temptress Jean Harlow. In early 1934, however, Gladys began a period of near continual hospitalization from which she rarely reemerged. Grace McKee accepted the responsibility for parenting her friend's daughter and quickly became the dominant influence in Norma Jean's life.

Norma Jean's life soon took yet another unexpected direction when McKee married Ervin Goddard, an aspiring actor who saw the child as an unwelcome burden. In 1935, Norma Jean was signed into the Los Angeles Orphans Home, which she was dragged in and out of for the next seven years. In 1942, at age sixteen, Norma Jean was dating Jim Dougherty, a twenty-one-year-old aircraft plant worker. Grace, who thought marriage a reasonable expedient, pushed the couple toward a June wedding, after which they moved into a rented cabin in Sherman Oaks. Although Norma Jean accepted the arrangement, she always felt that she "never had a choice." Not surprisingly, the marriage gradually unraveled. Dougherty, who joined the Merchant Marine, proved jealous and controlling. Norma Jean, increasingly dissatisfied and bored, found wartime work at the Radioplane Company, where she sprayed varnish on fuselage fabric. It was there in 1944 that David Conover, an army photographer working for *Yank* magazine, spotted her and recognized her uniqueness. "There was a luminous quality to her face," he remembered, "a fragility combined with astonishing vibrancy." In August 1945, she signed with the Blue Book Agency, which promised a path to fame for aspiring models and actresses. On the advice of her employer, who pointed out that "gentlemen prefer blondes," Norma Jean had her brown hair lightened to a golden blonde. It was the first of many cosmetic changes that would transform Norma Jean's appearance over the next half-dozen years.

Her career developed quickly; by spring 1946, she had appeared on the covers of thirty-three magazines. Part of the price of success in her chosen field, however, was personal compromise. Norma Jean accepted the prevailing practice of granting sexual favors to photographers who best promoted her interests. That August she was offered a screen test at Twentieth Century Fox Studios, where cinematographer Leon Shamroy recalled the startling impression she made: "I got a cold chill. Every frame of the test radiated sex. She didn't need a sound track—she was creating effects visually." She would be, he thought, "another Harlow." Having signed a contract with Fox, Norma Jean was summoned to studio head Ben Lyon's office to settle the still confusing matter of her name. Beginning a new life, she rejected both her maiden name and her married name, taking instead the surname of her mother's family. Pondering a new first name, Lyon recalled an actress he had once known by the name of Marilyn Miller. "I know who you are," he proclaimed, "you're Marilyn!" Assuming a name both memorable and euphonic, Marilyn Monroe stepped away from her past. Long dependent on the charity and approval of others, she was now poised to define herself and to realize her own ambitions. The last remaining immediate obstacle was her marriage to Jim Dougherty, which she ended that September.

It soon became apparent that a studio contract did not bring instant stardom. Monroe appeared in two forgettable 1947 films, *Scudda-Hoo! Scudda-Hay!* and *The Dangerous Years.* When her contract was not renewed that year, she attended classes at the Actors Laboratory, where she was exposed to serious drama. Her financial situation deteriorated, however, and following a chance meeting with actor John Carroll, Monroe confided that all her money went toward rent, acting classes, and auto repairs. She survived, she confessed, by prostituting herself near Hollywood Boulevard. Carroll and his wife, Lucille, were appalled at her misfortunes and temporarily took her in. In 1948, Monroe signed a six-month contract with Columbia Studios, contingent on her agreeing to cosmetic changes, including raising her hairline and further lightening her hair color. She was then turned over to Columbia's drama coach, the German-born Natasha Lytess. Strong-willed and opinionated, Lytess exercised considerable influence over Monroe until the actress ended the relationship in 1953.

In May 1949, Monroe dropped by the Hollywood studio of photographer Tom Kelley, who hired her for a beer advertisement. Impressed with what he saw, he called her back when he was asked to provide an artfully rendered nude photo for a calendar. Monroe accepted the assignment, for which she was paid $50. She never saw Kelley again, but two of his photos were destined to become famous three years later. In the next few years, Monroe's film career moved forward fitfully, gaining considerable momentum from her appearance in John Huston's crime thriller *The Asphalt Jungle*, but stalling in thirteen unremarkable films in which she was always relegated to the role of a vacuous, sexy blonde. Her loneliness and need for approbation drew her into a succession of affairs with agents, coaches, and others who could forward her ambitions—perhaps most notably with director Elia Kazan. A new seven-year contract with Fox in 1951 testified to her growing popularity, however, and offered promise of future success.

That same year, Monroe was introduced to Arthur Miller, who was collaborating to produce his play *The Hook* with Kazan. Miller later remembered how, when they shook hands, "the shock of her body's motion sped through me, a sensation at odds with her sadness." Monroe, whose personal experience predisposed her to empathize with life's victims, was immediately drawn to Miller, whom she saw as a brilliant, courageous man unjustly stigmatized for his left-wing political sentiments. Though the two parted only as acquaintances, Miller was clearly overwhelmed by the young actress. Even years later, the playwright recounted the impact of "the solemnity of feeling in her eyes" and her "childish voracity." "I knew," he recalled with perhaps unconscious melodrama, "I must flee or walk into a doom beyond all knowing." In early 1952, another admirer arranged to meet Monroe. Joe DiMaggio, at thirty-seven, was one of the most famous names in baseball history. Having signed with the New York Yankees in 1935, "Joltin' Joe" was the center fielder for nine world championship teams, attaining enduring national celebrity. Hampered by injuries, DiMaggio left the Yankees in late 1951 and accepted employment as host of a New York television show. His infatuation with Monroe was prompted by a photo of the actress dressed in a revealing "baseball" outfit. Following an initial dinner date, the couple began a passionate romance much remarked on in the press. Though their mutual attraction was sincere, the two held conflicting expectations for their relationship. Monroe saw in DiMaggio a strong, protective figure who would encourage her ambitions. DiMaggio was entranced by the idea of marriage to an exceptionally beautiful woman who would fulfill the role of housewife and mother as defined by the traditional Italian American culture he had grown up in. Like Monroe's former husband, the famous athlete was jealous and possessive. It was their mutual misfortune that they sought to make a life together at a point at which DiMaggio's fame had already peaked, whereas Monroe's star was ascendant.

In March, Fox Studios was confronted with a potentially damaging public relations problem involving its rising star. One of Kelley's nude photos that Monroe had posed for in 1949 had appeared on calendars in 1951 and 1952. In an era in which censorship was more the rule than the exception, Hollywood's films were expected to conform to the quasi-Victorian standards of the Motion Picture Production Code, and nude calendar photos were widely held to be vulgar, if not obscene. Much to the relief of studio heads, Monroe skillfully turned the controversy in her favor, explaining in an interview with a reporter that she had agreed to the nude photo session out of financial necessity. "That wasn't a terrible thing to do, was it?" she tearfully asked the correspondent. As the story broke in the *Los Angeles Herald Examiner*, the focus was on the actress's courage in owning up to a difficult decision she had made in earlier and more desperate circumstances. It was a brilliant strategy that stressed the empathetic dimension of Monroe's public image—the lost waif, vulnerable, innocent, and ultimately pure of heart.

The following year, Hugh Hefner, an aspiring writer and publisher, perceived the commercial potential of a magazine that would promote a new, hip lifestyle centered on the open expression and celebration of sexuality. As he prepared the first issue of *Playboy*, which would appear in December 1953, he concluded that the nude Monroe photo was the obvious choice for the cover. Hefner intended to create a classy, sophisticated magazine that would cater to a new universe of male fantasies that a stable and materially abundant postwar America made possible. *Playboy*, he explained, would be "a pleasure primer styled for the male taste." Hefner's genius, as sex researcher Paul Gebhard noted in 1967, was to link "sex with upward mobility." Though the magazine's most direct appeal was to young, single men, even older, married men could participate at least partially in the good life that Hefner defined. In the magazine's premiere issue, Hefner touted the material essentials of a new suburban hedonism: tailored Ivy League clothes, expensive liquors and stereo equipment, flashy sports cars. For those prosperous men whose family commitments precluded indulgence in libertine sexuality, the desire to live the sophisticated life could be at least partially fulfilled by the acquisition of its material symbols. For most single American males, guiltless sex for pleasure, as advocated in *Playboy*, remained an unfulfilled if alluring possibility. But according to magazine cofounder Victor Lownes, Hefner and *Playboy* had "stoked the rebellion against the idea that pleasure automatically equates to evil. . . . We felt that America had outgrown that attitude."

The same year that *Playboy* began publication, Monroe's movie career soared with the release of two films that allowed her to demonstrate a fuller range of talents. In *Niagara*, a suspenseful film noir, Monroe was the seductive and dangerous Rose Loomis, a role that went far beyond the cheery, superficial characters she had most often played. Her subsequent role as the beautiful, seemingly naive gold digger Lorelei Lee in the light comedy-musical *Gentlemen Prefer Blondes* showcased the actress's singing. Her rendition of "Diamonds Are a Girl's Best Friend" was later deemed legendary. Unfortunately, the role of Lorelei Lee did much to affirm an almost universal image of Monroe as an impossibly voluptuous, somewhat vacuous blonde bombshell. She was not, nor did she want to be, Lorelei Lee, but rather aspired to serious dramatic roles. Her final film that year, the comedy *How to Marry a Millionaire*, was well received, but it was not a vehicle for the realization of serious ambitions.

Monroe's growing stature as the embodiment of uninhibited sexuality coincided with the 1953 publication of Alfred Kinsey's *Sexual Behavior in the Human Female*. An Indiana University scientist, Kinsey had previously published *Sexual Behavior in the Human Male*, a lengthy, jargon-ridden statistical study that nonetheless achieved best-seller status in 1948. Kinsey's findings about male sexual behavior, especially extramarital sex and homosexuality, provoked outrage from a public that resisted acknowledging sexual behaviors that did not comport with professed values. Presented in similarly detached scientific language, Kinsey's study of female sexuality sold 185,000 copies in ten days and generated a firestorm of moral indignation, not least over the author's conclusion that significant numbers of women were engaging in sex outside of marriage and, single and otherwise, enjoying it. Evangelist Billy Graham condemned Kinsey for contributing to "the already deteriorating morals of America." The head of the Union Theological Seminary denounced the study as "revealing a prevailing degradation in American morality approximating the worst decadence of the Roman Empire." The head of Indiana's Roman Catholic diocese warned that Kinsey's studies helped "pave the way for people to believe in communism." Such heated denunciations of Kinsey's studies reflected a disjunction in American sexual values that was becoming manifest in the 1950s, suggesting that the reports conveyed behavioral realities that many preferred to dismiss. American society remained, as one historian observed, ("in the throes of a kind of adolescent confusion about sex.") A wider acceptance of sexual openness and broadened conceptions of sexuality were still a decade in the future. For the time being, the frank sexuality of Marilyn Monroe remained incompatible with the canons of traditional morality.

Monroe's growing fame as the embodiment of sexual availability was not without complications. Jealous and dismissive of Monroe's acting ambitions, DiMaggio frequently criticized her dress and behavior but nevertheless continued to profess his desire for marriage. Ignoring these warning signs, Monroe agreed, and they were married in a civil ceremony at city hall in San Francisco in early 1954. Shortly afterward, the couple departed for Japan, where DiMaggio hoped to maintain his public visibility by attending some rookie training sessions and exhibition games. It was from Japan that Monroe departed with the USO for Korea and the restoration of her self-confidence. The couple returned to the United States to find both challenges and affirmations that year. DiMaggio's resentment of his wife's fame and brazen sexuality only intensified with time, straining their marriage. Monroe, who had twenty-four films to her credit between 1947 and 1954, was determined to be more selective about her roles even if it meant making fewer films—she would complete only five more through the end of her life. She now assumed a look that reflected her admiration for Jean Harlow—her hair dyed platinum and her body regularly clothed in shimmering white fabrics (As the pressures in her personal and professional life mounted, she commonly relied on sedatives for sleep, and rumors soon circulated concerning her late arrival on sets, emotional outbursts, and frequent drowsy demeanor.)

Back at Fox following a brief disagreement, Monroe went to work on *The Seven Year Itch*, a comedy in which she played opposite Tom Ewell. In early September, the production crew flew to New York City for on-location filming and, on announced days, huge crowds turned up to catch a glimpse of the famous actress. On September 15, one of the most famous scenes in American film history was created when Monroe stood over a sidewalk grating in front of Lexington Avenue's Trans-Lux Theater. As cameras rolled, a fan beneath the grating lifted her pleated white skirt to reveal her underwear, as Monroe took on an expression of incongruously innocent delight. As the sequence was repeated multiple times, hundreds of still photographers captured the event from a number of vantage points. Few images of Marilyn Monroe so captured the public fancy, and probably none so enraged her jealous husband. Forewarned by columnist Walter Winchell about the Lexington Avenue shoot, DiMaggio had rushed to New York to witness the event. Infuriated by what he saw, DiMaggio stormed off to a bar. The next morning, in the aftermath of a loud nighttime quarrel between the two, Monroe's coach Natasha Lytess encountered a bruised and shaken actress. Two weeks later, she filed for divorce, publicly attributing the split to a "conflict of careers." Privately, she confided, "I couldn't be the Italian housewife he wanted me to be."

Monroe's continuing search for identity and independence led her away from the screen image that had brought fame. In 1955, intent on deepening her acting talents, she moved to New York to study at the Actors Studio with Lee and Paula Strasberg, who insisted that she would never realize her true potential until she came to grips with her personal past. Accordingly, Monroe began sessions with a psychotherapist, the first of several she consulted. Her therapy sessions kept her in a constant state of emotional turmoil, driving her to use more drugs to counter anxiety and sleeplessness. The search for personal happiness led Monroe back to Arthur Miller, who had been in her thoughts even during her marriage to DiMaggio. Though Miller was married, the two began a relationship in 1955. Monroe was impressed with the thirty-seven-year-old playwright's intellect and his determination to defend his work against allegations that it was subversive. She was, however, unaware that her association with Miller, who was under scrutiny by the Federal Bureau of Investigation, would cause the agency to open a file on her as well. In June 1956, shortly after he obtained a divorce, Miller and Monroe were married in White Plains, New York.

Monroe's blossoming relationship with Miller coincided with her return to Hollywood filmmaking in some well-received movies. Typifying the new acclaim, one critic declared that Monroe's performance in *Bus Stop* (1956) "effectively dispels once and for all the notion that she is merely a glamour personality." The following year, in *The Prince and the Showgirl*, Monroe delivered another performance that generally brought praise. In her private life, however, new problems arose. Monroe became pregnant and eventually suffered a miscarriage. The following year, an ectopic pregnancy resulted in a brief hospitalization. She also struggled to maintain her marriage with Miller, whom she feared she was losing due to the emotional distance between the two. Aware of her concern, Miller sought to demonstrate his commitment to her by crafting his short story "The Misfits" into a screenplay in which Monroe would play Roslyn, the female lead. Miller's Roslyn, however, was a beautiful naïf, an idealized version of his wife. Monroe was insulted by this condescending characterization, and as her relationship with Miller deteriorated, she increasingly sought refuge in alcohol and prescription drugs.

Even as Monroe's quest for personal fulfillment intensified during the late 1950s, there were continuing indications that American sexual attitudes were

66

shifting. In 1956, Grace Metalious, a previously unpublished writer, galvanized millions of readers with her novel *Peyton Place*, a steamy account of lust and marital infidelity in an otherwise conservative New England town. With more than 10 million copies sold within a few years, it was the best-selling novel to date. The barriers of censorship were further breached in 1958 with the publication of Vladimir Nabokov's scandalous *Lolita* and the long-suppressed D.H. Lawrence novel *Lady Chatterley's Lover*, which appeared the same year. The new openness about sexuality in literature coincided with Marilyn Monroe's continued ascent as a visual symbol of unrestrained sensuality. In early 1958, after a two-year hiatus from making films in Hollywood, Monroe agreed to appear in *Some Like It Hot* (1959), a comedy whose exploration of gender roles and sexuality was, in the socially conservative 1950s, considered risqué. Though the film proved a success, Monroe faced personal tragedy again when she miscarried in December. As tensions grew at the Miller/Monroe home in Bel Air, the actress was drawn into an affair with costar Yves Montand during the filming of *Let's Make Love* (1960). Increasingly distraught, she began regular sessions with Los Angeles psychoanalyst Ralph Greenson, an ardent advocate of drug therapy. It was the beginning of a dubious relationship. In contravention of all professional ethics, Greenson drew Monroe into his family, which only increased her dependence.

Events came to a climax in 1960 during the filming of *The Misfits*. Monroe's role in Miller's screenplay was a barely disguised recapitulation of all her past failed relationships with older men. As the production company went to work in the Nevada heat, Monroe soon succumbed to the emotional and physical stress. Filming was halted temporarily in late August when she suffered a "nervous breakdown." Though she returned to complete the film, it found little popular or critical favor. By the end of the year, the estrangement between Monroe and Miller was irredeemable and in early January 1961, they were divorced. In February 1961, after weeks of a reclusive routine of taking barbiturates and sleeping, Monroe was committed to the Payne Whitney Clinic in New York. Held against her will for several days, she desperately phoned Joe DiMaggio, who caught a flight from Florida to gain her release. The two spent some pleasant days together in the following weeks before Monroe returned to the house she had recently purchased in Brentwood, California. Desperate for happiness, she soon began a brief affair with Frank Sinatra. Her film career seemed to lose direction, though she committed to making *Something's Got to Give.*

During the last year of her life, Monroe seemed to revert to behavior that confirmed the image she had long sought to escape. The failure of her third marriage left her free to return to the dissolute Hollywood party scene. Her (belief that her career required some new boost that would gain favorable publicity may have played a role in her over-the-top performance at a Democratic National Committee birthday party for President John Kennedy in May 1962.) The extent of Monroe's relationship with the handsome Democrat has long been a topic of debate, but the best evidence suggests that the two met four times between October 1961 and August 1962 and on one of those occasions had sexual relations. Their encounters thrilled Monroe, who, according to friends, deluded herself into believing that the president could be persuaded to desert his wife for her. At the Madison Square Garden celebration on May 19, Monroe, wearing a dress that Adlai Stevenson described as "skin and beads," took center stage to moan an impossibly sultry "Happy Birthday" to the smirking, cigar-smoking Kennedy. As many onlookers recognized, Monroe's seductive performance more than hinted at intimacy with the president. Perceiving the potential political danger, Kennedy moved to end the relationship only days later (Tragically, the actress had become a parody of the image she hoped to transcend.)

(Monroe's decision that summer to once again marry Joe DiMaggio suggests a desperate desire to find the personal happiness that had so long eluded her.) In retrospect, her behavior during the several months prior to her death clearly pointed to a rapidly building emotional crisis. She failed to appear for work on *Something's Got to Give*, production of which was eventually suspended. On several occasions, friends found her secluded in her bedroom in a drug-induced stupor, agonizing over the personal and public failures of her life. A *Vogue* photographer, scheduled for a photo shoot, arrived at her hotel room to find her drunk and nude. Though she professed excitement over her pending August marriage to DiMaggio and a possible role in a musical version of *A Tree Grows in Brooklyn*, her public cheerfulness was a facade. On August 4, she was clearly troubled and spent much of the day with Dr. Greenson. (Sometime that evening, Monroe died alone in her bed; her housekeeper discovered the body in the early morning. The controversy over the actress's death continues, but the evidence suggests that the death was accidental. Monroe probably succumbed to an inadvertent but fatal combination of orally ingested Nembutal and an enema-induced dose of chloral hydrate.) Monroe had long resorted to enemas for purposes of weight-loss and the administration of tranquilizing drugs. Actor Peter Lawford later recounted that, in a final late-night phone conversation, a barely intelligible Monroe gave some indication that she knew she was dying before the line fell silent. "Say goodbye to Pat (Lawford's wife), say goodbye to the president, and say goodbye to yourself," she muttered, "because you're a nice guy."

News of Monroe's death stunned the nation. It was difficult to accept that such a vivacious life force could be stilled so suddenly, much less to accept that the carefree image that she projected had concealed such a deeply troubled individual. On August 8, the day he was to have remarried Monroe, DiMaggio joined other mourners at a small memorial service in Westwood to say goodbye. In later years, determined to preserve some dignity for his ex-wife, he refused to speak about her in public. (For the next twenty years, Joltin' Joe saw to it that flowers were delivered weekly to her grave.)

(Both used and abused in her lifetime, Marilyn Monroe endured as a popular but controversial icon in American culture. The circumstances of her death produced a multitude of conspiracy theories, the most common alleging that she was murdered to prevent public knowledge of a purported affair with U.S. Attorney General Robert F. Kennedy, a claim for which there is no reliable evidence. Monroe's continuing popularity resulted from the unforgettable persona that she created in the course of her career. Voluptuous, seductive, yet innocent, Monroe was the embodiment of male fantasies in an era in which traditional restraints on sexual behavior retained considerable force. In these circumstances, Monroe's cinematic persona offered vicarious indulgence in forbidden activities. The strength of her continuing appeal was evident in the decades following her death. Sixties pop artist Andy Warhol immortalized the actress in a famous artwork. Songwriter Elton John paid tribute to her in his 1974 song "Goodbye, Norma Jean." Monroe's films remained popular, and, in 1995, her portrait was featured on a thirty-two-cent commemorative U.S. postage stamp. Finally, in 1999, on the eve of the twenty-first century, Monroe was recognized by *People* magazine as the "Sexiest Woman of the Century." The same year, Hugh Hefner's *Playboy,* having enjoyed decades of relative respectability, designated Marilyn Monroe as the "Number One Sex Star of the 20th Century." It might not have been the tribute that Monroe had sought, but it testified to her enduring impact.)

ELVIS PRESLEY
Rock and Roll Rebel

Sam Phillips's Memphis Recording Service seemed an unlikely site for the beginning of a music revolution. The unimpressive building on Union Avenue housed a recording studio where one might at most hope to uncover talent of local or regional appeal. A radio engineer and disc jockey, Sam Phillips had grown increasingly bored with the insipid popular music of the era and was convinced that "the Negroes were the only ones who had any freshness left in their music." In 1950, determined to popularize that bold sound, he opened his recording studio and helped launch the careers of a number of black artists, including Howlin' Wolf and B.B. King. Having established the Sun Studios label in his continued search for African American music talent, Phillips endured frequent taunts from white acquaintances about "hanging around those niggers." Phillips understood that few whites were as yet receptive to what was then known as "race music." A coworker later recalled Phillips's reiterating, "If I could find a white man who had the Negro sound and the Negro feel, I could make a billion dollars."

In June 1954, Phillips was looking for some exciting new talent to record a song he had acquired. His secretary reminded him about a young man who had on several earlier occasions recorded at Sun Studios. Elvis Presley had first walked in the door of the studio on a Saturday in the summer of 1953, shortly after graduating from high school. The shy eighteen-year-old, a battered child's guitar in hand, had haltingly explained that he wanted to record a song. Asked whom he sounded like, Presley responded, "I don't sound like nobody." The young singer with the long sideburns and ducktail haircut recorded two ballads, "My Happiness" and "That's When Your Heartache Begins." Presley returned periodically in subsequent months to inquire about jobs as a vocalist and recorded another song in early 1954. He left a lingering impression on Phillips, who now summoned the aspiring singer to Sun Studios to record "Without You." In a grueling, frustrating session that lasted through the afternoon, Presley seemed unable to realize the song to Phillips's satisfaction. At Phillips's direction, Presley also performed a wide variety of other songs—pop, gospel, ballads. Presley's guitar playing was marginal, and nothing seemed to quite come together. Yet Phillips left the studio convinced that the teenager possessed an as yet unidentified quality that might hold potential.

Two weeks later, in early July, Phillips matched Presley with guitarist Scotty Moore and bassist Bill Black in hopes of uncovering Presley's latent talents. This studio session produced inconclusive results until, during a break, Presley spontaneously broke into Arthur Crudup's famous blues number, "That's All Right, Mama." Intrigued with Presley's unique vocalizations and unusual gyrations, Moore and Black joined in, producing a startling sound that caused Phillips, who was in the control room, to direct the trio to try it again so their efforts could be recorded. As they practiced through the evening, the essentials of Presley's unique appeal revealed themselves. His free, confident vocal stylizations, supported by an unadorned instrumental accompaniment, produced a sound that was, in Moore's words, "sort of raw and ragged." Finally committing the song to tape, the group then recorded a bluegrass number, "Blue Moon of Kentucky," as a "B" side. The resultant record—a rhythm and blues standard backed by a familiar bluegrass hit—captured Presley's genius, the ability to meld sounds and styles from disparate musical worlds into a new and very different whole.

71

Sam Phillips, convinced that the record would revolutionize popular music, played it for popular disc jockey Dewey Phillips, explaining that "it's not black, it's not white, it's not pop, it's not country." Intrigued, the DJ premiered the record for his Memphis audience. The enthusiastic response vindicated Sam Phillips's conviction that Elvis Presley was the man who could define a new genre of music, a sound grounded in black rhythm and blues but tempered by the gospel and country traditions of the South, with a style that would challenge conventional conceptions of performance. It was the beginning of a career that reshaped American music. In the years to come, Presley posted 149 songs on *Billboard*'s Hot 100 Pop Chart, 114 of which made it into the top forty and 18 of which achieved number one status. Of his 140 albums, 90 made it onto the charts and 10 reached the coveted number one spot. A protean talent, Presley left a huge imprint on popular music that future generations of musicians were quick to acknowledge. "Before Elvis," composer/musician John Lennon remarked with only slight exaggeration, "there was nothing."

Elvis Aaron Presley was one of twin sons born to Vernon Elvis Presley and Gladys Smith Presley on January 8, 1935, in the sleepy rural town of Tupelo, Mississippi. His brother, Jessie Garon, was stillborn and the Presleys had no other children. Consequently, Elvis was the sole recipient of his parents' attention throughout his childhood. Vernon Presley was an often-sullen man who struggled to provide for his small family, drifting through a variety of jobs as a farmer and truck driver. Crowded into a two-room shotgun house during the depths of the Great Depression, the Presleys lost their home in 1937 when Vernon went to prison for cashing a forged check. After an eight-month prison term, during which Gladys and Elvis were aided by their numerous Tupelo relatives, Vernon found temporary work in Pascagoula with a New Deal public works agency, then brought his family back to Tupelo, where Elvis began elementary school. His first significant exposure to music came at the Assembly of God Church, where he and his parents sang gospel hymns. At age ten, he won a talent contest at a fair in Tupelo and, the following year, received a guitar for his birthday. Relatives and the church pastor offered some basic lessons, and Elvis soon began providing musical accompaniment at church services. Within the next couple of years, he regularly took part in amateur hour radio shows broadcast from the town courthouse. His musical horizons grew as he listened to country and blue-grass musicians, both at local performances and on the radio's "Grand Old Opry" broadcasts. In 1948, as his family prepared to move to Memphis, Elvis performed a goodbye concert for his schoolmates. When a friend told him afterward, "Elvis, one of these days you're gonna be famous," the teenager replied, "I sure hope so."

In Memphis, the Presleys lived in a public housing project; both parents found modest employment and Elvis, enrolled at L.C. Humes High School, took a part-time job. In the city renowned for Beale Street, Elvis's musical universe quickly expanded. Country, gospel, jazz, and rhythm and blues filled the radio airwaves in Memphis, where disc jockey Dewey Phillips was a regional celebrity. Sam Phillips's Memphis Recording Service produced cutting-edge hits, including the Saddlemen's "Rocket 88," considered by some music historians as the first rock and roll record. Presley became a regular at the Ellis Auditorium All-Night Gospel Singings and performed informally not only at the housing project, but also with friends at area hospitals. Contemporaries noted a change in his demeanor and appearance by his junior year. Sporting sideburns and slicked-back hair, Presley developed an affinity for outrageous apparel. An acquaintance recalled how the "new" Elvis seemed almost deliberately provocative: "Everybody else wore jeans, but he wore dress pants. And he would wear a coat and fashion a scarf like an ascot tie, as if he were a movie star. . . (It was like he was already portraying something that he wanted to be.")

After graduating in 1953, Presley worked as a machinist and a theater usher before gaining employment as a truck driver. After having driven by Sam Phillips's studio many times without stopping, he eventually worked up the nerve to make his initial recording in 1953 and followed up with the breakthrough sessions in the summer of 1954. In the following months, the trio of Elvis, Scotty, and Bill found regular bookings at clubs and special events in the region. The group's first record showed up on *Billboard*'s regional charts in August as number three among the Country and Western Territorial Best Sellers. It was evident, however, that Presley's appeal went beyond the country and western audience. In September, the trio was featured at the grand opening of Memphis's Lamar-Airways Shopping Center, where, before a largely young audience, Scotty first became aware that "something was happening." "They liked Bill's clowning and Elvis' gyrations," he recalled, "but it was the beat that really got to them, and it was the kids' response that drove the music to another level. It was so out of control it was frightening.") Following an appearance at Nashville's Grand Old Opry, the group was signed to regular appearances on the radio show "Louisiana Hayride," a popular vehicle for regional country and bluegrass talent. The young singer's sound and on-stage antics drew growing attention, and 1955 proved to be the year that the Elvis Presley phenomenon swept the South. Taking on D.J. Fontana as drummer, Presley and his band toured the region extensively. Presley's appearances now regularly produced spirited, sometimes riotous reactions from audiences, especially on the part of young women. At the conclusion of a show at the Gator Bowl in Jacksonville, Florida, in May, Presley spontaneously announced to an audience of 14,000, "Girls, I'll see you all backstage." A shrieking mob chased the four musicians into the locker room, where Presley's clothes were literally torn from his back before police rescued him.

That day's events drew the attention of "Colonel" Tom Parker, co-owner of Hank Snow Attractions and an organizer of the "Hayride" tours, and Chick Crumpacker, RCA's country and western promotion manager. Both were convinced that Presley had tremendous appeal for the burgeoning youth market. Having witnessed a Presley concert, Crumpacker described the singer as "something else." "All the mannerisms were in place," he remembered. "The body language—I don't remember exactly what he sang, but there were frequent belches into the mike, and the clincher came when he took his chewing gum out and tossed it into the audience. This, of course, was shocking, it was wild—but what got the listeners were his energy and *the way he sang the songs*. The effect was galvanic." That August, Presley signed a management contract with Parker, who encouraged the large record companies to buy Presley's recording contract from Sam Phillips, who agreed to sell the singer's contract to RCA for $35,000. Only days after he turned twenty-one in January 1956, Presley appeared for his first RCA recording session at a Nashville studio. Among the songs recorded that day was "Heartbreak Hotel," which was released later in the month. The record sold 300,000 copies in three weeks, hit number one on both the popular and country charts, and went on to sell over 1 million copies, becoming Presley's first gold record. The Elvis Presley revolution was under way.

It was Presley's singular fortune to explode onto the national scene at this juncture. A number of circumstances combined in the mid-1950s to favor success for an innovative musician and performer. The music market of the early part of the decade was clearly demarcated for specific groups, correlating closely with social class or race. Classical music was marketed to those with sophisticated tastes, often meaning urban, educated Americans. Rhythm and blues, or race music, was largely targeted to African American audiences, while country and western was often the music of white rural and working-class Americans. Popular or pop music generally reflected the tastes of white middle-class America, with little delineation among age groups. As one historian has noted, such music was "very carefully made: mild, artificial, emotionless, cute," a reflection of the desire for "familiar security" and "bland perfection." The few black artists who appealed to white listeners, such as Nat King Cole, were those who accommodated white tastes in style, sound, and lyrics. As late as 1955, on the very eve of the rock and roll revolution, the top five songs on the pop charts reflected the stagnation in popular music. "Unchained Melody," "The Ballad of Davy Crockett," "Cherry Pink and Apple Blossom White," "The Yellow Rose of Texas," and "Melody of Love" were all gushy orchestrations or quasi-folk tunes that epitomized the sad state of American pop music.

Music historians disagree about the precise origins of rock and roll, but many trace its roots to the early 1950s, when Cleveland disc jockey Alan Freed saw the potential in a radio show aimed at white youth who were attracted to black rhythm and blues. Cognizant of the racial connotations of the term "rhythm and blues," Freed shrewdly introduced the name "rock and roll" to describe the new music that was evolving as race music began to make the crossover to white listeners. Freed's new radio show, *Moondog's Rock and Roll Party*, popularized the name for the new music. Broadcasting music targeted specifically at the youth market Freed began the reshaping of American popular music. One of the distinguishing characteristics of rock and roll was that its appeal was clearly demarcated along generational lines, and the music's themes reflected the same division. Rock and roll spoke directly to the feelings, aspirations, and tribulations of a young audience and was delivered with intensity, energy, and motion. Even as black artists like the Chords were crossing over onto white music charts, white groups were successfully incorporating many elements of black music. No group better exemplified this evolution than Bill Haley and the Comets, who, in their earlier incarnation as the Saddlemen, had recorded the seminal "Rocket 88" in 1951. Renamed the following year, the group recorded the blues stomper "Rock the Joint" and, in 1954, released "Rock Around the Clock," which musician Frank Zappa later dubbed the "Teenage National Anthem." The popularity of the song was enhanced immeasurably when it was adopted as the opening soundtrack for the youth rebellion film *The Blackboard Jungle* (1955). Hollywood, ever attentive to market and profits, was beginning to recognize the appeal of the new music.

Indeed, the young Americans who constituted the baby boom generation were emerging as a new consumer group in the 1950s, a development that fueled Elvis Presley's precipitous rise to fame. A 1956 *Scholastic* magazine survey revealed that American teens now numbered 13 million and, as a consequence of prosperous times, marshaled a combined income of $7 billion a year. With the average teenager earning a weekly income of $10.55, a figure close to the disposable income of an average American family only fifteen years before, the potential for youth-oriented merchandise markets was unprecedented. The 45-rpm record, introduced in 1948 by RCA, was a popular, affordable medium for the new music. In contrast to earlier eras when adults controlled what music was played on the family's radio or phonograph, teenagers could now afford to purchase portable record players and inexpensive radios, including the new transistor models. No longer limited by adult preferences, many teens enjoyed their generation's music in their own rooms, away from the supervision of disapproving adults. Merchandisers were also quick to perceive the profits in consumer items related to rock celebrities. As early as the end of 1957, Elvis Presley merchandise, including shoes, skirts, blouses, pajamas, pens, lipstick, and fluorescent Elvis portraits, had grossed $55 million in sales. If the baby boom produced an audience for the new music, the television boom of the 1950s provided a new medium through which it could be disseminated. Whereas in 1948 only 172,000 American households had television sets, by 1955, the number of television sets in use had grown to 32 million. Performers like Presley produced a visual excitement that was perfectly suited to the new medium. In 1957, Dick Clark's *American Bandstand* was first broadcast to a national audience on ABC and quickly became a major forum for the introduction of new music.

The confluence of these developments, together with Elvis Presley's unique talents, does much to explain the emergence of Presley and rock and roll as national phenomena by 1956. A *Time* magazine writer captured the Elvis performance that America was rapidly coming to know: "Without preamble, the three-piece band cuts loose. In the spotlight, the lanky singer flails furious rhythms on his guitar, every now and then breaking a string. In a pivoting stance, his hips swing sensuously from side to side and his entire body quivers, as if he had swallowed a jackhammer." It was a whirlwind year for the twenty-one-year-old singer. The extraordinary success of "Heartbreak Hotel" was quickly followed by the release of Presley's eponymous first album, which quickly went gold. Less than a month later, Presley was in Hollywood for a Paramount Studios screen test that resulted in a seven-year film contract. His first film, *Love Me Tender*, premiered in November to modest reviews but excellent ticket sales. Television appearances further propelled Presley's blossoming celebrity. In early 1956, Presley was signed to six appearances on CBS's *Stage Show*, a struggling variety program. Launching into an uninhibited version of "Shake, Rattle and Roll" during his first appearance, he left many viewers convinced that they had witnessed the beginning of something significant. Presley next appeared in April on *The Milton Berle Show*, where the audience responded to "Blue Suede Shoes" with exuberant appreciation. During his second appearance, he performed "Hound Dog," a number that drew wild applause from the youthful audience and haughty reprimands from adult critics.)In a comment that was characteristic of the burgeoning complaints about rock and roll, *New York Daily News* writer Ben Gross denounced "Elvis's grunt and groin antics,"(which he found "suggestive and vulgar, tinged with the kind of animalism that should be confined to dives and bordellos.")In a subsequent July appearance on *The Steve Allen Show*, Presley toned down his performance, bringing an avalanche of complaints from fans who wanted to see "the gyrating Elvis."

Presley's appearance on *The Ed Sullivan Show* in September 1956 proved the stuff of legend. Sullivan was a major arbiter of mainstream televised entertainment in the 1950s, renowned not only for his own bizarre, almost mechanical mannerisms but also for his distaste for any performer who might challenge accepted standards. But in the summer of 1956, Sullivan began to realize that Presley was a phenomenon that could not be wished away. On September 9, in the first of three appearances, Presley walked onto the stage and sang "Don't Be Cruel" and "Love Me Tender," both songs accompanied by the sensuous body movements that so worried critics. During his rendition of "Reddy Teddy," as Presley's movements became more unrestrained, the television camera moved in so as to show only his upper body. The screams from the audience in the studio, however, attested to what was occurring out of the television audience's field of view. Presley's second appearance, though more sedate, drew an equally enthusiastic response. Whatever Sullivan's private thoughts about Presley, he endorsed the young singer during Elvis's final appearance in early 1957, assuring his audience, "This is a real decent, fine boy." Ed Sullivan, the custodian of mainstream entertainment, had legitimated Presley with an adult audience. Elvis Presley had made it to the big time. Unknown to most, Presley's generally well-concealed self-doubts, which were manifest in(drug and alcohol abuse)as early as these years, followed him as he stepped into the national spotlight.

The following year offered little time for reflection. Production of a second Presley film, *Loving You*, got under way in January. Presley's fame quickly moved beyond national boundaries, spreading to Europe and even the Soviet Union, where, the *New York Times* reported, banned Presley records fetched high prices on the black market. In March, the working-class southern boy claimed his place in the region's aristocracy with the purchase of a colonial-style mansion in Memphis. For just over $100,000, Presley bought the Graceland estate that became home to himself, his parents, and his grandmother. In May, he began work on a third movie, *Jailhouse Rock*. A box office hit, it later earned a reputation among critics as a classic "rock opera" film, and its "Jailhouse Rock" number is considered the forerunner of contemporary music videos.

Even as Presley skyrocketed to fame, other participants in the rock and roll revolution were growing in prominence. Bill Haley and the Comets, Chuck Berry, Little Richard, Buddy Holly, Fats Domino, and Jerry Lee Lewis all found favor with young listeners. Not surprisingly, the on-stage antics of performers and the questionable lyrics of some rock songs provoked both concern and censorship. As early as mid-decade, a campaign to "clean up filth wax" sought to pressure distributors, record stores, and radio stations, with some local success. Both the U.S. Senate and the House of Representatives considered legislation to prohibit interstate commerce in "lewd, lascivious, or filthy" music recordings. The bills failed to pass, but many adults continued to express concern about the impact of the new music. Even before the advent of Elvis, the authors of *USA Confidential* (1952) had warned of the insidious effects of rock and roll: "Like a heathen religion, it is all tied up with tom-toms and hot jive and ritualistic orgies of erotic dancing, weed smoking and mass mania, with African jungle background." Critics of rock and roll warned that the new music would destroy Christian morality while promoting juvenile delinquency, interracial dating, and drug abuse. Presley, as the embodiment of the music revolution, was often singled out for special condemnation. Frank Sinatra, whose youthful fame and fan appeal in the 1940s had prefigured Presley's, denounced the young rocker: "His kind of music is deplorable, a rancid smelling aphrodisiac. It fosters almost totally negative and destructive responses in young people." Some derided Presley's musical abilities. A *Miami Herald* columnist described him as "the biggest freak in show business history," who "can't sing, can't play the guitar—and can't dance." A *New York Journal* critic bemoaned the "sight of young (21) Mr. Presley's caterwauling his unintelligible lyrics in an inadequate voice, during a display of primitive physical movement difficult to describe in terms suitable to a family newspaper."

Despite such criticism, Presley's career flourished. A succession of hit records, television appearances, concert tours, and movies testified to the continuing appeal of the man who would come to be known as the "King." By the late 1950s, as Presley proclaimed, "Rock and Roll Is Here to Stay." Yet this first phase of the rock and roll revolution was coming to a close. In March 1958, Presley was inducted into the army and in June, during a brief break, made his last recordings until 1960. In his absence, American popular music underwent some significant changes. The music industry was shaken by scandal and controversy over payola, which involved monetary inducements to feature certain artists on the airwaves. Subsequent federal investigations brought indictments against disc jockeys, ruining Alan Freed's career, while

Federal Communications Commission rulings and fear of prosecution caused many radio stations to abandon rock and roll in favor of more traditional programming. The loss of some of the leaders in the music revolution also temporarily derailed rock and roll. Elvis was posted to duty in West Germany. Little Richard abandoned rock in 1957 after reembracing the religion of his youth. Chuck Berry was sentenced to three years in prison in 1962 for bringing a young Mexican girl into the country for "illicit purposes." Southern rocker Jerry Lee Lewis offended public opinion by marrying his thirteen-year-old cousin Myra and was soon unwelcome in most venues. A 1959 plane crash killed Buddy Holly, Ritchie Valens, and Jiles Perry Richardson, known to fans as the Big Bopper. It was, as singer Don McLean proclaimed in his 1971 song, "The Day the Music Died."

The music did not die, of course, but the first wave of the rock and roll revolution certainly crested in the late 1950s. Innovative rock receded in the next several years, supplanted by boy and girl groups and less threatening vocalists like Fabian and Paul Anka. Presley was discharged from active duty in March 1960 and returned to general acclaim, but the course of his music and career was changing. Though he recorded some rock songs, he increasingly embraced ballads, many featured in the growing number of films he appeared in. Having attained his ambition of musical fame in the 1950s, Presley sought to gain recognition as a serious actor during the following decade, but found only frustration. The youth-oriented action and romance movies that he starred in gave him little chance to demonstrate serious acting abilities. No longer on the cutting edge of popular music, Presley seemed content to exploit the fame he had achieved and did not seek to forge new paths. Meanwhile, the pop music scene was being transformed by surf music, the mid-decade British Invasion and, within a few years, the advent of psychedelic acid rock. Increasingly, Presley seemed a dated remnant of an irrelevant era.

In the late 1960s, however, Presley began to reorder his life. In May 1967, he married Priscilla Beaulieu, whom he had met during his army stint in Germany; their daughter, Lisa Marie, was born in February 1968. Presley began preparations that spring for a television special that would be the catalyst for a comeback. Broadcast in December, *Elvis* was a musical autobiography, in which the singer recapitulated his past in both monologue and music, concluding with a profession of his own vitality and relevance in the song "I Can Dream." The broadcast was an enormous critical success and the soundtrack jumped to number eight on the pop chart. Greil Marcus's review epitomized the critical response: "It was the finest music of his life. If there ever was a music that bleeds, this was it." The comeback special did seem to infuse new life into Presley's career. Songs he recorded in early 1969 came to be regarded as some of his best, and some, like "In the Ghetto," spoke to contemporary social issues. Though Presley's films did not do well, his newly reestablished musical presence was evident on the airwaves, on television specials, in Las Vegas shows, and on tour. Elvis, it seemed, had established an enduring claim to superstardom.

Though Presley's recording and touring career continued unabated in the 1970s, the inner turmoil that troubled him proved increasingly damaging. An intermittent user and abuser of prescription drugs since the 1950s, Presley resorted more frequently to artificial stimulants. His marriage with Priscilla unraveled and the two were divorced in 1973. Health problems, some the product of drug abuse, became more frequent as Presley's weight ballooned. Though he remained a popular performer and maintained an arduous concert schedule through the summer of 1977, he was increasingly the subject of tabloid newspaper stories about his health, his weight, his eccentricities, and drug use. The harshest critics dismissed him as a parody of his former self. Presley died at home at Graceland on August 16, 1977, of advanced arteriosclerosis and congestive heart failure. It was a pathetic conclusion to a life and career that had begun with such energy and dynamism.

Presley's death shocked the nation and compelled an assessment of what the singer had meant to American popular culture. Composer and conductor Leonard Bernstein had surprised a group of friends in the late 1960s when he declared, "Elvis Presley is the greatest cultural force of the twentieth century." Pressed to elaborate, Bernstein continued, "It's Elvis. He introduced the beat to everything and he changed everything—music, language, clothes, it's a whole new social revolution—the Sixties come from it." Only in the aftermath of his death did a complete comprehension of his contribution find broad expression. Musicians and music historians alike have consistently testified to Presley's seminal role in creating modern popular music. In a recent summary of Presley's impact, musician Brian Setzer explained, "I don't think there is a musician alive today that hasn't been affected by Elvis' music. His definitive years—1954–1957—can only be described as rock's cornerstone. He was the original cool."

Conclusion

American popular culture began a remarkable transformation in the 1950s. Social stability, material abundance, and the baby boom provided the background for new cultural directions as a confident, prosperous, and increasingly youthful population explored new modes of expression in the entertainment arts. American music and film reflected a shift in social values that some embraced as liberating and others condemned as degenerate.(Marilyn Monroe rose rapidly to fame as an icon of sensuality in an era during which Americans were, however tentatively, reevaluating sexual mores.) For most Americans in the 1950s, unrestrained sexuality remained at most a tantalizing fantasy, a forbidden indulgence beyond realization. Nevertheless, the challenge to traditional sexual values reflected in the popular culture of the 1950s presaged a more radical reevaluation of sexuality in the following decade.

Elvis Presley, as much a cultural icon of the 1950s as was Monroe, was similarly provocative because of the allegedly(overt sexuality of both his music and performances.)Presley's greater importance, though, comes from his vanguard role in shaping a youth-oriented popular culture founded on the new music that would henceforth differentiate young Americans from the older generation.(Presley and other rock and roll greats of the decade succeeded in wresting the direction of popular culture from adult hands and giving it to American youth, now empowered not only by their sheer numbers but also by their new role as consumers.)Presley's musical innovations prefigured a radical transformation of popular music in the 1960s, which took the art into realms that could hardly have been imagined only a decade before. Through their contributions to the popular culture of the 1950s, Marilyn Monroe and Elvis Presley offered Americans a glimpse of things to come.

Study Questions

1. What developments suggest that American sexual values were in transition during the 1950s?
2. Given that Marilyn Monroe was not the only blonde bombshell of the 1950s, how would you explain her eventual status as the chief popular icon of the era?
(3. Why did so many adults perceive Elvis Presley and his music as threatening?)
4. What social and cultural factors helped make possible the emergence of youth music during the 1950s?
5. Were Monroe and Presley ultimately victims of their own weaknesses or of the pressures of being a celebrity?

Selected Bibliography

Altschuler, Glenn C. *All Shook Up: How Rock 'N' Roll Changed America*. New York: Oxford University Press, 2003.

Bertrand, Michael T. *Race, Rock and Elvis*. Champaign: University of Illinois Press, 2000.

Biskind, Peter. *Seeing Is Believing: How Hollywood Taught Us to Stop Worrying and Love the Fifties*. New York: Pantheon, 1983.

Curtis, Jim. *Rock Eras: Interpretations of Music and Society, 1954–1984*. Madison: University of Wisconsin Press, 1987.

Eisler, Benita. *Private Lives: Men and Women of the Fifties*. London: Franklin Watts, 1986.

Guralnick, Peter. *Last Train to Memphis: The Rise of Elvis Presley*. Boston: Little, Brown, 1994.

———. *Careless Love: The Unmaking of Elvis Presley*. Boston: Back Bay Books, 2000.

Halberstam, David. *The Fifties*. New York: Random House, 1993.

Leaming, Barbara. *Marilyn Monroe*. New York: Crown, 1998.

Miller, Douglas T., and Marion Nowak. *The Fifties: The Way We Really Were*. Garden City, NY: Doubleday, 1977.

Morgan, Michelle. *Marilyn Monroe: Private and Undisclosed*. London: Constable and Robinson, 2007.

Patterson, James T. *Grand Expectations: The United States, 1945–1974*. New York: Oxford University Press, 1996.

Spoto, Donald. *Marilyn Monroe: The Biography*. New York: HarperCollins, 1993.

Ward, Ed, Geoffrey Stokes, and Ken Tucker. *Rock of Ages: The* Rolling Stone *History of Rock and Roll*. New York: Rolling Stone Press, 1986.

Weyr, Thomas. *Reaching for Paradise: The Playboy Vision of America*. New York: New York Times Books, 1978.

Whitmer, Peter. *The Inner Elvis: A Psychological Biography of Elvis Aaron Presley*. New York: Hyperion, 1996.

4

Outsiders in a Conformist Society

In an era that seemed, on the surface at least, to be increasingly conformist, Jackie Robinson and Allen Ginsberg challenged prevailing social norms and traditions. While Ginsberg and the Beats appeared to deliberately flout conventional values, Robinson strove to be accepted by the society that flagrantly rejected him, yet defiantly challenged racial restrictions that shackled him and fellow African Americans.

Robinson's prowess in athletic competition enabled him to win fame and to become a pathfinder for others. A child of the American South whose family migrated to California in the 1930s, Robinson was a multisport star in high school and college. As a soldier during World War II, he challenged the racial segregation in the armed forces, resulting in a court martial proceeding involving a charge of insubordination. Robinson starred in the Negro Leagues before becoming the first African American player to enter baseball's major leagues in the twentieth century. Robinson's defiant grace under pressure as one of the "Boys of Summer," the Brooklyn Dodgers of the late 1940s and 1950s, helped to weaken the hold of discrimination on the American psyche.

By contrast, Ginsberg, the eldest son of radical Jewish immigrants, attempted, along with a small circle of friends, to articulate a "new vision" that contested barriers involving both body and mind, including proscriptions regarding homosexuality. Beginning immediately after World War II, the group, rejecting disapproving societal norms, fostered new modes of expression pertaining to literature, drugs, and sexuality. In the process, they helped to spawn the Beat movement, which in turn served as a harbinger for the much larger counterculture of the 1960s. Particularly following the reading in 1955 of his epic poem "Howl," which seemed to capture the spirit of a new, alienated generation, Ginsberg became an exemplar of cultural and political rebellion and a model of liberated sexuality.

JACKIE ROBINSON
Racial Torchbearer in the National Pastime

It was the morning of August 28, 1945. The location was 215 Montague Street in Brooklyn, the headquarters of the New York City borough's major league franchise. The receptionist ushered two men—a middle-aged white scout and a younger, ebony-colored man—into the office of sixty-three-year-old Branch Rickey, president, general manager, and part owner of the Brooklyn Dodgers. Clyde Sukeforth, a ten-year veteran of the major leagues, introduced the athlete he had recently scouted: twenty-six-year-old Jackie Robinson. Boasting a stellar athletic reputation from his collegiate days, the strikingly handsome, muscular Robinson was completing his first season as an All-Star shortstop with the Kansas City Monarchs of the Negro American League. Since the turn of the century, organized baseball, as the major and minor leagues were known, had shut its doors to African American players.

Robinson had heard that Rickey was seeking top black players for the Brooklyn Brown Dodgers, who would purportedly join a new Negro League. Wearing a sports jacket and bow tie, the bespectacled Rickey, holding his trademark cigar, greeted Robinson warmly before asking, "Do you know why you were brought here?" Robinson replied that he presumed it had something to do with the Brown Dodgers. Rickey responded, "You were brought here, Jackie, to play for the Brooklyn organization"—meaning not the Brown Dodgers but the major league team. "I want to win a pennant and we need ballplayers!" Rickey blurted out. "Do you think you can do it?" Robinson later remembered, "I was thrilled, scared, and excited. I was incredulous. Most of all, I was speechless." Finally, he answered, "Yes, if . . . if I got the chance." To explain the challenges Robinson would face as the only black member of the team, Rickey began role-playing, casting himself as "a room clerk in a southern hotel, an insulting waiter in a restaurant, and a sarcastic railroad conductor." Flinging off his jacket, Rickey then acted the part of an ill-tempered ballplayer who, after a hard slide into second, was tagged out by Robinson, yelled, "Don't hit me with a ball like that, you tar-baby son of a bitch," and belted him. Rickey insisted, "You cannot strike back."

Two hours after entering Rickey's office, Robinson departed, having signed a contract with the Dodgers, granting him a $3,500 bonus and setting his monthly salary with the Montreal Royals, the Dodgers' top minor league team, at $600. Robinson and Rickey agreed that, for now, they would remain mum about both their meeting and the contract. Consequently, news of the collapse of organized baseball's color barrier awaited a press conference by the Montreal Royals and Rickey on October 23.

The subject of that press conference, Jack Roosevelt Robinson, was born on the evening of January 31, 1919, to an itinerant farm laborer and a mother with a sixth-grade education, close to the town of Cairo, in southern Georgia. After Jerry Robinson abandoned his wife Mallie and their five children, she was evicted from the plantation where he had toiled. The deeply religious Mallie obtained a position as a maid for a white family in Pasadena, California, then the wealthiest community in America and one with a liberal reputation. Nevertheless, dwelling in a working-class district on Pepper Street, the Robinsons battled "a sort of slavery with the whites slowly, very slowly, getting used to us," Jackie's sister Willie Mae remembered. At the age of eight, Jackie heard a little girl cry out, "Nigger! Nigger! Nigger!" after which Jackie and the girl's father tossed rocks at each other.

Well-liked by his schoolteachers, Jackie remained an indifferent student who idolized his older brother Mack, runner-up to Jesse Owens in the 200-meter race at the 1936 Olympic Games in Berlin. Returning home, Mack was reduced to serving as a city street sweeper. In the meantime, Jackie, along with other members of the Pepper Street Gang, repeatedly got into trouble with the law, engaging in petty thefts and threatening to turn into "a full-fledged juvenile delinquent." However, at John Muir Technical High School, Robinson became a driven multisport star, joining future major league greats Ted Williams and Bob Lemon on a Pomona tournament all-star baseball contingent. Enrolled at Pasadena Junior College (PJC), Robinson participated in baseball, track and field, and football. In March 1937, Robinson performed so deftly in a pick-up game involving players from the Pasadena area against the Chicago White Sox, who were undergoing spring training, that White Sox manager Jimmy Dykes purportedly exclaimed, "Geez, if that kid was white I'd sign him right now."

During the 1938 fall football season, Robinson, who stood 5'11" and weighed about 175 pounds, with broad, muscular shoulders and tremendously powerful thighs, led PJC to an undefeated season. Playing before large crowds across the state, he attracted attention from a growing number of universities. He also starred on the baseball team, batting .417, and broad jumped 25'6", breaking Mack's national junior college record. The next year saw Robinson playing for the University of California at Los Angeles (UCLA). His brilliant punt return against the University of Washington induced one reporter to proclaim it "the prettiest piece of open field running ever witnessed on a football field." When the season ended, Robinson had compiled an astonishing 11.4-yard-per-carry rushing average for the unbeaten, but twice-tied Bruins. After World War II induced cancellation of the 1940 Olympic Games, where he had hoped to compete in the broad jump, Robinson joined the UCLA basketball team, leading the conference in scoring. He performed poorly for the university baseball nine, but won the National Collegiate Athletic Association (NCAA) broad jump championship, becoming a four-sport letterman. His senior football season saw the Bruins drop every game but one, although Robinson continued to star as quarterback and he established a national mark, averaging 21 yards per punt return. On the basketball court, Robinson again led the Pacific Coast Conference in scoring, but for the second straight year was denied a spot on the all-conference team, purportedly because of racism. Although nearing graduation, Robinson now determined to leave UCLA, certain, as he indicated in his autobiography, "that no amount of education would help a black man get a job."

With professional sports still crippled by Jim Crow barriers, Robinson briefly worked for the National Youth Administration as an assistant athletic director at a camp in Atascadero, California, receiving a $150 monthly salary. He participated in the annual charity contest put on by the *Chicago Tribune* that pitted the reigning champion of the National Football League against top college players. His performance during the game, when he snared a 36-yard touchdown pass, appeared to live up to a reporter's early reference to Robinson as "the Jim Thorpe of his race." After playing semipro ball with the Honolulu Bears, he returned to the mainland in early December, finding a position with Lockheed Aircraft in Burbank, California, and joining a semipro basketball squad, the Los Angeles Devils. On March 22, 1942, the Chicago White Sox held a tryout of sorts for Robinson and Nate Moreland, who had pitched in the Negro National League and in Mexico. The tryout resulted from an extensive campaign to break down the color barrier in organized baseball, an effort spearheaded by the black press and the *Daily Worker*, the tabloid run by the Communist Party. Now, Sox manager Jimmy Dykes purportedly indicated that Robinson, if afforded the opportunity, could readily draw $50,000 from a major league team, but organized baseball's unwritten segregation law precluded that.

No such offer was forthcoming, however, and in the spring of 1942, Robinson, having been drafted, was inducted into the U.S. armed forces. He completed his basic training at Fort Riley, Kansas. Although rated an expert marksman, his request to enter Officer Candidate School (OCS) was turned down with no explanation forthcoming. When he sought to join the baseball team, which included Dixie Walker and Pete Reiser of the Brooklyn Dodgers, a white soldier informed him that an officer had said, "I'll break the team before I'll have a nigger on it." Fortuitously, the arrival at the base of another celebrated black athlete, heavyweight-boxing champion Joe Louis, brought a change in circumstances for Robinson. On discovering that Robinson was also at Fort Riley, Louis went to meet him and the two became friends, with the boxer helping Robinson enter OCS. On January 28, 1943, Robinson received his gold bars and was sworn in as a lieutenant in the cavalry. While on leave, Robinson proposed to Rachel Isum, whom he had met at UCLA; Rachel was planning to become a nurse and wanted to complete her education before getting married.

In April, Robinson received orders to report to Camp Hood, Texas, which had a terrible reputation among African American soldiers. Fortunately, he was assigned to the all-black 761st Tank Battalion, Company B, under the command of Lieutenant Colonel Paul L. Bates, a white officer and former collegiate All-American football player who greatly respected Robinson. Troubled by a severely hobbled right ankle, first injured during a junior college football contest, which resulted in a determination that he was not fit for general duty, Robinson nevertheless helped to set up a softball team. As Bates later reflected, "When he hit a ball, it didn't come at you round, it came at you like a disk."

Robinson was told to prepare for shipment overseas with his company, but his ankle continuing bothering him. On July 6, 1944, he left McCloskey Hospital in Temple, located about thirty miles from the base, where he was undergoing an examination to determine what type of duty he could physically perform. Late that evening, he boarded a Camp Hood bus, but became involved in an altercation when the bus driver ordered him to head for the rear of the vehicle, rather than sit next to a friend, Virginia Jones, a light-skinned African American able to pass for white. Robinson refused to change his seat and warned the driver to leave him alone. Military police arrived and an interrogation followed, during which an MP admitted hearing Robinson cry out after a private referred to him with a racial epithet, "Look here, you son of a bitch, don't you ever call me no nigger. I'm an officer and God damn you, you better address me as one." Arrested because of both the fracas on the bus and an ensuing clash with the commander of the military police, Robinson was transported back to the hospital, where a white physician convinced him to take a blood alcohol test to refute a report that a drunken black officer had attempted to initiate a riot. During a subsequent four-hour court-martial, Colonel Bates, attesting to Robinson's "excellent" reputation and performance as a soldier, affirmed that "particularly with the enlisted men," Robinson was "held in high regard." Robinson was exonerated of all charges. On November 28, 1944, he was "honorably relieved from active duty . . . by reason of physical disqualification," an obvious reference to his weak ankle. The specific nature of the discharge troubled him, because, although "honorable," it did not entitle him to veterans' benefits.

Heeding advice from a former Negro League pitcher, Robinson contacted Thomas Y. Baird, co-owner of the Kansas City Monarchs, who invited him to attend the Monarchs' spring training camp. In the meantime, Robinson accepted a position as a physical education instructor at Sam Houston College in south Texas, where his friend, the Reverend Karl Downs, served as president. In late March 1945, Robinson joined the Monarchs' spring training camp in Houston. The Monarchs offered the best living and travel arrangements in black baseball, while their performance on the playing field was storied too, thanks to players like pitcher Satchel Paige, outfielder James "Cool Papa" Bell, and manager and first baseman Buck O'Neill. Robinson found the organization of black baseball, including scorekeeping and umpiring, haphazard at best. Nevertheless, the still unpolished player learned a great deal from some of the finest athletes ever to grace a baseball diamond. As fellow Monarch Newt Allen later reflected, "Jackie didn't have the ability at first, but he had the brains," which "made him a great ballplayer." In the forty-five games he played, Robinson excelled at the plate, batting .345, the seventh-best mark in the league; rapping ten doubles, the fourth top total; and belting five homers, second only to Alec Radcliff. Robinson was named to the West All-Star Team, but went hitless in the East-West Game.

That season Robinson obtained another tryout with a major league club. During World War II, the movement to integrate the game accelerated, receiving its greatest impetus with the death of Judge Kenesaw Mountain Landis, longtime baseball commissioner and intransigent foe of integrated baseball. On April 16, Robinson and two other Negro League players arrived at Boston's Fenway Park. Later, Boston councilman Isadore Muchnick remembered, "I'm telling you, you never saw anyone hit The Wall the way Robinson did that day. Bang, bang, bang: he rattled it." Clearly impressed with Robinson, Hugh Duffy, the top scout for Red Sox, commented, "Too bad he's the wrong color." Following the tryout, *Pittsburgh Courier* columnist Wendell Smith informed the Brooklyn Dodgers' Branch Rickey that Robinson was the most skilled of the three players that the Red Sox had examined. Rickey proceeded to track Robinson over the next several months. On August 28, the famous meeting at Rickey's Brooklyn office took place.

The signing of Robinson was a significant event, promising to undo decades of mistreatment of African American athletes. A small number of black ballplayers had played in organized baseball shortly after the Civil War, but by the late 1880s an almost impenetrable divide prevented even stellar dark-hued performers from competing against their white counterparts. As a result, blacks formed a league of their own, the Negro National League, in 1920, and a rival circuit, the Negro American League, soon arose as well. Financial difficulties, heightened by the Great Depression, threatened those enterprises but they generally held on, with the annual Negro League All-Star contest in Chicago each summer a particular highlight. Still, many observers of the game wanted to see players like Satchel Paige, Josh Gibson, and Buck Leonard go head to head against big league stars.

Throughout World War II, demands intensified that blacks receive the chance to compete on an even basis. Blacks began employing direct action tactics to challenge Jim Crow practices at home, while the epic book *An American Dilemma*, by Swedish diplomat and scholar Gunnar Myrdal, underscored how segregation and discrimination contradicted the supposedly sacrosanct American belief in equality of opportunity. The war itself, involving a fight against German Nazis and their horrific brand of racism, naturally threw theories of purported racial supremacy or inferiority into disrepute.

Having agreed to sign with the Dodgers, Robinson informed Rachel Isum, with whom he had maintained an on-again, off-again relationship, about his future plans. On October 23, Branch Rickey indicated during a news conference that Robinson was going to play for the Montreal Royals, the Dodgers' top minor league team. Talking with reporters, Robinson stated, "Of course, I can't begin to tell you how happy I am that I am the first member of my race in organized baseball. I realize how much it means to me, my race, and to baseball." The Dodgers, for their part, insisted that Robinson's signing was hardly to be seen as "as a gesture toward solution of a racial problem."

Both considerable criticism and support now came Rickey's way. Jimmy Powers of the *New York Daily News* considered Robinson merely a "1000-to-1 shot to make the grade," while Cleveland Indian fireballer Bob Feller also dismissed Robinson's prospects: "If he were a white man, I doubt if they would consider him big league material." Legendary pitcher Satchel Paige graciously offered, "They didn't make a mistake by signing Robinson. They couldn't have picked a better man," but many other Negro League participants were far less certain. Buck Leonard, the great first baseman with the Homestead Grays, admitted, "We didn't think he was that good." Robinson's mediocre performance on a barnstorming venture to Venezuela only reinforced notions that he was hardly the player to break organized baseball's color barrier.

Two weeks after Jackie and Rachel were married on February 10, 1946, they headed for the Dodgers' spring training camp in Daytona Beach, Florida, but they soon encountered Jim Crow practices that proved unsettling to both. Nevertheless, on the morning of March 4, Robinson and John Richard Wright, a twenty-seven-year-old Negro League veteran, became, as the *Daily Worker* reported, the first pair of African Americans "to crack modern organized baseball's Jim Crow." Mississippian Clay Hopper, manager of the Montreal Royals, queried the Dodgers' general manager at one point, "Mr. Rickey, do you really think a nigger's a human being?" Slumping badly at the plate, Robinson was forced out of an exhibition contest on April 7, when the local police chief in Sanford ordered Hopper to remove Jackie from the field. Rickey warned, "Without Robinson and Wright, there'll be no games!"

and proceeded to sign additional Negro Leaguers, catcher Roy Campanella and pitcher Don Newcombe. The Montreal Royals opened their season on April 18, before 25,000 fans at Roosevelt Stadium in Jersey City, New Jersey. Batting at 3:04 in the afternoon, Robinson weakly grounded to the Giants' shortstop. In the third inning, Robinson belted a fastball for a three-run homer and then beat out a bunt in the fifth, before stealing second. He took third base, despite a groundout to the third baseman. Then, inducing the rattled pitcher to balk, Robinson ambled home, causing the crowd to go wild. By game's end, Robinson had produced four hits in five at-bats, stolen two bases, scored four runs, and caused Montreal pitchers to balk twice. Only a throwing error marred his day, as the Royals won 14–1.

Robinson's stellar performance continued throughout the 1946 season, as he led the International League with a .349 batting average, tied for first in runs scored, finished second in stolen bases, and compiled the top fielding average for second basemen. He encountered expletives and projectiles on the diamond, but held his temper in check. He carried his team into the Junior World Series, which the Royals won in the sixth and final game, with Jackie scoring the winning run. At season's end, Royals manager Hopper readily shook Robinson's hand and said, "You're a great ballplayer and a fine gentleman. It's been wonderful having you on the team."

The off-season proved eventful in many ways. Jackie and Rachel had their first child, Jackie Junior, who was born in late November. Major league owners voted 15–1 against accepting black players, but Commissioner A.B. "Happy" Chandler, a former governor and U.S. senator from Kentucky, told Rickey to "bring him in. He'll play if he's got the capacity to play." Rickey moved the spring training camps of both the Dodgers and the Montreal Royals to Cuba, to mitigate publicity and problems regarding Jim Crow edicts. Arriving in camp, Robinson was stunned to discover that African American players would be housed at a run-down hotel in downtown Havana, while the white ballplayers stayed at the swanky Hotel Nacional or a recently opened boarding school.

As Robinson prepared to go against the Dodgers in a preseason contest, Rickey instructed him, "I want you to run wild, to steal the pants off them, to be the most conspicuous player on the field," thereby inducing fans to demand his promotion to the majors. Dodger manager Leo Durocher raved about Robinson: "He's a swell ball player. He's my type of ball player. Jackie can hit, run and field. What more can a manager ask of a player?" Nevertheless, spring training did not proceed smoothly. Stress resulted in stomach ailments, including an inflamed colon, for Robinson, who refused to rest. Playing first

91

base, he was knocked out by catcher Bruce Edwards, who ran into him, perhaps deliberately. Several other Dodger players expressed opposition to playing alongside African American teammates, but a trio of southerners, led by team leader and shortstop Pee Wee Reese, argued otherwise. For his part, Durocher angrily told his team, "I don't care if the guy is yellow or black, or if he has stripes like a fuckin' zebra! I'm the manager of this team, and I say he plays. What's more, I say he can make us all rich."

Durocher's year-long suspension for consorting with gamblers temporarily overshadowed Rickey's announcement on April 10, 1947, that the Dodgers had purchased Robinson's contract from the Montreal Royals. Handed a uniform boasting the number 42, Robinson signed a contract for $5,000 a year, the major league minimum. The *Pittsburgh Courier* warned, "If Robinson fails to make the grade, it will be many years before a Negro makes the grade. This is IT!" On April 15, Robinson appeared in his first major league game, before a packed crowd at Ebbets Field in Brooklyn. Throughout the season, fans turned out to see Robinson and the Dodgers, with Brooklyn eventually establishing a single-season attendance record. Dodger broadcaster Red Barber proclaimed the Dodger rookie the "biggest attraction in baseball since Babe Ruth." At the same time, Robinson had to overcome rookie jitters and taunts from opposing players and fans. Jimmy Cannon of the *New York Post* referred to Robinson as "the loneliest man I have ever seen in sports." The third series of the season, as Robinson later admitted, "brought me nearer to cracking up than I had ever been." The Dodgers were hosts to the Philadelphia Phillies, who were managed by Ben Chapman, an Alabaman known for his racist views. Led by Chapman, the Phillies hurled out a series of insults, such as "They're waiting for you in the jungles, black boy!" and "We don't want you here, nigger," when Robinson batted in the first inning. For a moment, Robinson admitted, he thought, "To hell with Mr. Rickey's noble experiment," and envisioned smashing "one of those white sons of bitches." Instead, he led the Dodgers to a 1–0 triumph, scoring the game's lone run. Undoubtedly helping to buck him up was the response of teammate Eddie Stanky, who hollered at the Phillies, "You yellow-bellied cowards, why don't you pick on somebody who can answer back!"

Other incidents imperiled baseball's "noble experiment." The Pittsburgh Pirates initially refused to take the field against the Dodgers at Forbes Field until threatened with a forfeit. In early May, National League president Ford Frick headed off a potential walkout by members of the defending World Series champion St. Louis Cardinals, warning that he would suspend strikers who would become "outcasts" in the press. Frick continued, "I do not care if half the league strikes. Those who do it will encounter quick retribution. All will be suspended and I don't care if it wrecks the National League for five years. This is the United States of America and one citizen has as much right to play as another." A series of hate-filled letters arrived, threatening Robinson's family with violence.

Through it all, Robinson persevered and soon began to excel, completing a 21-game hitting streak and gradually winning over teammates and even some opposing players. Along with Eddie Stanky, Hugh Casey and Dixie Walker, who had triggered the preseason campaign to keep Robinson off the Dodgers, began providing helpful advice. Younger players, like Duke Snider, who had grown up as a Robinson fan, befriended him. In the midst of one game as the opposition hurled "very vile names" at Robinson, the well-respected Pee Wee Reese purportedly stared at the name-callers, who soon grew silent. As the Dodgers captured the pennant, Robinson completed his initial regular season in the major leagues with a .297 batting average; 125 runs scored, the second-best mark in the National League; twelve homers; and a league high of twenty-nine stolen bases. Named Rookie of the Year by the *Sporting News*, Robinson brought speed back to a game that had been power-laden since Babe Ruth ushered in the era of the long ball in the 1920s. The Dodgers lost the World Series to the New York Yankees in seven hard-fought games, with Robinson batting .296 and fielding flawlessly.

Most significant of all, Robinson battered down the Jim Crow barrier that had long soiled the national pastime. Other Negro Leaguers entered the major leagues, with Roy Campanella and Don Newcombe soon starring for the Dodgers, and Satchel Paige and outfielder Larry Doby helping the Cleveland Indians to the 1948 World Series title. As the next decade began, Willie Mays, Hank Aaron, and Ernie Banks were among the other great ballplayers who moved over from the Negro leagues. Robinson, now playing second base, remained a star for several seasons, making the All-Star squad each year from 1949 to 1954 and compiling a lifetime batting average of .311 over ten campaigns. In 1949, he led the National League in hitting, with a .342 batting average, and in stolen bases, with thirty-seven thefts, knocked in 124 runs, and was named the Most Valuable Player. Altogether, he helped Brooklyn to six pennants and, in 1955, its only World Series crown, when the Dodgers finally bested their crosstown rivals, the hated Yankees.

Along the way, Robinson became a larger-than-life figure for many fans. In September 1947, he graced the cover of *Time* magazine and a nationwide poll placed him second in popularity, behind only entertainer Bing Crosby. The next year saw publication of his autobiography, *Jackie Robinson: My Own*

Story, while a film based on the book soon appeared. Increasingly, Robinson displayed greater interest in the wider world beyond baseball, including the Anti-Defamation League, run by B'nai B'rith; the YMCA facility located at 135th Street in Harlem; and a clothing store in Harlem. By the early 1950s, his fame was such that President Dwight Eisenhower, during a dinner for the Anti-Defamation League, made a point of coming over to Robinson's table to shake his hand. In January 1954, Robinson agreed to serve as chair of the Commission on Community Organizations of the National Conference of Christians and Jews. That same year, his now top salary and outside income enabled Jackie, Rachel, and their growing brood to move from a middle-class neighborhood in St. Albans, a residential district in the New York City borough of Queens, to a spacious home in the suburb of Stamford, Connecticut. Robinson became increasingly supportive of the National Association for the Advancement of Colored People's (NAACP) efforts to challenge racial strictures. The next year witnessed the unfolding of the Montgomery bus boycott, led by Martin Luther King Jr., who later acknowledged, "Jackie Robinson made it possible for me in the first place. Without him, I would never have been able to do what I did."

As King's epochal campaign of nonviolent protest continued, Robinson's playing career ended and a new phase of his life began. He refused to accept a trade to the New York Giants after the 1956 World Series, which the Dodgers lost to the Yankees, preferring instead to retire, as related in *Look* magazine, which paid $50,000 for his story. He took a job as vice president in charge of personnel for Chock Full o' Nuts, a chain of coffee shops, receiving an annual salary of $50,000 and benefits. He also served as chair of the NAACP's 1957 Freedom Fund drive and joined the organization's national board of directors. In 1959, Robinson wrote a column for the *New York Post,* while continuing to deliver a weekly radio show. He helped to establish the Student Emergency Fund, which collected several thousand dollars to support the young activists who were conducting sit-ins against Jim Crow practices in the South. In January 1962, Robinson received word that along with former nemesis Bob Feller, he would be inducted into the Baseball Hall of Fame in Cooperstown, New York—the first African American player and the first from the Negro Leagues to be so honored.

As the volatile 1960s wound on, the too rapidly aging Robinson—now battling diabetes and forced to use a cane—was castigated by black nationalists for his moderate viewpoints. Robinson flew to Birmingham to support King's fight against segregationist police commissioner Bull Connor, and he joined 200,000 protesters demanding jobs and freedom in the March on Washington

94

in August 1963. He accepted an appointment as chair of the New York State Athletic Commission, while continuing to deliver speeches for the Anti-Defamation League and the NAACP. In 1965, Robinson helped to establish the Freedom National Bank in Harlem, which he considered "symbolic of the determination of the Negro to become an integral part of the mainstream of our American economy." The next year found him serving as a special assistant to Governor Nelson Rockefeller for community affairs.

In other ways, Jackie, Rachel, and their three children experienced the highs and the lows of the zeitgeist of the 1960s and beyond. Rachel worked as a psychiatric nurse and became a professor at Yale University, while Jackie Jr., having dropped out of school and volunteered to serve in Vietnam, was charged in early 1968 with possession of heroin, marijuana, and a .22-caliber gun. Shortly after completing a detoxification program, Jackie Jr. was killed in a single-automobile crash on June 16, 1971. News of his son's death must have been shattering to Robinson, who was already suffering from hypertension, acute blockage of his arteries, advanced lung disease, diabetes, and near blindness.

Honors continued to come Robinson's way too, including *Sport* magazine's announcement in late 1971 that he had been chosen as "The Man of 25 Years of Sports." Saluted in the midst of the 1972 World Series for the twenty-fifth anniversary of his breaking of baseball's color barrier, Robinson characteristically declared, "I'm extremely proud and pleased. But I'll be more pleased when I can look over at third base and see a black man as manager." Days later, on October 24, Jackie Robinson died at age fifty-three of a massive heart attack. Civil rights leader Vernon Jordan lauded Robinson as "a trailblazer for all black people and a great spokesman for justice."

ALLEN GINSBERG
Avatar of the Beats

The date was October 7, 1955; the setting the dark and smoky Six Gallery, a former auto-repair shop located at Union and Fillmore, close to the Embarcadero in San Francisco; the occasion a spirited poetry reading organized by Kenneth Rexroth. An established fixture in Bay Area poetic circles, Rexroth provided an aura of legitimacy, if such were needed. The other poets included Michael McClure, Philip Whalen, Philip Lamantia, and Ruth Witt-Diamant, the lone woman in the otherwise all-male crowd. In fact, all the significant figures in the San Francisco poetry renaissance were present. Also in the audience of 150 or so was Jack Kerouac, who was too shy to read any of his own work but happily moved about the room, soliciting donations to purchase three large jugs of California burgundy.

As midnight approached amid generous imbibing of wine, an intoxicated Allen Ginsberg, conducting his first public reading, began to recite from ("Howl." His opening lines captured the spirit of the Beat Generation and soon catapulted him to the top rung of American poets.) Calling on his own experiences and that of many of his friends, Ginsberg sang out in the fashion of a cantor, "I saw the best minds of my generation destroyed by madness." Those "angelheaded hipsters" sought in drugs "the ancient heavenly connection to the starry dynamo in the machinery of night."

With Kerouac exclaiming, "Go!" "Yeah!" and "Correct!" in the background, Ginsberg delivered his still-incomplete epic work as if in a trance. Tears streamed from Rexroth's eyes as he listened to the younger man's ode to America, including a harsh condemnation of "Moloch" and a defiant announcement of his generation's arrival. For Ginsberg, his poem exuded "a rhythmic articulation of feeling . . . like an impulse that rises within—just like sexual impulses." Referring to his own experiences at Columbia University in the late 1940s, Ginsberg bemoaned those "who were expelled from the academies for crazy and publishing obscene odes on the windows of the skull." Alluding to his own sexual propensities, he extolled those "who howled on their knees in the subway and were dragged off the roof waving genitals and manuscripts." In the poem's second section, Ginsberg, in the fashion of a biblical prophet, condemned "Moloch the incomprehensible prison! . . . Moloch the vast stone of war! . . . Moloch whose blood is running money!" Afterward, Lawrence Ferlinghetti, whose City Lights Bookstore had agreed to publish "Howl," fired off a brief note: "I greet you at the beginning of a great career. When do I get the manuscript?" In the fall of 1956, City Lights/Pocket Poets released *Howl and Other Poems.*

One of the dominant figures of the Beat Generation, this offspring of radical Jewish immigrants helped to reshape America's cultural landscape. Irwin Allen Ginsberg was born in Newark, New Jersey, on June 3, 1926, the second child of Louis and Naomi Ginsberg, a pair of mismatched lovers. Their families, along with so many other immigrant Jews, had ended up on the Lower East Side of New York City, where Louis and Naomi, both seventeen, met at Barringer High School. Louis, drawn to the socialist beliefs of his parents, attended Rutgers University in Newark, while the Yiddish-speaking Naomi, attracted to communism, went to a normal school to become a grammar school teacher. Notwithstanding strong opposition from his parents, who disapproved of Naomi, the two married in 1919 and resided in Newark. Within a short while, Louis acquired a reputation as a poet, largely thanks to his 1920 work, "Roots." The two frequented Greenwich Village and were drawn to feminism, vegetarianism, and nudism, which especially appealed to Naomi. Louis coursed easily through New York literary circles, contributing to various literary publications, including the *New Masses,* which increasingly spouted a procommunist line.

The family moved to the Bronx in New York City and then to a dilapidated Jewish district in Paterson, New Jersey, where Louis taught English at a local high school. Pancreatic difficulties and mental illness afflicted Naomi, whose extended stays in sanatoriums, combined with incessant bickering between her and Louis, troubled their son Allen. Not surprisingly, he suffered some emotional difficulties of his own. At the age of five, he triggered a fire in his bedroom, while at school he was alienated from the other children. As the Ginsbergs moved from one apartment building to another, Allen experienced a series of crushes on prepubescent boys. At Central High School, this buck-toothed "mental ghoul," with his thick glasses, felt "totally disconnected from any reality," becoming enamored with musicians ranging from Ludwig van Beethoven to Bessie Smith and Huddie Ledbetter ("Leadbelly"). Compelled to transfer to East Side High, Ginsberg caught the attention of an English teacher who introduced him to the poetry of Walt Whitman.

In September 1943 Ginsberg entered Columbia University as a scholarship student who hoped to become a labor lawyer. He was drawn to the English department with its distinguished faculty, which included the literary critic and author Lionel Trilling and Pulitzer Prize–winning poet Mark Van Doren. Ginsberg pored over the writings of classical Greeks and Romans, St. Augustine, Dante, Machiavelli, and Shakespeare, among others, and became assistant editor of the *Columbia Review*. He eventually learned of both his mother's decision to leave her marriage and her subsequent involvement with Leon Luria, a communist physician who worked for the left-wing National Maritime Union.

With his friend Lucien Carr, Ginsberg frequented artistic and cultural haunts in Manhattan, including Greenwich Village. Through Carr, Ginsberg met first William Burroughs, a Harvard dropout and an heir to the Burroughs Corporation fortune, and then Jack Kerouac, a merchant seaman whose football career at Columbia had ended due to a leg injury and whose "indifferent character" had resulted in his early release from the U.S. Navy. As he had with Carr, Ginsberg fell in love with Kerouac, whom he idealized as an extraordinarily handsome, sensitive, intelligent, and compassionate young man. Carr recalled that this group of friends—especially Ginsberg and Kerouac—aspired to a "new vision" that involved "trying to look at the world in a new light, trying to look at the world in a way that gave it some meaning." By 1944, the group formed, as Kerouac put it, "a libertine circle" that sought to cultivate "the New Consciousness."

The proponents of this transformed consciousness were in keeping with an older bohemian tradition, initially associated with gypsies, outsiders, writers, and artists in nineteenth-century Europe. These individuals were determined to exist and create according to their own codes of behavior, which often deliberately contradicted more conventional practices. Bohemian enclaves sprouted in Paris's Montmartre and Montparnasse; London's Chelsea, Fitzrovia, and Soho; Munich's Schwabing; New York City's Greenwich Village; and San Francisco's North Beach. Columbia University in Morningside Heights in New York City served as an initial repository for the latest version of American bohemianism.

In the spring semester of 1945, Ginsberg—whose ideal of the "new vision" was leading him to question rationality itself—was suspended from Columbia after etching obscene, anti-Semitic graffiti on the windowpane of his dormitory room. He was required to undergo psychiatric counseling before being readmitted to the university. In the meantime, he took on a number of odd jobs, working as a welder, a dishwasher, and a clerk. He drew closer to Burroughs, who exposed him to the seamy underworld of Times Square. Determined to lose his virginity, Ginsberg had his first sexual encounters, including with Kerouac. Following his friend's lead, Ginsberg briefly joined the U.S. Maritime Service. He also smoked marijuana for the first time and took other drugs. His explorations with both homosexuality and drugs were illegal and viewed as immoral by the vast majority of Americans at the time. Indeed, psychiatrists were among those who deemed that such practices involved pathological behavior that should necessarily be curbed.

With a psychiatrist's letter in hand, Ginsberg reenrolled at Columbia for the fall semester in 1946. He was troubled about his sexual inclinations, while continuing to experiment with drugs. That fall, he met a friend of Jack Kerouac, a young, fast-talking hustler from Denver named Neal Cassady. Ginsberg engaged in a love affair with Cassady, whose sexual appetite included a fondness for numerous women and men as well. Soon, Ginsberg discovered that his mother's mental condition had worsened again and he worried about his own sanity. Shortly after completing a group of poems, "The Denver Doldrums," he had a religious sensation while reading William Blake's *Songs of Innocence and Songs of Experience*. Ginsberg remembered, "I suddenly realized that *this* experience was *it!*"

Still foundering, Ginsberg worked as a copyboy on the midnight shift for the Associated Press Radio News Service, situated at Rockefeller Center, and hung out with Kerouac and Cassady. Increasingly, Ginsberg and Kerouac sought to spread the word about each other's writing gifts, but to little avail. Petty criminals, including Herbert Huncke, another aspiring author, began storing stolen goods at Ginsberg's apartment in Lenox Hill, which led to Allen's arrest and his confinement at the Columbia Presbyterian Psychiatric Institute.

After his release in early 1950, Ginsberg became convinced that he could become content in heterosexual relations, an attitude undoubtedly influenced by the starkly homophobic nature of Cold War America.]Over the next several years, he did have a number of affairs with women, although he remained attracted to men as well. Temporarily serving on the staff of the *Labor Herald*, Ginsberg spent time at the San Remo bar, located on the corner of Bleecker and MacDougal streets in Greenwich Village. There, he encountered writers like James Agee and Paul Goodman, along with the composer John Cage. Ginsberg referred to the crowd at the bar as the "subterraneans,"(while Kerouac and John Clellon Holmes were already likening their friends to the Lost Generation of the 1920s. At one point, in fact, Kerouac exclaimed, "Ah, this is really a Beat Generation!")A new member soon arrived on the scene: a young, self-proclaimed poet, Gregory Corso. Like his compatriots, Corso embodied the unrestrained bohemianism—(characterized by a fondness for uninhibited sex, liberal consumption of alcohol, and drugs ranging from marijuana to heroin—of the small group of writers, artists, and less talented hangers-on, hustlers, and sociopaths.)Not yet a movement, this 1950s version of the Lost Generation suggested that the cusp of a counterculture was emerging, no matter how little recognized at the time(For Ginsberg, that counterculture demanded sexual liberation and the ability to explore alternative states of consciousness.)

Continuing to write and hang out in Greenwich Village, Ginsberg acquired work as a market researcher. In April 1952, he took peyote for the first time, recording in his notebook, "Heavens the universe is in order." Increasingly, poet and physician William Carlos Williams and Kerouac helped to mold his writing techniques, particularly after Williams agreed to serve as something of a mentor.(Another revelation came Ginsberg's way when, in early 1953, he began to explore Zen Buddhism.)Following a summer stint as a copyboy for the *New York World-Telegram*, he went to Havana and then Mexico, where he explored archaeological sites. Finally arriving at the home of Neal and Carolyn Cassady in San Jose, California, Ginsberg was soon ordered to leave by Carolyn, who was enraged by Allen's affair with her husband.

Having again taken a job with a market research firm, Ginsberg became a regular at the literary salon of Kenneth Rexroth, a leading figure in San Francisco poetry circles. He also began living with Sheila Williams Boucher at her apartment on fashionable Nob Hill, but that relationship soured after he revealed his sexual history to her. One evening, after yet another argument with Boucher, a drunken Ginsberg ended up at Foster's Cafeteria in Polk Gulch, where he joined a group of several young men, including the painter Robert LaVigne.(Later, at LaVigne's apartment, Ginsberg met twenty-one-year-old Peter Orlovsky, who would become the great love of his life.)

Soon, Ginsberg and Orlovsky shared an apartment in which they maintained separate bedrooms.

More than ever, Ginsberg was devoted to his writing and the literary scene in San Francisco. He ran into the poet Michael McClure at a reading by W.H. Auden and met Lawrence Ferlinghetti, a former World War II naval commander, poet, and owner of the City Lights Bookstore, which published first-rate paperbacks. In early August, Ginsberg began to write "Howl," determined to adopt the less inhibited style that Rexroth encouraged. The poem became a manifesto for the Beat Generation and a precursor of the counterculture of the 1960s. He drew on personal experiences and on those of his companions, including Huncke and Carl Solomon, who had experienced electroshock treatment. Rather than discussing Kerouac and Burroughs, Ginsberg pointed to other tortured souls, making the poem "a lament for the Lamb in America, with instances of remarkable lamb-like youths." Undoubtedly more hopeful than he was assured, Ginsberg envisioned a larger counterculture appearing in the middle of Eisenhower's America, which seemingly was still shaped far more by J. Edgar Hoover's FBI than by the "new vision."

The Six Gallery reading of October 7, 1955, heralded, as Ginsberg biographer Barry Miles noted, "the San Francisco chapter of the Beat Generation." Ginsberg now drew closer to fellow poets Gary Snyder and Philip Whalen, while exploring Zen Buddhism in greater depth. The following summer, Ginsberg served on the USNS *Sgt. Jack J. Pendleton*, headed for the Arctic Circle. He received bound copies of *Howl and Other Poems*, and he began reading the Torah, the Five Books of Moses. On September 2, 1956, the *New York Times* contained a lengthy article, "West Coast Rhythms," which saluted Ginsberg as a significant new poet. Referring to the San Francisco Beats, the *Times* reported that the past year's "most remarkable poem" produced by a band of young writers was "Howl," which was "profoundly Jewish in temper" and "Biblical in its repetitive grammatical build-up," a condemnation of "everything in our mechanistic civilization which kills the spirit." With his own fame now seemingly assured, Ginsberg continued to promote the work of other Beat writers, especially Kerouac, Burroughs, Corso, and Snyder. Although recognizing that the Beat Generation was just starting to take off, Ginsberg, "very conscious of leaving the scene to do something more serious and steady," decided to travel to Europe, hoping to broaden his horizons.

Through his far-flung adventures, drug experiments, and largely unrestrained sexual practices, Ginsberg served as a pathfinder for the counterculture that would emerge in the new decade. Determined to connect with well-known figures and those who promised to become acclaimed, as he now did himself, Ginsberg began his roundabout odyssey by encountering the writer Anaïs Nin in Los Angeles, the British poet Denise Levertov in Guadalajara in Mexico, and the poet Diane di Prima in New York City. Ginsberg introduced himself to the artist Salvador Dali at a gallery in Manhattan and went to see William Carlos Williams in New Jersey. In early March 1957, Ginsberg and Orlovsky sailed aboard a Yugoslav freighter for Casablanca in Morocco, where they indulged in the region's potent marijuana, hashish, and opium, while foreshadowing the adventures of the counterculture of the ensuing decade.

While traveling through Western Europe, Ginsberg fielded questions from *Time* magazine about an obscenity trial involving "Howl" that was taking place in San Francisco. The Juvenile Division of the San Francisco Police Department, clearly determined to prevent the release of "Howl," with its graphic use of language, including some obviously extolling homosexuality, had arrested Lawrence Ferlinghetti for publishing and selling Ginsberg's book of poems. In Paris, Ginsberg received word that the presiding judge in the case had declared that his epic poem was not "without redeeming social importance," even concluding "with a plea for holy living." Ironically, sales of "Howl" boomed, thanks to the publicity generated by the trial, with *Life* magazine presenting a lengthy piece on both.

Across the Atlantic, Jack Kerouac's frenetic account of the odysseys of the Beat Generation, *On the Road*, was published to mixed reviews but considerable fanfare. Herb Caen, a columnist for the *San Francisco Chronicle*, noted marijuana arrests in North Beach and the hassling of "beatniks" by the police. After a year and a half away, Ginsberg returned to the States in mid-1958. With Kerouac beset by alcoholism, Ginsberg became known as the "King of the Beats." Along with Orlovsky and Corso, he appeared in an experimental film called *Pull My Daisy*, a precursor of the underground cinema that would thrive in the ensuing decade.

Then, in early 1959, Ginsberg participated in a research experiment at the Mental Research Institute in Palo Alto, taking LSD 25—lysergic acid—for the first time. The experience proved revelatory for Ginsberg, who fell into a trance that he likened to that described in the English poet Samuel Taylor Coleridge's classic work, "Kubla Khan," seeming "permanent and transcendent" with "rather beautiful visual images too." Shortly after receiving news that Burroughs had published the long-awaited novel, *Naked Lunch*, Ginsberg began a trip through South America as the new decade opened, where he ingested large doses of a potent hallucinogen favored by Amazon Indians. Back in the States, he joined in an experiment involving psilocybin conducted by

Timothy Leary, then serving as a lecturer in psychology at Harvard. On that occasion, Ginsberg told Leary, "I'm the Messiah. I've come down to preach love to the world. We're going to walk through the streets and teach people to stop hating." In the fashion of Leary and Richard Alpert, Leary's colleague at Harvard, Ginsberg became a proselytizer for psychedelic drugs, seeking to turn on many creative performers and intellectuals, including the poet Robert Lowell and Lowell's lover, Elizabeth Hardwick.

Continuing his far-flung travels during the early 1960s, Ginsberg, joined by Orlovsky, visited the ashram of Swami Shivanda in the Himalayas, where Allen became versed in the Hare Krishna mantra that he would carry back to America. In the spring of 1963, Ginsberg flew to Saigon, where he met Neil Sheehan, a young journalist who was critical of American operations in Vietnam. In mid-August, Ginsberg, who now wore his thinning curly hair long and sported a full black beard, ended a poetry conference by chanting "Hare Krishna." Finally, back in San Francisco, Ginsberg participated in his first demonstration against the Vietnam War, helping to birth a new culture within the shell of the older one.

In early 1964, Ginsberg and Orlovsky hosted a number of orgies at their apartment in New York City, with Ginsberg noting, "Been making it with some nice young girls and boys—what a pleasure to be a clean old man—More I see it I think there is a big sex upsurge revolution which will alter and enlarge family unit." Ginsberg met up with Ken Kesey and the Merry Pranksters, who sought to foster a free-flowing psychedelic revolution, and included in their ranks Neal Cassady, driver of the brightly colored bus that transported them around the country. In late December, Ginsberg joined with the poet Ed Sanders in conducting a demonstration on the Lower East Side of New York City, calling for the legalization of marijuana.

The following year, Ginsberg was invited by the Cuban minister of culture to participate in a writers' conference at the Casa de las Americas in Havana. The homophobic nature of the Castro regime, which had been celebrated by many New Leftists, greatly disturbed Ginsberg, who was soon required to leave the Caribbean island. His next trip took him to Prague, which he considered "lovelier in miniature than Paris almost." A cultural and literary revolution was unfolding in Czechoslovakia, which ensured that Ginsberg was well received. His sexual antics continued unabated and he offered a reading of "Howl" and other poems before a large crowd at Charles University. At one point, Ginsberg took a train to Moscow, where he immediately headed for the Kremlin and Red Square. In the home station of Soviet communism, he encountered a series of relatives, who shared photos and stories about his mother. He also met the poet Yevgeny Yevtushenko, who said, "I respect you as a great man, a great poet." But Yevtushenko considered homosexuality and drugs "juvenile preoccupations," hardly as significant as Stalinism and the censorship that still afflicted Russian authors. Back in Prague, the students voted Ginsberg May King; he dedicated his "crown to the beautiful bureaucrat Franz Kafka." Soon, however, he suffered the theft of his notebook, a tailing by government security forces, and a beating at the hands of a man who shouted, "*Bouzerant! Bouzerant!* (homosexual)." The Czech government rescinded his visa. Arriving in London on May 8, 1965, Ginsberg met Bob Dylan, Joan Baez, and filmmaker Don Pennebaker at the Savoy Hotel. Soon, the Beatles sent for him. Then he delivered a series of poetry readings in the English and Welsh countrysides.

Returning home, he discovered that Orlovsky, who was battling drug addiction, had moved their possessions to a dilapidated district in New York City. Ginsberg received word that he had been awarded a Guggenheim Foundation grant, which enabled him to purchase a Volkswagen camper. Eventually, Ginsberg and Orlovsky went to see Cassady, who was residing at Ken Kesey's ranch in La Honda, outside Palo Alto.

On November 28, Ginsberg joined in an antiwar march bound for the Oakland Army Terminal, as both riot-trained police and members of the outlaw motorcycle gang, the Hell's Angels, threatened to disrupt the protest. Deflecting calls for the marchers to arm themselves, Ginsberg urged the use of street theater tactics instead. At a meeting orchestrated by Kesey at the home of Hell's Angels leader Sonny Barger, Ginsberg joined Cassady, several Merry Pranksters, and a score of Hell's Angels; only Ginsberg failed to take acid but the atmosphere initially remained icy. Then Ginsberg began to chant, which led one of the Angels to begin intoning, "Om, om zoom, zoom, zoom, om!" Eventually, everyone in the room joined in, to Ginsberg's delight.

Continuing to champion both the burgeoning counterculture and the antiwar movement, the poet-activist managed to be present at many of the era's most noteworthy happenings. On January 19, 1967, he joined with Snyder, Leary, and thousands of others in chanting mantras at Golden Gate Park in San Francisco, the scene of the Human Be-In. The publicity surrounding Ginsberg's appearance at the event, the poet Larry Fagin argued, "skyrocketed the whole Ginsberg cottage industry into outer space." In August 1968, Ginsberg watched as police attacked thousands of antiwar protesters, not all them well mannered, in Chicago during the Democratic Party presidential convention. At one point, after pacifist leader David Dellinger implored him to help calm both sides, Ginsberg took up a chant, resulting in a temporary quieting of tensions. Ginsberg was present for the Woodstock Festival in August 1969, when 400,000 people congregated on Max Yasgur's farm in upstate New York to listen to some of the era's top bands and poets.

Acclaim and attention continued to come Ginsberg's way, including a grant from the National Institute of Arts and Letters and *Time* magazine's acknowledgment that he had been "all but officially designated as a peculiar national treasure of sorts." In December 1969, he testified on behalf of the defense at the Chicago conspiracy trial, which saw Dellinger and antiwar activist Tom Hayden among those charged with having sought to incite a riot at the Democratic national convention. On October 9, 1971, Ginsberg was one of the select few gathered to celebrate John Lennon's thirty-first birthday in the former Beatle's hotel room in Syracuse, New York. In April 1974, Ginsberg was informed that his work, *The Fall of America*, had been granted the National Book Award in Poetry.

In the mid-1970s, Ginsberg joined Bob Dylan's Rolling Thunder Revue, a traveling cavalcade of musicians. In February 1979, he was given the National Arts Club gold medal, soon followed by his induction into the American Academy and Institute of Arts and Letters. In August 1981, he attended a writers' conference in Mexico City, along with Gunter Grass, Octavio Paz, and Jorge Luis Borges, among others. In Toronto, he witnessed a stage production of his poem "Kaddish." Appropriately enough, 1984 found Ginsberg, along with the great black writer James Baldwin and Coretta Scott King, Martin Luther King Jr.'s widow, on a list of speakers that the United States Information Agency blacklisted from government-backed performances abroad. Nevertheless, that fall, Ginsberg, Gary Snyder, and African American author Toni Morrison served as members of an American delegation to China, which was supposed to exchange ideas regarding the writing process. Remaining politically engaged, Ginsberg delivered poetry readings on behalf of the Polish Solidarity movement in Krakow and Warsaw. In January 1988, he showed up in Tel Aviv, condemning Israeli occupation policies regarding Palestine. In 1993, the French Minister of Culture named Ginsberg Chevalier de l'ordre des Arts et Lettres. On April 5, 1997, Ginsberg, who had been appointed Distinguished Professor of Poetry at Brooklyn College, succumbed to a heart attack, associated with the terminal liver cancer that afflicted him, in the East Village in New York City.

Ginsberg's friend Tom Hayden said, "He led quite a great life. He was an Old Testament figure railing against the establishment—a Jewish guy from New York who became a Buddhist, a poet, and a musician. Allen was like a prophet of the 1960s." Hayden continued, "He was a reflection of what was going on. The poem 'Howl' was a howl against the hypocrisy and silence of the generations of the 1950s—of the people who failed to perform their function as real elders."

Conclusion

They were both outsiders, whose very makeup contradicted the democratic overlay of the American nation. Jackie Robinson, with his very dark skin, confronted racial barriers that had afflicted African Americans for three centuries. Allen Ginsberg, because of his sexual orientation and his challenge to American material culture, similarly faced ostracism rooted in long-standing homophobia. Each man was an artist in his own fashion, the one with his athletic genius and the other with his flair for poetry, who battled against the kinds of impediments that continued to afflict democratic America as World War II ended. Robinson and Ginsberg opened doors for others to enter, dramatically serving to liberate the nation as a whole. The all-around athlete starred in America's favorite sport, part of a seemingly star-crossed team that was beloved in Brooklyn and many other corners of the United States. Robinson's performance on the baseball diamond enabled other gifted African Americans to enter organized baseball and demonstrated how readily they could compete if afforded something of a level playing field. The wordsmith acted as a missionary for an emancipated lifestyle, defiantly contesting sexual boundaries of many sorts. Although homosexuality and bisexuality remained highly controversial, Ginsberg's celebrity forced their public recognition. Restrictive sexual and racial boundaries, in the legal, cultural, and social realms, proved less acceptable as first Robinson's career and then Ginsberg's wound to a close.

Study Questions

1. The integration of major league baseball had enormous social, political, and cultural importance. Explain why this was so.
2. Dr. Martin Luther King Jr. and other civil rights leaders viewed Jackie Robinson as a hero. How did Robinson acquire this stature?
3. Discuss the significance of the Beats and their alternative vision of America in the early postwar years.
4. The public reading of Ginsberg's poem "Howl" was a figurative "shot across the bow" in the culture wars of the 1950s. Explain why this poem had such impact.

5. Robinson and Ginsberg were both outsiders and pathbreakers in post-war American society. Compare the roles of the two in challenging restrictive social and cultural barriers.

Selected Bibliography

Eig, Jonathan. *Opening Day: The Story of Jackie Robinson's First Season.* New York: Simon and Schuster, 2007.

Falkner, David. *Great Time Coming: The Life of Jackie Robinson from Baseball to Birmingham.* New York: Simon and Schuster, 1995.

Ginsberg, Allen. *Collected Poems 1947–1997.* New York: HarperCollins, 2007.

———. *Journals: Early Fifties, Early Sixties.* New York: Grove, 1977.

———. *Journals: Mid-Fifties, 1954–1958.* New York: HarperCollins, 1995.

Golenbock, Peter. *Bums: An Oral History of the Brooklyn Dodgers.* Lincolnwood, IL: Contemporary Books, 2000.

Kahn, Roger. *The Boys of Summer.* New York: Harper and Row, 1972.

Kramer, Jane. *Allen Ginsberg in America.* New York: Random House, 1969.

Long, Michael G. *First Class Citizenship: The Civil Rights Letters of Jackie Robinson.* New York: Times Books, 2007.

Miles, Barry. *Ginsberg: A Biography.* New York: Simon and Schuster, 1989.

Morgan, Bill. *I Celebrate Myself: The Somewhat Private Life of Allen Ginsberg.* New York: Penguin, 2006.

Rampersad, Arnold. *Jackie Robinson: A Biography.* New York: Ballantine, 1998.

Robinson, Jackie, and Alfred Duckett. *I Never Had It Made.* New York: Putnam, 1972.

Robinson, Rachel, and Lee Daniels. *Jackie Robinson: An Intimate Portrait.* New York: Harry N. Abrams, 1996.

Schumacher, Michael. *Dharma Lion: A Critical Biography of Allen Ginsberg.* New York: St. Martin's, 1992.

Tygiel, Jules. *Baseball's Great Experiment: Jackie Robinson and His Legacy.* New York: Oxford University Press, 1983.

5

Defending Democracy in the Nuclear Age

In the immediate postwar period, the development of nuclear weapons and the intensification of the Cold War confronted the American people with daunting challenges and sometimes seemingly stark choices. Given the unprecedented pressures of the atomic era, wherein national security needs sometimes came perilously close to encroaching on the democratic foundations of American life, one of the most critical tasks was to assure the continued existence of a democratic republic in a dangerous world. To some people, such as Curtis LeMay, commander of the Strategic Air Command, the preeminent threat was external and easily identifiable—the Soviet Union, with its immense military might and totalitarian ideology, was the greatest danger that the United States had ever faced. The gruff, cigar-smoking general, one of the foremost proponents of air power during World War II, viewed nuclear weapons as a means to ensure the nation's security, indeed survival, in a world dominated by the confrontation between the two superpowers. Individuals like LeMay, who considered themselves sober-minded realists, believed that nuclear armaments, as horrific as they were, offered the promise of deterring future conflict. Unlike those who considered major conflict in the atomic age unthinkable, LeMay advocated strategies that were premised on the possibility of nuclear Armageddon. Most alarmingly, LeMay spoke openly of situations in which the United States could resort to preemptive strikes against a threatening enemy. His duty, he was convinced, was to take those steps that would ensure the survival and victory of the United States in a nuclear war that few other people would even ponder.

For many other Americans, the greater danger to American democracy came from those who planned for hypothetical scenarios of nuclear destruction, the military strategists whose very determination to prepare for atomic war would assure its inevitability. They, together with powerful political and industrial leaders, constituted a "power elite" that was laying the foundations for what President Dwight Eisenhower termed the "military-industrial complex." The vastly heightened role of this small, insulated group of powerful men in postwar America, some began to argue, presented more danger to the nation's democratic traditions than did any foreign enemy. Some critics, like the radical sociologist C. Wright Mills, were deeply troubled by "the military metaphysic" fostered by LeMay, warning that "the causes of World War Three" could be traced to that mind-set. Peace activists focused on the consequences of accelerated nuclear testing, leading to the emergence of a test-ban movement in the 1950s. Mills was certainly sympathetic to the "ban the bomb" movement that arose in Great Britain and the United States, but largely confined his own activism to his writings and public addresses. By the time the antinuclear movement gathered momentum, Mills had become one of America's leading public intellectuals, known for his critical analyses of white-collar workers, the power elite that largely determined U.S. domestic and foreign policies, and the academic establishment, notwithstanding his own professorship at Columbia University. Mills's analyses spurred the growth of the New Left, whose members approved of his iconoclastic positions, particularly his willingness to speak truth to power, no matter what that might cost him.

CURTIS LEMAY
Apostle of Armageddon

In the early years of the Eisenhower presidency, American defense strategists were increasingly alarmed about the growing nuclear capabilities of the Soviet Union. Though the American monopoly on nuclear weapons had disappeared in 1949 when the first Soviet atomic bomb was tested, the United States had retained a clear superiority in nuclear arms and strategic bombers. Nonetheless, some strategists counseled that the American advantage would not last indefinitely and that it was imperative to consider the possibility of a first strike against the Soviet Union while circumstances still favored the United States. Curtis LeMay, commander of the Air Force's Strategic Air Command since 1948, was a consistent advocate of what many deemed an unthinkable action. As early as 1950, LeMay, already renowned for blunt and often impolitic remarks, had projected that 1954 would be the "year of maximum danger," when the Soviet nuclear arsenal and bomber force reached levels that would pose discernible threats to American security. By 1953, other government agencies confirmed the growing danger. A National Security Council (NSC) subcommittee concluded that existing U.S. defense programs were inadequate "to prevent, neutralize or seriously deter the military or covert attacks which the USSR is capable of launching." Other influential voices echoed the idea that national security required the United States to act while it held a clear advantage. In August, Nathan Twining, Air Force Chief of Staff, was presented with a staff report called "The Coming National Crisis," which warned that the nation would soon be compelled to choose between general war and submission to "the whims of a small group of proven barbarians." The report argued that a "no first-strike" policy guaranteed "disaster in a nuclear war." Increasingly, many high officials in the defense establishment were willing to consider a preventive war against the Soviet Union. In late 1954, President Eisenhower rejected this concept, declaring in a national security policy statement, "The United States and its allies must reject the concept of preventive war or acts intended to provoke war." A proponent of the "New Look" in defense strategy, Eisenhower advocated the deterrent quality of a policy of massive retaliation with nuclear weapons, not preventive war against potential enemies.

The president had not, however, disallowed a policy of preemption, and LeMay's Strategic Air Command (SAC) was authorized to plan for a preemptive attack on the USSR if SAC determined that the Soviet Union was preparing to attack the United States. Since Central Intelligence Agency (CIA) estimates concluded that the Soviets would require a month to assemble and deliver all their estimated 150 nuclear weapons, LeMay believed that he could easily carry out the full-scale "Sunday punch" strike that he had advocated for years—unleashing everything in the U.S. nuclear arsenal in a simultaneous, omnidirectional assault on the Soviet Union. A U.S. Navy officer later recounted his horrified reaction to a SAC briefing in March 1954 during which Air Force staffers summarized a proposed attack plan that seemed little short of apocalyptic—more than 1,000 U.S. strategic bombers were to rain as many as 750 atomic bombs on the USSR within a couple of hours. "The final impression," the stunned captain wrote, "was that virtually all of Russia would be nothing but a smoking, radiating ruin at the end of two hours." During the question-and-answer period after the briefing, LeMay casually remarked that, were war in Korea renewed, he would up the ante in such "poker games" by using atomic bombs on China, Manchuria, and southeastern Russia.

During his lengthy tenure as chief of Strategic Air Command, General LeMay established a reputation as a brusque, no-nonsense advocate of military preparedness, a convinced proponent of air power who endorsed uniquely

Plan for destro of Russia, Chin (handwritten marginal note)

111

aggressive nuclear strategies. Known variously by admirers and critics as the "Iron Eagle," "Iron Ass," and "Bomber" LeMay, the general came to personify the nuclear warrior—cold, unsentimental, committed to an increasingly ambiguous concept of victory in an era in which major warfare between the superpowers might well mean the destruction of world civilization. LeMay may have been the inspiration for the fictional General Jack D. Ripper, the renegade SAC wing commander who initiates a preemptive attack on the Soviet Union, with catastrophic results, in Stanley Kubrick's 1964 film *Dr. Strangelove, or How I Learned to Stop Worrying and Love the Bomb*. LeMay's embrace of an offensive nuclear strategy, some feared, might well result in a similar conflagration.

LeMay's experiences in World War II had been central in shaping his views about national defense—he had been appalled at America's lack of readiness in 1941. The effects of the American strategic bombing campaign against Germany and Japan, which he had done much to organize, also left a discernible imprint on his outlook. The immense destruction wrought by the strategic bombing of those two nations provided a lesson, he believed, that the United States could ignore only at its peril. In a postwar speech to Ohio State University alumni, LeMay warned, "If you love America, do everything you can do to make sure that what happened to Germany and Japan will never happen to our country." Only geography had spared the United States similar destruction—the enemy had lacked the capability to strike at the continental United States, granting the nation time to ready itself. In the next war, LeMay predicted, "distance will be academic and there will be no time for preparation." Given the rapid advances in weapons technology, the nation's security now rested with the Air Force, which, LeMay insisted, "must be allowed to develop unhindered and unchained. There must be no ceiling, no boundaries, no limitations to our air power development." As SAC commander, LeMay dedicated himself to the realization of that proposition. When he assumed his new command in 1948, he inherited a force of 837 combat aircraft, many aging and of questionable utility. Upon his promotion to Air Force Chief of Staff in 1957, Strategic Air Command boasted a massive fleet of 3,040 aircraft, including nearly 1,800 modern strategic bombers capable of delivering nuclear weapons to the Soviet heartland. Under LeMay's direction, SAC became, in the words of one historian, "the deadliest combat force of all time."

Curtis Emerson LeMay was born into modest circumstances in Columbus, Ohio, on November 15, 1906. His parents, Ernest and Arizona, were able to provide little in the way of material comforts to their six children, but instilled the values of hard work, duty, and morality. LeMay later recalled that he was about four years old when he saw his first airplane, and as a teenager, he concluded that attending college as a Reserve Officer Training cadet would be the best avenue to a career in aviation. In 1924, he enrolled at Ohio State University as an engineering major, but abandoned his studies four years later when he was accepted as a cadet in the U.S. Army Air Corps. Having completed flight training, LeMay was commissioned as a second lieutenant in the Air Corps Reserve in October 1929. His first assignment was to Selfridge Field, Michigan, where he served with the Twenty-Seventh Pursuit Squadron. During this assignment, the young Ohioan met Helen Maitland, a University of Michigan student whom he would marry in 1934.

During the 1930s, LeMay faced not only the financial challenges posed by the Depression, but also the glacial pace of promotion in peacetime; ultimately, he served eleven years as a lieutenant. It was a decade during which the Air Corps confronted slashed budgets and struggled to define its mission. In 1936, LeMay, who had trained as a fighter pilot, was assigned to the Second Bomb Group at Langley Field, Virginia. He was quick to discern the offensive capabilities of modern bombers such as Boeing's B-17 Flying Fortress, some of which arrived at Langley in early 1937. Though he and others recognized the aircraft's potential to carry massive amounts of destructive power into the enemy's heartland, neither the army nor the navy was receptive to this doctrine. LeMay and other like-minded airmen spent the next several years striving to demonstrate the bomber's utility as dramatically as possible through bombing exercises, long-range intercept missions, and long-distance intercontinental flights.

In 1941, as the United States entered World War II, the Air Corps was renamed the U.S. Army Air Force (USAAF) and LeMay finally received his captain's bars. During the next four years, he was an ardent advocate and practitioner of strategic bombing, first in Europe and then the Pacific. Commanding the 305 Bombardment Group in England and rising to the rank of major general by 1942, LeMay developed formation-flying procedures and bombing techniques that reduced Allied losses and improved bombing accuracy in raids across Nazi-occupied Europe. Though the effectiveness of the USAAF's strategic bombing campaign against Germany was debated during and for many years after the war, LeMay was widely credited with making the European bombing campaign feasible. Recognized as an innovative tactician and problem solver, LeMay was transferred to the Pacific theater in July 1944, where he organized a strategic bombing campaign against the Japanese homeland. Incorporating the new Boeing B-29 Superfortress into combat operations, LeMay devised a radical scheme for low-altitude incendiary raids on highly combustible Japanese cities. Stripped of armament, his B-29s roared over Japan at only 5,000 to 9,000 feet, scattering firebomb clusters across their targets. The effects were devastating—a raid on Tokyo on March 10, 1945, incinerated nearly seventeen square miles of the city and killed 100,000 Japanese. By war's end, sixty-three Japanese cities had been partially or wholly destroyed by these methods. LeMay never evinced moral qualms about the strategic bombing of populated areas. The greater lesson of the war for LeMay stemmed from the early years of the conflict, when the United States struggled furiously to develop its war-making capabilities. "There is nothing worse that I've found in life," he observed, "than going into battle ill-prepared or not prepared at all." The remainder of his career was dedicated to ensuring that his nation never again faced that dilemma.

The immediate postwar years brought challenges for professional soldiers like LeMay. Public sentiment for rapid demobilization and a reduction in military spending threatened the strength and readiness of all the armed services. The USAAF, which consisted of more than 2.25 million military personnel in August 1945, was reduced to only slightly over 300,000 as of May 1947. Of the branch's 25,000 aircraft, only 4,750 were combat-ready at that date. America's nuclear arsenal was miniscule, consisting of only thirteen atomic bombs in 1947. Anticipating such a postwar relaxation of defense readiness, LeMay had become an ardent advocate of preparedness from the moment hostilities concluded in September 1945. Warning against complacency, he told a War Department board in early 1946, "Our only defense is a striking-power-in-being of such size that it is capable of delivering a stronger blow than any of our potential enemies." Such a strike force, he was convinced, would not only deter attacks on the United States, but also ensure a U.S. advantage if such an attack did occur.

LeMay's first postwar assignment allowed him to ensure that U.S. defense capabilities kept pace with rapidly evolving technologies. Posted to the Pentagon as deputy chief for research and development, LeMay was at the forefront of the effort to develop and exploit new technologies. He organized Operation Paper Clip, which put captured German scientists to work on projects that would lay the foundation for the intercontinental ballistic missile (ICBM) program. He also engaged a consulting firm, the Rand Corporation, which became the most prominent defense think tank of the postwar era. He also headed a Joint Chiefs of Staff subcommittee to plan Operation Crossroads, which involved the test detonation of two atomic bombs at Bikini, an atoll in the Pacific, in 1946. These were the first nuclear explosions that LeMay witnessed, and he summarized the implications to Air Force chief Carl Spaatz, noting that in the near future, sufficient numbers of atomic bombs would exist to "nullify any nation's military effort." More ominously, LeMay observed that nuclear weapons made it possible to "depopulate vast areas of the earth's surface, leaving only vestigial remnants of man's material works." The lesson for LeMay was that "the most effective atomic bomb striking force possible" would be prerequisite to the full utilization of the new weapon and the realization of its deterrent value.

The passage of the National Security Act in 1947 brought a major reorganization of the armed services and the establishment of a separate U.S. Air Force (USAF). LeMay, now a three-star general, was reassigned to Germany, where antagonism between the Soviet Union and the western Allied powers was rapidly giving shape to the emergent Cold War. As commander of USAF forces in Europe as of October 1947, LeMay faced serious challenges in increasingly tense circumstances. Berlin, the former German capital, now divided and occupied by the four major Allied powers, sat in the heart of the Soviet occupation zone, ensuring that it would be the focus of numerous Cold War confrontations. On June 22, 1948, Soviet forces halted all ground traffic into the city in order to test the determination of the western allies, whose sectors composed West Berlin. Asked whether he could ensure that West Berlin could be supplied by the air force until a political resolution was found, LeMay responded confidently. His subsequent organization of the Berlin Airlift was one of the greatest American achievements of the Cold War. With help from Great Britain's Royal Air Force, LeMay mounted a continuous airlift that kept the city supplied until September 1949, when the Soviets ended their blockade. His aircrew completed 189,963 flights, bringing in food, fuel, medical supplies, and everything else that the citizens of West Berlin required.

In October 1948, LeMay returned to the United States to assume command of the Strategic Air Command, which together with Tactical Air Command and Air Defense Command now constituted the operational organizations within the USAF. SAC would clearly play a critical role in Cold War defense strategy, and it fell to LeMay to organize the command and define its mission. Forging the highly motivated, effective force that he envisioned required some effort. As personnel and equipment made the move from Andrews Air Force Base (AFB) outside of Washington, DC, to Offutt AFB on the outskirts of Omaha, Nebraska, LeMay perceived a multitude of operational problems that he quickly set about rectifying. He focused on training crews for specialized duties and implemented a rigorous program of realistic exercises, especially for flight crews. In addition to perfecting bombing proficiency, LeMay was adamant about developing aerial refueling capabilities for long-distance flights and training skilled radar technicians so as to improve early warning and navigational capabilities. He quickly affirmed his reputation as a commander who was unwilling to tolerate inefficiency. "My determination," he later recalled, "was to put everyone in SAC into this frame of mind: *We are at war now.*"

LeMay also strove to modernize the strategic bomber fleet, gradually updating or phasing out World War II–era aircraft. By the early 1950s, SAC's strategic bomber force was built around modern B-47 and B-52 jet bombers, which had greater range and speed than earlier propeller-driven aircraft. The SAC chief devoted equal attention to the careful basing of his bomber force. Bases in the continental United States were established with attention to distance and flying time from targeted sites in the USSR. Since SAC's mission required a global reach, SAC bases also sprang up as far afield as West Germany, Great Britain, Bermuda, the Azores Islands, Libya, and Saudi Arabia. At the point of its greatest strength, SAC boasted eighty-five bases around the world. Taken together, all these elements were crucial to the strike force that LeMay so ardently advocated. The fundamental mission of this imposing force was proclaimed in a motto of LeMay's devising, "Peace Is Our Profession," a bold declaration that soon marked SAC installations across the nation. To keep the peace, LeMay believed, SAC had to have the ability to initiate a preemptive strike. On assuming command in November 1948, he apprised Air Force Chief of Staff Hoyt Vandenberg that "the primary mission of SAC should be to establish a force in being capable of dropping 80% of the [nuclear] stockpile in one mission." LeMay's first "Emergency War Plan," presented in 1949 and expanding on his initial premise, proposed dropping the entire U.S. nuclear stockpile "in a single massive attack" on the USSR. The plan called for using 133 atomic bombs against seventy Soviet cities, killing an estimated 2.7 million civilians. Approved by the air force high command, this type of attack plan came to be known as "killing a nation," a horrific phrase characteristic of the cold-blooded terminology that evolved together with nuclear strategy.

[margin note: killing a nation]

Throughout the 1950s, LeMay aggressively defended his command. When the outbreak of the Korean War in June 1950 threatened to drain bomber strength from SAC, LeMay did his utmost to keep his force intact, confiding to an NBC correspondent his determination that the "Sunday punch" capability "not be pissed away in the Korean War." He was adamant that SAC retain control over targeting and he continued to advocate "urban area bombing" as a means of destroying crucial Soviet infrastructure. LeMay maintained that even inaccurately aimed bombs would produce what he termed "bonus damage" and "catastrophe bonus." Such terminology, which horrified critics, became a staple of the increasingly apocalyptic language commonly used by the SAC chief and defense strategists. LeMay's determination to gather precise targeting information led him to authorize dangerous and potentially provocative reconnaissance flights around the periphery of the Soviet Union and sometimes into Soviet airspace. Begun in 1950, these missions were meant to gather intelligence and probe Soviet defenses. The information gleaned came at high cost—some twenty U.S. aircraft were shot down and between 100 and 200 airmen were lost, some killed and others held for years in Soviet prisons. To ensure that SAC would be capable of carrying out its mission in the event of a surprise attack that interrupted chain-of-command communications, LeMay arranged for his bomber crews at Sandia Base, New Mexico, to have immediate access to nuclear weapons if "we woke up some morning and there wasn't any Washington or something." By 1957, he had succeeded in establishing SAC authority over the bombs. That same year, he astounded a civilian delegation by declaring, "If I see the Russians are amassing their planes for an attack, I'm going to knock the shit out of them before they take off the ground." Apprised that such individual initiative was not national policy, LeMay rejoined, "I don't care. It's my policy. That's what I'm going to do." Astonishingly, U.S. nuclear weapons were not equipped with permissive action links (which ensure presidential control) until the early 1960s.

The Soviet Union's successful launch of *Sputnik*, the first earth-orbiting satellite, in 1957 heightened concern about increased American vulnerability and created a new focus on the development of ICBMs. The military applications of rocket and missile technology had become evident during World War II, and by the early 1950s, the development of thermonuclear (or hydrogen) bombs suitably compact to be carried by missiles promised a significant alteration in the nature of nuclear warfare. Heretofore, U.S. nuclear defense strategy had been devised around weapons delivered by bombers. Whereas modern bombers proceeded to their targets at speeds of about 600 miles per hour, ballistic missiles flew at an almost incomprehensible 15,000 miles per hour. Previous advance warning times of hours thus dwindled to mere minutes. President Eisenhower gave high priority to an ICBM development program in 1955 and it was inevitable that the new weapons would become an integral component of SAC's arsenal. Given the task of creating a long-range ICBM, SAC oversaw development of the Atlas missile, which had a range of more than 10,000 miles. The 704th Strategic Missile Wing was established in January 1958, and the following year, a SAC crew carried out the first Atlas test launch at Vandenberg AFB. Housed primarily in underground silos, the

Atlas force grew to thirteen squadrons and 127 missiles by 1963. They were soon complemented by the newer Thor and Titan missiles, providing the United States with an unmatched ICBM capacity. Even as new technologies complicated the calculus of defense strategy, LeMay left his position at SAC to become air force vice chief of staff in 1957. Eisenhower's "New Look" policies had generally comported with LeMay's beliefs about the need for nuclear superiority, and developments late in the decade seemed to confirm the need for continued vigilance against the Soviet menace. The Gaither Report of 1958 warned of the nation's growing vulnerability to Soviet attack, and congressional Democrats railed against a "missile gap" that would fatally undermine national security.

Cold War tensions had not eased when LeMay was named air force chief of staff in 1961. The gruff general was often at odds with newly elected President John F. Kennedy's cabinet and advisers. LeMay distrusted Secretary of Defense Robert McNamara's management policies and the new "flexible response" strategy that was evolving as Kennedy and his cabinet pondered how to deal with issues such as the Berlin crisis without implementing LeMay's "Sunday punch" option. During the Cuban missile crisis in October 1962, LeMay stood with the Joint Chiefs of Staff in advocating a comprehensive surprise attack on Cuba and was infuriated by Kennedy's efforts to resolve the crisis without conflict. General David Burchinal, LeMay's deputy chief for plans and operations, later recalled that both LeMay and the new SAC commander, Thomas Power, were "eager to get World War III started." On October 24, when U.S. military forces went to Defense Condition 2, the condition prior to actual war, sixty-six SAC bombers armed with hydrogen bombs were already aloft on airborne alert, and some 3,000 nuclear weapons, including ICBMs, were placed on alert. In the midst of the most dangerous crisis of the Cold War, LeMay badgered Kennedy to call the Soviets' bluff in Cuba. "The Russian bear has always been eager to stick his paw in Latin American waters," LeMay declared at a White House meeting. "Now we've got him in a trap, let's take his leg off right up to his testicles. On second thought, let's take his testicles off, too." LeMay possibly hoped to use an invasion of Cuba as a pretext for his long-planned preemptive assault on the USSR. However, Kennedy rebuffed LeMay and the Cuban crisis was resolved peacefully. At a White House meeting to which Kennedy had invited the Joint Chiefs to thank them for their support, LeMay was unrepentant, claiming, "We lost! We ought to just go in there today and knock 'em off!"

Through the mid-1960s, LeMay remained a strong advocate for airpower, strenuously supporting the development of new weapons systems. As the war

118

in Vietnam was Americanized in 1965, LeMay emerged as a persistent critic of President Lyndon B. Johnson's policy of "enough but not too much." Gradual escalation, LeMay presciently warned, would drain American strength and enable the enemy to escalate correspondingly. In his most oft-quoted (and disputed) remark about Vietnam, LeMay purportedly exclaimed, "My solution to the problem would be to tell them [the North Vietnamese] frankly that they've got to draw in their horns and stop their aggression, or we're going to bomb them back into the Stone Age."

LeMay retired from the U.S. Air Force in 1965, but continued to warn about the menace presented by the USSR and communist China and to stress the value of a nuclear deterrent. In the fall of 1968, he inexplicably agreed to serve as the running mate of third-party presidential candidate George C. Wallace. LeMay astutely predicted the public response to his characteristically impolitic campaign utterances: "I'll be damned lucky if I don't appear as a drooling idiot whose only solution to any problem is to drop atomic bombs all over the world."

Curtis LeMay spent his later years in relative obscurity, living long enough to witness many of the final events of the Cold War. When he died on October 1, 1990, Eastern Europe was free of communist tyranny and the two Germanies were moving quickly toward unification; the Soviet Union was unraveling and would disappear from maps in slightly more than a year. The Cold War did not bring the nuclear Armageddon that so many had feared. As historical evaluations of the long confrontation began to appear in the 1990s, some historians argued that, ironically, it was the declared willingness to use the most destructive of weapons that had ensured the peace.

C. WRIGHT MILLS
Prophet of the New Left

The renowned author of *White Collar: The American Middle Classes* and *The Power Elite,* Columbia University sociologist C. Wright Mills turned to Ballantine Books to issue a mass-market paperback edition of *The Causes of World War Three*, which appeared in 1958 as antinuclear movements emerged in Great Britain and the United States. Declaring that an inexorable "drift" toward another world war defined the present era, (Mills denounced "crackpot realism," the supposedly realistic analysis of international events associated with Curtis LeMay. "Total war" obliterated the lines, Mills warned, "between military and civilian . . . attack and defense . . . strategic and tactical weapons.") In both the United States and the Soviet Union, "bureaucratic and lethal machineries" geared up for war, with the "ruling circles" guided by the "military metaphysic." The nuclear arms race that naturally followed offered only "the idiot's outlook."

At present, Mills argued, American intellectuals, drawn into anti-Stalinist politics, "the intellectual default of the apolitical fifties," assisted the drift toward total war. Western intellectuals in general, he charged, should humbly, even shamefacedly recall "that the first significant crack in the cold-war front" did not appear in the West. Rather, it was professors, writers, and students in Poland, Hungary, and Yugoslavia—"men who run the risk of being shot, imprisoned, driven to become nervous caricatures of human beings"—who had contested the status quo. Intellectuals in the West needed to view "democracy seriously and literally" and to stop performing as "intellectual dupes of political patrioteers," standing instead as conscientious objectors against "this disgraceful cold war."

Charging that "the politics of irresponsibility" characterized both the superpowers, Mills called for unmasking the "pretensions" of "men of power." At present, the very notion of responsibility was either submerged in liberal platitudes or devolved into "a trumped-up bloody purge." It was the responsibility of intellectuals, Mills wrote, to challenge "the cheerful robot . . . the technological idiot . . . the crackpot-realist." Typically, *The Causes of World War Three* drew mixed reviews, with conservative Russell Kirk declaring that Mills offered "dreams of setting this sorry old world aright by a few simple prescriptions," and the *Nation*'s Irving Howe worrying that the author was adopting "a mode or style of thought . . . unacceptable for the democratic left." Peace activist A.J. Muste, on the other hand, considered the slim volume "a sound, brilliant and most timely political tract." Members of the soon-to-emerge American New Left would agree with Muste, who, like Mills and I.F. Stone, was one of the few individuals associated with the Old Left that they honored.

Drawn from Irish, English, Dutch, and French stock, Charles Wright Mills, the second child of an insurance broker, Charles Grover Mills, and a housewife, Frances Wright Mills, was born in Waco, Texas, on August 28, 1916. Planning to become an engineer, Mills spent an unhappy freshman year at all-male Texas A&M University, in College Station, before transferring to the University of Texas in Austin and changing his major to sociology; there he met and married Dorothy Helen Smith. It was destined to be the first of three marriages for Mills.

In August 1939, Mills moved with his wife to Madison to pursue a PhD in sociology at the University of Wisconsin, working under sociologists Howard Becker and Hans Gerth and labor economist Selig Perlman. While still a graduate student, Mills published in both the *American Journal of Sociology* and the *American Sociological Review*. Adopting a pacifist stance as World

War II broke out, he voted for Norman Thomas, the Socialist Party candidate who opposed U.S. involvement. After he passed his doctoral exams in 1941, he accepted a position with a $3,000 annual salary at the University of Maryland in College Park. During his three-year stint in Maryland, Mills completed his doctoral dissertation—which focused on "a sociology of knowledge of pragmatism" through an examination of Charles S. Peirce, William James, and John Dewey—and was drawn to a trio of soon-to-be-celebrated historians —Richard Hofstadter, Frank Freidel, and Kenneth Stampp. The four often met for lunch, exchanging critical perspectives about President Franklin D. Roosevelt, capitalism, and conscription. Avoiding military service due to high blood pressure, Mills delved into the study of U.S. history so that he could "quote it at the sons of bitches who run American Big Business." Throughout the war years, he remained a prolific writer, working on a book with Gerth, academic articles, book reviews, and essays for publications like the *New Leader,* a social democratic weekly whose managing editor was his friend, the sociologist Daniel Bell. In an essay appearing in the *American Sociological Review* in 1942, Mills and Gerth declared that in modern times, revolutions required "revolutionary masses," not merely elites and political parties. In the December 19, 1942, issue of the *New Leader,* Mills's "Collectivism and the 'Mixed-Up' Economy" asked "why the aims of socialism" could not fit with those "of classic democracy."

Introduced to the radical intellectual Dwight Macdonald by Bell, Mills backed Macdonald's determination to create an unaffiliated, antiwar, radical magazine. In a letter dated October 10, 1943, Mills suggested that Macdonald's tentative name for his magazine, the *Radical Review*, would alienate potential readers; Mills also urged that the topic of radicalism should be developed "in detailed and compelling analyses, not in names and slogans." Macdonald eventually called his periodical *Politics,* and Mills's "The Social Role of Intellectuals" appeared in the third issue in April 1944. Adopting a theme he would later revisit, Mills proclaimed that American intellectuals, like the American population in general, appeared impotent, increasingly distanced from the levers of political power. Moreover, even at the large universities, the "freest of places . . . to work," faculty endured pressure to operate in a discreet, tasteful, or balanced fashion.

Increasingly displeased with the University of Maryland, which he saw as "a sinking ship," Mills inquired about other academic possibilities. In the fall of 1944, he submitted an application for a Guggenheim fellowship in which he underscored his desire to abandon "a crippling academic prose" and to reach a broader public. As a research associate at Columbia University, he was assigned to head a team examining opinion leaders in a Midwestern American community. In early 1945, Oxford University Press published *From Max Weber*, a collection of essays edited by Gerth and Mills. Also early that year, Mills received a call from the Smaller War Plants Corporation, asking him to serve as an expert when the U.S. Senate held hearings on establishing small businesses. Mills informed Gerth, "I'm so god damned excited I can hardly write!" and accepted the offer. In the spring of 1945, Mills reluctantly turned down a request from the U.S. State Department to travel to Germany to ferret out possible ties to "networks . . . the Nazis have set up—in all countries." Instead, with his marriage crumbling, Mills rented an apartment of his own in Greenwich Village.)

Pondering the state of the Left as World War II ended, Mills contended that no opposition was possible in the Soviet Union with its "nationalist, official, and, on due occasion, coercive" Communist Party (No Left even existed in his own country, Mills concluded; rather, "an irresponsible two-party system" prevailed. In Western Europe, the remnants "of the older Left" were "weak" and "inconsequential," having become "established" in places like Britain. "The right time is now" for an independent political movement, led by labor, that could provide the seeds for "a genuine democracy.")

In the spring of 1946, Mills received an appointment as a tenured professor at Columbia University, where he worked at the Bureau for Applied Social Research prior to becoming teaching faculty in February 1947. Having been awarded a Guggenhiem fellowship, Mills subsequently declined a position as full professor at the New School and in 1948, the thirty-two-year-old Mills completed *The New Men of Power: America's Labor Leaders*. Criticizing both labor leaders and liberals for their tepid attitudes, Mills sadly observed that "American liberalism . . . has lived off a collection of ideas put together before World War I." At the same time, he criticized the Left for being disdainful "of politics and even of life." Arthur Schlesinger Jr. of Harvard University offered a blurb for Harcourt Brace, deeming Mills's book "brilliant, original . . . provocative . . . genuinely democratic and boldly radical." Reviews of *The New Men of Power* proved mixed, although generally favorable, with Irving Howe applauding Mills for firmly opposing "quietism, advocacy of preventive atomic war, and a truce with the right because of a fear of Stalinism."

The year 1950 saw Mills obtain a promotion as associate professor of sociology at Columbia and Harper Brothers publish *The Puerto Rican Journey: New York's Newest Migrants*, which he coauthored with Clarence Senior and Rose K. Goldsen. In 1951, Oxford University Press published his *White Collar: The American Middle Classes*, which likened America society to "a new universe of management and manipulation." The long celebrated white-collar workers, "the new little people, the unwilling vanguard of modern society," exuded malaise and alienation, thus suffering the fate that nineteenth-century socialist theorist Karl Marx had foreseen for the industrial proletariat. Indeed, Mills believed that the white-collar worker suffered a "Kafka-like" existence, exhibiting no craftsmanship, becoming bored on the job, and failing to take a stand, becoming "alienated from work and . . . from self; expropriated of individual rationality, and politically apathetic." Like Mills's earlier work, *White Collar* earned both criticism and high praise. The *Management Review* argued that Mills had adopted the stance of a Luddite, hearkening back to the "good old days" of "independent small businessmen and craftsmen." By contrast, the *New Republic* extolled *White Collar* as "truly brilliant." In the *Nation*, Irving Howe deemed the book "exciting to read" but worried about the author's "occasional tone of tough, professional power-consciousness."

Mills proceeded to tackle his next subject, which he referred to as "The American Elite. Or the High and Mighty. Or the upper classes!" Oxford University Press signed him to a contract with a then-substantial advance of $5,000. In early 1952, Mills turned down a well-paying job with publisher William Randolph Hearst, while the next year, he declined a second offer from Brandeis University. Also in 1953, Brace published *Character and Social Structure: The Psychology of Social Institutions*, coauthored by Mills and Gerth, which charged that "individualistic, sexual, hedonistic, and pecuniary vocabularies of motive" appeared prevalent throughout the United States.

In the winter of 1954, *Dissent* magazine, edited by Irving Howe, published Mills's essay "The Conservative Mood." In postwar America, where material abundance and "crackpot realism" prevailed, Mills proclaimed, certain writers unsuccessfully sought to discover a conservative ideology, discarding the rationality that had guided both "classic liberalism" and "classic socialism" and championing instead tradition and a kind of natural aristocracy. Ultimately, however, he contended, a conservative ideology could not be sustained in the United States, notwithstanding Russell Kirk's recent efforts in *The Conservative Mind*. At the same time, Western thought presently suffered through "the tiredness of the liberal and the deflation of radicalism," with Soviet machinations, the Red Scare, and "plain and fancy fright" cowing American intellectuals, as their nation, "a conservative country without any conservative ideology," stood "before the world a naked and arbitrary power."

In 1956, Mills published *The Power Elite*, which contested the then fashionable notion that American society was characterized by countervailing interests, ensuring that no particular group became too dominant.) In the opening pages, Mills discussed the small group of men who operated in a manner far removed from "ordinary men and women," dominating large corporations, government policy, and "the military establishment." While the corporate rich both controlled "the privately incorporated economy" and the major political parties, the warlords and "their military metaphysics" largely influenced U.S. foreign policy. Mills warned that fully blown "American militarism" would dominate "all other ways of life." A number of reviews of *The Power Elite* appeared. Comparing Mills to social theorist Thorstein Veblen, sociologist Talcott Parsons questioned whether Mills had adequately verified the existence of a power elite. Sociologist Daniel Bell was also skeptical of Mills's contentions, and wondered, "Is there a ruling class in America?"

Meanwhile, Mills benefited from a Fulbright Fellowship to spend considerable time in Copenhagen. During his stay overseas, Mills closely followed Cold War developments. Preparing to speak to a student audience in Copenhagen, Mills bemoaned the fact that he was not in Eastern Europe, where a revolution supporting both socialism and democracy erupted in the fall of 1956. "Why in God's name am I not in Hungary?" he questioned in a letter to friends back in the States. He was "always on the edges when the center doesn't hold." Perhaps influenced by developments in Hungary, Mills determined to closely examine "Marxism today" when he returned to the States. He acknowledged having railed against liberalism, but recognized that he could even more readily criticize Marxism. What his critics failed to realize, Mills said, "is that way down deep and systematically I'm a goddamned anarchist." In that spirit, Mills began conducting a literary conversation with a fictional Tovarich (friend) from the Soviet Union. Mills operated under the assumptions that "zones of real freedom" existed in the communist behemoth or soon would. Along with Ralph Miliband, a Marxist scholar, he went to Warsaw, Poland, in mid-1957; they encountered several intellectuals critical of the communist state but still sympathetic to socialism. Having already visited Yugoslavia, Mills now indicated that such experiences had "deepened my own socialism." Writing in the fall of 1957, Mills noted his own "constitutional inability to sympathize with the upper dogs," but he also considered the American middle-class pretentious and prejudiced. Consequently, "I have been intellectually, politically, morally alone." He viewed himself as "outside the whale," disliking "bosses—capitalistic or communistic."

Notwithstanding a determination to produce more popular works, including *The Causes of World War Three*, Mills completed *The Sociological Imagination*, which Oxford University Press published in 1959. Here Mills challenged the dominant sociological schools, insisting on the need for a more humanist approach and castigating supposedly "disinterested" social science. All too often, he wrote, intellectuals became "manipulators or coercers or both, rather than persuaders." Later among his most celebrated books, *The Sociological Imagination* provoked reviews characterizing its critique as "hard-hitting, cogent, clearly put, and at times brilliant" (*Spectator*) and declaring that it "performs an essential task in the service of intellectual lucidity and truth" (*American Scholar*). At the same time, the book produced something of a firestorm at Columbia itself, especially within the discipline of sociology, as attested by Edward Shils's biting review in *Encounter.* Sarcastically, Shils referred to "a burly cowpuncher," engaged in a "long, slow ride from the Panhandle of Texas to Columbia University," who discovered "Madison Avenue, that street full of reeking phantasies of the manipulation of the human will and of what is painful to America's well-wishers and enjoyable to its detractors." All this culminated, Shills stated, with "an imaginary grand tour" in *The Sociological Imagination.*

Befitting his heightened alienation from academia and his nation's foreign policy, including its nuclear strategy, Mills delivered a lecture for the British Broadcasting Company on "the decline of the Left." To his credit, Mills admitted that left-wing figures sometimes proved "as confining in their values, as snobbish in their assignment of prestige as any national establishment." He recognized that presently "there is no Left establishment anywhere that is truly international and insurgent—and at the same time, consequential." Communism served "one national elite," while its political action in many countries proved "as reactionary as that of any other great power." The identification of many left-wing circles with Stalinist communism had resulted in the dissipating of those groups. In the United States, he complained, many former communists turned doctrinaire in a different fashion, becoming "professional anti-Communists." Nevertheless, American intellectuals possessed "a unique opportunity to make a new beginning," to act as "independent craftsmen." Mills demanded that his fellow intellectuals operate as "free men" and democrats who "take our heritage seriously," promote civil liberties, and stop complaining about alienation, allowing them to produce "radical critiques, audacious programs, commanding views of the future." He asked, "If *we* do not do these things, who will?" "We cannot expect to create a Left with mere slogans," he argued, "much less with the tired old slogans that bore us so." Most important, "We cannot create a Left by abdicating our roles as intellectuals to become working-class agitators or machine-politicians, or by play-acting at any other direct political action." Intellectuals had to confront the possibility of a third world war and "become internationalists again" by declining to participate in the Cold War.

While planning to write an essay for the *New Left Review*, Mills—who had recently moved with his third wife, the artist Yaroslava Surmach, to West Nyack, where he built a home twenty-five miles from Manhattan—again sought a broader audience. He signed a contract with Dell Publishing Company to produce a volume on Marxism that would compel him, as he admitted, "to straighten out my view of Marx & Co. before I can lay it on the line about socialism." In the meantime, he accepted an invitation to visit the Soviet Union, traveling there in April 1960. During his visit, Mills spoke with several party officials, undoubtedly hoping, as his biographer Irving Louis Horowitz suggests, to produce a "Soviet Journal" similar to *The Power Elite*. Mills found disconcerting the "chauvinism and ethnocentrism" that characterized Soviet leaders, as well as their propensity to subscribe to the theory "my party, right or wrong, for in the end it will be right." In June 1960, as Yaroslava delivered an eight-and-a-half pound baby boy, Mills, still working on the volume he initially called *The Marxians*, reflected on the possibility of resigning from Columbia University to devote himself to writing full-time. Instead, he maintained his association with Columbia and took a sabbatical, believing he had "four, yes four books bubbling up inside me." That summer, Mills confessed that he had often criticized the academic life "because I have loved that life, and because I do esteem many of my colleagues." He bemoaned the fact, however, that some refused to take advantage "of their marvelous intellectual opportunities," failing to exhibit freedom of thought.

In the same vein, Mills produced his "Letter to the New Left," which served as a harbinger of developments to come. The essay appeared in the September/October 1960 issue of *New Left Review*, a British publication influenced by radical historian E.P. Thompson and other intellectuals who were determined to foster Marxist humanism following both Khrushchev's denunciation of Stalinist crimes in the USSR and the organization of the Campaign for Nuclear Disarmament in the West. "Letter to the New Left" pointed to the recent upsurge in student activism in Turkey, South Korea, Cuba, Taiwan, Okinawa, Great Britain, Japan, and the United States. Its author criticized seemingly complacent intellectuals, such as Daniel Bell, who contended that "an end of ideology" had emerged in Western societies. There, Bell had concluded, democratic practices and moderated capitalism had proven superior to extremist ideologies like fascism and communism. Mills blasted the "very wearied discourse" conducted by "smug conservatives, tired liberals and disillusioned radicals" in both Britain and the United

States. The result of such discussion was "the sickness of complacency" and "bi-partisan banality." The latest vogue, he continued, involved talk of the passé nature of ideology, a notion offered by the Congress of Cultural Freedom and *Encounter* magazine (both of which were later proven to have been sponsored, at least in part, by the Central Intelligence Agency). This is what passed for liberalism, Mills charged, but served as an "uncriticized" means to castigate Marxism. Forgotten, as a consequence, was the "power to outrage," the "power to truly enlighten in a political way." The proclaimed disengagement from ideology resulted from "disillusionment with any real commitment to socialism." He emphasized, *"That* is the only 'ideology' that has really ended for these writers."

Mills criticized the end-of-ideology concept for other reasons too, arguing that it suggested a design to avoid "an explicit political philosophy" and "political relevance." The necessity of carving out a political stance, Mills pointed out, did not demand an insistence on "A Fanatical and Apocalyptic Lever of Change" or "Dogmatic Ideology," the type of "bogeymen" or "red herrings" denounced by "our political enemies." While those individuals insisted, "ordinary men can't always be political 'heroes,'" Mills declared that individuals did indeed need to discover how to act heroically. Proponents of New Left politics, often condemned for their "utopian" orientation, had to address "the problem of the historical agency of change," discarding the earlier hope of socialists that the working class would spearhead needed social transformation. Instead, intellectuals "on the Left today" might well serve "as a possible, immediate, radical agency of change," as borne out by recent student protests. Indeed, Mills identified "the young intelligentsia" as the group that "is getting fed up . . . getting disgusted with what Marx called 'all the old crap.'" In the Soviet bloc, in states lined up against the USSR, and in those nations drawn to "a third way," it was young intellectuals who were "thinking and acting in radical ways." Discarding the apathy that afflicted others, they largely favored nonviolent tactics and could instruct others in creating "new forms of action." Mills proclaimed, "The Age of Complacency is ending. . . . We are beginning to move again." Members of the budding American New Left, particularly those associated with Students for a Democratic Society, eagerly passed around copies of Mills's essay, which they reprinted in *Studies on the Left.* Many viewed its author as a mentor and role model of the public intellectual willing to contest seemingly sacrosanct ideas, no matter how isolated that left him in certain quarters.

August 1960 found Mills in Cuba, where Fidel Castro's revolution, which the American New Left had praised, was adopting a more strident tone, perhaps in response to the United States' hard-line policies. Mills spoke to a variety of Cubans, including Castro, who was familiar with *The Power Elite*, and also to revolutionary Che Guevara, then head of the National Bank of Cuba. McGraw-Hill subsequently published Mills's *Listen, Yankee! The Revolution in Cuba*, a condemnation of American actions written from the vantage point of Cubans supportive of the revolution. "A world-wide competition" for hearts and minds was taking place, Mills maintained. The Cubans had elected to obtain assistance from the Soviet Union but hardly intended to exchange "one tyranny" for "some other yoke—any other yoke." *Listen, Yankee!* urged the American people "to smash Yankee imperialism from inside the United States." Castro, Mills insisted, was "a new and distinct type of left-wing thinker and actor . . . neither capitalist nor Communist. He is socialist in a manner, I believe, both practical and humane." Should Cuba be allowed to chart its own course, Mills suggested, its people would possess a real opportunity "to keep the socialist society they are building practical and humane."

J. Edgar Hoover's FBI, which had investigated Mills as early as 1949, was warned of the potentially subversive character of Mills's latest work, which sold 400,000 paperback copies by March 1961 and was excerpted in *Harper's* magazine. One informant referred to *Listen, Yankee!* as "an artfully written piece of pro-Castro and pro-Communist propaganda." Most reviews tended to be quite positive, although the *New York Herald-Tribune* warned that Castro and Guevara both "sound like noises from the Kremlin." Historian Frank Freidel charged that Mills had failed to denote the Cuban revolution's "excesses and unpleasantness." In a letter to Freidel, Mills acknowledged having recognized "a lot of 'unpleasantness' in the Cuban possibilities," but he insisted that "most . . . are being brought on by U.S. action and inaction." In Irving Horowitz's estimation, the release of *Listen, Yankee!* brought Mills "the celebrity status" that had previously eluded him. NBC television scheduled a debate on "U.S. policy towards Latin America" between Mills and former State Department official Adolf A. Berle Jr.—an encounter that Mills prepared for diligently.

Shortly before the debate was to occur, Mills, who had a history of cardiac problems, experienced a heart attack, leading to the debate's cancellation and an extended convalescence. He angrily followed the Bay of Pigs fiasco, in which Cuban exiles backed by the Kennedy administration attempted to oust Castro. In an extended trip overseas, Mills completed *The Marxists*, while spending time with existentialist writer Jean Paul Sartre and feminist author Simone de Beauvoir in Paris. In August, Mills, Yaroslava, and several friends drove through Poland to Moscow. One of those friends, Saul Landau, recalled

Mills as having observed that the Soviets had discarded "some of the state machinery and replaced it by perhaps even more rigid societal control" while reverting "to a primitive kind of law and control." Castro's pronouncement of allegiance to Marxism-Leninism, delivered in December 1961, could hardly have pleased Mills either.

On March 20, 1962, shortly after his return to the United States, the forty-five-year-old Mills suffered a fatal heart attack. Yaroslava received a telegram from I.F. Stone stating, "Terribly sorry. We are all impoverished by the death of your wonderful and courageous husband." Ralph Miliband later noted that Mills "never belonged to any party or faction . . . did not think of himself as a 'Marxist'; he had the most profound contempt for orthodox Social Democrats . . . for closed minds in the Communist world . . . smug liberals and . . . hand wringing radicals." Rather, Mills, "a man on his own . . . was on the Left, but not of the Left, a deliberately lone guerrilla, not a regular soldier." He "occupied a unique position in American radicalism," Miliband asserted, and "his death leaves a gaping void," for "in a trapped and inhumane world, he taught what it means to be a free and humane intellect."

Appearing the very month Mills died, *The Marxists* took to task both liberalism and Marxism. The former, a once "insurgent creed," had become conservative, "serving to justify capitalist democracy"; the Stalinist proponents of the latter had become apologists for the Soviet Union and the Eastern bloc nations, relying on "ideological uniformity and doctrinaire realignment" to follow Soviet "twists and turns." The quest for emancipation discussed in *The Marxists* provided guidance for many of the young rebels who made up the New Left. They appreciated Mills's determination to battle against academic canons, but more important, they celebrated his critical perspectives regarding white-collar workers, the power elite, U.S. foreign policy, Soviet maneuvering, reckless nuclear strategies, and the need for the intellectual to operate as an "independent craftsman." New Leftists also welcomed Mills's insistence that students could play a key role in world events. Consequently, as New Left leader Paul Booth remembered, "Mills was a model." Author James Miller believed that "in Mills, the young radicals found a theory of power, an image of democracy, a kindred spirit," as well as some of the seeds for the idea that "'the personal' is 'political.'" Tom Hayden drew on Mills's analyses as he helped to shape "The Port Huron Statement," a seminal New Left document and founding manifesto of Students for a Democratic Society, an organization destined to challenge complacent liberalism and Cold War orthodoxies during the 1960s.

Conclusion

Though the postwar years brought America unprecedented material abundance, they also brought unprecedented challenges. The Cold War confrontation with the Soviet Union and the communist bloc that took shape after 1945 posed new dangers that could hardly have been imagined even only a short while before. The advent and spread of ever more powerful nuclear weapons, together with new means of delivering them more rapidly and accurately, created the potential for warfare so catastrophic in its consequences as to threaten the continued existence of humankind. Some people, like Curtis LeMay, saw nuclear weapons as merely the latest stage in weapons development, following the introduction of progressively more powerful and destructive weapons during World War II. To win America's war against Japan, LeMay had been willing to employ weapons and tactics that wreaked horrific damage on Japanese cities, and he had expressed few, if any, moral qualms about them. The atomic bomb, with all its destructive potential, held no special mystery for LeMay, who saw it as a logical and necessary weapon in America's strategic arsenal. As chief of the Strategic Air Command, LeMay was convinced that international realities required the United States to develop a nuclear strategy that took into consideration the grimmest possible scenarios, and he tailored the American response accordingly.

Other Americans, such as C. Wright Mills, were horrified by the direction that U.S. defense policy took in the postwar years. Nuclear armaments, Mills reasoned, did in fact fundamentally alter the meaning and consequences of war in the modern world. His conviction that such weapons would inevitably be deployed in a third world war only strengthened his belief that the perspectives of the power elites, both in the United States and the Soviet Union, had to be challenged. Such a challenge would, he hoped, lead to more rational policy making and a more democratic and humane social order. Backers of LeMay's strategies contended that the kind of approach Mills favored was simpleminded at best, if not outright defeatist. They argued that LeMay's hard-nosed approach to nuclear-based defense achieved a "balance of terror" between the United States and the Soviet Union, assuring something of a standoff and thus avoiding atomic apocalypse. For their part, Mills and the New Left he influenced challenged U.S. foreign policy issues ranging from nuclear weapons to Cuba, while encouraging a young intelligentsia to lead the fight to restrain the power elite's most dangerous propensities. Mills's critical analysis of American policies in the underdeveloped world provided a theoretical framework for New Leftists who would later condemn U.S.

policies in Vietnam. Mills's views were antithetical to those of LeMay, who advocated escalating America's role in Indochina and urged that nuclear weapons be considered for deployment. The contrasting perspectives of LeMay and Mills received a hearing in New Right and New Left circles, respectively, throughout the 1960s. The public debate over the utility of an aggressive U.S. foreign policy, guided by a nuclear strategy of the sort LeMay favored, versus a foreign policy predicated on accepting, even welcoming, revolutionary transformations worldwide, in the manner of Mills, continued well into the 1980s, at least in academic circles. It quieted, albeit only temporarily, with the near end of the Cold War in the later years of that decade.

Study Questions

1. What events shaped Curtis LeMay's views on national defense?
2. Was LeMay's concept of a nuclear "striking-power-in-being" a threat to international peace, or did it, as some argue, ensure world peace by establishing a nuclear "balance of terror"?
3. What intellectual influences shaped Mills's critical perspectives on American society and foreign policy?
4. The idea of a power elite has proven one of the most controversial ever offered by an American social scientist. How did Mills arrive at this conclusion, which seemed to contravene popular conceptions about American democracy?
5. How did LeMay and Mills differ as to how the United States might best confront the challenges of the Cold War?

Selected Bibliography

Boyer, Paul. *By the Bomb's Early Light: American Thought and Culture at the Dawn of the Atomic Age.* New York: Pantheon, 1985.
Boyne, Walter J. *Beyond the Wild Blue: A History of the U.S. Air Force, 1947–1997.* New York: Thomas Dunne, 1997.
Brands, H.W. *The Devil We Knew: Americans and the Cold War.* New York: Oxford University Press, 1993.
Coffey, Thomas M. *Iron Eagle: The Turbulent Life of General Curtis LeMay.* New York: Random House, 1986.
Horowitz, Irving Louis. *C. Wright Mills: An American Utopian.* New York: Free Press, 1983.
Kaplan, Fred. *The Wizards of Armageddon.* New York: Simon and Schuster, 1983.
LeMay, Curtis, and MacKinlay Kantor. *Mission with LeMay.* New York: Doubleday, 1965.

McEnaney, Laura. *Civil Defense Begins at Home: Militarization Meets Everyday Life in the Fifties*. Princeton: Princeton University Press, 2000.

Miller, James. *"Democracy Is in the Streets": From Port Huron to the Siege of Chicago*. New York: Simon and Schuster, 1987.

Mills, C. Wright. *The Causes of World War Three*. New York: Simon and Schuster, 1958.

———. *Letters and Autobiographical Writings*. Edited by Kathryn Mills with Pamela Mills. Berkeley: University of California Press, 2000.

———. *Listen, Yankee! The Revolution in Cuba*. New York: Ballantine, 1960.

———. *The Marxists*. New York: Dell, 1963.

———. *The New Men of Power: America's Labor Leaders*. Urbana: University of Illinois, 2001.

———. *The Power Elite*. New York: Oxford University Press, 1956.

———. *Power, Politics and People: The Collected Essays of C. Wright Mills*. Edited by Irving Louis Horowitz. New York: Oxford University Press, 1963.

———. *White Collar: The American Middle Classes*. New York: Oxford University Press, 1951.

Press, Howard. *C. Wright Mills*. Independence, KY: Twayne, 1978.

Rhodes, Richard. *Dark Sun: The Making of the Hydrogen Bomb*. New York: Simon and Schuster, 1995.

Rose, Lisle A. *The Cold War Comes to Main Street: America in 1950*. Lawrence: University Press of Kansas, 1999.

Tillman, Barrett. *LeMay*. New York: Palgrave, 2007.

Tilman, Rick. *C. Wright Mills: A Native Radical and His American Intellectual Roots*. University Park: Pennsylvania State University Press, 1984.

Part II

From Confidence to Crisis, 1960–1980

Few presidents have so effectively set the tone for an era as did John F. Kennedy in his inaugural address in January 1961. Invoking America's revolutionary heritage and commitment to liberty, Kennedy sought to establish an ambitious, idealistic course for a powerful, prosperous nation. The brief address was rich in memorable and moving phrases. "The torch has been passed to a new generation," the young president asserted; "the trumpet summons us again." Indeed, as the American people entered the 1960s, expectations for the nation's prospects were high, given a burgeoning economy and the absence of any evident threat to social stability. The civil rights movement, having gained momentum throughout the 1950s, was becoming a mass movement, poised to realize long-deferred rights for black Americans. That struggle inspired other ethnic groups and women to examine their status in society and to organize their own movements to effect change. During the early 1960s, many Americans believed that these issues could be successfully resolved within the established system, with a minimum of social disruption. Though the "long twilight struggle," as John F. Kennedy characterized the Cold War, always hovered in the background during these years, sometimes assuming a frightening imminence, public support for policies aimed at containing the communist threat remained largely unshaken.

By mid-decade, much of the promise of the early 1960s had faded. The limits of liberalism, the ideology that had guided the Democratic Party since the 1930s, seemed increasingly evident to critics on both the left and the right.

A New Left emerged during these years, producing new groups that questioned whether liberalism was capable of bringing about the fundamental social and economic transformations necessary to rectify the glaring inequities in American society. Almost simultaneously, the roots of a new conservatism were being set down by those on the right who feared that liberalism had encouraged the growth of a dangerously interventionist state that had to be restrained. The Americanization of the war in Vietnam catalyzed protest from both left and right, marking the end of the foreign policy consensus that had prevailed since the 1950s. By 1968, all the fundamental components of the postwar consensus were called into doubt in a whirlwind of war, violent protest, assassinations, and political chaos. By decade's end, the limits of political and cultural radicalism were manifest, as the New Left and the counterculture self-destructed. The chief casualty, however, was the consensus society born out of World War II. The 1960s left the American people badly divided and facing uncertainties that could not have been imagined at the decade's beginning.

Events in the 1970s brought new anxieties. Even as the nation drifted into the uncertainties of a postindustrial economy, worsened by growing concern about the country's dependence on imported oil, public confidence in the nation's leadership was shaken by two failed presidencies, separated by a third that was at best ineffective. New social issues emerged as conservative activists began to challenge the changes wrought by the social protest movements of the previous decade, most notably the women's movement. The New Right that had begun to coalesce in the 1960s now emerged as a popular movement, organized to turn back what were perceived as dangerous threats to traditional gender roles, religious beliefs, and social values. As liberalism went into eclipse, the new conservatism gained momentum and influence.

6

Civil Rights and Social Justice

The decade of the 1960s witnessed the shattering of racial barriers that had long contradicted the very essence of American democracy. A series of civil rights organizations and activists emerged who tenaciously contested long-standing practices that relegated people of color to second-class status. Fannie Lou Hamer and César Chávez were two of the most charismatic figures to loosen the shackles that had burdened African Americans and Mexican Americans. Their own struggles against racial oppression convinced them that the empowerment of black and brown Americans required more than the eradication of Jim Crow laws and an end to racial discrimination. Hamer and Chávez soon realized that a considerable measure of economic democracy was also warranted to empower those who had long been disenfranchised. Initially, they worked under the auspices of the Student Nonviolent Coordinating Committee, the Southern Christian Leadership Conference, or the Community Service Organization, all founded by other progressives. Eventually, outgrowing those organizations, Hamer and Chávez branched out to create the Mississippi Freedom Democratic Party and the United Farm Workers.

Both Hamer and Chávez, like many in the civil rights campaigns of the early 1960s, employed nonviolent tactics in their attempts to transform American society. Hamer became somewhat disenchanted with the purely Gandhian style of activism that Martin Luther King Jr. steadfastly championed. Frustrated by the mounting numbers of beatings and vigilante killings of movement activists and the seemingly inadequate pace of liberal reform, Hamer was attracted to Black Power ideals; her own rhetoric became more heated and she diligently strove to create the Freedom Farm Corporation, which sought to improve economic opportunities for black families in the Mississippi Delta. By contrast, Chávez, throughout the volatile 1960s and far beyond, insisted that his followers adhere to nonviolence notwithstanding the verbal and physical abuse they endured. To demonstrate his belief in nonviolence as his movement's moral touchstone, Chávez resorted to a series of life-threatening fasts. The difficulty of organizing field laborers led Chávez to adopt an organizational style that some condemned as authoritarian. Nevertheless, he continued to insist that a peaceful path to change would be successful: *Se puede*; *si se puede* (It can be done; yes, it can be done).

FANNIE LOU HAMER
Mississippi Freedom Fighter

On June 9, 1963, a group of Mississippians, including a forty-five-year-old rural black woman named Fannie Lou Hamer, embarked on a freedom ride like those undertaken by members of the Congress of Racial Equality (CORE) back in 1947 and repeated fourteen years later. Hamer and her compatriots were served at a segregated lunch counter in Columbus, Mississippi. They then boarded a bus for Winona in Montgomery County. The bus driver, insisting "Niggers were not to be in front of the line," apparently called ahead, for a large number of police officers awaited the bus as it entered Winona just before noon. When members of the delegation sought service at a lunch counter, one of the waitresses threw aside her dishcloth and exclaimed, "I can't take no more." Police soon ordered the black patrons to "get out" and arrested them for refusing to leave. Sheriff Earl Wayne Patrick kicked and cursed Hamer en route to the jail.

On arriving at the jail, the activists encountered "white folks [who] appeared from everywhere with guns." Several of the group endured terrible beatings. Hamer was questioned by John L. Basinger, a highway patrol officer, who wanted to know where she lived. Hurling obscenities at her, Basinger warned, "You bitch, we going to make you wish you was dead." Taken to a cell known as the bullpen, Hamer heard Basinger order an African American male inmate to beat her. As she later reported, Hamer had to lie "on the bed flat on my stomach, and that man beat me—that man beat me until he give out." At one point, when she cried out, a police officer, who appeared "so hot and worked off," began pounding the back of Hamer's head. Finally, returning to her cell, Hamer collapsed along the way and was simply tossed inside. The beating, which damaged Hamer's kidneys, haunted her for the rest of her life.

Threatening the group members with deadly violence, the police induced them to sign statements indicating that other activists had injured them. Charged with disorderly conduct and resisting arrest, Hamer and her companions were convicted on June 10 and received $100 fines. Two days later, following pressure brought to bear by both the Student Nonviolent Coordinating Committee (SNCC) and the Southern Christian Leadership Conference (SCLC), Hamer and the other prisoners left the Winona jail. On June 17, the U.S. Justice Department, headed by Attorney General Robert F. Kennedy, filed suit to toss aside the convictions and also sought to prevent state officials in Mississippi from violating interstate transportation guidelines. In early September, the Justice Department brought criminal charges against Sheriff Patrick and others for violating the constitutional rights of the freedom riders. It was only the beginnings of justice long denied for many black Americans like Hamer, whose life had been a long sequence of the travails consequent to poverty and prejudice.

On October 6, 1917, James and Lou Ella Townsend, sharecroppers in Montgomery County, Mississippi, welcomed the birth of their sixth girl and twentieth child, Fannie Lou. The arrival of their latest child provided something of a financial bounty for the Townsends: the plantation owner, undoubtedly anticipating another field hand, gave them fifty dollars. However, within two years, the family relocated to the plantation of E.W. Brandon some sixty miles to the west in Sunflower County. Most African Americans in Sunflower County suffered grinding poverty, made worse by the ever-present threat of violence in their segregated community.

While Lou Ella Townsend toiled as a poorly paid domestic servant, James, who occasionally served as a Baptist preacher, sharecropped and bootlegged so his family could survive. Their children picked cotton up to fourteen hours daily, with Fannie Lou, who had recently acquired a lifelong limp due to polio, joining them in the fields when she was only six. Her career began when Brandon, driving by one day, spotted her playing alongside a gravel road and promised to provide treats, including Cracker Jack, gingerbread, and sardines, if she picked thirty pounds of cotton within a week. Grabbing a cloth flour sack, the child went to work, with her assignment doubled almost immediately but no additional reward coming her way. By the time she was a teenager, she was picking hundreds of pounds of cotton each day, receiving a mere dollar for her labors. Her education, like that of her siblings, suffered accordingly, thanks to her attendance at segregated schools that were sorely underfunded, offered reduced academic schedules, and proved difficult for the inadequately dressed child to even reach during rainy, stormy, or cold seasons. Nevertheless, Lou Ella instructed her daughter, "You respect yourself as a little black child. And as you grow older, respect yourself as a black woman."

At one point during her childhood, conditions appeared to improve for the family, albeit temporarily. Having managed to set aside funds from his meager earnings, Jim Townsend planned to rent a plot of land and refurbish the Townsend home, which lacked electricity, running water, and indoor plumbing. He purchased three mules, two cows, tools, and a car. One evening, the family spent the night elsewhere because the repairs on the house were not completed. During the night, a white man poured Paris green, a highly toxic insecticide, into the stock feed, which poisoned their animals. As Fannie Lou Hamer later recalled, the loss "knocked us right back down flat. We never did get back up again." Her father returned to sharecropping, his hopes for economic independence dashed. Soon afterward, Fannie Lou, having reached the sixth grade, left school for good.

Her siblings began departing from rural Mississippi, seeking a better life in places like Chicago, but she remained behind to care for her increasingly ailing parents. James died shortly after suffering a stroke in 1939, while Lou Ella, following an eye injury in the fields, became a blind invalid who continued to reside with her youngest daughter. In 1944, at the age of twenty-seven,

Fannie Lou Townsend married thirty-two-year-old Perry "Pap" Hamer, a sharecropper who enjoyed hunting and fishing. Following their marriage, the Hamers moved to the plantation of W.D. Marlow, outside Ruleville. There, they dwelled in a small house, which did possess running water, a bathtub, and an ill-functioning indoor toilet. Hamer served as the plantation's timekeeper, a domestic servant for Marlow and, along with her husband, operator of the juke joint once owned by her father. The Hamers peddled bootleg liquor, while Fannie Lou also sold insurance. Notwithstanding their own tough economic circumstances, the Hamers adopted a pair of young girls, whose parents were unable to provide for them. In 1961, Hamer went to a local hospital to have a "knot" or small cyst on her stomach removed and, on awakening from the surgery, discovered that she had been given a hysterectomy. Although possibly past her childbearing years at that point and apparently having miscarried on at least two occasions, Hamer thus still suffered, in effect, from involuntary sterilization—a fate that had befallen many African American women throughout the first several decades of the twentieth century.

Shortly after this surgery, Hamer became directly involved with the civil rights movement in the South. In August 1962, she received an invitation from Mary Tucker, an elder woman and longtime friend of Fannie Lou's family, who was holding a meeting to teach African Americans how to register and vote. Hamer declined to attend the session but did show up at William Chapel Church that evening, where the Reverend James Bevel of the Southern Christian Leadership Conference was discussing voter registration at a meeting sponsored by the Council of Federated Organizations (COFO). Also speaking at the church were James Forman, Bob Moses, and Reginald Robinson, all key figures in SNCC. Prior to this point, as she later admitted, Hamer had "never heard of no mass meeting and I didn't know that a Negro could register and vote." On August 31, Hamer, along with seventeen other blacks, boarded a bus for Indianola, where they went to the circuit clerk's office at the courthouse. The clerk, Cecil B. Campbell, unhappily greeted them by asking, "What do you want?" Hamer replied, "We are here to register." Campbell refused their request.

On the heels of this unsuccessful attempt to register, Hamer, like many other civil rights activists, experienced continued harassment. Plantation owner W.D. Marlow warned her to forget about voting, threatening to take away the Hamers' furniture and to fire Pap, who had worked for him for almost two decades. Hamer felt compelled to leave her home, but Pap was soon tossed out of his job anyway, having also lost the furniture and car. Forced to exist like fugitives, Hamer and her two daughters stayed with friends. Soon shots were fired into the friends' house. Undoubtedly well aware that vigilantes, shooting into the house of another African American family, had killed two young women, both students at Jackson State College, Hamer insisted, "Killing or no killing, I'm going to stick with civil rights."

In the fall of 1962, Hamer went to Fisk University in Nashville, Tennessee, to participate in a leadership training conference held by SNCC. Movement activists like Bob Moses viewed Hamer as an ideal "prospect" who could provide the kind of local leadership that the civil rights crusade desperately needed. After the gathering in Nashville, Hamer joined with the SNCC Freedom Singers in traveling around the country, seeking financial support for the movement. Back home in new quarters, Hamer again sought, unsuccessfully, to register to vote. Purportedly, she informed the white registrar, "You'll see me every 30 days till I pass." Finally, in early January 1963, after poring over the state constitution, Hamer passed the literacy test, although she still had to obtain poll-tax receipts. Although she began leading citizenship classes orchestrated by SCLC, she increasingly drew closer to members of SNCC, whose direct action techniques appealed to her.

The terrible beating she endured in Winona only further emboldened Hamer, now operating as a SNCC field secretary, to participate in the movement to eradicate racial discrimination in the United States. The struggle for elementary citizen rights continued in Mississippi and throughout the Deep South, resulting in both an outpouring of support and a wellspring of embittered, frequently violent opposition. The Voter Education Project, which had helped to finance the operations of COFO, dramatically reduced the funding it was spending on Mississippi in late 1963. "My family and I have suffered greatly since I started working with the movement," Hamer admitted, but she remained "determined to become a first-class citizen." She insisted that change was demanded in her home state: "I'm sick of being hungry, naked, and looking at my children and so many other children crying for bread."

A new campaign, orchestrated by COFO activists, resulted in 80,000 Mississippians delivering "freedom votes" for Aaron Henry, an important National Association for the Advancement of Colored People (NAACP) figure, and Ed King, a white chaplain at Tougaloo College, candidates for governor and lieutenant governor, respectively. Hamer undertook her own bid for public office, running as the candidate of the newly formed Mississippi Freedom Democratic Party (MFDP), founded in late April 1964, against longtime congressman Jamie L. Whitten, who was running for reelection to a seat he had held since 1941. During the campaign, she received a death threat, her campaign workers suffered violence and harassment, and her husband lost his job at a cotton mill.

Hamer received a mere 621 votes against more than 35,000 cast for Whitten. Nevertheless, Bob Moses recognized the importance of her candidacy. "When Mrs. Hamer talks she speaks of her life. She concretizes abstract problems for her peers," he said. "Here the question of human dignity is crucial."

Although most civil rights leaders continued to express allegiance to the ethos of nonviolence, the physical terror that rained down on the movement sometimes led to compromises considered necessary by all but the most ardent pacifists. These compromises included keeping weapons in automobiles and movement offices to provide a modicum of protection for movement leaders. The movement still endured a considerable amount of violence during this period, as when three young civil rights workers, participating in the Mississippi Freedom Summer project to register Delta blacks to vote, disappeared in 1964. The badly decomposed bodies of Andrew Goodman, Michael Schwerner, and James Chaney were uncovered months later. Vigilantes had brutalized and then murdered the two Jews and the African American, whose body had been horrifically broken before he was summarily executed.

To provide support for their campaign, Freedom Summer organizers established a panel in Washington, DC, to publicize the reasons why the voting rights push was necessary. Among those speaking before the distinguished panelists was Fannie Lou Hamer, who explained, "We have a curfew only for Negroes," and told of two policemen arriving at the Hamer home at five o'clock in the morning one day to ask Pap why he was awake at that hour. Hamer also reported that a telephone operator had called her, asking, "Do you have any outsiders in your house?" Undaunted, Hamer provided support for the Freedom Summer project, exhorting volunteers during training sessions to avoid hatred and to communicate with southern whites. Despite the disappearance of Goodman, Schwerner, and Chaney, volunteers continued to arrive, with one, Len Edwards, a law student whose father was Congressman Don Edwards of California, viewing Hamer as "the most inspirational person I've ever met . . . the purest of heart." The Hamer household served as a movement center for the Mississippi Freedom Summer participants, who dropped by at all hours.

As the national Democratic Party's nominating convention approached, Hamer was one of sixty-eight delegates and alternates selected to represent the Mississippi Freedom Democrats. The convention in Atlantic City promised to be something of a coronation for President Lyndon B. Johnson, whose recent signing of the 1964 Civil Rights Act helped to batter down many of the legal edifices of Jim Crow. Fearing a white backlash, Johnson fretted about the Mississippi Freedom Democrats' attempt to unseat the all-white, regular

Mississippi delegation, which refused to promise to vote for the Democratic Party nominee.

Both the MFDP and the regular Mississippi delegates sought support from the credentials committee, with the MFDP's challenge backed by Martin Luther King Jr., NAACP head Roy Wilkins, and Rita Schwerner, widow of the murdered Freedom Summer volunteer. Many considered forty-six-year-old Fannie Lou Hamer's the most moving presentation. Her description of the terrible experiences at the Winona jail the previous summer evoked tears from many in attendance. Weeping herself, Hamer concluded that Mississippi Freedom Summer involved a desire to register to vote, to enable its participants to become "first-class citizens." If the MFDP failed to be seated, she said, she had to wonder why people's lives could be threatened daily simply because they "want to live as decent human beings in America." SNCC chair John L. Lewis remembered this as "a stunning moment. So dramatic. So riveting."

Television networks replayed Hamer's testimony, while the *New York Times* and other leading newspapers presented biographical sketches of her. But despite such favorable publicity, convention planners refused to certify the MFDP delegates. The best offer the MFDP representatives received was to have two members awarded at-large seats on the convention floor, a possibility Hamer disdainfully dismissed. During one session with Minnesota senator Hubert Humphrey, Hamer told the presumptive vice presidential nominee, "You just want this job, and I know a lot of people have lost their jobs, and God will take care of you, even if you lose this job. But Mr. Humphrey, if you take this job, you won't be worth anything. Mr. Humphrey, I'm going to pray for you again." Eventually, even Martin Luther King Jr., SCLC's Andrew Young, MFDP chair Henry, and attorney Joseph Rauh backed the proposal for two at-large representatives, with the other would-be delegates to be seated in the gallery. Hamer refused to accept the notion of a moral victory, crying out "We ain't getting nothing" and even warning Henry that, if he accepted the compromise, "I'm going to cut your throat." After the deal was completed, Hamer eloquently informed reporters, "We didn't come all this way for no two seats."

The experience in Atlantic City proved catalytic for Hamer and many other civil rights activists, who proved increasingly distrustful of the so-called liberal establishment. As Hamer recorded in her autobiography, "We followed all the laws that the white people themselves made. . . . But we learned the hard way that even though we had all the laws and all the righteousness on our side—that white man is not going to give up his power to us." Instead, Hamer and an increasing number of civil rights figures determined, "We have to take for ourselves." Thus, the Democratic national convention, coupled with mounting anger and frustration over seemingly ever-present racial discrimination and the beatings and deaths of compatriots, spurred the militancy that increasingly characterized the civil rights movement.

To overcome the burnout and disillusionment of the convention, the singer and social activist Harry Belafonte organized a trip to Guinea for civil rights leaders, including Hamer, Moses, CORE's James Forman, and SNCC's John L. Lewis and Julian Bond. The three-week trip, initiated only days after the heartbreak in Atlantic City, proved enthralling for Hamer, who was warmly greeted by President Sekou Toure with a big hug. The adventure empowered Hamer, who witnessed sights she never had before: "I saw black men flying the airplanes, driving buses, sitting behind the big desks in the bank and just doing everything that I was used to seeing white people do."

Returning to the States in October, Hamer helped to orchestrate Freedom Vote, which allowed all adult Mississippians to cast ballots "without intimidation or discrimination as to race and color." In sharp contrast to the Democratic Party primary results earlier, the unofficial Freedom Vote proceedings saw Hamer gather 33,000 ballots, while Congressman Whitten pulled down only 59. Later that year, Hamer met Malcolm X, the influential black nationalist who had recently broken away from Elijah Muhammad and the Nation of Islam, which insisted on racial separation from "white devils." Undergoing his own process of evolution, Malcolm, after a pilgrimage to the Middle East, was discarding Elijah Muhammad's dogmatism but continued to insist that blacks possessed the right to defend themselves from white-generated violence. On December 20, Malcolm and Hamer both spoke in Harlem at a rally at the Williams Institutional Church, with Hamer talking of the beating she endured in Winona and of the need to unseat racist southern legislators. Malcolm told the crowd, "The language that they were speaking to Mrs. Hamer was the language of brutality." He invited her to participate in a rally that evening held by the Organization of Afro-American Unity. Speaking at the Audubon Ballroom in Harlem, Malcolm introduced Hamer as "the country's number one freedom-fighting woman." As he noted, "She's from Mississippi, and you've got to be a freedom fighter to even live in Mississippi."

In early January 1965, Hamer and Annie Devine, and Victoria Gray, both MFDP candidates, traveled to the nation's capital, where a challenge to Mississippi's congressional delegation was to occur as the Eighty-ninth Congress began operations. Hamer announced, "We are here for our own people—and we are here for all the people." The three women, along with MFDP attorneys Arthur Kinoy and William Kunstler, were denied entry into the chambers of the House of Representatives. As the session opened, New York congressman William Ryan objected to the seating of five white Mississippi Democrats, including Whitten. Scores of congressional representatives supported Ryan's position, but following a 276–149 roll call vote, Whitten and the other Mississippians were sworn into office.

That spring, a *Newsweek* article referred to Hamer as the MFDP's "leading mouthpiece" who supposedly showed "disturbingly demagogic tendencies" in her criticism of middle-class members of the civil rights movement, U.S. actions in Indochina, and Dr. Martin Luther King Jr. By contrast, Andrew Kopkind of the *New Republic* applauded Hamer for demonstrating "little respect for traditions of political compromise." Hamer was also in the midst of other controversies, including one pitting the increasingly strident SNCC against MFDP, which was criticized for not being radical enough.

Although she had become a national figure, Hamer remained intimately involved with social and political campaigns back home, as befitting her grassroots origins as a civil rights proponent. She strongly supported the Mississippi Freedom Labor Union (MFLU), which sought better conditions for domestics, truck drivers, and day workers, but imploded because of internal schisms.

In its wake and as her relations with SNCC deteriorated, Hamer became immersed in another community action program, the Associated Communities of Sunflower County (ACSC), which attempted to participate in the antipoverty program of the Office of Economic Opportunity (OEO). Testifying at a congressional hearing in April 1967, Hamer acknowledged the importance of Head Start—the federal program designed to assist preschool children from low-income families—"because not only does it give the children a head start but also it will give the adults a head start." Accusations soon followed that ACSC improperly managed its programs, while Mississippi governor John Bell Williams attempted to redirect Head Start grants. Eventually, Hamer battled with another civil rights activist, Head Start's well-regarded Cora Fleming, resulting in charges that Hamer, noted for having refused to compromise in Atlantic City, had pushed for that deal in order to satisfy OEO.

Hamer was happier when she was involved with her own enterprise, the Freedom Farm Corporation, which sought to empower Mississippi Delta blacks economically. Starting operations in 1969, the Freedom Farm bred pigs, purchased forty acres of land to cultivate vegetables and cotton, and ran the Co-Op, which instructed poor blacks in how to obtain low-cost loans for houses and farms. Within two years, the Freedom Farm acquired 640 additional acres; by 1972, it had constructed seventy affordable homes. It also offered grants to enable students to continue their education, provided seed money for opening or expanding local businesses, and helped local residents attain disaster relief and food stamps. Soliciting financial support for the Freedom Farm, Assistant Director Hamer traveled around the country, visiting Harvard University and appearing on the *David Frost* television program. Eventually, however, poor management, economic difficulties, and Hamer's own ill health doomed the Freedom Farm.

Despite two electoral setbacks, Hamer was chosen to second the vice presidential nomination of Frances Farenthold at the Democratic Party national convention in 1972. But during the next few years, Hamer suffered from high blood pressure, diabetes, a nervous breakdown, exhaustion, breast cancer, and pervasive depression. On March 14, 1976, Hamer's heart gave out, and her funeral followed six days later at the William Chapel Baptist Church in Ruleville. Among those in attendance were Andrew Young, U.S. ambassador to the United Nations; Hodding Carter, Assistant Secretary of State; Vernon Jordan of the National Urban League; and Ella Baker, Stokely Carmichael, and H. Rap Brown of SNCC. Delivering an oration, Carmichael asserted that Hamer represented "the very best of us." Later, John Lewis pointedly declared, "Without her and hundreds of women like her, we would never have been able to achieve what we did." Nearly penniless, Hamer was buried on property previously owned by the Freedom Farm, beneath a headstone bearing the epitaph, "I am sick and tired of being sick and tired."

CÉSAR CHÁVEZ
Guardian of the United Farm Workers Union

On February 14, 1968, César Chávez, the head of the United Farm Workers (UFW), initiated a fast that would last twenty-five days in order to protest labor conditions and support his movement. Following a series of fund-raising efforts across the nation, he had heard, to his dismay, threats of violent

148

action from militant members of his own organization in Delano, California. During a UFW union meeting, Chávez exploded: "Goddamn it! We'll never be able to get anywhere if we start using tactics of violence. . . . You have to believe in that!" Determined to demonstrate his movement's commitment to nonviolence, Chávez talked to striking farm workers and staff members at a special meeting held on the fifth day of his fast. As he explained, "I thought that I had to bring the Movement to a halt, do something that would force them and me to deal with the whole question of violence and ourselves." He spoke of the war in Vietnam, which had intensified dramatically after the Tet Offensive began in January 1968, and of the civil rights campaign and the mounting frustrations that had resulted in race riots. The UFW, Chávez reminded the audience, had instilled hope in many previously disillusioned farm workers, but a resort to violence would violate the trust it had cultivated. Calling on the words of Mahatma Gandhi and St. Paul, Chávez said that his fast would demonstrate penance and love for his fellow UFW members.

While many of the people closest to him—including his wife, Helen, who called him "ridiculous" and "crazy," and his mentor, Fred Ross—worried about the damage that might result to Chávez's health, the UFW chieftain maintained his fast day after day. Approaching the third full week of the fast, Chávez spurned a physician's demand that he take medication, bouillon, and grapefruit juice. Media attention heightened, due to genuine concern or perhaps morbid fascination that the fast could fell him. He received numerous letters of support, many from high-powered political, labor, and religious figures. The junior senator from New York, Robert F. Kennedy, fired off a telegram, expressing concern about Chávez's well being.

On March 10, the twenty-fifth day of the fast, Kennedy, who had earlier demonstrated support for the UFW, sat down with Chávez to end his fast by sharing a piece of bread. Kennedy asked, "Well, how goes the boycott, César?" Alluding to rumors that Kennedy was about to make a run for the presidency, Chávez replied with a question of his own: "How goes running for president, Bob?" In a message intended for public distribution, Chávez acknowledged, "Our struggle is not easy," for it was opposed by the wealthy and the powerful. The farm workers, by contrast, were poor and lacked allies. However, they possessed "something the rich do not own. We have our own bodies and spirits and the justice of our cause as our weapons."

César Estrada Chávez, the man who became famous for organizing farm laborers into a powerful economic and political force, was born on March 31, 1927, the second of five children raised on an 80-acre farm outside Yuma, Arizona. His grandfather Césario Chávez, affectionately called "Papa Chayo," had come from Chihuahua, Mexico, where he endured a feudal existence on a large ranch or hacienda. Escaping from the ranch, the illiterate Césario worked as a muleskinner in Arizona before purchasing some land of his own. He married Dorotea, "Mama Tella," an orphan who had grown up in a convent where she learned both Spanish and Latin. Césario and Dorotea had fifteen children. Their son Librado, who helped manage the family's farm, married Juana Estrada in 1924; the two ran a small grocery store, a garage, and a pool hall on land they purchased, while residing in an apartment above the store. Their children enjoyed a somewhat privileged existence, with César and his brother Richard hiking together, swimming, helping out at the garage, and shooting pool.

The Great Depression crippled the Chávez family, as it did so many others. By 1932, the Chávezes were compelled to sell their businesses and return to the ranch of the now widowed Mama Tella. The next year saw drought envelop the Colorado River Basin, resulting in harder times still for Librado and Juana. After struggling along for the next five years, Librado went to California to find work, soon sending for Juana and their children to join him. There, the family endured a humiliating encounter with officers of the border patrol, who demanded papers verifying U.S. citizenship. Finally allowed to move on, the Chávezes went to Oxnard, where Librado was hired as a day laborer and Juana sold items she had crocheted. After returning to Yuma, the Chávezes were tossed off their land, reduced to the status of migrant workers, and forced to take the road in a 1927 Studebaker with clothing, linens, and $40 in hand, received through the sale of cows and chickens.

Back in California, Librado, Juana, and their children once again experienced the all-too-familiar existence of migrant workers. Picking the abundant crops of the Golden State, the Chávezes toiled for long hours of backbreaking work with short-handled hoes, enduring discriminatory treatment. Frequently, the family lived in migrant camps or slept in their aging car. The children could attend school only sporadically; bouncing around from school to school, nearly forty altogether, César encountered racial tension on playgrounds and in classrooms. At times, he and his siblings were the only Mexican children attending integrated schools. Chávez later reflected, "We were like monkeys in a cage. There were lots of racist remarks that still hurt my ears when I think of them. And we couldn't do anything except sit there and take it." They were not allowed to speak Spanish on school grounds and were subjected to raps on their knuckles for ignoring that admonition. Still, César Chávez managed to finish the eighth grade.

Conditions were little better for Librado in the fields, where he frequently participated in strikes due to the exploitative treatment farm workers endured. Indeed, California had a long history of such labor strife, with radical unions like the Cannery and Agricultural Workers Industrial Union pitted against the powerful Associated Farmers, which employed vigilantes to crush labor activism. Even the path-breaking National Labor Relations Act, known as the Wagner Act, passed in 1935; the emergence of the Congress of Industrial Organizations, established the next year; and a sympathetic administration in Washington, DC, headed by President Franklin Delano Roosevelt, did little to improve the plight of America's farm workers. For its part, the Wagner Act failed to provide protections for domestic and farm laborers, the vast bulk of whom were people of color.

After picking up work whenever they could, the Chávezes settled in Delano, California, in the San Joaquin Valley, where, during the height of the Depression, a great communist-led strike by cotton workers had been brutally repressed. As a teenager, César Chávez disavowed Juana's religiosity and affected the zoot-suit style of the pachucos, who sported long coats worn over baggy, pegged trousers, large hats, key chains, and thick-soled shoes; he smoked cigarettes, combed his thick, dark hair back in a ducktail, and favored big band performers like Duke Ellington and Billy Eckstine. Regarding the zoot suits, which became controversial precisely because they were associated with young Hispanics, Chávez noted, "We needed a lot of guts to wear those pants, and we had to be rebellious to do it, because the police and a few of the older people would harass us. But it was the style, and I wasn't going to be a square." Perhaps fortunately for Chávez, he was toiling in the fields in spring 1943 when thousands of soldiers and civilians attacked young zoot-suiters in Los Angeles; city officials responded to the so-called zoot-suit riots by making it a misdemeanor to wear a zoot suit.

Tired of "sugar-beet thinning, the worst backbreaking job," the seventeen-year-old Chávez enlisted in the U.S. Navy in 1944, despite his parents' opposition. Following boot camp in San Diego, the five-foot, six-inch Chávez was stationed in the Mariana Islands in the South Pacific, where he worked as a coxswain apprentice, before moving on to Guam to work as a painter. His experience in the military proved unhappy, but he received an honorable discharge in 1946 and returned to Delano. He soon joined his father as a fellow member of the National Farm Laborers Union (NFLU), headed by Hank Hasiwar and Ernesto Galarza. In 1948, Chávez married his sweetheart Helen Fabela, whom he had met six years earlier and who had also dropped out of school to work in the fields. Desperately poor, César and Helen lived in a one-room shack in a labor camp. After working with his brother Richard on an apricot ranch, Chávez toiled as a sharecropper, picking strawberries. Two years of daily labor and no financial reward led to a decision to head north to Crescent City, where a lumber company was seeking workers. After a year and a half in Crescent City, where Helen was depressed by the stormy weather, the Chávezes decided to move back south. With their first two children, César and a pregnant Helen went to San Jose, where he worked in a lumber mill and they resided in a barrio known as *Sal Si Puedes* ("Get Out If You Can").

In 1952, Chávez met Father Daniel McDonnell, a socially conscious Roman Catholic priest who was struggling to construct a parish in Sal Si Puedes. Along with another priest, Thomas McCullough, Father McDonnell was determined that the impoverished farm workers of the San Joaquin Valley should be schooled in the Catholic Church's ethos of social justice and labor organizing. McDonnell taught Chávez about St. Francis of Assisi, the papal edicts on labor conditions by Leo XIII, and the Indian pacifist Mahatma Gandhi. Having received word of Chávez's friendship with McDonnell, Fred Ross, a radical organizer with the Community Service Organization (CSO) in Los Angeles, came to speak with the young Mexican American. CSO was associated with Saul Alinsky, the renowned social activist who sought to empower local community members. After being informed that Ross wanted to see him, a distrustful César arranged to have friends come to the Chávez home, prepared "to run him out of the house" if they saw a signal.

Ross visited his reluctant host in June 1952, with Helen and a host of neighbors present too. Initially hostile, César found himself warming up to his guest, who obviously knew something about the ailments afflicting the San Jose barrio. César was surprised to hear Ross condemn politicians for failing to clean up a contaminated creek that coursed through the neighborhood. Ross indicated that in his travels across the region he had encountered similar conditions in other Mexican American communities: "the same kind of cops beating up young guys and 'breaking and entering' without warrants. The same mean streets and walkways and lack of streetlights and traffic signals. The same poor drainage, overflowing cesspools, and amoebic dysentery." Ross reported that the CSO had challenged segregation in education and recreation in such communities and condemned police brutality against young Chicanos.

Clearly impressed, Chávez agreed to attend a meeting, sponsored by CSO, that night in East San Jose. That evening, Ross inscribed the following entry in his diary: "I think I've found the guy I'm looking for." The next day, Chávez, who came to consider Ross a hero of a kind, joined the CSO voter registration drive in Chicano districts. Eventually, Alinsky agreed to pay Chávez a small weekly salary that enabled him to devote full-time to organizing. Chávez's involvement with CSO, beginning during the zenith of the postwar Red Scare, led to questions about his involvement with communism, a charge leveled by the Republican Central Committee. The anger Chávez displayed on confronting such an accusation convinced FBI agents, who were investigating him, that the Republicans were attempting to smear Chávez and to intimidate would-be voters. Nevertheless, some of his coworkers refused to deal with Chávez until Father McDonnell joined with other priests in applauding the brand-new organizer.

After being assigned by Ross to initiate a CSO chapter in Oakland, Chávez headed into the San Joaquin Valley to guide the organization's operations there. In Madera, rumors again circulated that Chávez was a communist and his own chapter decided to investigate him. As Chávez later reflected, this "taught me the most important lesson in my life about organizing. When people are fearful, when it's their skin, they don't care about anybody." Ross, on the other hand, determinedly supported his protégé, sending him on new organizing assignments over the next several years. An activist later explained part of Chávez's appeal: "He looked mestizo. He was dark skinned, short, with high cheekbones, piercir g black eyes, and sparse facial hair. He was the embodiment of the Chicano. Chicanos could see themselves in César: clothes, personal style, demeanor and commitment."

After a meeting with Alinsky and other top CSO figures in mid-1958, Chávez took on the task of helping the United Packinghouse Workers Union, based in Oxnard, organize workers who toiled in sheds, packing lemons in boxes. Chávez discovered that farmers preferred hiring thousands of Mexican braceros (seasonal laborers), rather than members of the local community in need of work. In 1942, Congress had initiated the Bracero Program to import Mexican workers in the midst of a labor shortage brought on by U.S. participation in World War II. When the war ended, Congress maintained the program, acceding to the wishes of western farmers who welcomed the cheap labor. While the program supposedly established a minimum wage and other safeguards, employers kept wages low, provided inadequate housing for workers, and overcharged them for basic necessities, sometimes meting out racist epithets and physical violence as well. Moreover, growers turned to braceros as strikebreakers, a practice that also drove down wages.

In Oxnard and surrounding communities, Chávez adopted the kinds of tactics that he would turn to repeatedly. He organized economic boycotts directed at merchants who supported the Bracero Program, sit-down strikes conducted in the fields, the picketing of a meeting in Ventura attended by

Secretary of Labor James Mitchell, lobbying, and marching. He determined "that the growers weren't invincible." Nevertheless, his experiences in Oxnard were not altogether happy. The CSO vetoed his bid to create a union that would compete with the United Packinghouse Workers, and factionalism within the local CSO branch followed his departure from Oxnard. Consequently, to Chávez's dismay, growers continued hiring braceros. As he later admitted, "I was so mad—I don't know at whom, at the leadership and at the people for not fighting for what I was sure was there."

During this same period, other activists were striving to create a farm workers' union. Father McCullough, Father McDonnell, Fred Ross, and Dolores Huerta—soon to become one of Chávez's closest associates—were involved in such an enterprise in Stockton. Eventually, they helped to found the Agricultural Workers Organizing Committee (AWOC). Serving as the CSO's executive director in California, Chávez worked closely with Huerta and Gil Padilla, another CSO member interested in organizing farm workers. In Los Angeles, Chávez also linked up with the Mexican-American Political Association and the Viva Kennedy Clubs, which sought to register voters in urban barrios. Having failed to convince the CSO board to back the formation of a new union of farm laborers, a "heartbroken" Chávez stood up at the organization's convention, held in Calexico in March 1962, and declared, "I resign." Subsequently, he received offers to serve as an organizer for AWOC, but Chávez, disillusioned with standard labor union tactics and wanting a position with "no strings attached," turned them down. That April, the now thirty-five-year-old Chávez returned with his family to Delano, renting an inexpensive house near the downtown sector. To survive financially, Helen picked grapes at the mammoth Sierra Vista Ranch run by the DiGiorgio family, while César, who had a nest egg of about $1,000, picked peas part-time.

Even more than before, Chávez was committed to La Causa ("the cause"), the effort to win fair labor conditions for farm workers. Indeed, his efforts soon amounted to the formation of a movement, similar to the campaign to empower poor African Americans that Martin Luther King Jr. had helped to trigger in the South. In September 1962, a new grassroots organization, the National Farm Workers Association (NFWA), emerged, with Chávez named president; the organization's three vice presidents were Huerta, Padilla, and Julio Hernandez. The NFWA's motto was Viva La Causa! Its flag showed a black eagle inside a white circle against a red backdrop. Chávez said about the flag, "A symbol is an important thing. That is why we chose an Aztec eagle. It gives pride. . . . When people see it they know it means dignity." As chroniclers Susan Ferris and Ricardo Sandoval indicate, the union's newspaper,

El Malcriado ("ill-bred") demanded decent wages and condemned growers who were angered that the Bracero Program was finally ending in 1965. Union dues ran $3.50 monthly, but the NFWA initially possessed a tenuous financial life. Nevertheless, Chávez turned down a $50,000 foundation grant, preferring to rely on the contributions of farm workers instead. His own family often made inordinate economic sacrifices, and Chávez himself declined a job offer as a Peace Corps director in Latin America that paid $21,000 annually. Instead, the union used the collateral on a small house that Richard Chávez had built in Delano in order to provide loans to farm workers.

The NFWA participated in its first strike activities in 1965, a volatile year in which frustration intensified within the civil rights movement and U.S. involvement in Vietnam deepened dramatically. The union helped flower workers in McFarland obtain higher wages and supported a strike of migrant laborers in Porterville, who were enraged by rent increases in migrant camps. Nevertheless, the NFWA just limped along, lacking financial resources and powerful allies. Then the union and Chávez became involved in an epochal labor struggle that focused national attention on *La Causa*. The battle arose from a grape strike in Delano. The Labor Department had allowed growers in the Coachella Valley to hire braceros to pick grapes at an hourly rate of $1.40, fifteen cents more than Filipino workers received and twenty-five cents more than Mexican Americans were paid. In May, AWOC called for a strike to oppose the wage differentials, quickly winning raises for the underpaid Filipinos and Mexican Americans.

As the grape-harvesting season arrived in the San Joaquin Valley that summer, growers reverted to paying both Filipinos and Mexican Americans the lower-wage rates. Insisting on equitable wages, members of AWOC kicked off a strike in Delano on September 8. While police targeted strikers for harassment, growers drove Filipinos from labor camps. Responding to requests for assistance, Chávez and the NFWA urged members of the AWOC not to cross picket lines. On the evening of September 16, several hundred farm laborers and their families met at Our Lady of Guadalupe's church hall. Cries of "Viva La Causa!" rang out. Those present listened attentively as Chávez spoke. After referring to the struggle for Mexican independence led by Father Miguel Hidalgo a century and a half before, Chávez declared that individuals of Mexican ancestry who resided in the United States, like farm workers in general, were involved in a quest "for the freedom and dignity which poverty denies us." Soon, the gathered throng voted unanimously to support the Filipino workers.

Throughout the Great Delano Grape Strike, Chávez demanded that the farm workers use nonviolent tactics. He contended that strike activity could empower previously downtrodden laborers, for the picket line enabled a worker to make an "irrevocable" commitment: "The lengthier one's involvement in such an affair . . . the stronger the commitment." For both practical and spiritual reasons, Chávez maintained, nonviolence had to characterize the farm workers' behavior at the picket line and across the several hundred square miles that the strike covered. Arguing that the growers' violence directed at "a nonviolent movement" would generate sympathy for the strikers, he insisted that, in the end, "we can turn the world if we can do it nonviolently."

Though eventually buttressed by hundreds of volunteers from outside the area, including clergy influenced by liberation theology, members of both SNCC and CORE, and other students too, the strike encountered tremendous hostility from growers and their employees. Resentful ranchers believed that they were taking care of their workers, paying them more for their labor than did growers elsewhere. Consequently, members of the clergy were taunted as "communists" and "fairies," ranchers hurled racist epithets at strikers, and growers jabbed their fists into the ribs of individuals standing on picket lines. Despite having his own ribs battered, Chávez declared, "Love is the most important ingredient in nonviolent work—love the opponent." He also suggested, "If we're full of hatred, we can't really do our work. Hatred saps all that strength and energy we need to plan."

In mid-October, with the atmosphere in Kern County fraught with tension, Sheriff Roy Galyen began issuing a series of edicts undoubtedly intended to provoke Chávez and the striking farm workers. Galyen announced that strikers who congregated along or shouted from roadsides would be arrested for "disturbing the peace." He insisted that strikers who used the word *huelga* (strike) would also face arrest. On October 19, with television and newspaper reporters in attendance, Helen Chávez and other picketers repeatedly tossed out the forbidden word, leading to their arrests. Chávez received word of the arrests while he was speaking to a large crowd of students at the University of California at Berkeley. More than $6,000 in contributions followed, along with telegrams protesting the arrests. More attention resulted from the showing of the 1960 CBS documentary, "The Harvest of Shame," which presented the plight of migrant workers.

As the year wound down, the NFWA initiated a boycott to pressure growers to accept union demands. Particularly singled out were the biggest growers in Delano, including Schenley Industries, the DiGiorgio Fruit Corporation, and TreeSweet. On December 16, after the AFL-CIO had voted to support the strike, Walter Reuther, head of the United Auto Workers (UAW), came to Delano to march side by side with Chávez and deliver a speech at Filipino Hall. With the UAW providing $5,000 monthly to both the NFWA and AWOC, the strike continued into the spring, when the California State Senate Factfinding Subcommittee on Un-American Activities initiated an exploratory investigation of the labor unrest. More important, however, the U.S. Senate Subcommittee on Migratory Labor began its own hearings on March 14, 1966, with Senator Robert F. Kennedy as one of the panelists. Testifying before the subcommittee, Chávez offered affidavits indicating that growers were illegally bringing in Mexican strikebreakers. He spoke of measures proposed in Congress to establish a minimum wage standard for farm workers, guarantee the right to bargain collectively, and abolish child labor in the fields. Chávez asserted, "All that these bills do is say that people who work on farms should have the same human rights as people who work in construction crews, or in factories, or in offices." Three days later, Chávez and a group of farm workers began a 300-mile march from Delano to Sacramento, under a banner proclaiming "Pilgrimage, Penitence, and Revolution." He again indicated that those participating in *La Causa* "wanted to be fit not only physically but also spiritually, and . . . to stress nonviolence even more, build confidence, and have more visible nonviolent tactics." In the midst of the march, Chávez spoke to a representative from the Schenley Industries, which agreed on April 7 to a contract with AWOC and to recognize the NFWA.

Almost immediately after the march came to an end, Chávez directed his attention to DiGiorgio, one of the state's great agribusiness concerns. Even in the face of opposition by the powerful Teamsters union, the NFWA undertook a boycott of the company's products. After field workers in Delano voted to affiliate with the NFWA rather than with the Teamsters, Martin Luther King Jr. fired off a congratulatory note to Chávez and declared, "The fight for equality must be fought on many fronts." The apparent successes in Delano further solidified Chávez's reputation as perhaps the nation's foremost Chicano figure and placed the farm workers' movement among the era's most noteworthy. Chávez's union soon merged with the AWOC to become the National Farm Workers Organizing Committee (NFWOC). During a strike against the Perelli-Minetti vineyards, Chávez undertook his first fast as a spiritual and political act. In early April 1967, the NFWOC garnered another significant victory in Delano when DiGiorgio signed an agreement establishing health and welfare benefits, unemployment compensation, and paid vacations and holidays for farm workers.

In January 1968, the NFWOC began a boycott of California table grapes. It became one of the most important labor fights of the period and proved symbolic of both class conflict and nonviolent protest. As this latest strike threatened to turn violent, Chávez resorted to the soon-to-become legendary fast that lasted twenty-five days, purportedly longer than any fast Gandhi carried out. The publicity surrounding Chávez's protest, which underscored the importance of nonviolent action, provided considerable impetus for the grape boycott. Three weeks after Chávez broke bread with Senator Kennedy to end the fast, an assassin gunned down one of the movement's foremost allies, Martin Luther King Jr., undoubtedly the nation's leading apostle of nonviolence. In early June, Senator Kennedy was also murdered. Notwithstanding the loss of such noteworthy supporters, the grape boycott continued, focusing on Safeway stores by the spring of 1969. The new Nixon administration purchased millions of pounds of grapes to be sent to soldiers in Vietnam, but Chávez's campaign failed to dissipate, now being directed against all California grape growers. In an open letter to the head of the California Grape and Tree Fruit League, Chávez challenged E.L. Barr Jr.'s assertions that the farm workers' movement employed violence and terrorism. Recalling his own nearly month-long fast the previous year, Chávez wrote, "We advocate militant nonviolence as our means for social revolution and to achieve justice for our people."

Finally, on July 16, 1970, Chávez and NFWOC staff attorney Jerry Cohen met John Giumarra Jr. and his father, John Giumarra Sr., whose family held 12,000 acres of grapes, at the Stardust Motel in Delano. The negotiations continued for several hours, with Cohen insisting that the ranchers bring together all growers that the union was targeting. The following evening, twenty-nine grape growers signed a contract with the NFWOC at Reuther Hall in Forty Acres, just outside Delano. Negotiations were finalized the next night, with the grape pickers obtaining a hiring hall, a fifteen-cent hourly increase to $1.80, the promise of joint committees that would regulate the use of pesticides in the fields, and employer contributions to a health and welfare program. While acknowledging that most of the striking workers had lost "their worldly possessions," Chávez applauded their commitment to nonviolence.

In the face of hostile administrations in Washington, DC, and Sacramento, the latter headed by Republican governor Ronald Reagan, and the difficulties the American economy endured in the early 1970s, the gains that the farm workers' movement had attained proved tenuous only. On the heels of the agreement with the Giumarras and other grape growers, Chávez again confronted redbaiting, threats of violence, and competition posed by the Teamsters regarding the allegiance of farm workers. While the NFWOC achieved successes, it also faced repeated court injunctions forbidding picketing, a drying up of financial resources, and flagging energy. In December 1970, Chávez ended up in jail again, having been arrested in Salinas for failing to adhere to a court order that prohibited boycotting one grower's lettuce crop, although the injunction was soon declared unconstitutional.

In 1971, Chávez's organization became an AFL-CIO affiliate and was renamed the United Farm Workers of America; the change led to the loss of a substantial subsidy from the national union. The union also relocated to an abandoned tuberculosis sanatorium in the Tehachapi Mountains, outside Bakersfield; the UFW called the new site *La Paz* ("The Peace"). The UFW fought attempts by state legislatures to enact statutes that would outlaw boycotts and restrict strikes. It faced continued competition from the Teamsters; an outbreak of violence in Modesto during the spring of 1973 resulted in the killing of two union members. Urging his members to fast for three days, Chávez worried about the loss of 90 percent of grape contracts to the Teamsters and the dramatic shrinkage of UFW membership rolls. In 1974, however, the Teamsters abandoned efforts to organize farm laborers. Meanwhile, Chávez continued an ongoing boycott against Ernest and Julio Gallo. The following February, Chávez and the UFW began a 110-mile procession from San Francisco to Modesto, the home base of the Gallo vineyards. Governor Jerry Brown came to support the California Agricultural Labor Relations Act, which guaranteed farm workers the right to bargain collectively. Unfortunately, the next year witnessed the resounding defeat of Proposition 14, which would have afforded increased funding for the Agricultural Labor Relations Board.

The heyday of the farm labor movement appeared to have passed, and media reports that Chávez had adopted increasingly autocratic control over the UFW generated negative publicity. Still, 1979 saw a massive strike by lettuce workers that spread to Arizona and reenergized Chávez, who announced, "We have thirty years of struggle behind us, but I am spirited and encouraged." Some workers refused to adhere to Chávez's nonviolent approach, physically assaulting strikebreakers. After months of strife, rallies, and marches, growers began to sign generous contracts. The UFW again increased in size, boasting 45,000 members by 1980, with new agreements even providing medical coverage. The union increasingly resorted to lobbying to protect the gains it had achieved, but the 1980s saw union membership again drop significantly. Nevertheless, the UFW, spurred by Chávez, initiated new campaigns, including one in the middle of the decade urging statutory restrictions on pesticide use, the type of government action he had long demanded. In 1986, Congress passed legislation affording amnesty to hundreds of thousands of illegal immigrants; Chávez, who worried about the call for a new bracero-style program, nevertheless hoped that the union might gain additional members from among the newly legalized workers. By the early 1990s, the UFW was again urging support for a grape boycott, and Chávez could be seen, ironically enough, marching through Salinas side by side with Teamsters. He experienced the deaths of several individuals closest to him, including his mother, Juana, and his aging mentor, Fred Ross.

On April 22, 1993, César Chávez, having just completed yet another fast, died at the age of sixty-six. He had remained true to his ideals, to *La Causa* and the practice of nonviolence. State senator Art Torres lauded Chávez as "our Gandhi . . . our Dr. Martin Luther King." The funeral took place in Delano on April 29, with some 40,000 people coming to pay tribute. Among those in attendance were civil rights leader Jesse Jackson, former governor Jerry Brown, and Ethel Kennedy, widow of the slain U.S. senator. The next year, Helen Chávez received the Medal of Freedom citation from President Bill Clinton, who termed her husband "a Moses figure" for Chicanos.

Conclusion

At the height of the civil rights movement, Fannie Lou Hamer and César Chávez challenged racial boundaries that continued to tarnish the American ideal of equality of opportunity. Both generally adhered to nonviolent tactics, although Hamer proved less steadfast in that regard than Chávez, who believed, like Martin Luther King Jr., that means and ends were inextricably connected. Older than many of the participants in SNCC, CORE, the MFDP and UFW's Hamer and Chávez, well before they joined the civil rights movement and *La Causa*, had already endured the kind of racial discrimination that economically shackled many African Americans and Hispanics. Once they began participating in those crusades, Hamer and Chávez proved willing to make lifelong commitments, no matter how taxing and perilous they became. In the fashion of Dr. King, the black activist and the Mexican American labor leader determined that racial justice required, at a bare minimum, a semblance of economic equity, to be achieved by economic boycotts, cooperative endeavors, marches, sit-ins, and fasts. Their challenge to the political and economic powers-that-were ensured that controversies swirled about these sparsely educated, but highly charismatic figures. Their very lives demonstrated how discriminatory treatment contradicted fundamental American tenets of democracy and equality.

Study Questions

1. In contrast to many of the leaders of the civil rights movement, who came from middle-class backgrounds, Fannie Lou Hamer represented

the African American underclass. Explain how her background drew her into the civil rights movement.

2. Analyze the impact of Hamer's speech at the 1964 Democratic National Convention.

3. Economic circumstances also drew César Chávez into the struggle for social justice. Discuss how Chávez's family history played a role in his activism.

4. The United Farm Workers became a powerful force in agitating for better working conditions for its members. What was Chávez's role in making the UFW a significant actor in the American labor movement?

5. Compare and contrast the different strategies and tactics that Hamer and Chávez employed to bring about social change.

Selected Bibliography

Belfrage, Sally. *Freedom Summer*. New York: Viking, 1965.

Dunne, John Gregory. *Delano: The Story of the California Grape Strike*. New York: Farrar, Straus and Giroux, 1971.

Ferris, Susan, and Ricardo Sandoval. *The Fight in the Fields: César Chávez and the Farmworkers Movement*. New York: Harcourt Brace, 1997.

Fusco, Paul. *La Causa: The California Grape Strike*. New York: Collier Books, 1970.

Hamer, Fannie Lou. *To Praise Our Bridges: An Autobiography*. Jackson, MS: No publisher, 1967.

Jensen, Richard J., and John C. Hammerback. *The Words of César Chávez*. College Station: Texas A&M University Press, 2002.

Jordan, June. *Fannie Lou Hamer*. New York: Ty Crowell, 1972.

Kling, Susan. *Fannie Lou Hamer: A Biography*. Chicago: National Women's History Project, 1979.

Lee, Chana Kai. *For Freedom's Sake: The Life of Fannie Lou Hamer*. Urbana: University of Illinois Press, 2000.

Levy, Jacques E. *César Chávez: Autobiography of La Causa*. New York: W.W. Norton, 1975.

McAdam, Doug. *Freedom Summer*. New York: Oxford University Press, 1988.

Mills, Kay. *This Little Light of Mine: The Life of Fannie Lou Hamer*. Louisville: University Press of Kentucky, 2007.

Nelson, Eugene. *Huelga: The First Hundred Days of the Great Delano Grape Strike*. Delano, CA: Farm Workers Press, 1966.

Taylor, Ronald. *Chávez and the Farm Workers*. Boston: Beacon, 1975.

Yinger, Winthrop. *César Chávez: The Rhetoric of Nonviolence*. Hicksville, NY: Exposition Press of Florida, 1975.

Young, Jan. *The Migrant Workers and César Chávez*. New York: J. Messner, 1972.

7

Challenges to the Liberal Consensus

The presidential election campaign of 1960 seemed to signal that the ideological fervor of the recent past had slackened. Style rather than substance seemed to distinguish Massachusetts senator John F. Kennedy from Vice President Richard M. Nixon, as suggested by the razor-thin margin that catapulted the handsome Democrat into the White House. The British social analyst Godfrey Hodgson has suggested that a moderately liberal consensus dominated the American political landscape during the quarter-century following the end of World War II. Democrats and Republicans, liberals and conservatives generally agreed on the following premise: the nation was well served by its capitalist economic system, leavened by the humanizing qualities offered by the welfare state, and by an anticommunist policy that promised to protect America from purported enemies at home or abroad. Both Kennedy and Nixon supported this liberal consensus, with the vice president insisting that the country remain strong, as it had been throughout the Eisenhower administration, and his challenger somewhat more aggressively calling for a beefed-up response to Cold War events.

Few people foresaw the budding challenges to the American welfare state and the warfare or imperial state that the decade of the sixties witnessed. As the period began, the American Left was moribund, thanks to the identification of many of its adherents with Soviet-style communism and to the debilitating effects of the postwar Red Scare. The American Communist Party limped along in the wake of both Nikita Khrushchev's 1956 revelations about Stalinist terrors and the Soviet invasion of Hungary. The American Right, at least its farthest reaches, had earlier been discredited by its association with the kind of fascism that failed to find fertile ground in the United States. In the late 1930s, American Bundists, proponents of German Nazism, and other would-be fascists had cropped up briefly, but never posed a significant threat after the United States entered World War II, thanks to government prosecution of right-wing leaders and a general renewal of public confidence in the "American Way." The end of the 1950s did witness the emergence of groups like the American Nazi Party and the John Birch Society, which roundly condemned both the welfare state and the foreign policy of Democratic and Republican administrations as un-American and traitorous.

Organizations like the Anti-Defamation League warned about the rise of an extremist right, and prescient social critics like I.F. Stone and C. Wright Mills hoped or suggested that a new left was emerging on university campuses. But most observers of the contemporary scene spoke of "an end of ideology" and the creation of general consensus in an increasingly comfortable nation that remained at peace, notwithstanding the Cold War. They failed to appreciate what Stone and Mills recognized: the zeitgeist was beginning to shift both abroad and at home. In the so-called third world—in Asia, Africa, the Middle East, and Latin America—ferment was evident in the Vietminh triumph in French Indochina, the Algerian guerrillas' struggle against French colonial rule, and Castro's revolution in Cuba. At home, the civil rights campaign, the beats, the antinuclear movement, and a new youth subculture all suggested that change was in the offing.

Operating from opposite ends of the ideological spectrum, Tom Hayden, a founder of Students for a Democratic Society (SDS), and Arizona senator Barry Goldwater, who helped to shape the conservative movement in America, challenged the liberal consensus.

Following the lead of civil rights activists, Hayden, a student at the University of Michigan, chose to confront social injustice directly and challenge American society's structural ailments. His 1962 manifesto, the Port Huron statement, served as a rallying cry for New Leftists throughout most of the decade. He also participated in community action projects, fervently opposed U.S. involvement in Vietnam, and remained an influential figure in student and New Left circles. Later, Hayden became involved with the Campaign for Economic Democracy in California, where he eventually served as a well-regarded state legislator.

In 1960, Goldwater produced *The Conscience of a Conservative*, a brief book that provided intellectual ammunition for a strident condemnation of communism, the liberal consensus, and the American welfare state. His dedicated followers helped him garner the 1964 Republican Party nomination for the presidency, although a poor showing in the general election led to suggestions that conservatism had seen its best days in the United States. In fact, the Goldwater forces helped to found the New Right, which became increasingly important within the ranks of the GOP, setting the stage for the presidency of Ronald Reagan and his Republican successors. Goldwater himself had a long tenure in the U.S. Senate, where he acquired a reputation as a dedicated conservative, but one whose attitudes regarding social issues sometimes put him at odds with the New Right he had helped to spawn.

TOM HAYDEN
New Left Activist

Students for a Democratic Society, a New Left organization founded in 1960, held its national convention in June 1962 at a camp owned by the United Automobile Workers, in Port Huron, Michigan, forty miles north of Detroit.

Five days of discussion engaged fifty-nine SDS members and a sprinkling of delegates boasting credentials from groups like the Student Nonviolent Co-ordinating Committee (SNCC), the Congress of Racial Equality (CORE), the Student Peace Union, the Young People's Socialist League (YPSL), and Young Democrats. Also present were some elder statesmen of the Left—although some were not much older than the college students—including Michael Harrington and Harry Fleischman of the League for Industrial Democracy (LID), an early sponsor of SDS, and Arnold Kaufman, a professor of philosophy at the University of Michigan, who advocated "participatory democracy."

At the time, SDS possessed only 800 members, a dozen chapters scattered across the country, and a $10,000 annual budget that was covered by LID. Nevertheless, the convention produced a document that proved seminal for the New Left and the decade of the 1960s: the *Port Huron Statement*. This manifesto articulated the ideal of participatory democracy, the empowerment of the people. Tom Hayden, a twenty-two-year-old student at the University of Michigan, largely shaped the *Port Huron Statement* after extensive discussions among those in attendance. Hayden was particularly influenced by the French author Albert Camus and the radical American sociologist C. Wright Mills. The recipient of the 1957 Nobel Prize for Literature, Camus seemed to personify a committed adherence to existentialist thought, striving to remain true to a personal code of honor in the face of the absurdities of modern life. Mills contended that a power elite, highly undemocratic and insular, shaped American foreign and domestic policies, diminishing democratic possibilities in the United States and elsewhere.

At the SDS convention, the thirty-two-year-old Harrington, a committed socialist and the soon-to-be author of the path-breaking *The Other America: Poverty in the United States*, blasted Hayden's criticisms of organized labor and his failure to adopt a more hard-line anticommunist perspective. After Harrington departed from the conference, Hayden submitted a new introduction to the SDS manifesto, which declared, "We are people of this generation, bred in at least modest comfort, housed now in universities, looking uncomfortably at the world we inherit." Hayden's draft referred to the disillusioning realities that his generation had experienced, ranging from the continuation of Jim Crow practices to the Cold War, so starkly "symbolized by the presence of the Bomb." In addition, as a young Karl Marx had warned, deadening labor produced alienation in millions of workers, and the United States was failing to respond adequately to a worldwide revolutionary upsurge. Old illusions, even those on the left side of the political spectrum, appeared inadequate, while "few new prophets" had arisen.

On a more positive note, Hayden's document asserted that members of SDS "regard men as infinitely precious and possessed of unfulfilled capacities for reason, freedom, and love." To nurture such possibilities, SDS sought to "replace power rooted in possession, privilege, or circumstance by power and uniqueness rooted in love, reflectiveness, reason, and creativity." Although American students had to contend with the deadening bureaucratization that afflicted modern academia, they could still help to bring about such a transformation; the university could act to usher in social change. Throughout much of the remainder of the decade, the Port Huron statement served as a model for New Leftists.

Tom Hayden was born on December 11, 1939, the son of John Francis Hayden and Genevieve Isabelle Garity, both descendants of Irish Catholic immigrants from Ulster who had traveled to Wisconsin before the Civil War. Having settled in Detroit, John became an accountant for Chrysler before serving in the Marine Corps during World War II. Later, the Haydens divorced, with Genevieve, who became a school librarian, taking care of their only child, Tom, in the largely Protestant suburb of Royal Oak. Tom spent weekends with his father, tagging along to sporting events. Hayden attended a Catholic school run by the Shrine of the Little Flower Church and its pastor, Father Charles Coughlin, the "Radio Priest" of the 1930s, who became infamous for his anti-Semitic diatribes and shrill attacks on President Franklin D. Roosevelt.

Hayden played sports regularly, particularly baseball, but really excelled in the classroom and as editor of the high school newspaper. He idolized James Dean, the brooding young film star of *Rebel Without a Cause* who died in an automobile accident in 1955; J.D. Salinger's novel *The Catcher in the Rye*, with its anguished adolescent protagonist Holden Caulfield; and *Mad* magazine, featuring the irreverent Alfred E. Neuman. During the fall of 1957, Hayden entered the University of Michigan at Ann Arbor, where he "was interested in the bohemians, the beatniks, the coffeehouse set, the interracial crowd," but remained apart from them. His most important connections developed through his work as a reporter for the campus newspaper, the *Michigan Daily*, and through Al Haber, the "campus radical" and the son of a faculty member who had served as an economic adviser to President Harry S Truman.

Hayden's work for the *Michigan Daily* helped to politicize him, as he followed Haber and other sympathy pickets in front of Kresge Department Store in their effort to back students conducting sit-ins to challenge segregation ordinances in the South. Named editor of the *Michigan Daily* for the upcoming academic year, Hayden hitchhiked to Berkeley in June 1960 to report on youthful activists in the Bay Area. He encountered a group of individuals who had founded SLATE, a student-based organization that insisted on the right to discuss issues like racial discrimination, free speech violations, and the nuclear arms race. That summer, Hayden covered the Democratic Party's national convention in Los Angeles, recognizing Massachusetts senator John F. Kennedy's potential and "promise of youth," but proving more impressed with Martin Luther King Jr.'s directive, "Ultimately, you have to take a stand with your life."

Hayden subsequently attended the annual conference of the National Student Association (NSA), a liberal organization that was covertly receiving funding from the CIA and the State Department. He met several delegates from SNCC, including Sandra Cason, a SNCC activist from Austin, Texas, who had been involved with both the YWCA and the Christian Faith and Life Community, which opposed Jim Crow practices. Back in Ann Arbor for his senior year, Hayden shipped Cason a copy of Hermann Hesse's *Siddhartha,* which deals with an existentialist quest, and pored over the writings of Jean-Paul Sartre and Camus. In the *Michigan Daily*, the paper's new editor poignantly asked, "Why This Erupting Generation?" and suggested the need "to serve justice so as not to add to the injustice of the human condition." The university administration warned Hayden that his paper's editorials were "demagogic." Hayden helped to establish a new student organization at the university, VOICE, which followed SLATE's lead in championing progressive programs. Hoping to transform SDS into a national organization, Haber, its initial president, appointed Hayden field secretary, which enabled Tom to join his new wife, Sandra "Casey" Cason Hayden, in Atlanta, to establish an SDS office there.

Both SDS and SNCC were part of the New Left, which emerged after the demise of its predecessor and the waning of the McCarthyite phase of the Red Scare. In their infancy, both organizations deliberately avoided the ideological fixations of the Old Left, as well as the identification, warranted or not, with the Soviet Union and communism. Prominent New Leftists like Hayden and Todd Gitlin, another SDS leader, greatly respected the Socialist Party's Norman Thomas, the pacifist A.J. Muste, and the journalist I.F. Stone, all of whom had fought in the ideologically driven internecine wars of the 1930s. The New Leftists also admired the rebellious style of antiheroic figures from the 1950s, ranging from film star James Dean to Beat writer Jack Kerouac and rock and roller Elvis Presley. As the 1960s began, the New Left also drew inspiration from the anti-colonial movements that had sprouted in the third world, leading to revolts in places as far-flung as Vietnam, Algeria, and Cuba.

At that point, SNCC in particular served as a model for many New Leftists.

Hayden praised this "good, pure struggle . . . that we have every reason to begin in a revolutionary way across the country, in every place of discrimination that exists." In early September 1961, Tom and Casey Hayden traveled to rural Mississippi, where the black activist Bob Moses had just established a Freedom School in McComb to help trigger a voter registration drive by SNCC. On October 11, Hayden and SDS's Paul Potter were yanked from the car in which they were riding and pummeled by segregationists, then arrested and charged with vagrancy. Forced to leave town, the two flew to Washington, DC, where Hayden asked Assistant Attorney General Burke Marshall if vigilante forces were "outside the reach of the law." Effectively indicating that the federal government was powerless to stop those groups, Marshall feared that Bob Moses and civil rights activists would be murdered if they remained in Mississippi. In early December, after participating in a Freedom Ride, Hayden, Casey, and other SNCC activists were arrested after leaving the train station in Albany, Georgia, for "blocking the sidewalk" and "obstructing traffic."

In late December 1961, forty-five activists gathered in Ann Arbor to chart the future of SDS. Many were familiar with an article Hayden had written, "A Letter to the New (Young) Left," a response to C. Wright Mills's earlier suggestion in "Letter to the New Left" that intellectuals and students could become the new agents of change. Having devised the initial draft of "a political manifesto of the Left," Hayden headed for SDS's national convention in early June 1962. The Port Huron conclave resulted in the discarding of an exclusionary clause pertaining to "advocates of dictatorship and totalitarianism" that the LID, SDS's parent organization, retained. Attempting to placate LID, SDS declared itself "an organization of democrats," affirmed "opposition to any totalitarian principle" and denied admission to "advocates or apologists for such a principle." Nevertheless, LID soon withdrew all financial and logistical support for SDS. Hayden's influence over the student-based organization only continued in the fall of 1962, when he became SDS president.

Thanks to the influence of the *Port Huron Statement*, SDS began to make deeper inroads onto university campuses. Shortly after the Cuban missile crisis in October 1962, Hayden and Richard Flacks, a graduate student in sociology at the University of Michigan, initiated SDS's Peace Research and Education Project. All the while, Hayden failed to appreciate how unhappy Casey was. She found Ann Arbor, where the Haydens were now residing so Tom could set up an SDS headquarters and go to graduate school there, cold and sterile and was troubled by the affairs he had with other movement women. Within months, she returned to Atlanta to rejoin SNCC's campaign to transform the American South. The collapse of the Haydens' marriage proved unsettling to many of their friends; Bob Ross, another SDS leader at the University of Michigan, lamented, "that our seamless, loving, and romantic community was breaking up." Hayden remained in Ann Arbor, where he completed a master's thesis on C. Wright Mills. He pondered whether "the methods of SNCC" might be carried up north or if SDS, which at the time tended to draw most of its support from elite schools, particularly located in the east, in addition to the University of Michigan, would be relegated "to a vague educational role in a society . . . increasingly . . . deaf to the sounds of protest." To Hayden's delight, the United Auto Workers agreed to provide a $5,000 grant to SDS, enabling it in September to begin its Economic Research and Action Project (ERAP). Through ERAP, SDS hoped to organize the poor and the unemployed, with Hayden favoring the targeting of out-of-work young people. With several hundred ERAP members adopting a communal, indigent lifestyle, SDS ran ten inner-city projects in 1964. For three years, Hayden participated in the ERAP program in the black ghetto in Newark, New Jersey, a city largely run by white, liberal Democrats but saddled with Mafia-laden corruption in government circles. SDS's Newark Community Union Project triggered rent strikes, picketed units owned by slumlords, and held block meetings. However, SDS's "cult of the ghetto," as Haber referred to ERAP, proved short-lived, as city after city, including Newark in the summer of 1967, experienced race riots that some people attempted to blame on supposed outside agitators like Hayden. The FBI deemed him "a trained agitator" and "recommended that he be placed on the Rabble Rouser Index."

During this same period, SDS increasingly focused on events in Indochina, where U.S. involvement dramatically escalated following the assassination of President John F. Kennedy. Concerned about the passage, in August 1964, of a congressional resolution that apparently gave Kennedy's successor, Lyndon B. Johnson, something of a blank check to wage the war in Vietnam, SDS's Peace Research and Action Project directed more attention to the conflict there. In December, SDS's National Council, influenced by I.F. Stone's impassioned plea for young radicals to take a stand against the war, called for a mass march in Washington. On April 17, 1965, some 25,000 people gathered in the capital to protest U.S. engagement in Vietnam, the nation's largest antiwar rally up to that point. By now, new recruits—many, like Jeff Shero and thirty-year-old Carl Oglesby, from the heartland—viewed Hayden and the SDS Old Guard with suspicion, considering them too ideological, too intellectual, and too tied to the sectarian wars that had long afflicted the American left.

In the fall of 1965, Hayden joined radical historians Staughton Lynd and Herbert Aptheker on a trip to Hanoi, via a circuitous route through Prague, Moscow, and Beijing, thereby violating a State Department directive prohibiting travel to North Vietnam. In Hanoi, they met North Vietnamese prime minister Pham Van Dong and convinced communist leaders to allow *New York Times* correspondent Harrison Salisbury to visit Hanoi; Salisbury subsequently reported on the impact of American bombing on civilian targets in the North Vietnamese capital. The Justice Department considered prosecuting Hayden, Lynd, and Aptheker, but worried that a "furor" might result; in April 1966, the FBI placed Hayden on its Security Index. Along with Lynd, Hayden wrote *The Other Side*, which romantically extolled Vietnamese attempts to create "rice-roots democracy" and "a socialism of the heart." In speeches on university campuses across the United States, Hayden condemned the war. In 1967, Hayden and Lynd met with New York senator Robert F. Kennedy, whose charisma and increasingly critical stance regarding the Vietnam War impressed Hayden.

The antiwar movement continued to garner support as U.S. involvement in Vietnam—and the consequent casualty figures—increased, and the worst race riots yet occurred during the summer of 1967. Frustrated New Leftists spoke of the need to move from "protest" to "resistance." The left-wing journalist Andrew Kopkind reported, "To be white and a radical in America this summer is to see horror and feel impotence." This was when Hayden left Newark, the attempt to establish participatory democracy there having collapsed. Indeed, on July 12, 1967, Newark began experiencing a violent racial cataclysm that took the lives of twenty-four black residents. Hayden had recently suggested, "Urban guerrillas are the only realistic alternative at this time to electoral politics and mass armed resistance." In the pages of the *New York Review of Books* and a new volume, *Rebellion in Newark*, Hayden warned against "radical illusions about revolution" but also declared, "a riot represents people making history."

That fall, Hayden again traveled overseas, going to Bratislava, Czechoslovakia, where he joined with other American radicals, including the pacifist Dave Dellinger and SDS leader Rennie Davis, in speaking to North Vietnamese representatives. In Bratislava, Hayden saw something of the "Prague Spring," as communists and noncommunists alike undertook an ill-fated attempt to liberalize Czech society. Accompanied by Davis, whose father had been a top economic adviser to President Truman, and a handful of other antiwar activists, Hayden then traveled to Phnom Penh in Cambodia, Hanoi, Paris, and back to Phnom Penh, where he was informed in early November that the North Vietnamese government was releasing three American prisoners of war, the first to be freed.

As 1967 neared an end, Hayden and Davis attended a session of the National Mobilization to End the War in Vietnam, where activists discussed the impending presidential campaign. Wide-ranging differences were apparent, with Hayden believing that a massive protest at the next year's Democratic National Convention in Chicago could demonstrate "the power of the people." In January 1968, Hayden also attended the International Cultural Congress in Havana, Cuba. The following month, Hayden and Davis drafted a memo for the Mobilization to End the War, urging an "election year offensive." They called for "non-violent . . . legal" protest at the Democratic National Convention as a way to "delegitimate the Democratic Party while building support for an independent people's movement." The proposal to disavow violence angered many movement activists, including Youth International Party (Yippies) leaders Abbie Hoffman and Jerry Rubin, radicals with a heavy counterculture focus who envisioned a "Theater of Disruption" in Chicago.

On April 4, while conversing with W. Averell Harriman, longtime diplomat, former cabinet official, and one-time governor of New York, at the State Department, Hayden spotted parts of the nation's capital that had been torched in response to Martin Luther King Jr.'s assassination. Less than three weeks later, Hayden joined in the takeover of a series of buildings by white and black radicals at Columbia University. The campus chapter of SDS, headed by twenty-year-old Mark Rudd, condemned the Ivy League university for its complicity with the military-industrial complex that President Eisenhower had earlier criticized. The now twenty-nine-year-old Hayden raced to the Morningside Heights campus in New York City, where he joined Abbie Hoffman and others activists holding Mathematics Hall. After several days, the police moved to clear the occupied buildings, beating many protesters and arresting more than 700. One of those arrested, Hayden recast the words of Argentine revolutionary Ernesto "Che" Guevara, slain the previous year by the CIA-backed Bolivian army: "Create two, three, many Columbias."

Resuming his travels in support of mass action at the Democratic National Convention, Hayden again met Senator Robert Kennedy, who was running in the California presidential primary; Hayden expressed a readiness to work with Kennedy's people on planning antiwar demonstrations in Chicago. After Kennedy was assassinated on the morning of June 5, Hayden, with a beret from Castro's Cuba in hand, joined the journalist Jack Newfield in attending the funeral mass at St. Patrick's Cathedral in New York City. For Hayden, as for many others, the death of Senator Kennedy appeared to foreclose the possibility of peaceful change once championed by the New Left as a whole. Only days after the killing of the man who Hayden thought might bridge the chasm between indigent whites and blacks, SDS veered off in a far more radical direction.

That summer, with 540,000 American soldiers stationed in Vietnam, Hayden flew to Paris to help ensure the release of a number of American POWs. In the meantime, many activists rethought their original plans to show up in Chicago for the Democratic Party's national convention. They worried about the episodic violence rocking the nation and Chicago mayor Richard Daley's "shoot to kill" order during the riots that followed King's assassination. The newly elected president of SDS, Mike Klonsky—once a "red-diaper baby," born to communist parents—indicated, "whatever the politics of New Left oriented Hayden and Rennie Davis may be (it is still unclear to many of us), it probably doesn't even matter." The pacifist David Dellinger proved critical too, believing that Hayden and Davis "were strongly committed to the idea that in the long run the movement would have to move to violent resistance and armed struggle."

At the Democratic convention in August, fighting erupted in the streets of Chicago, resulting in what a presidential commission would later describe as a "police riot." Antiwar demonstrators hurled epithets, rocks, and bags filled with urine at the police, who sometimes appeared determined to beat anyone in sight, including innocent bystanders, journalists, and individuals associated with mainstream political candidates. Hayden wrote that the protesters were "forced into a military style not because we are 'destructive' and 'nihilistic,' but because our normal rights are insecure and we must be able to survive in the jaws of Leviathan." Condemning the "illegitimacy and criminality" of the Democratic Party, he charged that "a police state" appeared to be battling "a people's movement" in Chicago.

Hayden was arrested twice in Chicago, with both detentions resulting in warnings that he was going to be killed or sent "away for a long time." *Ramparts* magazine quoted him as declaring, "We can only call on free people everywhere to keep fighting in the open—in the parks and the streets—for the right to get together on their own terms." Out on bail, Hayden, semi-disguised with a fake beard and hat, returned to Grant Park, Chicago's most prominent downtown park, on Wednesday, August 28, the day Vice President Hubert Humphrey obtained his party's presidential nomination. Having watched the police beat Davis, an enraged Hayden urged a gathered throng to spread throughout Chicago to "turn this overheated military machine against itself. Let us make sure that if blood flows, it flows all over the city. If they use gas against us, let us make sure they use it against their own citizens." He told the *New York Times*, "We're going to create little Chicagos everywhere the candidates appear." In early November, Republican presidential nominee Richard Nixon, having promised a restoration of "law and order," narrowly defeated Humphrey.

In March 1969, Hayden, along with Davis, Dellinger, Hoffman, Rubin, Black Panther Bobby Seale, and two others, was charged with having conspired to kindle riots at the Democratic National Convention. The trial of the so-called Chicago Seven (a bound and gagged Seale ultimately had his case severed from the others), also known as the Chicago conspiracy trial, proved farcical in many ways, as Judge Julius J. Hoffman unprofessionally bantered with the defendants and their attorneys. In February 1970 the trial concluded and the judge delivered lengthy prison sentences for contempt of court, with Hayden handed a fourteen-month, thirteen-day sentence. Allowed to speak, Hayden declared that the system "does not hold together." Judge Hoffman admonished him, "Oh, don't be so pessimistic. Our system isn't collapsing. Fellows as smart as you could do awfully well under this system." The jury found Dellinger, Davis, Rubin, Hoffman, and Hayden guilty of incitement, but not of conspiracy. Released on bail, the defendants continued speaking out against the war and the system that allowed it to go on. On November 1, 1972, Hayden received word that the Seventh Circuit Court of Appeals, condemning the "demeanor of the judge and prosecutors," had overturned the convictions resulting from the Chicago Seven trial. In October 1973, Hayden returned to Chicago for another trial on the contempt charges; ultimately, he was cleared altogether.

Meanwhile, Hayden, advocating "free territories in the mother country" and "a new generation of American revolutionaries," saw the birth of Weatherman, a violent offshoot of SDS. Calling for bringing the war home and initiating urban guerrilla warfare, the Weathermen conducted the Days of Rage in early October 1969, shortly after the Chicago Seven trial began. Before the Weathermen undertook a rampage through the streets of Chicago's Gold Coast, Hayden, who had considered joining them, spoke through a bullhorn: "The conspiracy defendants send their greetings; we welcome any efforts to intensify the struggle." One of the leaders of the Weathermen, Bernardine Dohrn, urged Hayden to go underground, warning that he would be killed in prison.

Other troubling events both at home and abroad seemed to indicate that the early high hopes of the New Left and the counterculture had faded. In December 1969, the Rolling Stones' free concert at Altamont failed to recapture the seeming innocence of Woodstock, a high point of the counterculture where 400,000 congregated in the Catskills, located northeast of New York City; a number of women were raped and one man was murdered by the Hell's Angels, who were serving as dubious "security guards." In San Francisco, the sociopathic Charles Manson assembled a cult of drug-befuddled followers who, at his behest, murdered pregnant actress Sharon Tate and several others in the Los Angeles area. In December 1969, Dohrn applauded Manson's actions, while the Weathermen called white babies "pigs." That same month, Chicago police fired repeatedly into a Black Panther apartment, killing Fred Hampton and Mark Clark in what many in the New Left described as "police murders." In early March, three Weathermen died when a Greenwich Village townhouse blew up, destroyed by the bomb they were attempting to build as part of an urban guerrilla campaign. That spring, the United States expanded military operations in Southeast Asia with a massive incursion into Cambodia, leading to campus eruptions across the United States. National Guardsmen fired on antiwar protesters at Kent State University in Ohio on May 4, killing four, and police killed two students at Jackson State University in Mississippi ten days later.

Hayden joined an urban commune, the Red Family, near the University of California campus, where he soon endured lengthy consciousness-raising sessions in which he was denounced as a "politician" and accused of "male chauvinism." Hopping into his old Volkswagen convertible, a stunned Hayden moved to Venice, California, long a haven for bohemian types. By the fall of 1971, he was teaching a series of classes on Indochinese history at colleges and universities in the Los Angeles area. He purchased his first house, a two-story dwelling situated a block from the ocean in Santa Monica. On January 19, 1973, he married actress Jane Fonda, who was three months pregnant with their first child, Troy. Fonda was an antiwar activist who supported the Vietnam Veterans Against the War. Hayden and Fonda established the Indochina Peace Campaign, hoping to sustain the recently signed Vietnam peace accords. They traveled extensively around the country, demanding the termination of American military funding for Southeast Asia.

Increasingly, Hayden became drawn to mainstream politics, establishing "very close" ties to Jerry Brown, the newly elected governor of California. In 1976, Hayden ran against U.S. senator John Tunney, a liberal up for reelection. Hayden's late surge fell short, with Tunney prevailing by a 54–36.7 percent margin, with fringe candidates also picking up votes. Hayden then helped found the grassroots Campaign for Economic Democracy (CED, later known as Campaign California). The CED, emphasizing the need for rent control, took over the Santa Monica City Council and assisted scores of successful candidates in elections throughout the state. In 1982, Hayden was elected to the California state assembly and, ten years later, entered the state senate, where he served until term limits forced him from office. Hayden's legislative career was marked by controversy, with some legislators condemning him because of his radical past and others respecting his dedication to legislative responsibilities. He steadfastly championed progressive legislation intended to empower the powerless, including people of color, women, and sweatshop workers. Continuing to write prolifically, Hayden came to be admired for his work on behalf of environmental and academic issues. Dan Walters, political columnist for the *Sacramento Bee*, labeled Hayden "the conscience of the Senate." During the 1990s, he undertook unsuccessful campaigns for the governorship of California and the mayoralty of Los Angeles and, in 2000, narrowly lost a bid for a seat on the Los Angeles city council.

In 1990, Hayden and Fonda divorced; three years later, he married Barbara Williams, a Canadian actress. In 2002, the Haydens adopted a baby boy, Liam. Having successfully undergone open-heart surgery, Hayden worked as a professor at Occidental College and served as social science adviser for several public school districts in California, including the one in Venice. He also put out his own provocative Internet blog, offered radio commentary, and acted as codirector of No More Sweatshop!, a coalition of progressive groups demanding "enforceable labor standards for corporate behavior." He also served on the advisory board for Progressive Democrats of America, a grassroots organization determined to strengthen the progressive wing of the Democratic Party. As for many others drawn to the New Left, the demise of radical politics and the politics of the street did not signal the end of a life committed to activism for Tom Hayden.

BARRY GOLDWATER
Hero of the New Right

At San Francisco's Cow Palace on July 16, 1964, bespectacled, silver-haired Barry Goldwater presented a fiery speech before the Republican Party's national convention. Accepting the party's nomination as its presidential candidate, the fifty-five-year-old senator from Arizona refused to equivocate, condemning the liberal consensus and heralding the emergence of the New Right. Insisting that his movement was "dedicated to the ultimate and undeniable greatness of the whole man," Goldwater declared, "The tide has been running against freedom." The American people, he said, had "followed false prophets." The Republican Party, however, possessed "but a single resolve, and that is freedom."

Goldwater proceeded to condemn Democratic Party governance under John Kennedy and Lyndon Johnson, when freedom, as he saw it, had been heralded but not secured. He pointed to the Berlin Wall, the Bay of Pigs fiasco, difficulties in Southeast Asia, and the weakening of the NATO alliance. Such setbacks, the Republican Party presidential nominee claimed, resulted from "lost leadership, obscure purpose, weakening wills and the risk of inciting our sworn enemies to new aggressions and to new excesses." The Kennedy-Johnson administration was to be faulted, Goldwater continued, for ensuring that there stood "a world divided" and "a nation becalmed." At home, he stated, the American people endured "centralized planning, red tape, rules without responsibility and regimentation without recourse." In language strikingly similar to that employed by New Leftists, Goldwater referred to the "aimlessness" afflicting American youth and contended that Republicanism should ensure that "power remains in the hands of the people." Turning to the matter of the Cold War, Goldwater promised that he would not "let peace or freedom be torn from our grasp because of lack of strength, or lack of will." Closing, he defiantly thundered, "I would remind you that extremism in the defense of liberty is no vice. And let me remind you also that moderation in the pursuit of justice is no virtue." These words would come back to haunt him during the campaign, but Goldwater's ultimate impact on the course of American national politics would not become evident until many years after the Republican's ignominious electoral failure. Derided in 1964 as the voice of a reckless, extreme brand of conservatism, Goldwater would be vindicated in subsequent decades as his proposals found their way into the heart of the national political dialogue.

Barry Goldwater's grandfather, Michael Goldwasser, came from a family of observant Polish Jews, whom the Russian czar forced to reside in the Pale of Settlement. Emigrating to the Arizona territory in the early 1860s, he eventually established a thriving general merchandise store in Prescott, where his son Morris served as mayor before helping to found the Arizona Democratic Party and entering the state legislature. In 1896, Michael's other son, the fashion-conscious Baron, disinclined to practice the Judaism of his ancestors, began running Goldwater's Department Store that opened in Phoenix, emphasizing high-quality goods. Federal projects, including the Roosevelt Dam, spurred economic development in the region, making Phoenix a large, prosperous urban center and allowing Baron to offer his patrons "a Palace of Feminine Finery," which opened its door in late 1910. By that point, Baron had met and married Josephine Williams, a nurse who traced her family ancestry to the Puritan dissenter Roger Williams. Their first child, Barry Morris, arrived on January 1, 1909, in the Arizona territory.

Life for Barry and his two younger siblings proved comfortable, as the Goldwaters had a nurse, chauffeur, and maid in their spacious home. The Goldwaters became one of the leading families in Phoenix, with Baron and JoJo, who grew up a Presbyterian, joining the socially conscious Trinity Episcopal Church. Baron largely left the job of parenting to his wife, who had difficulty displaying affection; nevertheless, the children were fond of her, and she encouraged her eldest to hunt, fish, and camp out in the Arizona wilderness. "He was the first," she recalled, "so we tried to make him perfect," emphasizing self-reliance, community service, and honesty. An inadequate student, Goldwater frequently proved a disciplinary problem, leading his father to place him at the Staunton Military Academy in Virginia, where he encountered anti-Semitic barbs for the first time. During his junior year, influenced by a military instructor, Goldwater began to temper his rebellious streak. His grades improved and he became a fine athlete and popular student who was named the school's top cadet, guaranteeing acceptance to West Point. However, his father's poor health compelled Goldwater to return to Arizona, where he enrolled at the University of Arizona. Goldwater left school, where he was struggling academically, after Baron died in March 1929, leaving behind a substantial estate and a thriving business.

Soon joining the family store's management team, Goldwater also participated in various business and civic organizations, including the Chamber of Commerce, the Masons, the Shriners, and the Elks. A member of the elite Phoenix Country Club, he hobnobbed with powerful city figures, including the realtor Del Webb. Regretting his inability to attend West Point, Goldwater served in the U.S. Army reserve corps, becoming a first lieutenant in 1933. During his leisure time, he hiked, shot photographs of the Arizona countryside and Native American tribes, and logged time as a pilot. He courted Peggy Johnson, whose wealthy Indiana family was connected to the Warner Gear Company, which produced automobile equipment. The handsome couple married in 1934 and subsequently had four children. Peggy also proved active in community affairs, joining the Birth Control Federation of America (later known as Planned Parenthood) and helping to establish the Mothers' Health Clinic, which assisted Mexican American women.

The financial ravages of the Great Depression failed to affect the Goldwaters, who watched as federal money, tied to President Franklin Roosevelt's New Deal, poured into the state. Although federal largesse improved Arizona's economy, Goldwater viewed the New Deal and Roosevelt with disdain. In mid-1938, Goldwater, who remained enamored with former president Herbert Hoover, offered "A Fireside Chat with Mr. Roosevelt" through the pages of the *Phoenix Gazette*; the editorial condemned the "queer antics of those in Washington," blasting higher taxes, public spending, and labor "racketeering." Along with his brother Bob, who helped to run the family store, Goldwater favored their own system of paternal capitalism, which provided a forty-hour workweek, good wages, health coverage, access to company records, and recreational facilities.

Bored with the family business, Goldwater drank heavily at times and experienced bouts of depression, but increasingly acquired a reputation as a leading civic figure in Arizona. World War II seemingly rescued Goldwater, who became a captain in the U.S. Army Air Corps in mid-1942. Afflicted with poor eyesight and now thirty-three years old, he nevertheless was eventually stationed in India, from which he undertook perilous five-hundred-mile flights over the Himalayan Mountains to western China. In August 1944, Goldwater, already sporting gray hair, returned to a training unit in California, and in November 1945, he left the army air corps, having attained the rank of Lieutenant Colonel. Joining the Air Force Reserve, Goldwater helped to found the Arizona Air National Guard shortly after the war. Without any publicity, he also integrated the Arizona Air National Guard, for which he eventually served as a major general and its chief.

During the war, the federal government became more involved in the rapid development of the American Southwest, including Arizona, which acquired a series of military bases and defense-related businesses. The sunbelt experienced steady growth in the postwar period, as federal money continued to pour into the region, providing support for the mining, oil, and gas industries, along with agriculture, electronics, and aerospace. Notwithstanding the region's dependence on support from Washington, DC, Goldwater and other proponents of laissez-faire capitalism continued to chafe at federal restrictions, including labor legislation. Goldwater became a leader in the right-to-work campaign that condemned the closed shop and also served on his state's Colorado River Commission, which was involved in a struggle over water rights.

In late 1947, Mayor Ray Busey named Goldwater, to the Phoenix Charter Revision Committee, which called for a competent city manager and denounced government inefficiency. Subsequently, Goldwater won a seat on the city council, serving as vice mayor. In 1950, he helped elect Howard Pyle governor of the state, ending long-standing Democratic control, and increasingly aspired to higher office himself. In mid-1950, the family department store produced an advertisement warning that the "dark clouds of socialism . . . may roll across the American scene." Angered by President Harry S Truman's firing of General Douglas MacArthur, who had headed United Nations troops in the Korean War, Goldwater accused the president of "appeasement" and wondered if "poor judgment or . . . design" had produced a stalemate in the conflict. Damning Senator Ernest McFarland, the Democratic majority leader in the upper chamber, as he did the increasingly unpopular Truman, Goldwater initiated his own political campaign to replace McFarland in the U.S. Senate in September 1952. He blasted the purported domestic and foreign policy failings of President Truman, claiming that Roosevelt's New Deal and his successor's Fair Deal amounted to a "devilish plan to eventually socialize this country." Nevertheless, at this stage, Goldwater denied any determination to abolish a series of federal programs, including Social Security. He did accuse both the Roosevelt and Truman administrations of letting "communists . . . infiltrate into high places" and of having "sanctioned that infiltration." Wisconsin Senator Joseph McCarthy campaigned on behalf of Goldwater, who benefited from Dwight Eisenhower's landslide victory over Democratic Party presidential nominee Adlai Stevenson to eke out a narrow victory.

Goldwater welcomed the new administration's emphasis on nuclear deterrence and the seeming determination of the new secretary of state, John Foster Dulles, to liberate nations that had fallen under communist dominance. At the same time, Goldwater condemned French colonialism in Vietnam, Cambodia, and Laos and feared the United States might slide into another quagmire in Southeast Asia, in the fashion of the Korean conflict. He also disapproved of Eisenhower's apparent readiness to safeguard the welfare state, and he remained a stalwart ally of Joseph McCarthy even when sixty-seven senators voted in December 1954 to censure their demagogic colleague. Goldwater soon became chair of the Senate Republican Campaign Committee, establishing connections with conservative forces around the country and garnering national publicity. *Time* magazine produced a favorable article, "Jet-Age Senator with a Warning," and Goldwater began appearing regularly on national news programs, blasting labor unions and embracing private property, aggressive anticommunism, and restraints on federal power. He disapproved of Eisenhower's "modern Republicanism," which had resulted in basic adherence to the liberal consensus.

This disapproval was significant in a period when many distinguished political analysts, including Louis Hartz, suggested that liberalism of a mild variety remained the essential philosophy of the American people. Such a perspective did not appear to be at odds with Daniel Bell's pronouncement about "an end to ideology." Coming on the heels of fiery ideological struggles, such beliefs undoubtedly represented wishful thinking on the part of many American intellectuals, many of whom had once been committed radicals. Tempered by the Great Depression, internecine battles on the left, the ferocity of fascism, the excesses of communism, and the horrors of world wars, those intellectuals desired more placid times. However, the successful quashing of fascism failed to lead to halcyon days as a new struggle pitting East against West unfolded. Violent anti-colonial eruptions cropped up around the globe, while age-old fights to sustain ever-expanding national populations resulted in disastrously conceived policies, as in Mao Zedong's People's Republic of China.

For Goldwater, such developments only underscored his belief in American capitalism and democracy, provided they remained untainted by excesses involving the welfare state and government-sponsored encroachments on individual attainments. Such a perspective was hardly unique to Goldwater. In the very period when social analysts contended that conservatism was something of an alien philosophy in the United States, individuals like William F. Buckley Jr., Russell Kirk, and Milton Friedman were helping to build a new conservative movement. Like Goldwater, they hearkened to such works as Austrian economist Friedrich A. Hayek's *Road to Serfdom*, published in 1944, which contended that the New Deal, in the fashion of radical ideologies of the left and right, gravitated to "collectivism." In 1953, Kirk's *The Conservative Mind* argued that a distinct conservative tradition had indeed long been present in the American pantheon. Two years later, Buckley began publishing the *National Review*, a forum for right-of-center perspectives on domestic and international affairs.

During the later 1950s, the conservative movement branched out and became more militant, while Goldwater became known as a leading critic of the liberal consensus. Through the Senate Select Committee on Improper Activities in the Labor or Management Field, Goldwater particularly directed his ire at Walter Reuther, socialist head of the United Automobile Workers union. The year 1958 proved critical in many regards. Goldwater—backed by right-wing multimillionaires on the order of H.L. Hunt, a Texas oilman, and Robert Welch, founder of the John Birch Society—won a new term in the Senate although Republicans suffered a shellacking in national and state elections. Goldwater again received good press as the embodiment of the new

American West; *Newsweek* referred to him as a "statesman" who possessed "rare courage," and the *Saturday Evening Post* offered a piece on "The Glittering Mr. Goldwater." The *National Review* expanded its readership, along with *Human Events*, another right-wing publication. In December 1958, Welch established the extremist John Birch Society, which called for "less government and more responsibility." Goldwater, who had just become a brigadier general in the air force, affirmed that members of Welch's organization "are the finest people in my community, while Welch praised Goldwater highly: "He is absolutely sound in his Americanism. . . . I'd like to see him President of the United States."

A leading Bircher, Clarence Manion, dean of the Notre Dame Law School, urged Goldwater to produce a book heralding conservative tenets. Eventually, Manion got L. Brent Bozell, Buckley's brother-in-law, to ghostwrite *The Conscience of a Conservative*, which appeared in early 1960 and became a best seller, proving particularly popular on university campuses. The thin volume opened with the pronouncement "that to regard man as part of an undifferentiated mass is to consign him to ultimate slavery," the kind of statement Tom Hayden also produced, albeit from a different ideological vantage point. Wrongheaded liberals, Goldwater warned, had created "a Leviathan, a vast national authority out of touch with the people, and out of control." In contrast, conservatives sought to bring about "the maximum amount of freedom for individuals . . . consistent with the maintenance of social order." Goldwater championed states' rights, "our chief bulwark against the encroachments of individual freedom by Big Government." Although personally adverse to discriminatory practices, he contended that constitutional restrictions prevented the federal government from establishing policy involving education, such as the U.S. Supreme Court's decision in *Brown v. Board of Education of Topeka, Kansas* (1954) had apparently mandated. Goldwater closed his book by attacking U.S. foreign policy, urging instead "a war of attrition . . . to bring about the international disintegration of the Communist empire."

The success of *The Conscience of a Conservative* induced Manion to support a Goldwater presidential run in 1960, but Goldwater, recognizing that Vice President Richard Nixon had virtually cinched the nomination, demanded that conservatives demonstrate party unity. Speaking at the Republican National Convention in Chicago in July, Goldwater condemned the Democratic "blueprint for socialism," then exclaimed, "Let's grow up, conservatives." He continued, "If we want to take this party back, and I think we can someday, let's get to work." In early September, young conservatives, possibly emboldened by Goldwater's exhortation, gathered at the Buckley estate in Sharon, Connecticut, where they formed the Young Americans for Freedom (YAF), which soon issued the Sharon statement. Echoing Goldwater, the manifesto asserted that "among the transcendent values" was "the individual's use of his God-given free will." Liberty, the document indicated, was "indivisible," with political freedom requiring economic freedom. Government was designed to preserve internal order, provide for the national defense, and administer justice. International communism, the YAF warned, most endangered American freedoms.

The conservative movement proliferated in other ways, thanks to the right-wing radio ministries of individuals like Billy James Hargis and Carl McIntire, Fred C. Schwarz's evangelizing Christian Anti-Communist Crusade, and speakers on the order of Hollywood actor Ronald Reagan. No star loomed any brighter in the conservative pantheon than Barry Goldwater, who continued to receive plaudits from the mainstream press. A *Newsweek* cover featured him, "a handsome jet aircraft pilot with curly gray hair, dazzling white teeth, and a tan on his desert-cured face," while *Time* referred to him as the "hottest political figure this side of Jack Kennedy." In early 1961, following Kennedy's election, Goldwater offered a statement of conservative principles on the floor of the U.S. Senate, praising his "forgotten" and "silent" countrymen "who quietly go about the business of paying and praying, working and saving . . . meet their responsibilities on a day-to-day basis . . . (but) for too long, have had their voices drowned out by the clamor of pressure groups." For Goldwater, the silent Americans of the sunbelt and the American heartland, as well as the blue-collar families in the north, constituted "the Republican Party's natural constituency and future majority."

Like many on the right, Goldwater disliked the policies of the Kennedy administration, especially what he considered its tepid response to communism worldwide and support for civil disobedience as conducted by civil rights activists in the South. A small band of conservative stalwarts, led by William Rusher, F. Clifton White, and Congressman John Ashbrook, gathered in Chicago in October 1961 to devise plans to take over the Republican Party and orchestrate a presidential campaign for Goldwater, who feigned disinterest in that very possibility. Nevertheless, he maintained a high profile, writing *Why Not Victory? A Fresh Look at American Foreign Policy*, which came out in early 1962 and warned that Americans must thwart communist aggression. During the midst of the Cuban missile crisis, Goldwater recommended that President Kennedy "move on Cuba militarily."

The following year, it appeared increasingly likely that the 1964 presidential race would pit Kennedy against Goldwater, although the Arizona senator's press coverage had become more mixed. One interviewer, Stewart Alsop, who was writing a piece for the *Saturday Evening Post*, appeared stunned when Goldwater suggested the possibility of selling the Tennessee Valley Authority, a highly successful government-run operation dating back to the New Deal. Nor was Goldwater's image improved by his admission to Alsop, "You know, I haven't got a really first-class brain." Still, Kennedy and Goldwater evidently considered campaigning together to provide a clean-spirited discussion of issues that would enable voters to choose between a liberal and a conservative perspective. Kennedy's assassination on November 22, 1963, depressed Goldwater, who attended the slain president's funeral and determined not to continue his quest for national office.

Encouraged by conservative cohorts, Goldwater soon discarded his reticence, affirming on January 3, 1964, that he would seek the Republican presidential nomination. Asserting that he was no "'me-too' Republican," Goldwater declared, "I will not change my beliefs to win votes. I will offer a choice, not an echo." His campaign, however, soon foundered, thanks to his penchant for extreme or seemingly flippant statements. He proposed during a press conference that Social Security should be made voluntary, and he performed poorly on NBC's *Meet the Press*, suggesting the need to violate the recently drawn test ban treaty if that would benefit the U.S. militarily. He informed the West German periodical *Der Spiegel* that the commander of NATO should be afforded "great leeway" in deciding to use nuclear weapons and that "low-yield nuclear devices" could obliterate foliage shielding guerrilla forces in Vietnam. Such comments earned sharp criticism from the same media that had so recently idolized Goldwater, now seen as delivering simplistic interpretations of complex political and international events. Talk proliferated that an American brand of fascism might emerge if Goldwater were elected.

During the Republican Party's national convention in San Francisco, Goldwater did little to assuage such concerns. Although moderate forces inside the Republican Party attempted to rally around Henry Cabot Lodge, U.S. ambassador to South Vietnam; New York governor Nelson Rockefeller, himself politically wounded because of a recent divorce and remarriage; or Pennsylvania governor William Scranton, Goldwater won the nomination. Yet many Americans, including former president Dwight D. Eisenhower, were disturbed by the rhetoric of his oration: "Extremism in the defense of liberty is no vice. And . . . moderation in the pursuit of justice is no virtue." Hardly helpful was Goldwater's choice of a running mate, a right-wing congressman from New York State, William E. Miller. A campaign slogan, "In Your Heart You Know He's Right," appeared provocative, with its almost Freudian call to ideological arms. Equally unfortunate for Goldwater, he was running against

Kennedy's successor, Lyndon Baines Johnson, who had compiled an impressive record of his own involving civil rights and antipoverty legislation. The country appeared economically prosperous and the war in Vietnam had yet to become fully Americanized. Moreover, troubling incidents in the Gulf of Tonkin, involving the purported North Vietnamese attacks on an American destroyer and a retaliatory strike, caused many to "rally around the flag," providing Johnson with a decided bounce in the polls.

Johnson presented himself as a steady hand who would not send American boys off to fight in another Asian land war, while the Democratic Party portrayed Goldwater as hardly one to be trusted with the nation's nuclear capabilities. Goldwater soldiered onward, urging reduction of income taxes annually over a five-year period. Ecstatic crowds turned out in the Deep South, while Goldwater welcomed South Carolina senator Strom Thurmond's decision to bolt from the Democratic Party. Speaking in Chicago in mid-October, Goldwater, who had voted against the 1964 Civil Rights Act, defiantly stated, "It is just as wrong to compel children to attend certain schools for the sake of so-called integration as for the sake of segregation." He focused on social issues, condemning "wave after wave of crime in our streets and in our homes . . . . riot and disorder in our cities. . . . A breakdown of morals of our young people. . . . A flood of obscene literature."

Goldwater suffered a landslide defeat, receiving only 39 percent of the popular vote, although he captured several southern states in addition to Arizona. This result boded well for the future of the Republican Party in the South, indicating that Kennedy and Johnson's civil rights position was dampening white southerners' affection for the Democratic Party. Other telling signs, too little noticed at the time, also proved portents of American politics to come. Notwithstanding Goldwater's electoral shellacking, a million individuals contributed to his campaign, many offering only small amounts but proving loyal to the conservative cause. The Goldwater campaign had also attracted conservative leaders Jesse Helms, Phyllis Schlafly, and Ronald Reagan, all of whom proved instrumental in holding aloft the banner for conservative causes in the years ahead. Conservative activist Richard Viguerie established a direct-mail operation culled from lists of Goldwater supporters that would be turned to for future fund-raising efforts. Leading national publications saw the liberal tilt only and suggested that the conservative movement and possibly the Republican Party had suffered fatal blows. In fact, the seeds were planted for conservatism's regeneration and eventual triumph.

Temporarily out of office, Goldwater remained in the public limelight, regularly delivering speeches or columns that extolled conservative ideals.

As the war in Vietnam intensified, he urged the application of overwhelming air power and insisted that the generals be allowed to determine strategy. He viewed critics of the war disdainfully, calling for the resignation of Arkansas senator J. William Fulbright, then chairing televised hearings on the conflict. Goldwater watched with satisfaction as anger over the war and race riots at home produced Republican and conservative gains during the midterm election. In 1969, Goldwater returned to the Senate, where he took on the role of elder statesman. While remaining true to conservative principles, he supported solar energy, condemned environmental decay, temporarily backed the equal rights amendment for women, and even favored the legalization of marijuana. But he also backed the Pentagon's calls for more sophisticated military hardware and opposed passage of the 1973 War Powers Act, which sought to limit a president's prerogative to send American troops into action. Although long supportive of Richard Nixon as the Watergate scandal unfolded, Goldwater finally determined that Nixon had indeed engaged in a cover-up and should resign.

During the last half of the 1970s and the early 1980s, the New Right emerged as a major political force, drawing on many of the themes and tactics earlier employed by Goldwater or his campaign operatives. New Right proponents demanded sharp tax reductions, deregulation of business, a curbing of street crime, school prayer, an end to busing, and a staunch anticommunist foreign policy. They also used the direct-mail techniques that Goldwater's 1964 presidential run had helped to spawn. The presidency of Ronald Reagan, which became possible because of the ascendancy of the New Right, adopted many of the themes that Goldwater had long highlighted, championing supply side economics and a militant anti-Soviet posture. However, Goldwater was far less comfortable with the New Right's seeming insistence on legislating morality; rather, he considered the right to privacy as sacred. He also was enraged to discover that CIA director William Casey had failed to consult Congress—and had lied to Goldwater—about illicit covert operations in Central America.

In early 1987, Goldwater, who had recently suffered the death of his wife, left public office, having completed five terms in the U.S. Senate. Beset by depression, he remained revered as the single most important figure in the reenergizing of the conservative movement. Still, in the early 1990s, he again adopted maverick stances for a conservative, supporting abortion rights, a state holiday honoring Martin Luther King Jr., and gay and lesbian rights. On nationwide television, he reiterated his basic dictum, "Government should stay out of people's private lives." His spirits lifting after his marriage to Susan Schaffer Wechsler in 1992, Goldwater declared, "I've got one hell of a good life." In 1996, he suffered a stroke and the beginnings of Alzheimer's disease. He died at his home in Paradise Valley, Arizona, on May 29, 1998, at the age of eighty-nine.

Conclusion

Operating from opposite sides of the ideological spectrum, Tom Hayden and Barry Goldwater contested the liberal consensus that largely shaped American domestic and foreign policies by the 1960s. Each sharply criticized the liberal administrations of John F. Kennedy and Lyndon B. Johnson, hoping that a brighter day lay ahead for their country but fearing the worst. Indeed, although their dreams of a newborn America differed markedly, Hayden and Goldwater seemed to anticipate that the apocalypse was closer in coming than any new millennium.

Neither man was comfortable with the welfare state, with Hayden viewing it as a liberal palliative designed to prevent necessary revolt—nonviolent or otherwise—and Goldwater damning it as a coercive force that best served government bureaucracy and lethargy. Notwithstanding their ideological differences, they both disliked the bureaucracy associated with the welfare state, favoring a less top-down approach. Hayden pointed to the need for participatory democracy, and Goldwater favored diminished federal authority and strengthened state rights. Neither was comfortable with postwar U.S. foreign policy, although here their analyses were disparate. Hayden worried about a Pax Americana designed to suppress third world liberation movements, while Goldwater condemned the containment policy that appeared to guide U.S. policy makers, emphasizing instead the need for unrivaled American military strength that would help liberate countries from communist tyranny. The Vietnam War mirrored their differences, with Hayden often appearing to favor a triumph by the National Liberation Front the coalition group in South Vietnam backed by the communist government in Hanoi, whose guerrilla fighters were known as the Vietcong, and Goldwater demanding that military planners be allowed to pursue an aggressive strategy that would vanquish North Vietnam. While both remained politically active well into the late twentieth century, it was Goldwater's ideology that dominated the political discourse for the last quarter of that century.

Study Questions

1. The New Left emerged in the early 1960s. Compare and contrast the perspectives and methods of SNCC and SDS during the first half of the decade.

2. Tom Hayden is largely credited with drafting the *Port Huron Statement*. Analyze the key ideas presented in that document.
3. Barry Goldwater was a firm believer in limiting the role of government in the lives of Americans. Discuss the consistencies and contradictions in Goldwater's conservative philosophy.
4. Analyze Goldwater's role in the emergence of the New Right.
5. Both Hayden and Goldwater advocated citizen engagement. Examine the similarities and differences in their philosophies.

Selected Bibliography

Anderson, Terry. *The Movement and the Sixties*. New York: Oxford University Press, 1995.

Brennan, Mary C. *Turning Right in the Sixties: The Conservative Capture of the GOP*. Chapel Hill: University of North Carolina Press, 1995.

Gitlin, Todd. *The Sixties: Years of Hope, Days of Rage*. New York: Bantam, 1987.

Goldberg, Robert Alan. *Barry Goldwater*. New Haven: Yale University Press, 1995.

Goldwater, Barry M. *The Conscience of a Conservative*. Shepherdsille, KY: Victor, 1960.

———. *With No Apologies: The Personal and Political Memoirs of United States Senator Barry M. Goldwater*. New York: Morrow, 1979.

Goldwater, Barry M., with Jack Casserly. *Goldwater*. New York: Doubleday, 1988.

Hayden, Tom. *Reunion: A Memoir*. New York: Collier, 1989.

———. *Writings for a Democratic Society: The Tom Hayden Reader*. San Francisco: City Lights Books, 2008.

Himmelstein, Jerome L. *To the Right: The Transformation of American Conservatism*. Berkeley: University of California Press, 1990.

Hodgson, Godfrey. *America in Our Time: From World War II to Nixon—What Happened and Why*. Princeton: Princeton University Press, 2005.

Iverson, Peter. *Barry Goldwater: Native Arizonan*. Norman: University of Oklahoma Press, 1997.

Middendorf, William, and John William Middendorf. *Glorious Disaster: Barry Goldwater's Presidential Campaign and the Origins of the Conservative Movement*. New York: Basic Books, 2006.

Miller, James. *"Democracy Is in the Streets": From Port Huron to the Siege of Chicago*. New York: Simon and Schuster, 1987.

Nash, George H. *The Conservative Intellectual Movement Since 1945*. New York: Basic Books, 1976.

O'Neill, William. *The New Left: A History*. Wheeling, IL: Harlan Davidson, 2001.

Perlstein, Rick. *Before the Storm: Barry Goldwater and the Unmaking of the American Consensus*. New York: Hill and Wang, 2002.

Sale, Kirkpatrick. *SDS*. New York: Random House, 1973.

Unger, Irwin. *The Movement: A History of the New Left, 1959–1972*. New York: Dodd, Mead, 1974.

8

1968: The Hope and the Fear

Scholars of contemporary American history have struggled to find the words that adequately convey the magnitude of the crises that shook America in 1968, a year in which Americans, as one historian explained, "experienced too much history." Book and film titles have characterized 1968 variously as "the year that rocked the world," "the year the dream died," and "the year that shaped a generation." Historian Garry Wills succinctly captured the tone of that epochal year when he wrote, "There was a sense everywhere in 1968, that things were giving. That man had not merely lost control of his history, but might never regain it."

Several social and political currents came together that year to comprise a volatile whole. The civil rights movement began to divide over means and objectives as younger, often more militant voices challenged the leadership and direction offered by an older generation of activists committed to non-violence. The heated rhetoric of the new militants, questioning the utility of pursuing racial justice within a fundamentally racist society, inevitably stoked resentment and fear among white Americans. White backlash, fueled by a growing belief that costly federal social programs primarily benefited minorities, was fanned into tangible antagonism by ghetto rebellions that regularly swept urban centers by mid-decade. Years of inner-city violence and rising crime fed the anxieties of Middle America, which began to feel under siege. The blossoming counterculture was yet another source of social conflict. To most people in Middle America, the youth rebellion, born of a repudiation of

190

traditional values and morality, threatened to produce a younger generation committed to little other than self-indulgence under the guise of self-liberation. By the late 1960s, the excesses of the counterculture were matched by rising alarm among tradition-minded Americans who saw their society threatened by the new barbarians.

These tensions and others were folded into the increasingly acrimonious debate over the war in Vietnam, which ultimately overshadowed all other issues as of 1968. To many Americans, the conflict in Southeast Asia was a justifiable extension of the wider struggle to contain communism, a national commitment that demanded fulfillment. To a growing number of dissidents, however, the war was not only a strategic error but also a gross contravention of the nation's ideals. As the conflict continued, the more radical dissenters interpreted it as a symptom of the fundamental corruption of the American system. Politically, the Vietnam War was fatal for President Lyndon Johnson and catastrophic for the Democratic Party, which was shattered by fratricidal quarrels over the rationale for and morality of the conflict. The Democratic Party was, in many ways, a microcosm of the nation that year—the battle lines drawn between liberals and conservatives, young and old, black and white were as marked within the party as they were in American society.

Among the contenders for the Democratic Party's presidential nomination that year, New York senator Robert F. Kennedy emerged as a candidate promising a restoration of both party and national unity, which he believed was possible through rational discourse, tolerance, and inclusiveness. Those seeking hope, he argued, needed only to reflect on the nation's history. In the face of the greatest dangers, the American people had always overcome their differences and triumphed. Though often ambiguous about specific resolutions to difficult issues like the Vietnam War, Kennedy exuded a deep confidence in the basic goodness of the American character and the power of idealism. The crowds that flocked to his campaign rallies seemed proof of his potential to reunite the disparate constituencies of the Democratic Party and perhaps even the nation. Blue-collar workers, liberals, antiwar Democrats, blacks, Asians, and Hispanics mixed easily at Kennedy gatherings. His greatest challenge in winning the Democratic nomination would be in securing enough popular support to overcome the inevitable resistance of party officials opposed to his insurgent candidacy.

All of 1968's tensions were inevitably amplified by the political rhetoric generated by that year's presidential election. Seeking to capitalize on growing public anxieties, both Republican candidate Richard Nixon and American Party candidate George C. Wallace identified liberalism as the chief cause of the nation's many ills and offered instead conservative policies and the restoration of "law and order," a phrase that resonated with an alarmed electorate. Less restrained than Nixon, who sought to establish himself as a responsible conservative, Wallace built an astonishingly successful campaign around vitriolic denunciations of an intrusive federal government, welfare cheats, black rioters, hippies, and antiwar protesters. Practicing what one scholar terms "the politics of rage," Wallace evoked visceral emotions from his audiences of ethnic working-class whites, who regularly cheered his promises to institute extreme measures to restore order to the land. To many journalists who followed the Wallace campaign, the former Alabama governor seemed a dangerous demagogue, extraordinarily adept at exploiting the multitude of fears that had arisen by 1968. The very violence of his rhetoric, some surmised, fed the hot sentiments pervading the nation. Indeed, the violence hovering around the margins of American life took center stage in dramatic fashion on two occasions that year. On April 4, Martin Luther King Jr. was murdered on the balcony of the Lorraine Motel in Memphis, Tennessee. The death of the leading American apostle of nonviolence drove thousands of enraged and frustrated rioters into the streets of 125 American cities, some of which burned for days. Even before the country could absorb the meaning of King's murder, a second and equally incomprehensible tragedy occurred. In June, shortly after winning California's Democratic presidential primary, Robert Kennedy was fatally shot in the kitchen of the Ambassador Hotel in Los Angeles. His death, a historian later wrote, constituted the "murder of hope." Those assassinations were perhaps the most shattering events that defined 1968.

ROBERT KENNEDY
Herald of the New Politics

The year 1968 did not begin auspiciously for the United States. Years of rising racial tensions, urban riots, and expanding social protest movements had already divided the nation, and now the intensification of the Vietnam War further shook the country. In late January, that far-off conflict escalated sharply during the Tet Offensive, when communist forces launched a surprise attack across much of South Vietnam during the Vietnamese New Year celebration. The event seemed to cloud the assurances over the years by President Lyndon

Johnson's administration that the war was being won, and it induced New York senator Robert F. Kennedy to take the step he had hesitated over for nearly a year.

The forty-three-year-old Democrat had undergone a grueling personal odyssey in the years after his brother's assassination in 1963. Struggling to rebuild a world shattered by grief, Kennedy had fundamentally reexamined his faith, his values, and his ambitions in the dark months after John Kennedy was killed in Dallas. Most of Robert Kennedy's adult life had been given over to securing the political ambitions of his brother, which he had done with a single-mindedness that left him with a ruthless and calculating reputation. He had emerged from his soul-searching strengthened, convinced that he could give new purpose to his life. Having won one of New York's U.S. Senate seats in 1966, Kennedy committed himself to championing the cause of those who were relegated to the margins of American society. Social justice, he had come to believe, demanded that the plight of the poor and the racially oppressed be addressed immediately and comprehensively. Any insinuation that Lyndon Johnson's Great Society had not adequately met these needs was bound to raise the hackles of the president, an egotistical man who invariably responded to critics with vindictive wrath. Boding even worse for Kennedy's relationship with Johnson, which one historian aptly describes as involving "mutual contempt," the senator was among a growing number of congressional Democrats who had begun to question the administration's Vietnam policy. Three years of military escalation, Kennedy believed, had brought no discernible gains, but rather only rising casualties and the prospect of continued conflict. Torn between his growing doubts about the war and the potential political consequences of challenging his own president, Kennedy had hesitated perhaps overly long to voice his opposition. Democratic senator Eugene McCarthy had announced in late 1967 that he would challenge Johnson for the party's nomination, campaigning on a pledge to end the war. Now, with the 1968 presidential primary season looming, Kennedy was compelled to act.

On February 8, speaking in Chicago to the Book and Author luncheon, where the audience included important Democratic officials, Kennedy forsook the opportunity to discuss his new book *To Seek a Newer World* and instead addressed his remarks to recent developments in Vietnam. January's offensive, he declared, "finally shattered the mask of official illusion with which we have concealed our true circumstances, even from ourselves." There was no longer any reason to credit administration claims that victory in Vietnam was near. "Those dreams are gone," the senator proclaimed. He continued with a comprehensive assault on the premises of administration policy, arguing that the United States could not win a war that the South Vietnamese could not win for themselves and that the U.S. reliance on a military solution was wrongheaded. Finally, Kennedy rejected the idea "that the American national interest" was in any way conjoined with the survival of "the selfish interest of an incompetent military regime" in Saigon. He summarily dismissed the validity of the domino theory, long a justification for U.S. intervention in Vietnam. He went on to suggest that the conflict had to be viewed in a broader historical context if American policy makers were to understand that it was folly to seek to resolve the conflict through military means. "First the French and then the United States have been predicting victory in Vietnam," Kennedy observed. "Once in 1962," he conceded, "I participated in such predictions myself." But the time for illusion was over. "The best way to save our most precious stake in Vietnam—the lives of our soldiers—is to stop the enlargement of the war," he insisted. "The best way to end the casualties is to end the war." The speech marked a dramatic turning point in Kennedy's life. He had called for an end to the conflict that his brother had escalated. He had attacked the policies of a powerful and unforgiving Democratic president. And he had taken the first step toward a presidential campaign during one of the most volatile years in modern American history.

Robert Francis Kennedy was born on November 20, 1925, into a Boston family that was wealthy, influential, and, to a significant degree, dysfunctional. His father, Joseph P. Kennedy, was ambitious in the pursuit of wealth, social status, and political influence. After World War I, Joseph Kennedy demonstrated his business acumen in the stock market, real estate, and the film industry, acquiring two movie studios. More prescient than most, he liquidated his stock holdings before the crash of 1929, ensuring that his family was well insulated from the deprivations of the Great Depression. Profits from bootlegging liquor during Prohibition further enhanced his wealth. He had married Rose Fitzgerald in 1914, and though the couple eventually produced nine children, their marriage was little more than an uncomfortable arrangement. Joe was a shameless philanderer, often flaunting his infidelities before his wife. Rose responded by distancing herself emotionally from her husband and focusing on her expanding family. A stern disciplinarian, she discouraged emotional displays and often withheld her affections from her children. Kennedy spent his young years largely in the shadows of his older brothers Joseph Jr. and John, growing up among his sisters. Neither childhood nor adolescence was easy for Kennedy, who was undistinguished in his studies at ten different schools and established no lasting friendships. Having led privileged lives in an era of want during the 1930s, the Kennedy children also had the exceptional experience of living in London during their father's term as U.S. ambassador to Great Britain from 1937 to 1940.

Returning to the United States when his father was recalled from London, Kennedy drifted through a number of preparatory schools. Whereas his brothers Joe Jr. and John sought glory abroad in World War II, Kennedy had to be content with enrolling in the Navy's V-12 officer training program. In February 1946, he left the program and entered the U.S. Navy as a seaman, serving only through May, when he was discharged. Ironically, he sailed on the maiden voyage of the USS *Joseph P. Kennedy, Jr.*, a destroyer named in honor of his older brother, who died while serving in the European theater of war. His death was the first among a number of tragedies that the family endured during that decade. Kennedy's sister, Kathleen Kennedy Harrington, would die in a plane crash in 1948. John, who commanded a Navy torpedo boat in the Pacific, gained some minor acclaim when he heroically rescued several crewmen after his boat was rammed and sunk by a Japanese destroyer, and Joe Sr.'s political hopes were soon vested in his eldest surviving son. John mounted his first congressional campaign in 1946, greatly aided by his father's money and influence. Kennedy, enlisting as a campaign worker, proved tireless and politically adept as he walked Cambridge's wards, securing votes for his brother. Following John's election, Kennedy, again confronting the issue of his own future, enrolled at Harvard, graduating with a bachelor's degree in government in 1948. That September, he began studying law at the University of Virginia, graduating in 1951. It was during this period that he married Ethel Skakel. Though the couple enjoyed a mutually supportive relationship, Kennedy proved unwilling or unable to escape the pattern of adulterous behavior that his father had bequeathed to his sons, engaging in several extramarital affairs in subsequent years. Nonetheless, he and Ethel established a family that grew to include eleven children.

Since his childhood, when it became obvious that he would always be relegated to a secondary role in the family, Robert Kennedy had committed himself to defending the family name and prospects rather than advancing his own. In 1952, with a Justice Department position secured through his father's influence, he was urged to turn his talents to aiding John's U.S. Senate campaign. Once again, Kennedy deferred his own future to advance his brother's political career, working strenuously to assure John's victory over Republican Henry Cabot Lodge. Joe Sr. demonstrated little gratitude after the election, telling Kennedy, "You've got to get to work. *You* haven't been elected to anything." Nonetheless, Joe Sr. soon turned to an old family friend to gain advancement for his son. Republican senator Joseph R. McCarthy agreed to take Kennedy on as assistant counsel to the Senate Permanent Subcommittee on Investigations, then a chief instrument of the Wisconsin senator's red-hunting activities. Kennedy, often assigned to tedious research duties, found little to like about the job and resigned the position in July 1953. Still unfocused, he returned to the subcommittee in February 1954, this time as chief counsel to the committee's Democratic minority. As such, Kennedy played a minor role in one of the most dramatic political skirmishes of the decade when McCarthy's allegations of communist influence in the U.S. Army led to the Army-McCarthy hearings, which culminated with McCarthy's public humiliation. Though Kennedy coauthored a Democratic minority report that judged McCarthy guilty of "gross misconduct," his association with the controversial redbaiter proved embarrassing in the future.

When the Democrats regained control of the Senate in 1955, Kennedy remained as chief counsel to the permanent subcommittee and, the following year, participated in an often-contentious Senate select committee investigation into the alleged malfeasances of Teamsters boss Jimmy Hoffa. Despite Kennedy's obsessive efforts to see Hoffa convicted for labor racketeering, the defiant Teamsters chief was acquitted. Nonetheless, Kennedy had gained prominence as a national figure and won considerable admiration for his unrelenting pursuit of the slippery Hoffa. His efforts to chart a path for himself, however, came to an abrupt halt as the presidential election year of 1960 approached.

Aware of his reputation for ruthless efficiency, John Kennedy asked his brother to manage his 1960 presidential campaign. Kennedy's energies were once again poured into realizing his brother's political ambitions, and after John's victory, Kennedy was appointed attorney general in the new administration. Sensitive to allegations that he was unqualified for the job, Kennedy nevertheless dedicated himself to ensuring the success of his brother's presidency, running interference in difficult situations and serving as the president's closest adviser. The early 1960s were tumultuous years, testing the abilities of both the president and the attorney general, to whom the media increasingly referred to as RFK. As head of the Justice Department, RFK was often at the center of difficult confrontations between segregationist southern officials, civil rights activists, and a White House that feared alienating southern Democrats before the 1964 elections. In the course of frustrating negotiations with crude, manipulative racists like Mississippi governor Ross Barnett, RFK gained a fuller comprehension of the depth of southern racial animosity. Although the actions of civil rights activists often posed political difficulties for the Kennedy administration, RFK could not help but admire their moral courage.

Cold War crises brought additional challenges. The Bay of Pigs fiasco in

April 1961 infuriated Kennedy, leaving him all the more determined to ensure that his brother never again suffered such a humiliation. The vindictive element in Kennedy's character was evident in his organization of Operation Mongoose, a clandestine project to overthrow Fidel Castro, by assassination if necessary. Cuba was again the focus of concern in October 1962, when the discovery of Soviet missiles on the island produced a major international crisis. Kennedy revealed several sides of himself during the tense thirteen days that followed. Although he sometimes appeared impulsive and overly eager to endorse proposed air strikes on the island, his brashness was moderated by more deliberate judgments, and ultimately he was instrumental in formulating the compromise that broke the dangerous Soviet-U.S. deadlock. The war in Vietnam, however, posed seemingly endless difficulties for the administration. Kennedy steadfastly supported his brother's decisions to expand the U.S. role in the conflict, a position that caused an immense political dilemma for him in later years. Despite these controversies, President Kennedy seemed to have weathered the worst of the political storm by the fall of 1963. It was the president's concern about the upcoming 1964 election that took him to Texas in November.

President Kennedy's assassination fundamentally altered the direction of Robert Kennedy's life. Though a pillar of strength during the public ceremonies following his brother's death, Kennedy was devastated by the loss and was inconsolable for months. As he worked through his grief, he began an intellectual and spiritual quest that led him to reexamine, though not to reject, his Catholic faith. He turned to the tragic Greek poets and dramatists, from whom he took the idea that men's actions determined their destiny. In the years to come, this search for meaning also led him to the writings of French essayist and novelist Albert Camus, who argued that life was a sometimes seemingly futile struggle for which people must provide their own meaning. With his brother dead, Kennedy was compelled to address the question of his own ambitions. Though retained as attorney general, he was never comfortable in the new administration. Aware of Lyndon Johnson's visceral disdain for him, Kennedy resigned in 1964. Given time for reflection, he concluded that there were significant national issues that had not yet been adequately tackled. Convinced that he could effectively speak to those problems, he sought and won a U.S. Senate seat in New York in 1964. The exuberant rally crowds that jostled to get near him confirmed the resilience of the Kennedy magic. "These were people out of control, like pop-music crowds," wrote a *New York Times* reporter. "Here was Jack come back."

But Robert Kennedy did not desire to be "Jack come back." Finally free to chart his own political course, he addressed the issues of nuclear proliferation,

U.S. policy in Latin America, and, increasingly important, poverty in America. Kennedy believed that Johnson's Great Society programs had not adequately confronted the roots of the problem. These concerns were quickly overshadowed, however, by the shifting course of U.S. policy in Vietnam. Shortly after Kennedy had assumed his Senate seat in 1965, the top policy makers in the Johnson administration had decided to Americanize the conflict by sending more troops. By summer's end, 125,000 U.S. troops were committed to the Asian war. Aware of his vulnerability on the issue, given his support for his brother's Vietnam policies, Kennedy was hesitant to challenge administration policy, but he began by cautiously suggesting that U.S. objectives might be better gained by political rather than military means.

Not surprisingly, Johnson saw Kennedy's muted criticism as crass political opportunism and disloyalty. As the war expanded in scope, Kennedy's doubts increased, as did Johnson's suspicion that the New York senator was seeking to undermine his policies. Following a trip to Europe in early 1967, Kennedy was summoned to the White House to face an irate president, who had heard rumors that Kennedy had discussed a negotiated settlement of the war while in Paris. Johnson's ire quickly turned to threats as he warned Kennedy, "I'll destroy you and every one of your dove friends. You'll be politically dead within six months." Kennedy's careless talk about a political settlement, Johnson declared, gave aid and comfort to the enemy and the senator had, in effect, "blood on his hands." Stunned by the tirade, Kennedy replied, "Look, I don't have to take that from you" and walked out of the Oval Office. Several weeks later, Kennedy addressed the Senate chamber, urging that U.S. policy makers reevaluate the direction of the war.

Kennedy was not the first Democrat to question administration policy. In 1964, Senators Ernest Gruening and Wayne Morse had strongly voiced their concerns about the consequences of the Gulf of Tonkin Resolution, which gave President Johnson broad latitude in responding to events in Vietnam. In 1966, Arkansas senator J. William Fulbright had chaired committee hearings on the direction of the Southeast Asian conflict. In retaliation, President Johnson ordered the FBI to monitor Fulbright's phone calls. The growing rift within the Democratic Party over Vietnam prefigured broader internal divisions yet to be revealed.

When Robert Kennedy gave his February speech assailing administration policy in Vietnam, many of the dynamics of the 1968 election year were already evident. Abroad, the war in Vietnam had assumed an increasingly violent character, taking more American lives every day. At home, the consensus that had bound the nation together since the end of World War II was clearly unraveling, rent not only by division over the war, but also by rising crime, campus violence, racial polarization, and a growing perception that events were spiraling out of control. The fragmenting of the Democratic Party had already produced a candidate willing to challenge the sitting president. In November 1967, as Kennedy hesitated, still unsure of himself and wary of dividing his party and opposing an incumbent president, Minnesota senator Eugene McCarthy announced that he would enter the Democratic primaries in early 1968. Reserved and professorial in manner, McCarthy quickly became the standard-bearer for antiwar activists both within and outside the Democratic Party. Though far from charismatic, McCarthy had the advantage of the enthusiastic support of his generally youthful campaign workers. He won an astounding 42.2 percent of the vote in the New Hampshire primary in March, less than Johnson's 49.4 percent, but a clear indication that the president was vulnerable.

Hearing of these results, Kennedy feared that his indecisiveness had proven politically fatal. "I think I blew it," he confided to an aide. Yet he soon found justification to announce his candidacy. President Johnson had rejected proposals for a commission to reevaluate Vietnam policy, and it appeared that the war would continue to escalate. The war also diverted attention from still pressing racial issues at a time when a continuing succession of inner-city rebellions provoked white backlash, even on the part of the president. Johnson's dismissal of the Kerner Commission Report on urban riots, which concluded that racial polarization was dividing America into "two societies, one black, one white—separate and unequal," was a major factor in Kennedy's decision to run. Thus, on March 16, only days after McCarthy's New Hampshire success, Robert Kennedy announced his candidacy. "I do not run for the presidency merely to oppose any man," he declared, "but to propose new policies. I run because I am convinced that this country is on a perilous course and because I have such strong feelings about what must be done, and I feel that I'm obliged to do all I can."

Although many Americans were thrilled at the prospect of a Kennedy candidacy in 1968, the senator still had many detractors. Much editorial comment across the nation denounced Kennedy's candidacy as opportunistic and self-serving. Many in the McCarthy campaign likewise viewed Kennedy's belated announcement as evidence of his unwillingness to challenge the administration until he was certain of Johnson's vulnerability. Equally troubling, a Kennedy candidacy could well split antiwar Democrats, who faced an uphill battle at the upcoming national convention. The Johnson White House immediately launched a campaign to undercut Kennedy, depicting him as disingenuous and self-serving. Johnson's own political viability, however, was eroding with each passing week. Earlier in the year, one of the chief architects of the country's Vietnam policy, Robert McNamara, distraught over the course that the war had taken, had resigned as secretary of defense. His successor, Clark Clifford, had arranged for a meeting of the "Wise Men," the influential elder statesmen who in 1967 had advised Johnson to stay the course in Vietnam. Now, in the aftermath of the Tet Offensive, the "Wise Men" counseled Johnson to seek an end to the conflict. Though stunned and suspicious, Johnson realized that his political position was untenable. On March 31, in a televised speech in which he offered hope of new negotiations to end the war, the president announced that he would not seek reelection. Johnson's withdrawal transformed the political dynamics of 1968 and presented Robert Kennedy and his supporters with new prospects and challenges.

The chief challenge was in devising an appeal that might pull together the disparate threads of a rapidly fraying Democratic Party. The Vietnam controversy was only the most prominent of numerous issues that threatened to fatally divide the party. Many southern Democrats, never comfortable with their party's willingness to use federal authority to end segregation and ensure the rights of black Americans, were increasingly resentful over what they perceived as special benefits for minorities. Southerners also lamented the breakdown of "law and order" and the assaults on traditional social conventions by youthful rebels. Nor were southerners alone in these concerns. Among other Democratic constituencies, such as urban blue-collar workers, northeastern ethnic groups, and farmers, all of whom had generally supported Democratic economic policies since the New Deal, there was growing concern about social disorder, coupled with worry that the Democratic Party was forsaking their interests for the causes of new special interest groups. Their own party, many historically Democratic constituencies worried, seemed overly tolerant of social protest and the "new morality," which was dismissive of traditional restraints and values.

Kennedy's strategy for victory rested on uniting traditional Democratic constituencies with newer ones and winning his party's nomination through the "new politics." This meant sidestepping the traditional nomination process of winning over party managers, influential Democratic office-holders, and leaders of powerful interest groups such as organized labor. Instead, Kennedy would take his campaign directly to the Democratic electorate through state primaries, allowing voters, not party bosses, to pass judgment on his candidacy. Kennedy's relative youth, charisma, and ability to effectively communicate would be important advantages in this type of campaign. He was confident that he could direct the electorate's focus to issues of social and economic justice, thus appealing to the sometimes-antagonistic elements of a shaky Democratic coalition. His criticism of the Vietnam War would be aimed at the failed policies that placed America's sons in unnecessary jeopardy in defense of a corrupt Saigon regime. Kennedy was not averse to appealing to Americans' passions or to employing his charismatic appeal. As a Kennedy campaign official explained, "Our strategy is to change the rules of nominating a president. We're going to do it a new way. In the streets."

On the campaign trail, Kennedy proved willing to take provocative stands on controversial issues. Two days after he entered the race, in an address to students at Kansas State University, he delivered a withering assault on Johnson's Vietnam policies. The president's "only response to failure," Kennedy declared, was "to repeat it on a larger scale." "I am concerned that at the end of it all," he concluded, "there will only be more Americans killed; more of our treasure spilled out; and because of the bitterness and hatred on every side in this war, more hundreds of thousands of Vietnamese slaughtered." The American legacy in Vietnam, he feared, would mirror Tacitus's description of the Roman way of war: "They made a desert, and called it peace." Kennedy's rhetorical eloquence and presence gave energy to his campaign, but the year brought a succession of unforeseen developments that compelled frequent reevaluations of strategy. President Johnson's announcement that he would not run for reelection deprived Kennedy of a major issue, as the administration now seemed receptive to a political settlement in Vietnam. Increasingly, Kennedy focused on issues of economic and social justice as he sought to build a coalition that would transcend the racial, cultural, and class boundaries that had hardened by the late 1960s. On April 4, Kennedy was standing before an audience in Indianapolis, Indiana, when he was apprised of Martin Luther King Jr.'s assassination. It fell to Kennedy to inform the largely black campaign crowd that the leading advocate of nonviolence had been murdered by a white gunman. In an unsteady but moving extemporaneous speech, Kennedy urged the crowd of 2,000 not to resort to violence. In the days to come, as riots broke out across the nation, Indianapolis remained quiet. In the aftermath of King's murder, Kennedy more frequently stressed the need for social justice in American life. Even before he had announced his candidacy, he had demonstrated a growing concern for disadvantaged minorities, meeting in California with Cesar Chávez, head of the United Farm Workers, a union that represented mostly Hispanic migrant laborers. Their quest for equitable treatment by the powerful growers was the type of cause that increasingly gained the senator's support.

Another major issue was the tenacious poverty that still gripped parts of America. Earlier in his senatorial career, Kennedy had witnessed the appalling poverty of Mississippi sharecroppers and the inner-city residents of the Bedford-Stuyvesant section of New York City. He believed that a nation as wealthy as the United States should demonstrate a greater commitment to the disadvantaged. While that issue appealed to constituencies such as disadvantaged minorities and the poor, Kennedy recognized the need to balance it with expressions of support for "law and order" issues when speaking to predominantly white, ethnic, blue-collar audiences. It was imperative that he capture these traditional Democratic constituencies if he were to wrest his party's nomination from Vice President Hubert H. Humphrey, who entered the race as the administration candidate in late April, too late to run in the primaries.

As spring wore on, Kennedy demonstrated his political strength in a number of primaries, consistently showing greater popularity than Humphrey stand-ins and defeating McCarthy in Indiana and Nebraska. Kennedy's political fortunes seemed to be improving as the Oregon primary approached in late May. That election proved a setback, however, when McCarthy won a clear victory, making the California primary on June 4 all the more crucial to Kennedy's campaign. The winner would gain 174 delegates for the Democratic National Convention in Chicago, scheduled in August. The Kennedy campaign maintained a frenetic pace in order to cover the huge state. The senator met McCarthy in a televised debate on June 1. Follow-up polls suggested that Kennedy had easily bested the laconic McCarthy, and indeed, when the primary votes were tallied, Kennedy had defeated the Minnesota senator by 46.3 percent to 41.8 percent. Kennedy had won six of the seven primaries that he had entered. Though his party's nomination was far from assured, he now had reason to believe that he could mount a credible challenge against Humphrey at the national convention in August.

The official vote count was almost finished when Kennedy entered the ballroom of the Ambassador Hotel in Los Angeles to address his exuberant supporters. His message was one of healing and unity, expressing his faith in the fundamental goodness of the American people. "I think in the end we can end the divisions in the United States . . . we can work together in the last analysis," Kennedy affirmed. "The divisions, whether it's between blacks and whites, between the poor and the more affluent, or between the age groups, or over the war in Vietnam—we can start to work together again. We are a great country, an unselfish country, and a compassionate country. And I intend to make that the basis for my running over the period of the next few months." Concluding, "It's on to Chicago, and let's win there," the senator waved, gave the V-for-victory sign (or was it the peace sign?) and turned to exit through the kitchen.

Moments later, as Kennedy worked his way through the crowded kitchen, five pistol shots rang out and he fell to the floor. Horrified bystanders wrestled his assailant, Sirhan Sirhan, a young Palestinian, to the ground. Later, Sirhan stated that he had shot Kennedy because of the senator's support for Israel. Word of the shooting produced pandemonium in the ballroom when Kennedy's stunned supporters learned that their candidate had become the latest victim of a very violent year. Kennedy died the next morning and with him, in the minds of many, the hope that civility and unity might be restored in a badly battered nation. President Johnson, shaken by the event, offered a thoughtful public eulogy, but privately described Kennedy's death as "too horrible for words." As the senator's funeral train traveled from New York City to the nation's capital, thousands of people spontaneously gathered along the route to stand in silent witness.

The death of the man marked the beginning of the myth, and many of Kennedy's anguished supporters were convinced that, but for Sirhan's irrational act, Robert Kennedy would have gone on to inevitable triumph at the Democratic convention in August. A second Kennedy presidency, some maintained, might well have brought the tranquility, unity, and healing that the nation so desperately needed. Others argued that would have brought an end to the war in Vietnam, saving countless lives. This scenario was at best improbable. Kennedy's claim to the Democratic nomination was by no means assured by his primary victories; his party was still in the hands of Lyndon Johnson, whose convention managers could have been expected to do everything in their power to deny Kennedy the nomination. Even had Kennedy triumphed and defeated Republican candidate Richard Nixon in the national election, the problems facing a Kennedy administration would have been no less resistant to resolution than they subsequently proved to be for Nixon. The public romance with Robert Kennedy grew quite understandably from the despair that attended unrealized hopes. The redeemer was dead and, for many, any hope for national redemption seemed to recede beyond reclamation. Internally weakened by the travails of 1968, the Democratic Party was entering a lengthy era of declining electoral strength, battered by the conservative impulses unleashed that year. Even then, as the hopes that Kennedy had raised faded, other forces driven by far different passions were gaining momentum in a campaign that was shaking the foundations of national politics.

GEORGE C. WALLACE
Practitioner of the Politics of Rage

Many of the journalists assigned to cover the presidential campaign of third-party candidate George C. Wallace in 1968 noted the intense sentiments that the former Alabama governor's fiery rhetoric seemed to unleash. Richard Stout, columnist for the *New Republic*, was alarmed by the seething anger he perceived at a Wallace rally at New York City's Madison Square Garden in October. "There is menace in the blood shout of the crowd," Stout reported. "You feel you have known this all somewhere; never again will you read about Berlin in the 30's without remembering this wild confrontation here of two irrational forces." Wallace was, Stout declared, "the ablest demagogue of our time, with a bugle voice of venom and a gut knowledge of the prejudices of the low-income class." A writer for the *Washington Post* concurred, noting that Wallace had "found a way to translate the raw racism of Alabama politics into a potent expression of the uncertainties, discontents and hates of millions of Americans." The Wallace phenomenon, some warned, might well be the harbinger of a uniquely American form of fascism. It mattered little, as other correspondents observed, that the candidate himself lacked the slickly polished media image that the major party candidates, especially Republican Richard Nixon, sought to fashion that year. Journalist Theodore H. White was among those who found Wallace both crude and sinister. "Occasionally he would run a comb through his sleek, glossy hair," White observed. "His close-set eyes were shrunken into deep, dark hollows under the great eyebrows. He was a very little man." Historian Garry Wills uncharitably described Wallace as having "the dingy attractive air of a B-movie idol, the kind who plays a handsome garage attendant." But in 1968, George Wallace's physical attributes and alleged crude manners were of little concern to his supporters. They filled arenas and high school gymnasiums across the country to hear his message, the subtext of which was largely lost to the cosmopolitan journalists and historians who saw only a dangerous demagogue. His was the voice of the "angry white man," a political force that found dramatic expression in Wallace's "Stand Up for America" campaign and established itself as an enduring, dynamic factor in national politics.

George Corley Wallace could honestly lay claim to a working-class background, having been born on August 25, 1919, to a farming family in rural Clio, Alabama, a cotton-belt town. His father, George Wallace Sr., and mother, Mozell Smith Wallace, struggled to make a living in an impoverished state made poorer by the Depression, circumstances that largely shaped George's early years. Though a short five-feet-six in height and weighing about ninety-five pounds in his teens, George possessed the aggressiveness requisite to boxing and eventually became the state Golden Gloves bantamweight champion. Contemporaries confirm that from an early point his passion was politics, and he managed to win appointment as a page in the state legislature. In young George's Alabama, as in the rest of the Deep South, the Democratic Party had dominated since the end of Reconstruction, establishing white supremacy in all areas of public life. Wallace unquestioningly embraced this political heritage as he made his entrée into public life, and he was determined to defend it. He later remembered that on his first day in the capitol he stood on the bronze star that marked the spot where Jefferson Davis had assumed the presidency of the Confederacy in 1861: "I knew I would return to that spot. I knew I would be governor." His path to politics diverged temporarily in 1937 when he enrolled at the University of Alabama, where his interest in student and state politics far exceeded his dedication to academics. Nonetheless, Wallace graduated with a law degree in 1942, the same year he met Lurleen Burns, whom he married shortly after his induction into the U.S. Army Air Force. Eventually trained as a flight engineer, Wallace flew combat missions on B-29 bombers out of the Mariana Islands in the Pacific before being discharged in 1945.

Wallace's first foray into politics began only months later when he convinced Alabama governor Chauncey Sparks to employ him in the state attorney general's office. Wallace took a leave of absence only three months later to run for the state legislature. His successful 1946 campaign paralleled that of gubernatorial candidate James "Big Jim" Folsom, who won election as a populist Democrat. Folsom's campaign stressed political democracy and economic justice and, in contravention of Alabama tradition, rejected appeals to racism. As a neophyte Democratic legislator, Wallace was drawn to the earthy Folsom, whose support for improved public services made him a major force in the state. Wallace left the legislature for the state circuit court in 1950 and was on the bench when the consequences of the 1954 Supreme Court decision *Brown v. Board of Education of Topeka, Kansas* began spilling into Alabama politics. Folsom's moderation on the race issue was now a liability, and Judge Wallace quickly moved to distance himself from the besieged governor, publicly promising to block FBI efforts to investigate discriminatory grand jury selection in the state. Deftly bringing together two themes that served him repeatedly in coming years, Wallace reassured white Alabamans that he would not permit an intrusive federal government to determine the racial composition of their juries. Such a "gross violation of *State Sovereignty*," Wallace proclaimed, was "illegal" and if the FBI persisted in its "Gestapo methods," he would have its agents arrested and jailed.

It was the first public shot in George Wallace's long rhetorical war against the national government, which many southerners now saw as a threat to their way of life. As the concept of massive resistance to federally mandated integration swept the South, the region's political landscape shifted rapidly. Folsom, constitutionally barred from a second term and disgraced by public drunkenness and corruption charges, was denounced as "too liberal" on the race issue. The 1958 governor's race was thrown open and Wallace, sensing opportunity, entered the contest. Much to his surprise, he was blindsided on the race issue by John Patterson, the state attorney general, whose blatantly racist campaign stressed his success in legally crippling the NAACP in Alabama and implied that Wallace, a former Folsom supporter, was soft on defending segregation. Decisively defeated, Wallace absorbed a valuable lesson from the campaign. "Well, boys," he confided to a group of supporters on the day of his defeat, "no other son-of-a-bitch will ever out-nigger me again." Wallace was quick to realize that resistance to integration and civil rights could be cloaked in the rhetoric of states' rights and opposition to federal "tyranny." In 1962, these themes ensured that Wallace did in fact return to Montgomery as governor, having won more votes than any Alabama governor to that date. At his inauguration in 1963, Wallace spat out the creed that he came to embody. "I draw the line in the dust," he announced to cheering supporters, "and toss the gauntlet before the feet of tyranny, and I say, 'Segregation now, segregation tomorrow, and segregation forever!'"

The state that George Wallace now governed had a well-deserved reputation for violent resistance to integration and black civil rights. In previous years, civil rights activists had been routinely brutalized, often with the connivance of local police. A continuing series of dynamite bomb attacks on black-owned buildings and homes in Birmingham had won the city the nickname "Bombingham." The violence escalated under Wallace, whose loud denunciations of federal authority and provocative public declarations encouraged official and vigilante brutality against blacks. In April, Birmingham police commissioner Eugene "Bull" Connor's police turned high-pressure fire hoses and police dogs on peaceful black demonstrators, including many schoolchildren. Though much of the nation was horrified and shamed when the brutality was televised on the evening news, Wallace remained defiant. In June, he carried out his campaign promise to "stand in the schoolhouse door" to block integration at the University of Alabama, where two black applicants sought admission. In a carefully stage-managed event, Wallace stepped aside only after denouncing the illegality of the federal government's enforced integration of the university. Only weeks after Martin Luther King's March on Washington in August, the volatile mood in Alabama was made manifest when a bomb destroyed a black church in Birmingham, killing four young girls. Much of the national press ascribed the murders directly to Wallace's frequent endorsements of white resistance. Martin Luther King Jr. alleged that the Alabama governor's hands were "dripping with blood" and that Wallace was "perhaps the most dangerous racist in America today." His genius, the civil rights leader observed, was to focus on a few simple but compelling themes in his stock speeches: federal tyranny, liberal judges, states rights, and law and order. "He works on them and hones them so that they are little minor classics," the civil rights leader observed.

By 1964, Wallace was the acknowledged champion of southern resistance to federal integration policies and federal protection of civil rights. That summer, he was a featured speaker at the Patriots' Rally Against Tyranny held in Atlanta and presided over by Georgia governor Lester "Pickhandle" Maddox. Wallace presented himself as a spokesman for truth, which he claimed was being suppressed by a national media "run and operated by leftwing liberals, Communist sympathizers and members of the Americans for Democratic Action and other Communist front organizations." The fiery Alabaman denounced the recently passed Civil Rights Act of 1964 as "straight out of the *Communist Manifesto*." A liberal Supreme Court, he alleged, had chiefly served the interests of "convicted criminals, Communists, atheists, and clients of vociferous leftwing minority groups." Though such sentiments had become common fare in southern rhetoric, Wallace perceived that there was a growing national audience that was receptive to such themes. The governor tested his national appeal in three Democratic primaries that year and was gratified by the results: he garnered 33.9 percent of the vote in Wisconsin, 29.9 percent in Indiana, and 42.7 percent in Maryland. Though he ultimately conceded the conservative cause to Republican standard-bearer Senator Barry Goldwater and withdrew from the race, it was clear that there was a potential constituency for a conservative candidate willing to challenge the basic precepts of liberal, activist government. Though routed almost everywhere else, Goldwater had carried five Deep South states, an early indication of the major shift in national politics that was on the horizon.

Sensing that his particular abilities and command of the issues might prove a highly effective combination in the volatile political climate of the late 1960s, Wallace began to lay the foundations for a presidential campaign in the fall of 1967. He had already resolved a potentially troublesome political problem—he was constitutionally barred from running for governor again in 1966. Having failed in 1965 to secure a constitutional amendment permitting him to run again, Wallace persuaded his reluctant wife, Lurleen, to run as a stand-in for him. She won handily, and in the months between her January 1967 inauguration and her death from cancer in May 1968, Lurleen acted as George's surrogate in the governor's office and served as the figurehead of his Stand Up for Alabama campaign. With his political base secured, Wallace devoted his energies to organizing a third-party campaign, no small task in a nation in which the two-party system generally doomed such efforts to abject failure. Wallace, like most southern politicians in the 1960s, was at best a nominal Democrat. While southern Democrats had in the past often supported their party's economic populism, few could abide the liberal direction that Democratic social policy took in the Kennedy and Johnson years, much less the growing willingness of both administrations to use federal power to implement changes in racial relationships. Wallace's political genius was to perceive that the popular resentment generated by these policies and their consequences was not restricted to the South, but had become national in scope. In 1968, the sentiments behind Wallace's earlier Stand Up for Alabama campaign could easily be turned to the service of a Stand Up for America movement.

It had become evident early in 1968 that there was significant grassroots support for a Wallace candidacy. The first challenge was to organize a national campaign, which required getting Wallace and his party, generally known as the American Independent Party, on the ballot in all fifty states. Indicative of the enthusiasm that the Wallace candidacy generated, thousands of volunteers offered their time in signature-gathering drives, and by the fall of 1968, Wallace's name was added to the ballot in the fiftieth state, Ohio. Prior to June, however, the Wallace phenomenon appeared to be little more than a sideshow. Only after Kennedy's assassination in early June did the Alabama governor's polling numbers begin to rise, moving into low double-digits. Some commentators later attributed this rise to a growing national perception that events were dangerously out of control. By early summer, the Wallace campaign had established a rhythm that provided surprising momentum. Traveling about the country in a loud, smoking, obsolete four-engine propeller-driven aircraft, the candidate clearly lacked the financial underpinnings that major party candidates enjoyed. Wallace, however, self-consciously aimed his appeal at the "little man," that archetypal working-class or lower-middle-class American who felt that the government, in its rush to meet the demands of undeserving minorities, had forsaken his interests. In many ways, Wallace targeted the same groups that Richard Nixon would later refer to as the "Silent Majority"—hardworking, taxpaying Americans who loved their country, attended church, did not protest, and never asked for special favors. This large, amorphous group, Wallace realized, nurtured deep resentments against those whom he identified as the source of the nation's ills: the welfare cheaters, black militants, antiwar protesters, dope-smoking hippies, liberal judges who strengthened criminal rights, and faceless federal bureaucrats. His success as a candidate was contingent on his ability to effectively speak to these resentments and convince his audience that he alone had the courage to voice the hard truths and take the necessary corrective measures. In an interview with journalist James J. Kilpatrick, Wallace demonstrated his mastery of the rhetoric of populist rage. Asked about the issues of 1968, Wallace was quick to respond. "Schools, that'll be one thing," he asserted. "By the fall of 1968, the people of Cleveland and Chicago and Gary and St. Louis will be so goddamned sick of federal interference in their local schools, they'll be ready to vote for Wallace by the thousands." Another issue, he declared, would be "law and order." "The people are going to be fed up with the sissy attitude of Lyndon Johnson and the intellectual morons and theoreticians he has around him," Wallace sneered. "They're fed up with a Supreme Court [that is] a sorry, no-account outfit." Wallace was unequivocal about the divisive conflict in Vietnam: "I think we got to pour it on. We've got to win this war."

On the campaign trail, Wallace established a pattern that was repeated at almost all his rallies, whether they were held in arenas, civic centers, or strip malls and regardless of region. Preceded by patriotic band music, Wallace's appearance often coincided with a rendition of "Dixie," inevitably provoking an enthusiastic response from expectant crowds. Once on the podium, he alternately glowered, snarled, and mocked as he recited a litany of federal misdeeds and liberal failures that had brought the nation to its current sorry state. He readily identified those responsible: "bearded Washington bureaucrats," "pointy-headed intellectuals who couldn't park a tricycle straight," and "intellectual morons." Wallace's proposed solutions were as improbable as they were unequivocal. Once elected, he proclaimed, protesters would be dealt with summarily. "If any demonstrator lies down in front of my car when I'm president," Wallace often promised, "that'll be the last car he lies down in front of! Just try me and see!" Alternately, he vowed that troublemakers would be "drug before the courts by the hair of their heads and thrown under a good strong jail." For those who still insisted on disturbing the public peace, "a good crease in the skull" from a police baton was the proper corrective. It might be beneficial, Wallace maintained, to simply "turn the country over to the police for two or three years." The governor frequently contrasted the congenial state of order in Alabama with nationwide lawlessness. At his Madison Square Garden rally, he declared, "We don't have riots in Alabama. They start a riot down there, first one of 'em to pick up a brick gets a bullet in the brain, that's all. And then you walk over to the next one and say, 'All right, pick up a brick. We just want to see you pick up one of them bricks, now!'" Though it went unspoken, Wallace's audience knew who "they" were—blacks, whom many white Americans held responsible for the breakdown of civic order. More than one commentator noted Wallace's effective use of "code words" such as "law and order" to emphasize the necessity of curtailing the ostensibly criminal and irresponsible behavior of African Americans. The nation's ills, Wallace inevitably concluded, could never be resolved by the two major parties, as "there isn't a dime's worth of difference between them." Wallace, it seemed, was the solution.

By late September, Wallace was pulling 21 percent in some presidential polls and seemed likely to go higher. Political commentators pointed with alarm to his growing popularity and the size of the crowds he was attracting: 10,000 in Kansas City and Dallas and perhaps 25,000 in a series of Florida rallies. It appeared that Wallace might in fact be capable of accomplishing what once had seemed an improbable threat—depriving the major-party candidates of an electoral majority and throwing the election into the House of Representatives. But as quickly as Wallace's fortunes had risen, they plummeted. One factor was his selection of former air force general Curtis LeMay as his vice presidential running mate in early October. The former head of the Strategic Air Command, never known for verbal restraint, was characteristically blunt in his first press conference, suggesting that most Americans had a "phobia" about nuclear weapons, the use of which he considered to be "no worse than a rusty knife." Wallace's frantic efforts at damage control were futile, and Democratic candidate Hubert Humphrey, among others, began referring to the duo as the "Bombsey Twins."

Perhaps more damaging to the Wallace campaign, however, was the violence that inevitably accompanied the candidate's appearances. Wallace positively fed on hecklers, often inviting them to "c'mon down and have your sandals autographed" or offering them a free haircut. Not infrequently, verbal exchanges between Wallace supporters and protesters escalated into physical violence. At a Detroit rally, Wallace fans and hecklers fought each other with fists and folding chairs as the candidate glowered from the podium and remarked, "Well, ya asked for trouble and ya got it." By October, Wallace's poll numbers were falling off rapidly as voters, deterred by the violence attendant to his campaign and his lack of realistic solutions for the nation's ills, drifted back toward the major parties. The November election saw Wallace capture 13.5 percent of the popular vote, winning fifty-eight electoral votes in the South, which had been a Democratic enclave since Reconstruction.

Though George Wallace was defeated, his message was alive and well. Successful Republican presidential candidate Richard Nixon, among the first to recognize the potential appeal of Wallace's message, had presented himself as the respectable "law and order" candidate in 1968, part of a "southern strategy" aimed at bringing the South over to the Republican electoral column. Once elected, Nixon quickly positioned himself as the spokesman for the "Silent Majority," dedicated to defending its interests against intrusive government and ensuring that the values of "middle America," rather than those of the "elite intellectuals" and the counterculture, would prevail. In 1969, Republican strategist Kevin Phillips published an astute analysis of the shifting tides of national politics. *The Emerging Republican Majority* concluded that demographic trends would provide a solid foundation for a conservative political impulse, driven by resentment among the same predominantly white, ethnic, working-class groups that Wallace had targeted. As president, Nixon moved to reshape Republican policies so as to effectively capture these constituencies and wean them from their historically Democratic allegiance. By the late 1970s, the Republican Party was strengthening its political reach in the South as well as other historically Democratic strongholds and seemed well on the way to becoming the majority party.

George Wallace was disappointed by his 1968 defeat, but not deterred. By 1972, Wallace, now remarried, once again Alabama's governor, and convinced that many of the same issues that he had based his first national campaign on were still viable, proceeded to organize a second presidential campaign. Nixon, concerned about the electoral impact of another Wallace third-party candidacy on his reelection fortunes, persuaded Wallace to run instead as a Democrat. Urging voters to "Send Them a Message," Wallace hammered his Democratic primary opponents on the issues of forced busing, taxes, gun control, drugs, and welfare abuse. He won a stunning 42 percent of the Florida primary vote and came in a close second to liberal South Dakota senator George McGovern in Wisconsin. Wallace seemed poised to wreak further havoc in the Democratic Party when, on May 15, at a shopping center rally in suburban Maryland, a deranged gunman shot him five times at close range. Though the hospitalized candidate still won primaries in Maryland, Michigan, Tennessee, and North Carolina, his wounds effectively removed him from this and any future presidential campaigns.

The attempted assassination radically altered what remained of Wallace's life. Partially paralyzed, in constant pain, and largely confined to a wheelchair, he nonetheless won reelection as governor in 1974, his path cleared by a 1968 amendment to the Alabama state constitution that repealed the existing law prohibiting "self-succession." He forsook another presidential campaign in 1976, focusing his energies on social and economic reforms in Alabama. During the next two decades, many of the issues that Wallace had advanced as a presidential candidate moved to the center stage of national politics, where the Republican Party effectively capitalized on them, not only dominating national politics in the 1980s, but also asserting increasing political strength in the historically Democratic southern states. The Wallace phenomenon prefigured what some scholars term the "southernization of America," a reference to the rapidly growing populations and thus congressional representation of the sun belt states of the south and southwest, where conservative social and cultural traditions prevailed. Those values figured largely in the shaping of national legislation as southern conservatives, beginning in the 1980s, rose to leadership positions in the increasingly right-wing national Republican Party.

This was the period during which Wallace fought his last and arguably most difficult campaign. Overwhelmed by the collapse of his second marriage and the limited, painful existence to which he was reduced, Wallace entered into a lengthy period of introspection during the late 1970s. Considerable soul-searching led him to begin making amends to those whom he feared he had most hurt during his career. In 1979, Wallace met with black activist John Lewis, now a congressman, telling him, "I've come to ask your forgiveness." Moved by Wallace's tragic fate and his evident sincerity, Lewis clasped his hand while the two men prayed together. In the months and years to come, Wallace met with dozens of civil rights activists, politicians, and clergy, always to seek forgiveness and usually receiving it. After a four-year hiatus from office, Wallace undertook his last gubernatorial campaign in 1982, decisively winning a final four-year term with the support of black voters, who turned out in unprecedented numbers to support the man who had once been their nemesis. During the next four years, Wallace pursued an astonishingly progressive agenda, supported by the "Wallace Coalition," an alliance including educators, organized labor, black political organizations, and trial lawyers. Education funding, tax equity, and employee rights dominated the agenda of Wallace's last governorship.

Some years before, Wallace had been summoned to the Oval Office for a meeting with President Johnson, who turned his immense skills of persuasion to the task of convincing the segregationist governor to abandon his obstruction of integration efforts and his provocative racial rhetoric. Johnson asked the defiant Wallace whether, when he was dead, he would prefer that his memorial be a shabby marker with the epitaph "George Wallace—He Hated" or a dignified monument with the inscription "George Wallace—He Built." By the end of his public career in 1987, Wallace could legitimately lay claim to the latter legacy. In the minds of many Americans, black and white alike, George Wallace was a redeemed man when he died in 1998. Still, his political legacy was clearly manifest at the time of his death. As early as 1964, Wallace had exposed the latent power of the "politics of rage," tapping into a new strain of populist conservatism that resonated widely with the electorate. Interventionist government, the breakdown of social order, liberal policies that seemed to favor minorities, and an increasingly libertine culture were all issues that enabled Wallace to successfully mobilize voters not only in the historically Democratic South, but in other regions as well. The fiery Alabaman was, as biographer Dan T. Carter has written, "the alchemist of the new social conservatism . . . that laid the foundation for the conservative counter-revolution that reshaped American politics in the 1970s and 1980s." By 2000, this conservative tide brought about Republican control of both houses of Congress, the presidency, and a growing number of governorships and state legislatures, ending a long era of Democratic dominance. Carter offered the most succinct assessment of George Wallace's impact: "He was the most influential loser in twentieth-century American politics."

Conclusion

The year 1968 was a definitive landmark in contemporary American history. Its horrors erased the last vestiges of the confident mood that prevailed in

214

the decade's early years. To some degree, Robert Kennedy's presidential campaign represented the potential resurrection of that earlier idealism, and many Americans saw in the young senator some hope of recapturing what had slipped away. His quixotic presidential campaign was a beacon to those who desperately longed to believe that their nation still was, as Kennedy himself had proclaimed, "a great country, an unselfish country, and a compassionate country." After Kennedy's murder, fear eclipsed hope as the dominant passion of 1968. One aspect of that fear was growing anxiety about social disorder, a concern that George Wallace effectively capitalized on in his presidential campaign. Successfully articulating the fears of many average Americans, Wallace laid the groundwork for a populist conservatism born of resentment of elites, minorities, dissidents, and the liberal policies that many saw as responsible for the nation's ills. The Republican Party was the most direct beneficiary. The year 1968 marked the advent of a long era of Republican dominance of presidential politics, as well as the beginnings of a grassroots conservative impulse that decisively transformed national politics in subsequent decades.

Study Questions

1. What major issues brought about the deep divisions that strained American society in 1968?
2. How would you explain George Wallace's appeal as a presidential candidate?
3. What long-term problems did Wallace's candidacy suggest for the national Democratic Party?
4. What was meant by the observation that Robert Kennedy's assassination in 1968 marked "the murder of hope"?
5. Undertake an exercise in alternative history in which Robert Kennedy won the Democratic Party's presidential nomination in 1968. How might subsequent history have differed?

Selected Bibliography

Applebome, Peter. *Dixie Rising: How the South Is Shaping American Values.* New York: Harvest, 1996.

Carter, Dan T. *The Politics of Rage: George Wallace, the Origins of the New Conservatism, and the Transformation of American Politics.* New York: Simon and Schuster, 1995.

Chester, Lewis, Godfrey Hodgson, and Bruce Page. *An American Melodrama: The Presidential Campaign of 1968.* New York: Viking, 1969.

Egerton, John. *The Americanization of Dixie: The Southernization of America.* New York: Harpers Magazine Press, 1973.

Frady, Marshal. *Wallace.* New York: Dutton, 1968.

Heyman, C. David. *RFK: A Candid Biography of Robert Kennedy.* New York: Dutton, 1998.

Kurlansky, Mark. *1968: The Year That Rocked the World.* New York: Ballantine, 2003.

Lesher, Stephan. *George Wallace: American Populist.* Boston: Addison-Wesley, 1994.

Mahoney, Richard D. *Sons and Brothers: The Days of Jack and Bobby Kennedy.* New York: Arcade, 1999.

Palermo, Joseph A. *In His Own Right: The Political Odyssey of Senator Robert F. Kennedy.* New York: Columbia University Press, 2001.

Sherrill, Robert. *Gothic Politics in the Deep South.* New York: Ballantine, 1968.

Shesol, Jeff. *Mutual Contempt: Lyndon Johnson, Robert Kennedy and the Feud That Defined a Decade.* New York: W.W. Norton, 1997.

Steel, Ronald. *In Love with Night: The American Romance with Robert Kennedy.* New York: Simon and Schuster, 2000.

Talbot, David. *Brothers: The Hidden History of the Kennedy Years.* New York: Free Press, 2007.

Thomas, Evan. *Robert Kennedy: His Life.* New York: Simon and Schuster, 2000.

White, Theodore. *The Making of the President: 1968.* New York: Atheneum, 1969.

Witcover, Jules. *The Year the Dream Died: Revisiting America in 1968.* New York: Warner, 1998.

9

Implosions

Collapse of the Counterculture and the New Left

By the late 1960s, two impulses that had been gaining momentum since the decade's early years accelerated rapidly toward self-destruction. Both were grounded in the decade's dynamic youth movement; one was cultural in nature, the other political. The counterculture, in large part a reaction to the abundant, conformist 1950s, had coalesced by the mid-1960s. Its advocates, rejecting the prevailing material ethos and conventional morality of mainstream society, extolled new habits of body and mind that included consciousness-raising drugs, sexual liberation, new spiritualities, and a renewal of communal bonds. The cultural rebels discovered a common language in the new music of the era, which evolved rapidly after 1964, often reflecting the counterculture's rejection of conventional society while celebrating the virtues of the unfolding youth culture.(Unsurprisingly, many people came to see rock stars as the avatars of the new culture,)the chief celebrants of the new self-indulgence. In time, some critics would reduce the significance of the counterculture to "sex, drugs, and rock and roll," a phrase that did little justice to its serious intellectual roots. Since the 1950s, an eclectic group of cultural dissidents, including writers, musicians, psychologists, and social critics, had been tentatively exploring the various paths to self-liberation that the counterculture was to embrace. The potential dangers became evident in the late 1960s as the remaining obstacles to self-liberation were rapidly cast aside in the quest for complete personal freedom. The character of the counterculture changed as it became a mass phenomenon, its ranks swelled by many drawn by the promise of unfettered self-indulgence. The inability to set limits inevitably cost lives, perhaps nowhere more noticeably than among musicians. Guitarist Jimi Hendrix, an innovative musician and flamboyant performer, exemplified the potential dangers inherent in the unrestrained exuberance that the counterculture celebrated. His death in 1971 signaled the end of the cultural rebellion that he personified.

The origins of the New Left also go back to the 1950s, when disaffection with Cold War conservatism and with the increasingly irrelevant Marxism of the Old Left shaped a new generation of reform-minded activists. Founded in 1960, Students for a Democratic Society (SDS) was the largest and most influential New Left organization. Its adherents were optimistic and idealistic, dedicated to defining a new ideology that would remedy the political alienation of Americans. SDS and the New Left underwent a rapid transformation beginning in the mid-1960s, driven by events that seemed to render moderate reform through peaceful means impracticable. Pushed beyond advocating reform to embracing resistance and finally revolution, SDS began to unravel in 1969, irreparably riven by intense sectarian disputes. Among those who witnessed this process was Bernardine Dohrn, a young law school graduate-turned-activist drawn into the organization as it turned toward radicalism in the late 1960s. Dohrn was among those few who embraced revolutionary violence as the only means of bringing down a militaristic, racist American empire. She was a founding member and leader of Weatherman, an SDS remnant that advocated revolutionary struggle; later, Dohrn and Weatherman went underground to carry on the revolutionary struggle through terrorism. Weatherman was destined to act out the revolutionary fantasy that proved a dead end for the New Left.

JIMI HENDRIX
Troubadour of Psychedelia

It was called the Human Be-In and it marked mainstream America's introduction to what would soon be referred to as the counterculture. The setting was San Francisco's Golden Gate Park, where a generally youthful crowd of some

219

20,000 gathered on January 14, 1967, an unusually warm and sunny winter day. Organizers of the Be-In proclaimed that it would inaugurate a new age of peace and love, promising to "shower the country with waves of ecstasy and purification." "Fear will be washed away," they asserted; "ignorance will be exposed to sunlight; profits and empire will lie drying on deserted beaches." Music critic Ralph Gleason noted in the *San Francisco Chronicle* that the prevalent fashions at the Be-In reflected "a wild polyglot mixture of Mod, Palladin, Ringling Brothers, Cochise and Hell's Angels Formal." At 1:00 PM, poet Gary Snyder blew loudly on a conch shell, signaling the beginning of an anarchic sequence of festivities.

Over the next four hours, a parade of counterculture icons spoke and performed on the makeshift stage. Beat poet Allen Ginsberg, activist Jerry Rubin, and LSD (lysergic acid diethylamide, a powerful hallucinogen) advocate Timothy Leary were among those who addressed a not always attentive crowd, which was distracted in part by the distribution of free LSD tablets. The distinctive San Francisco Sound echoed across the park as Jefferson Airplane, the Grateful Dead, Quicksilver Messenger Service, and Big Brother and the Holding Company performed for the crowd. Helen Swick, a sociologist who attended the Human Be-In, thought she detected something more, something "mystical," in the atmosphere at this assemblage of the "peace and love" generation. "The dogs did not fight," she noted, "and the children did not cry." Such was the early promise of the counterculture.

The San Francisco Be-In was only a prelude to a broader celebration of the counterculture. Only months later, the Summer of Love unfolded in the same city. The nation's media focused on the Haight-Ashbury district of San Francisco, where an estimated 75,000 young people had gravitated to the promise of a new society built on a celebration of life, love, and community. A Top 40 song, Scott McKenzie's "San Francisco (Be Sure to Wear Some Flowers in Your Hair)," sounded a national clarion call to join the migration. Indeed, as many commentators were noting, music was the common language that united the many threads of the counterculture and gave it a powerful voice. Ralph Gleason observed, "At no time in American history has youth possessed the strength it possesses now. Trained by music and linked by music, it has the power for good to change the world." If rock and roll was the lingua franca of the youth movement, rock festivals were its semiofficial convocations, and during the Summer of Love, the Monterey International Pop Festival marked the first major summoning of the tribes. The festival took shape in early 1967 as a nonprofit event, and during the planning stages Beatle Paul McCartney pressed festival organizers to include a new but already explosive act—the Jimi Hendrix Experience.

Thus it was that Jimi Hendrix, a twenty-four-year-old African American guitarist who neither read nor wrote music, arrived in Monterey in June 1967 for his American debut as a rising superstar. His band, which consisted of Noel Redding and drummer Mitch Mitchell, had toured widely in Europe and the United Kingdom during the previous year and was already watching its first album, *Are You Experienced?*, climb rapidly up the charts. Hendrix baffled music critics. His colorful, hippie attire, his unruly Afro hairstyle, and his unique sound—built around thunderous chords, pounding rhythms, and soaring electric guitar solos, joined to poetic and often mystical lyrics—seemed to defy categorization. Some spoke of the theatrical and overtly sexual Hendrix as "Black Elvis." A writer for *Melody Maker* used the terms "mau-mau" (referring to the fierce Kenyan rebels of the 1950s), and "wild man" to describe the guitarist. A writer for *Ebony* magazine described Hendrix as looking "like a cross between Bob Dylan and the Wild Man of Borneo." Indeed, one of the ongoing challenges that Hendrix confronted was defining who he was and whom his music was for. His appeal was not primarily to blacks, few of whom attended his concerts. Rather, his lifestyle, his clothes, his music, and his use of hallucinogenic drugs all seemed to place him squarely within the blossoming counterculture, a predominantly white phenomenon. At Monterey, an American audience was given its first opportunity to evaluate the unique musician firsthand.

The Monterey Pop Festival, which took place June 16–18 at the city's fairgrounds, offered an artist lineup that mirrored the rapidly changing face of popular music in the late 1960s. The program for the first day included an eclectic mix of individuals, groups, and styles: the Association, Lou Rawls, Johnny Rivers, Eric Burdon and the Animals, and Simon and Garfunkel. Most belonged to a period that was already being eclipsed by the more avant-garde sounds of electric psychedelia. The second day brought acts of both ephemeral and enduring fame, among them Canned Heat, Big Brother and the Holding Company with Janis Joplin, Al Kooper, the Quicksilver Messenger Service, the Electric Flag, Moby Grape, and Country Joe and the Fish.

Only hours before he went on stage on Sunday night, Hendrix confided to the Animals' Eric Burdon, "I'm looking forward to tonight, man. I'm so high, living on my nerves. The spaceship's really gonna take off tonight." The tall, slender, left-handed guitarist, whose large hands afforded him a reach that few others had, did not disappoint. That evening, the Experience astounded the audience with thunderous versions of "Killing Floor," "Foxy Lady," "Like a Rolling Stone," and finally the oft-covered "Wild Thing." The crowd roared approval as Hendrix played his guitar between his legs, behind his back, then rammed it into a column of speakers before hurling it to the stage floor and pounding on it. In a riotous finale, he sprayed the much-abused guitar with lighter fluid and ignited it before smashing the still-burning instrument to pieces on the stage. The moment, famously captured in a later documentary film of the event, may well have been what inspired a music critic for the *Los Angeles Times* to declare that Hendrix "had graduated from rumor to legend." The members of the Jimi Hendrix Experience left the stage that night with twenty minutes of applause and cheers echoing in their heads.

The festival was brought to a close that evening with an appropriate bow to the West Coast origins of the counterculture. Scott McKenzie performed "San Francisco," which had already achieved the stature of the hippie anthem, and was followed by the Mamas and the Papas, whose vocal harmonies on songs like "California Dreamin'" and "Monday, Monday" already seemed redolent of another musical era. The vibes at the event were good; though drug use was widespread, there was little antisocial activity. Monterey was, some commentators proclaimed, solid evidence that the counterculture values of the young could produce a peaceful, harmonious society. Jimi Hendrix left Monterey elated at his performance, though many music critics remained unconvinced of his genuineness. *Rolling Stone*'s John Morthland offered one of the least charitable assessments, describing Hendrix as "the flower generation's electric nigger dandy, its king stud and golden calf, its maker of mighty dope music, its most outrageously visible force." White critic Robert Christgau dismissed the guitarist as "a psychedelic Uncle Tom."

Hendrix was not, however, as some critics implied, a contemporary black minstrel affecting ridiculous clothing and exaggerated theatrics for the entertainment of white people. Race never figured prominently in his consciousness or music, though he was well versed in the tradition of African American blues and more than proficient in their performance. His extraordinary musical style was drawn from his familiarity with blues and jazz, but built around his innovative ability with the electric guitar and lyrics that reflected his personal fascination with science fiction, outer space, extraterrestrials, and even West Indian magic. His music was a product of his own creative genius, rather than of the counterculture. Nonetheless, his art resonated with the blossoming youth culture, and Hendrix was inevitably borne along by its currents. His tendencies toward self-indulgence in drugs, sexual promiscuity, and a freewheeling lifestyle were amplified in the counterculture context, which celebrated unlimited personal freedom. Like many swept up by the phenomenon, Hendrix disregarded the necessity of setting personal limits, and his celebrity undoubtedly accelerated the process of self-destruction.

The son born to Al and Lucille Hendrix on November 27, 1942, was destined to experience an unstable early childhood. Lucille was only sixteen when her son was born in Seattle, Washington. Her twenty-three-year-old husband, James Allen, or Al, had been inducted into the army and was stationed in Alabama at the time, and Lucille registered her son as Johnny Allen Hendrix. Like his mother, the child had a light complexion, and like his father, he exhibited evidence of his part-Cherokee ancestry. For the first several years of his life, Johnny Allen did not have a permanent home. Lucille was too emotionally immature for either marriage or motherhood, so, given her irresponsibility, Johnny Allen was often cared for by other female relatives. When Al was discharged from the army in November 1945, he headed to Berkeley, California, where Johnny Allen was living with an aunt's friend. Retrieving his son, Al returned to Seattle, where he hoped to find his errant wife. Having had no say in his son's birth name, Al had it changed to James Marshall Hendrix. Al and Lucille struggled to salvage their marriage, reuniting in 1947 and producing another son, Leon, in early 1948. Jimi Hendrix later offered his own eulogy for his hard-living mother: "She died when I was ten, but she was a real groovy mother."

Al Hendrix struggled to keep his family together during the early 1950s, working at a sequence of menial jobs. James Marshall, now Jimmy, proved a marginal student in elementary school, doing poorly in music class but displaying a talent for fantasy in artwork. An introverted child, he demonstrated an early interest in music, playing "broom guitar" around the house until he got his first acoustic guitar in 1958. A fan of Elvis Presley and Little Richard, Jimmy quickly developed his skills as a guitarist. He was soon playing local gigs and steeping himself in the combination of rock, jazz, and blues that echoed through Seattle's black nightclubs. It was the blues guitarists, men like B.B. King, Muddy Waters, Jimmy Reed, and John Lee Hooker, who most impressed the young musician. In 1960 he dropped out of high school, drifting for a number of months until he was arrested twice in the span of three days for auto theft in May 1961. His two-year sentence was suspended when he agreed to join the military. Jimmy's experience as a Screaming Eagle, a paratrooper with the 101st Airborne Division at Fort Ord, California, was mixed. Though parachuting from aircraft exhilarated him, he disdained the authoritarianism of the military. Bored, he and Billy Cox, a West Virginia bass player, formed several short-lived groups that performed in nearby clubs during off-duty hours. In July 1962, a few months after breaking his ankle in a parachuting accident, he was discharged from the army.

For the next four years, Hendrix led a transient existence backing artists like the Marvellettes, Curtis Mayfield, and the Isley Brothers. He was beginning to test the capabilities of the electric guitar by this point, experimenting with the effects of volume, feedback, and new techniques to draw unusual sounds from the instrument. He bought his first new guitar—a Fender Duosonic—and shortly afterward, at New York City's Lodi Club, performed in the presence of electric guitar pioneer Les Paul, who remarked that he had "never seen anyone so radical." Bouncing between Chicago and New York, Hendrix performed and recorded with a number of artists, including Little Richard, Joey Dee and the Starlighters, the Squires, and King Curtis. He began to establish himself as a unique musical presence on the Greenwich Village scene in 1966 with his new band, Jimmy James and the Blue Flames. Now equipped with a Fender Stratocaster and moving away from soul music and blues, Hendrix tested new musical boundaries with lengthy solos and feedback. He was inevitably drawn into the Village's drug culture, trying both marijuana and methedrine. His unrestrained lifestyle also included random relationships with a growing series of women, several of whom would, in future years, allege that he had fathered children with them.

The guitarist's prospects improved in the summer of 1966 when Chas Chandler, bass player for the Animals and an aspiring manager and producer, signed Hendrix up for an English tour. In late September, Hendrix flew to London, where he rapidly achieved celebrity. On Chandler's advice, the guitarist now billed himself as "Jimi," and The Jimi Hendrix Experience came into being on October 12, 1966, with British bassist Noel Redding and drummer Mitch Mitchell joining the American guitarist. London was a focal point for the tremendous talent that was driving English rock and roll, and the bushy-haired Hendrix was soon socializing with stars like Mick Jagger and Eric Clapton. The band's crucial breakthrough came in December with the release of "Hey Joe," not an original composition, but one that revealed the group's potential. The year 1967 marked the beginning of Hendrix's meteoric rise to stardom. It was a seminal year for the budding youth culture, bringing the release of the Beatles' *Sgt. Pepper's Lonely Hearts Club Band*, the first issue of *Rolling Stone* magazine, and the unfolding of the counterculture in San Francisco. In May, the Experience released its first album, *Are You Experienced?* It was a stellar debut, demonstrating the full range of Hendrix's talent in songs that ranged from pop and free-form jazz to rhythm and blues. While songs like "Purple Haze" and "Manic Depression" spoke directly to the counterculture's infatuation with psychedelia, there is no evidence that they had their genesis in drugs. As Hendrix explained, "I put a lot of dreams down as songs." The Experience crafted a sound that drew enthusiastic concert audiences across

England, the Netherlands, Sweden, Finland, France, and West Germany that spring. In June, the band departed for the United States.

The American music scene that Jimi Hendrix exploded into during 1967 was the product of a rapid evolution that paralleled broader cultural developments. The first post-Elvis revolution in American pop music began in February 1964, when the Beatles arrived in New York City as the advance guard of the "British Invasion," infusing new energy, creativity, and irreverence into the American music universe. The Yardbirds, the Kinks, the Animals, and the Rolling Stones, many influenced by black rhythm and blues, brought to America an edgier, rawer music. During these same years, advocates of the mind-expanding qualities of hallucinogenic drugs were finding a wide audience within the growing counterculture. This psychedelic movement attracted an ever-widening circle of musicians, artists, and intellectuals, such as writer Aldous Huxley, psychologists Timothy Leary and Richard Alpert, author Ken Kesey, Zen philosopher Alan Watts, and psychiatrist R.D. Laing, who all celebrated the liberating, consciousness-altering effects of drugs like mescaline and "acid" (LSD). Some, like Watts, were also advocates of Eastern religion as an instrument of self-exploration. Concurrent with these developments, a coterie of social critics, philosophers, and psychologists, including Wilhelm Reich, Herbert Marcuse, and Norman O. Brown, began to establish an intellectual rationale for the liberating nature of open and unrestricted sexuality. These themes of sexual liberation and expanded consciousness, either through drugs or Eastern spirituality, broadly pervaded much popular music by the late 1960s. Rock musicians became, in essence, the troubadours for these counterculture values.

Having arrived in the United States, the Jimi Hendrix Experience was an immediate popular sensation. Attired in colorful, chaotic apparel, Hendrix developed an unpretentious stage manner in which he addressed his audience conversationally, often seeming to be talking to himself. Once the music began, however, he was transported by the sounds and focused on his performance. The band's first nationwide tour was somewhat oddly conceived, as the Experience was paired with the Monkees, a group assembled specifically to appeal to teenyboppers, young adolescents renowned more for their adoration of uncontroversial celebrity than for their discerning musical tastes. Nonetheless, the tour succeeded in introducing Hendrix to audiences outside his West Coast base. The Experience headed back to England in late August, establishing a pattern of frequent transatlantic travel that would continue over the next two years, arguably the most creative period of Hendrix's career. Hendrix concentrated on putting together another groundbreaking album, *Axis: Bold as Love*, released in the United States in January 1968. Fans and critics alike hailed the album's diverse creativity, evident in "Little Wing," "Bold as Love," and "If 6 Was 9." A *Rolling Stone* reviewer declared, "*Axis* demonstrates conclusively that he [Hendrix] is one of rock's greatest guitar players in his mastery and exploration of every possible gimmick." *Axis* was, the reviewer wrote, "the finest Voodoo album that any rock group has produced to date."

The Experience, which returned to the United States in early 1968, gained similar critical success with the release of *Electric Ladyland* that October. This album again featured an astonishing diversity of genres, including blues, soul, pop, rhythm and blues, rock and roll, and electronic music. Songs ranged from a captivating cover of Dylan's "All Along the Watchtower" to the apocalyptic "Voodoo Child (Slight Return)." The album's "House Burning Down" marked Jimi's first overtly political song, a comment on an increasingly polarized America. Hendrix was no political activist. Though he had offered a musical tribute to the martyred Martin Luther King Jr. at a concert in April, he was ambivalent about the growing black power movement. On several occasions, Black Panthers pressured Hendrix for donations, denouncing the guitarist as a "white nigger" and a "coconut." But as a long-term friend remarked about Hendrix, "He never talked in terms of color." Race simply had no acknowledged place in his internal universe.

By 1969, Hendrix had other things on his mind. Having rediscovered his American roots, he was distancing himself from his British sidemen Redding and Mitchell, even as he was coming to believe that the Experience had outlived its usefulness as an artistic vehicle; the group would, in fact, disband by late June. Hendrix began talking about a new group, an "electric church," built around expanded instrumentation and musical experimentation. The construction of Electric Lady Studios in New York that summer was a major step in that direction. A more serious distraction came in May 1969, when airport customs officers in Toronto, Canada, arrested Hendrix for possession of heroin and hashish. All these developments made Hendrix somewhat testy, but most critics who heard him that summer confirmed that his talent was undiminished. A writer for the Los Angeles *Image* proclaimed, "He seems to know the instrument and its nearly limitless possibilities better than any electric guitarist who has ever lived." Hendrix was, in the critic's words, "Wes Montgomery, B.B. King, Eric Clapton and you name it all wrapped up in one package of artistic fury."

Hendrix lived up to his reputation with his performance at the Woodstock Music and Arts Festival of August 15–17, 1969. Performing now with the new Gypsy Suns and Rainbows, which included his old friend Billy Cox, he went on stage early on the morning of the final day. Offering his audience both old and new tunes, he brought the festival to a close with "Purple Haze" and his pyrotechnic version of "The Star-Spangled Banner." After leaving the stage, Hendrix collapsed from nervous exhaustion and was flown out by helicopter. His breakdown was an apt metaphor for the state of the counterculture in 1969. Although the Woodstock Festival was hailed as evidence of the vitality of the counterculture, it became clear in retrospect that the event actually marked its decline. As early as the summer of 1967, there were those who realized that the popularization of the counterculture, driven by media hype, was destroying its authenticity. Its unofficial capital, the Haight-Ashbury district, showed signs of deterioration even as the Summer of Love came to an end, with crime, drugs, and racial violence pervading the area. In October 1967, some of the founders of "the Haight" organized the "Death of Hippie" ceremony, complete with a mock funeral ending with the incineration of a coffin filled with hippie paraphernalia. The affair proved a prescient comment on the direction of the counterculture.

The absorption of the counterculture into mainstream culture, perhaps nowhere more symbolically than in the immensely successful 1968 musical *Hair*, with its celebration of a new "Age of Aquarius," quickly drained the movement of any genuineness. As masses of American youth adopted long hair and outrageous fashions and delved into drugs for recreational rather than spiritual purposes, the meaning and force of the counterculture were dissipated, leaving behind only a shallow celebration of life without boundaries. While the most extreme manifestation of this development was evident in the horrendous Manson family murders in 1969, the broader legitimization of personal irresponsibility that had taken root was evident in growing drug abuse, sexually transmitted disease, and illegitimate births, along with a conviction among many youth that life's commodities, especially music, should be free. The potential anarchy and violence that hovered at the edge of the counterculture became starkly evident at California's Altamont Festival in December 1969. Only four months after Woodstock's "Three Days of Peace, Love and Music," the Altamont Festival was a nightmare of bad drugs, violence, and death. Organized by the Rolling Stones as a free concert, the poorly planned event drew an unruly crowd of 300,000, most of whom were high on drugs, liquor, or both. Hell's Angels bikers, hired as security in return for $500 worth of beer, attacked audience members as well as some performers. Four people died at the concert, one stabbed to death by a Hell's Angel. The chaos was captured on film in the documentary *Gimme Shelter.*

Hendrix, who witnessed the violence at Altamont, had little time to contemplate its meaning before flying to Toronto for his drug possession trial the day after the concert. Though found not guilty, he remained burdened with a multitude of problems: quarrels over contracts and royalties, disputes with musicians and girlfriends, and uncertainty over his future direction. The formation of the Band of Gypsys, a trio with Billy Cox and drummer Buddy Miles, offered some hope, but after a successful New Year's Eve show at the Fillmore East, portions of which were released as *Band of Gypsys* (1970), things went quickly awry. At a benefit concert for the Vietnam Moratorium Committee in January 1970, Hendrix seemed disoriented, possibly as a result of bad LSD, and walked off stage. Band of Gypsys never played again. Struggling futilely against a growing drug habit, Hendrix brought the old members of the Experience back together for a concert tour stretching from April to August. He also tried to focus on a projected album to be called *First Rays of the New Rising Sun*, which he hoped would redefine his image, and contracted to provide music for *Rainbow Bridge*, a film being made in Hawaii to counter the negative image of the youth culture.

Hendrix's ambitions failed to offset his deteriorating physical health, which many around him observed with alarm. The combination of ulcers, anxiety, and drug abuse was manifest in the guitarist's growing moodiness and periodic, private, violent outbursts. Hendrix found that the temper of concert audiences had also changed for the worse; unruliness, hostility, and gatecrashing were becoming more frequent. After witnessing the disorderly Isle of Wight concert in August, Hendrix roadie Gerry Stickells commented, "It was the end of the love and peace era. People broke down fences, there was violence. It had run its course—the love and peace bit." The Love and Peace Concert on the Isle of Fehmarn in West Germany on September 7 was far worse. In the midst of a howling gale, armed German bikers terrorized the audience, robbing the box office and extorting money from concertgoers. The rowdy crowd booed and taunted Hendrix, bikers assaulted Stickells, and a stagehand was shot. The band fled upon finishing its set, after which the bikers burned the stage. It was Jimi Hendrix's last concert.

The remainder of the tour was canceled when bassist Billy Cox fell victim to some punch spiked with LSD, became psychotic, and was hospitalized in a vegetative state for more than a week. Friends and associates were uneasy about Hendrix's frame of mind; many interpreted his distracted demeanor, erratic behavior, and inability to keep appointments as indications of a deeply troubled individual. On September 17, while staying at London's Samarkand Hotel, Hendrix attended a party where he was seen to take methedrine and later LSD. The next morning, girlfriend Monika Danneman was unable to awaken him and, discovering some of her sleeping pills missing, called an ambulance. About an hour later, at St. Mary's Abbot Hospital, Hendrix was declared dead. The coroner's report listed "inhalation of vomit" and "barbiturate intoxication" as the causes of death, noting that "insufficient evidence of circumstances" compelled an "open verdict."

Jimi Hendrix was not the first celebrity to die from drug abuse, but as a renowned rock and roll icon, his death was of great symbolic significance for America's youth culture. Those who rejected all restraints in a quest to "kiss the sky," it seemed, did so at great personal risk. The same excesses that claimed Jimi Hendrix soon took others. Less than a month after Hendrix's death, singer Janis Joplin died of a heroin overdose. Jim Morrison of the Doors, the self-proclaimed "Lizard King," died of heart failure in July 1971. Cass Elliot of the Mamas and Papas succumbed to a heart attack in 1974. It can be argued that they were victims not of the counterculture but of their own excesses, but the counterculture offered a context in which the excesses of personal freedom were extolled as liberation. The counterculture itself did not long outlast these rock and roll icons. Absorbed, tamed, and marketed by mainstream society, the counterculture was stripped of any remaining authenticity by the early 1970s. Jimi Hendrix's legacy survived, however, and he is still celebrated as an accomplished, innovative musician. In 1992, he was posthumously inducted into the Rock and Roll Hall of Fame.

BERNARDINE DOHRN
Reformer, Radical, Revolutionary

It was called the Days of Rage. Organized in the summer of 1969, the proposed National Action was intended to demonstrate the newly proclaimed revolutionary fervor of Weatherman, a radical splinter group that had emerged from the wreckage of the final, tumultuous convention of Students for a Democratic Society (SDS) that June. SDS, like much of the New Left, had been driven in an ever more radical direction by the pressure of events. An increasingly violent war in Vietnam, racial polarization, political assassinations, and growing government repression combined to convince radicals that peaceful protest and hopes of reforming American institutions were in vain. When SDS members met at the cavernous Chicago Coliseum in June, a group drawn from the leadership of the National Office provoked near-riotous debate among the attendees by presenting a new position paper, "You Don't Need a Weatherman to Know Which Way the Wind Blows." Its name taken from the lyrics of a Bob Dylan song, the manifesto renounced nonviolent protest and proclaimed solidarity with third-world revolutionary movements. The time had come, the "Weatherman" document proclaimed, for American youth to accept the need for "armed struggle."

SDS national secretary Bernardine Dohrn was at the forefront of the drive to establish Weatherman as the new incarnation of SDS. A twenty-six-year-old law school graduate who had been drawn into SDS in 1968, Dohrn had rapidly established a presence in the organization. To many around her, the attractive, long-haired brunette, with her affinity for fashionable leather miniskirts and knee-high boots, was the epitome of the new radical—intellectually acute, dynamic, and wholeheartedly committed to the cause. Now, in early October, Weatherman prepared to carry out the National Action, to "bring the war home" with a frenzy of violence in the streets of Chicago. Long weeks had been spent forging revolutionary bonds and practicing martial arts in anticipation of combat with the notoriously brutal Chicago police. The rationale for the Days of Rage, scheduled for October 8–12, was to mobilize tens of thousands of disaffected youth for the coming war against "Pig Amerika." On Monday October 6, as a prelude to the main events, Weatherman members dynamited the police memorial in the city's Haymarket Square. On the evening of October 8, about 600 would-be revolutionaries assembled in Lincoln Park, many equipped with helmets, steel-toed boots, gas masks, chains, pipes, and clubs. Dohrn, a member of the Weatherbureau, as the leadership was known, mounted a makeshift podium to exhort the crowd, reminding them that it was the second anniversary of the death of Argentine revolutionary Che Guevara. After additional verbal encouragements, Dohrn led the assembled troops southward out of the park. Walking briskly, then breaking into a run, the young radicals poured into the streets of Chicago's Loop, shouting revolutionary slogans, smashing storefront windows and car windshields, and assaulting surprised police officers. Some twenty minutes of mayhem elapsed before police were able to organize a counterattack. Both sides fought fiercely. Weathermen injured twenty-one officers, beating one unconscious, while police gunfire injured half a dozen radicals. The battle was over in an hour, but it was only the opening action of a four-day campaign of revolutionary violence.

The following day, Dohrn headed up the Women's Militia action. Meeting at Grant Park, some seventy militant women equipped with helmets and sticks prepared to assault a nearby army induction office. Seeking to steel her compatriots' nerves, Dohrn reminded them "a few buckshot wounds, a few pellets, mean we're doing the right thing here." As the street fighters marched off toward their target, police ordered them to drop their weapons and disperse. Disregarding a tactical situation that pitted six dozen militants against some 300 officers, Dohrn led an enthusiastic charge into police lines, initiating a wild melee. The battle ended with a dozen or so arrests before the police allowed the rest of the women's militia to walk away.

On Saturday, the radicals, numbering about 300, gathered at Haymarket Square for a mass march through the Loop. The week's final and most violent action unfolded early in the afternoon as the radicals again smashed windows and charged police lines. Better prepared for this confrontation, police over-whelmed the militants in a thirty-minute battle. The Days of Rage came to an end with 284 militants, including Dohrn and most of the Weatherbureau, under arrest and facing cumulative bail charges of $1.5 million. With most of the leadership in custody, the final day of rage, Sunday, was anticlimacti-cally quiet.

In subsequent days, however, as it became evident that the expected revo-lutionary masses were not emerging, the Weatherbureau revised its strategy. Only a dedicated cadre operating underground and employing terrorism as its chief weapon, the leadership concluded, could realize the revolution. With the formation of the new Weather Underground, Dohrn and her colleagues began a fugitive existence, committed to a delusional faith in revolutionary violence. The underground group marked the terminal phase in the collapse of the New Left, which had been inexorably driven toward increasingly radical strategies that pushed it to the fringe of American politics. Dohrn's leadership role in the Weather Underground led FBI director J. Edgar Hoover to deem her "the most dangerous woman in America."

Like the great majority of the student radicals of the 1960s, Bernardine Dohrn came from an unexceptional middle-class background. Born in Mil-waukee, Wisconsin, on January 12, 1943, she grew up in suburban Whitefish Bay, daughter of Bernard Ohrnstein, a Jewish businessman, and a Christian Scientist mother. Her father, concerned about anti-Semitism affecting his ca-reer, changed the original family name of Ohrnstein to Dohrn when Bernardine was a teenager. Bernardine was known as an above-average high school student who sought social acceptance and pursued the usual extracurricular activities. Graduating in 1959, she attended Miami University of Ohio before transfer-ring to the University of Chicago. She graduated with honors in political science and education in 1963, and then gained admission to the university's law school. During her years as a law student at Chicago, Bernardine was drawn to activism. She spent a summer in New York City working with an antipoverty program before returning to Chicago to support the efforts of Martin Luther King Jr. to integrate all-white suburbs. Dohrn was providing legal services to rent strikers in the city's ghetto when she was introduced to organizers for JOIN (Jobs or Income Now), an SDS community-organizing project. After completing her law degree in 1967, Dohrn went to work for the National Lawyer's Guild (NLG), an organization dedicated to providing legal support for unpopular radical groups and individuals.

The decision marked the beginning of Dohrn's commitment to what was generally referred to as "the Movement," a loose term encompassing a variety of leftist causes and organizations. By 1967, many movement activists had lost confidence in liberalism and the Democratic Party as effective agents of change. Perhaps more than anything else, the escalating violence in Vietnam discredited the liberal administration of President Lyndon Johnson and suggested the systemic failure of fundamental institutions. Dohrn, like many young adults who became politically aware in the years 1965 to 1967, underwent a rapid political evolution, shaped by an accelerating course of often-dramatic events. The distance from liberalism to radicalism, from activism to militancy, was strikingly compressed in these years, as many in the movement were driven toward ever more extreme positions. No New Left organization better exemplified this trend than did Students for a Democratic Society, founded in 1960 by young activists seeking to define a new reform ideology. By 1968, it was indisputably the most influential of New Left groups. That same year, Bernardine Dohrn became an active participant in SDS, destined to play a central role in the radicalization of the organization.

As an assistant executive director of the NLG in early 1968, Dohrn focused on organizing law students at eastern schools to offer legal counsel to draft resisters. She made an immediate impression on her colleagues, perhaps best summarized by a coworker who remembered, "First of all there was her sex appeal. . . . People would come from miles around just to see *her.* But she was regarded as a good 'political person' at a time when other women in the movement weren't given any responsibility at all. Students really turned on to her." It was during these hectic months that Dohrn, working in the New York NLG office, developed friendships with local SDS activists and was invited to participate in a conference on women's liberation. In late March, she attended an SDS National Council meeting in Lexington, Kentucky, where the delegates recognized nineteen new chapters, bringing the national total to about 300. As ever, the central issue was a national strategy for the organization. The new focus, delegates agreed, should be on supporting black liberation. "We must see our job," a resolution read, "as one of moving the white population into a position of rebellion which joins the black struggle of revolution to make the American revolution." Subsequent events seemed to confirm the need for radical change.

On April 4, Martin Luther King Jr. was assassinated. Sporadic violence broke out in New York's Times Square, as it did in more than a hundred American cities over the next several days. A friend recalled Dohrn's reaction: "She was really stunned. . . . She cried for a while and she talked about Chicago, when she had worked with King. . . . Then she went home and changed her clothes . . . she said she was changing into her riot clothes: pants." Dohrn and her friend made their way to Times Square, where they joined in the "trashing," involving generally minor property destruction. "Bernardine really dug it," her friend remembered. "She was still crying, but afterward we had a long talk about urban guerrilla warfare, and what had to be done now—by any means necessary." That final phrase, popularized by the black radical Malcolm X, increasingly resonated with New Left radicals, and events of the next several months seemed to confirm the logic of revolutionary violence. In late April, student protests at Columbia University culminated in a brutal police assault on demonstrators occupying administration buildings. Having witnessed the event, Dohrn was among a number of NLG staff assigned to aid the arrestees in posting bail and arranging their defense.

The Columbia revolt galvanized the New Left, as did a massive student rebellion in Paris in May, when radicals fought police for days. With the scent of revolution in the air, membership in the national SDS organization swelled to 7,000, while local chapter memberships were estimated at more than 40,000. According to an Educational Testing Association poll that year, more than 140,000 college students described themselves as affiliated with SDS. Many in the movement felt that history itself was speeding up, creating a press of events that compelled people to seize the day or be left behind. The assassination of presidential candidate Robert Kennedy on June 4 only seemed to confirm the bankruptcy of the system. Days later, Dohrn caught a flight for East Lansing, Michigan—the site of the 1968 SDS convention. The events of the next few days changed the direction of her life.

Dohrn and others who gathered for the convention at Michigan State University's student union walked into a meeting room that reflected the ideological distance that SDS had traveled since 1960—the walls were festooned with huge posters of Vladimir Lenin and Leon Trotsky, communist and anarchist banners decorated the stage, and delegates waved Mao Zedong's "Little Red Book." The disparate perspectives of those in attendance reflected the growing divisions within the organization. While many of the experienced National Office delegates remained skeptical about the prospects for revolution, Mark Rudd and others from Columbia expressed disdain for the advocates of restraint. Stalemated by sectarian squabbles, the convention failed to arrive at any coherent program for advancing the revolution. Dohrn, however, gained a leadership role in the organization when she was nominated for interorganizational secretary for the National Office. On the evening of June 10, she stood before the assembly to answer questions relating to her ideological suitability for the post. "Do you consider yourself a socialist?" a delegate shouted. Without hesitation, Dohrn replied, "I consider myself a revolutionary communist." Elected without opposition, Dohrn joined the National Office staff in Chicago.

The internal strife evident at East Lansing left SDS directionless during the next several months, arguably some of the most politically volatile in American history. The leadership had only belatedly supported demonstrations at the Democratic National Convention in Chicago in August, but some SDSers drew fateful conclusions from the "police riot" unleashed against protesters in the streets. Official violence, many reasoned, justified revolutionary violence in response. And many who had witnessed the street fighting were impressed with the willingness of black militants and working-class white youths to engage the police. However, SDS leaders still struggled to define a revolutionary ideology. At a National Council meeting in Ann Arbor in December 1968, delegates were offered a way out of the dilemma. Michael Klonsky's position paper, "Toward a Revolutionary Youth Movement" (to be known as RYM I), concluded that students alone could not "bring about the downfall of capitalism." To accomplish that end, it was necessary to turn "SDS into a youth movement that is revolutionary," fusing class-conscious students with alienated and working-class youth. SDSers narrowly approved RYM I, embracing the Marxist analysis that had been dismissed as a strategic dead end in 1960. To bring about the revolution, SDS would go back to the future.

Events during the spring of 1969 encouraged those who believed that a revolutionary situation was building. Some 300 campuses experienced major, often violent, demonstrations that spring and there were eighty-four campus bombings during the first half of the year. It was becoming increasingly difficult for radicals to resist the idea that revolution was a realistic possibility. Yet SDS seemed an ever more unlikely vehicle for that revolution. Endless ideological quarrels, internal fragmentation, and growing paranoia had badly eroded the organization's campus base. At the annual convention in Chicago beginning on June 18, the fatal fractures within the organization quickly became evident. Dohrn and a dozen colleagues from the National Office, who had spent the preceding months forging a close-knit "national collective," arrived at the convention determined to make their recently composed "Weatherman" statement the focus of discussion among the 2,000 attendees.

Hoping to give revolutionary authenticity to their position, Dohrn and her colleagues had invited members of the Illinois Black Panther Party to the convention's second session, expecting that the black militants would lend credibility to the Weatherman cause and undercut members of Progressive Labor (PL), a disputatious Maoist faction within SDS. Onstage at the podium, Panther minister of information Rufus "Chaka" Walls seemed to do just that, deriding PL members as "armchair Marxists." Unexpectedly, however, Walls digressed to the issue of women's liberation, a topic of growing importance to committed feminists like Dohrn. Baffled delegates listened with growing incomprehension as Walls explained the Panthers' perspective on women's liberation. "We believe in freedom of love," he declared. "We believe in pussy power." Shouts of outrage broke the momentary stunned silence, followed by catcalls from gleeful PL members who sensed that Walls had discredited himself and the National Office faction. The surreal situation deteriorated further when Panther Jewel Cook walked to the podium to offer support for Walls, insisting that the "brother was only trying to say to you sisters that you have a strategic position in the revolution—the position for you sisters is . . . prone!" A reporter in attendance described the audience's response to Cook's outrageous remark as "pandemonium." The moment effectively captured the increasingly incoherent essence of the end-stage radicalism of 1969.

The Panther fiasco was a setback for Dohrn and the National Office faction, and they returned to the hall determined to defeat PL. They appeared to gain traction when a Panther delegation reappeared and read a statement denouncing PL for "having deviated from Marxist-Leninist ideology." The allegation reignited the previous day's shouting match. With the assembly in an uproar, a now furious Dohrn rushed to the stage, denounced PL, and demanded that right-thinking radicals follow her in a walkout. Supporters of the National Office followed her out of the hall and, the next morning, the group voted to expel PL from SDS. That evening, the National Office group returned to the main hall to proclaim itself the legitimate convention, then marched out. Retaining the keys to the Chicago office with its membership files, Dohrn and her supporters considered themselves the true SDS. Not to be outfoxed, PL delegates met in the Coliseum the following day and proclaimed themselves the real SDS, voting to move the headquarters to Boston. The June convention marked the end of SDS as a coherent organization. One disillusioned radical succinctly expressed the growing disgust with SDS in a devastating parody of the now-famous Weatherman slogan. "You don't need a rectal thermometer," he observed, "to know who the assholes are."

Whereas PL and SDS were destined to fade into oblivion by 1972, Weatherman took shape around a core group including, among others, Dohrn, Mark Rudd, Bill Ayers, Jeff Jones, Terry Robbins, and Kathy Boudin. Michael Klonsky, the originator of the initial "revolutionary youth" position, was soon expelled following disagreements over strategy. Striving to forge themselves and their 500 adherents into "political collectives," the Chicago group took the lead in implementing revolutionary discipline aimed at eradicating lingering vestiges of "bourgeois individualism." This discipline included relentless "self-criticism" sessions aimed at instilling ideological conformity, martial arts practice, stringent diets, abstinence from drugs and alcohol, discarding the concepts of privacy and personal property, and a "smash monogamy" campaign. The latter involved compulsory sexual relations, including homosexual practices and group orgies, intended to destroy individual emotional attachments and strengthen solidarity within each collective. Dohrn, who had developed a relationship with Jeff Jones, managed to avoid the group activities through strategic absences.

That summer, Weatherman collectives prepared to launch an offensive aimed at stirring disaffected white and working-class youth into revolutionary action. The most dramatic tactic was the "jailbreak," in which Weatherman members stormed classrooms on high school and college campuses. On July 31, ten women from the Detroit collective invaded a classroom at Macomb County Community College, where they barricaded the door, subdued the instructor and uncooperative students, and subjected the stunned class to a tirade about imperialism, racism, and sexism. A similar action was undertaken in early September at South Hills High School in Pittsburgh. Some seventy-five Weatherwomen invaded the campus, rampaging through hallways, shouting slogans, and exposing their breasts before regrouping outside around a Vietcong flag, where they exhorted baffled students to join the planned National Action in Chicago in October. The radical women attacked the first police officers on the scene, fleeing only after eight carloads of reinforcements arrived. Weatherman's isolation from the rest of the New Left deepened that summer, as the alliance with the Black Panthers unraveled in early August. Panther chair Bobby Seale denounced the white radicals as "a bunch of jive bourgeois national socialists and national chauvinists." Clarifying any remaining ambiguities about Panther relations with Weatherman, Panther chief of staff David Hilliard warned, "We'll beat those little sissies', those little schoolboys' asses if they don't straighten up their politics."

These setbacks came even as Weatherman efforts to organize a revolutionary army of working-class youth brought little success. The leadership soon concluded that Weatherman could succeed only if it joined with genuine third-world revolutionary movements. In July 1969, Dohrn and a Weatherman delegation traveled to Cuba for a five-week stay. There the radicals discussed ideology, worked in the sugarcane fields, and met with representatives of the North Vietnamese government and the Vietcong. Steeled by these experiences, the leadership returned to Chicago for the much-anticipated National Action in October. In the prior weeks, collectives carried out seven more "jailbreaks" at high schools, in some cases assaulting and tying up teachers who objected.

Twenty Weathermen invaded the Harvard Center for International Affairs, destroying property and attacking staff. In Cleveland, the radicals attempted to disrupt the Davis Cup tennis matches. These actions, however dramatic, were ultimately as unproductive as were the Days of Rage in October. By the end of the year, as the expected masses of revolutionary youths failed to emerge, Weatherman was driven to conclude that only a campaign of unrelenting terrorism, carried out by an underground army, could bring down the state.

Weatherman's final public meeting, billed as the National War Council, took place in Flint, Michigan, in December 1969. A giant cardboard automatic weapon, suspended from the ceiling of the squalid ballroom, together with superheated rhetoric, hinted at the new direction. Some 400 attendees listened as speakers proclaimed the need for armed resistance alongside black and third-world revolutionaries. Mark Rudd denounced those under the spell of "white skin privilege" and advocated "the destruction of the mother country." John Jacobs declared, "We're against everything that's 'good and decent' in honky America. We will burn and loot and destroy. We are the incubation of your mother's worst nightmare." It was Dohrn's remarks, however, that would be most widely quoted in the nation's media. Weatherman regularly celebrated a number of revolutionary heroes, including Che Guevara, Ho Chi Minh, and Fidel Castro, but now, from the podium, Dohrn hailed Charles Manson, who had recently achieved public infamy as the instigator of the murders of actress Sharon Tate and four others in Los Angeles. Extolling Manson and his homicidal "family" as the epitome of white America's fears, Dohrn exulted, "Dig it, first they killed these pigs and then they ate dinner in the same room with them, then they even stuck a fork into the victim's stomach! Wild!" Dohrn later conceded that she regretted the comments, but they were uniquely representative of Weatherman's descent into the depths of irrationality. The war council ended with about 100 radicals organizing into "affinity groups" that would operate as underground terrorist cells.

The Weatherman Underground took shape in early 1970 as Dohrn and other leaders in Chicago oversaw the process of going underground. Closing the national SDS office in February, they gathered together remaining funds and set about establishing new identities, safe houses, mail drops, and a code for telephone calls. Three main "tribes" eventually coalesced, one on each coast and one in the Midwest, but Weather cells existed in a number of cities. Even as the new Central Committee set about mapping a strategy of terror bombings and kidnappings, the potential cost of such activities was driven home in dramatic fashion. Much of the New York tribe had taken up residence in a Greenwich Village townhouse owned by Cathy Wilkerson's father, and by early March they were busily assembling antipersonnel dynamite bombs. On March 6, one of the bomb makers connected the wrong wires, touching off a massive explosion that completely destroyed the townhouse. Ted Gold, Diana Oughton, and Terry Robbins died in the blast; Wilkerson and Kathy Boudin stumbled out of the smoking ruins and fled the scene.

The Greenwich Village explosion led the FBI to intensify its efforts to identify and pursue the new terrorist band, and weeks later federal indictments of twelve of those involved in the Days of Rage were issued. By year's end, Dohrn was one of six Weatherman radicals added to the FBI's Ten Most Wanted list. The townhouse deaths shook the Weatherman leadership, but failed to deter them from their campaign of terror. The volatility on the nation's campuses that spring offered further encouragement. During the 1969–70 academic year, there were at least 174 bombings on campuses and hundreds elsewhere, targeting corporate offices and government buildings. The Treasury Department noted about 5,000 bombing incidents nationwide during the same period, and the American Council on Education recorded 9,408 campus demonstrations. On May 21, the Weatherman Underground issued a taped communiqué signaling its support of the protests. "Hello, this is Bernardine Dohrn," the message began. "I'm going to read a declaration of a state of war." Dohrn extolled the revolutionary potential of the expanding youth culture and warned that Weatherman was poised to attack a symbol of "American injustice."

Beginning in early June, Weatherman made good on Dohrn's promise. That month, a bomb damaged the second floor of New York City police headquarters. In late July, a bomb was detonated at a military police post at the Presidio army base in San Francisco. Another explosion damaged a Bank of America branch in Manhattan. The greater sensation was the group's success in freeing LSD advocate Timothy Leary from a California prison in September. The Weatherman Underground continued its terror campaign that fall, responding to perceived acts of state injustice with bombings around the nation. Yet Dohrn and the leadership soon rejected this "military strategy" as inadequate, addressing the issue in a December communiqué called "New Morning–Changing Weather." In it, Dohrn embraced the importance of the youth culture and an active aboveground movement. In the future, bombings would aim at property damage, while kidnappings and assassinations "were off the table." Weatherman itself would adopt a "holistic" approach to the revolutionary struggle, recognizing the importance of feminism to the new society and abandoning collectives in favor of "families." In recognition of the expanded role accorded to women, the organization became the Weather Underground Organization (WUO).

During the next two years, the WUO retaliated for numerous "Amerikan injustices." WUO terrorists bombed the Senate wing of the U.S. Capitol, offices of the California prison system, a state office building in Albany, New York, and, in 1972, a restroom in the Pentagon. Ironically, the end of the Vietnam War posed a dilemma for the militants; peace drained much of the energy from domestic radicalism. In San Francisco, Dohrn, now living with Bill Ayers, was among those who argued for yet another reevaluation of the group's direction. Though WUO continued the bombing campaign, it was increasingly evident that armed struggle alone was a dead end. The short life of the Symbionese Liberation Army, a small group of radicals who kidnapped newspaper heiress Patty Hearst in 1974, offered proof enough of that. In May of that year, an army of 500 police ran the principals to ground in a suburban house in Compton, California, killing six of the radicals in a fusillade of teargas and bullets. In the aftermath of this debacle, the next permutation of the Weather Underground, and the final one in which Dohrn would participate, took shape in the summer of 1974.

Since 1972, the WUO had moved away from its focus on the importance of counterculture youth. By 1973, Clayton Van Lydegraf, a former member of the American Communist Party, exercised growing ideological influence over the group's principals, pushing them back toward Marxist orthodoxy and away from the idea of imminent revolution. The triumph of that position was evident in *Prairie Fire: The Politics of Revolutionary Anti-Imperialism*, a booklet published in July 1974. Dohrn was a major contributor to the new thesis, which argued for both clandestine actions and the organization of a mass revolutionary base. To this end, the Prairie Fire Organizing Committee (PFOC) was created. Within WUO-PFOC, a new Revolutionary Committee purged the New York PFOC, where most of the Weather leadership, including Dohrn and Ayers, had gravitated. Denounced as deviationists, Dohrn, Ayers, Jones, Boudin, and the remnants of the longtime leadership were either expelled from or left the organization that they had founded.

WUO-PFOC struggled to navigate the changing political currents of the late 1970s, periodically carrying out bombings, but Weatherman was in its last days. The revolutionary tide of the previous decade had long since ebbed, and the organization seemed an anachronistic remnant of a distant time. Dohrn and Ayers remained underground in Manhattan, where their first son, Zayd Shakur, was born in 1977; a second son, Malik, followed within a few years. Working at a variety of jobs, including as a waitress and a baker, Dohrn and Ayers continued to follow developments in radical politics, still unwilling to consider resurfacing. Nonetheless, many Weather radicals had wearied of life underground and, as the years passed, both arrests and voluntary surrenders

thinned the ranks of the fugitives. Mark Rudd, facing possible fines and probation, was the first to surface in 1977. In 1980, Cathy Wilkerson surrendered
and was sentenced to three years in prison. Finally, in early December 1980,
Dohrn and Ayers, after eleven years underground, surfaced. After a brief press
conference during which Dohrn defended her past activities, they caught a
plane for Chicago to face charges. She was given three years' probation and
a $1,500 fine for earlier crimes. Charges against Ayers had been dropped
earlier. Jeff Jones, arrested in the Bronx in October 1981, was also sentenced
to probation. Only days later, Kathy Boudin and members of a Black Liberation Army "family" were arrested following the botched robbery of a Brinks
armored truck and the deaths of two police officers. During the lengthy trial
period, Dohrn served seven months in prison for refusing to answer a grand
jury's questions. Boudin received a sentence of twenty years to life imprison-
ment, and was released in September 2003.

Like many former radicals, Dohrn turned to social activism in subsequent
years, becoming an advocate for children's rights. She eventually joined the
faculty of Northwestern University's School of Law, where her appointment
provoked angry criticism from some alumni. As director of the school's Children and Family Justice Center, founded in 1992, Dohrn has generally avoided
interviews that focus on her past, preferring to concentrate on the contemporary
issues that she addresses. In a 1995 interview, she still maintained that the
resort to violence in the late 1960s was appropriate, though she conceded that
the revolutionary scenario hailed by the Weather Underground was a fantasy.
Asked if SDS were a failure, Dohrn agreed that SDS "failed at our larger goals,"
but argued that tens of thousands of former radicals retained their idealism
and had dedicated their lives to improving some aspect of American society.
Like many of her fellow radicals, she said, she would always remember the
1960s as "scary times, but absolutely, intoxicating, heroic times."

Conclusion

During the 1960s, the counterculture and the New Left promised to transform
America, the first offering the complete liberation of the individual, the second
the realization of a truly participatory democracy grounded in a renewed sense
of community. Both movements followed roughly parallel paths, born of an
initial idealism and optimism about the future, but fatally drawn to ever more
radical positions as the decade wore on. Cultural radicals, enthusiastic about
the potential for self-liberation, were increasingly unwilling to concede the
legitimacy of any restraints on individual behavior. The political radicals of

the New Left, facing frustrating obstacles to the establishment of participatory democracy and interpreting continuing social injustices and the Vietnam War as symptoms of the fundamental sickness of the Establishment, easily rationalized an escalation from protest to resistance and, finally, revolution.

Jimi Hendrix was not a creator of or spokesman for the counterculture, but more appropriately a fellow traveler. Long before he became a counterculture icon, he had adopted values and behaviors that the counterculture seemed to legitimate. His musical art, born of his own personal vision, easily comported with the psychedelic style that emerged after the mid-1960s. For many, Hendrix, who was present at the seminal musical events of the late 1960s, was the embodiment of the counterculture's musical art. There were no boundaries to his music, which seemed to constantly evolve in new directions. Like many other counterculture icons, Hendrix established few boundaries in his lifestyle, with predictably tragic results. His death was a metaphor for the fate of the counterculture itself.

Bernardine Dohrn's activities in SDS offer in microcosm a history of the rise and fall of the New Left in the tumultuous 1960s. Drawn to the organization at the point at which early idealism was being rapidly supplanted by increasingly militant radicalism, Dohrn, like the New Left itself, underwent an extremely rapid ideological transformation in the late 1960s. As official government repression and violence grew, Dohrn and like-minded radicals embraced the intoxicating logic of ever-greater militancy. Weatherman and its subsequent permutations were the ultimate incarnations of a radical terrorism dedicated to the destruction of what was seen as a thoroughly corrupted American system. In a period of ten years, SDS and other New Left organizations gravitated toward increasingly dogmatic ideological positions and eventually turned into the dead end of self-destructive revolutionary fantasy.

Study Questions

1. What was the promise of the counterculture?
2. Some critics maintain that counterculture youth were "rebels without a cause." Do you agree or disagree?
3. Was Jimi Hendrix a victim of the excesses of the counterculture or of his own irresponsibility?
4. Given that SDS began as an organization dedicated to reforming the American political and social system, explain the group's drift toward radicalism and violence by the late 1960s.
5. Did the counterculture and the New Left leave any positive legacies?

Selected Bibliography

Ayers, Bill. *Fugitive Days*. Boston: Beacon, 2001.

Barber, David. *A Hard Rain Fell: SDS and Why It Failed*. Jackson: University Press of Mississippi, 2008.

Berger, Dan. *Outlaws of America: The Weather Underground and the Politics of Solidarity*. Oakland, CA: AK Press, 2006.

Black, Johnny. *Jimi Hendrix: The Ultimate Experience*. New York: Thunder's Mouth, 1999.

Chepesiuk, Ron. *Sixties Radicals, Then and Now: Candid Conversations with Those Who Shaped the Era*. Jefferson, NC: McFarland, 1995.

Collier, Peter, and David Horowitz. *Destructive Generation: Second Thoughts About the '60s*. New York: Free Press, 1989.

Cross, Charles R. *Room Full of Mirrors: A Biography of Jimi Hendrix*. New York: Hyperion, 2005.

Gitlin, Todd. *The Sixties: Years of Hope, Days of Rage*. New York: Bantam, 1987.

———. *The Whole World Is Watching: The Mass Media in the Unmaking of the New Left*. Berlekey: University of California Press, 1980.

Goode, Stephen. *Affluent Revolutionaries: A Portrait of the New Left*. London: Franklin Watts, 1974.

Henderson, David. *'Scuse Me While I Kiss the Sky: The Life of Jimi Hendrix*. New York: Bantam, 1983.

Jacobs, Ron. *The Way the Wind Blew*. New York: Verso, 1997.

Matusow, Allen. *The Unraveling of America: A History of Liberalism in the1960s*. New York: Perennial, 1984.

McKeen, William, ed. *Rock and Roll Is Here to Stay*. New York: W.W. Norton, 2000.

Sale, Kirkpatrick. *SDS*. New York: Vintage, 1973.

Shapiro, Harry, and Caesar Glebeek. *Jimi Hendrix: Electric Gypsy*. Boston: St. Martin's Griffin, 1995.

Tate, Greg. *Midnight Lightning: Jimi Hendrix and the Black Experience*. Chicago: Lawrence Hill, 2003.

Unger, Irwin. *The Movement: A History of the American New Left, 1959–72*. Lanham, MD: University Press of America, 1974.

Unger, Irwin, and Debbie Unger. *America in the 1960s*. Malchen, MA: Blackwell, 1988.

Varon, Jeremy. *Bringing the War Home: The Weather Underground, the Red Army Faction and Revolutionary Violence in the Sixties and Seventies*. Berkeley: University of California Press, 2004.

10

The Women's Movement

Revolution and Reaction

During the 1970s, a cultural war in the United States resulted in a growing national debate about major social issues and matters of the most intimate personal nature regarding the family, gender roles, and sexual relations. Two extremely bright, well-educated, and attractive women were at the forefront of this cultural contest: the journalist Gloria Steinem, a graduate of Smith College, and Phyllis Schlafly, who received a master's degree from Radcliffe College and both an undergraduate and a law degree from Washington University in St. Louis. Journalism and law were two of the battlegrounds on which Steinem and Schlafly fought in the cultural conflict that only mounted in intensity as the decade continued. While Steinem was in the vanguard of the women's movement that reemerged in the 1960s, Schlafly was a key figure in the development of the New Right, which contested the changes in personal and social relations that many Americans considered essential.

Both women were deeply involved with a series of social and political campaigns that rippled through the America of the 1960s. Steinem strongly supported women's liberation and helped found *Ms.* magazine, the National Women's Political Caucus, and the Women's Political Alliance. Schlafly, an early member of the right-wing John Birch Society, fervently backed Barry Goldwater's 1964 presidential campaign before becoming the dominant figure in the Stop ERA (equal rights amendment) and Eagle Forum organizations, which supported "family values" and condemned the purported excesses of the women's movement. The 1970s particularly saw the two women on opposite sides of a cultural chasm regarding an equal rights amendment, with Steinem insisting that the U.S. Constitution and American democracy demanded its ratification and Schlafly warning that its passage would lead to moral decay and social pathologies.

GLORIA STEINEM
Feminist Icon
(on left holding poster)

In late 1970, Brenda Feigen Fasteau—a graduate of Harvard Law School and a strong proponent of the ERA—and Gloria Steinem began formulating plans for the Women's Action Alliance (WAA), which would assist women in grappling with everyday concerns, including a dearth of employment opportunities and childcare centers. Meeting with several leading writers in the women's movement, including Susan Brownmiller, Adrienne Rich, Robin Morgan, and Vivian Gornick, they were soon exploring the possibility of establishing a national newsletter that would focus on women's issues. These writers welcomed the possibility of a magazine run by women. They were all familiar with the difficulty of getting the mainstream press to focus on feminist subjects or even well-known women, other than those considered to embody sex appeal, and they knew that even when feminist articles were accepted by the mainstream press, "anti–women's movement" writings were invariably offered as counterweights. Following one of the planning sessions, Susan Braudy informed Steinem, "The only person I could see really heading it was her, even if she kept saying she didn't want to. . . . She was very level-headed and calm, she would be a great person to be in charge of the magazine and she shouldn't shirk that."

In the meantime, requisite funding for the magazine had to be obtained. Fasteau, who soon decided to concentrate on the WAA, introduced Steinem to Elizabeth Forsling Harris, a skilled fund-raiser who was seeking to establish a newsletter, *Women—The Majority Report*. Steinem and Harris joined with Patricia Carbine, the editor of *McCall's*, in an effort to establish a national women's magazine. Harris and Carbine soon convinced Steinem that a popularly based women's magazine should be their goal, rather than a publication that appealed largely to activists. The publisher of the *Washington Post,* Katharine Graham, provided $20,000 in seed money, while Clay Felker of *New York* magazine, where Steinem wrote a political column, promised to include a thirty-page preview on "the contagion of feminism" in his close-of-the-year issue. Newsstand profits were to be divided equally between Felker and *Ms.*, while *New York* would retain any advertising revenue. Shortly after the new *Ms.* magazine appeared, its founders claimed that Felker "had begun to believe, like us, that something deep, irresistible, and possibly historic, was happening to women."

In the meantime, the special issue of *New York* containing the *Ms.* preview quickly sold out—300,000 copies in eight days—garnering an enthusiastic response from readers and interest from possible financial investors. Those investors were put off, however, according to writer Amy Erdman Farrell, by the insistence of Steinem and the other founders that their staff possess full control of the proposed magazine's finances and editorial stance, including authority to decline antifeminist advertising. Still, Warner Communications agreed to invest $1 million in return for 25 percent of the magazine's stock. One other issue needed to be immediately resolved: the naming of the new publication. Steinem favored the name *Sisters*, to express affinity with the women's movement, but Carbine worried that such a title would prove disconcerting to individuals with a Catholic school upbringing. By contrast, *Ms.*, with its deliberate disclaimer of marital status, possessed several advantages, having long been employed by secretaries, Congress, and women who disliked being labeled by their relationship with male partners. The magazine's editors declared, "The use of Ms. isn't meant to protect either the married or the unmarried from social pressure—only to signify a human being. It's symbolic, and important. There's a lot in a name."

One of the founders of *Ms.* magazine, Gloria Marie Steinem was born in Toledo, Ohio, on March 25, 1934, to Ruth Nuneviller Steinem and an antiques dealer and would-be resort operator, Leo Steinem. Ruth, a third-generation German American, and Leo, whose parents were born in Germany, met as students at the University of Toledo. His mother, Pauline, an early member of the Hebrew Ladies' Benevolent Society, was a distinguished enough suffragist to end up in *Who's Who in America*. She was drawn to the theosophical movement, which blended occidental and oriental religious tenets, while Ruth also became an ardent theosophist. Unhappy as a teacher, she began writing columns for local newspapers, while Leo, whose parents were affluent, flitted from job to job, working in real estate and as a freelance journalist. In 1930, five years after the birth of Suzanne, her first child, Ruth experienced a nervous breakdown.

Gloria Steinem was aware of her mother's insecurities and anxieties, but her childhood appeared charmed, at least on the surface. Her father, an easy-going romantic, doted on her, and his purchase of a resort at Clark Lake, Michigan, enabled her to spend summers there. Winters found the Steinems on the move from their three-bedroom home, invariably heading for warm weather spots in Florida or California. On occasion, Gloria attended local schools, but at other times her mother tutored her; following Ruth's lead, Gloria devoured books, particularly those by Louisa May Alcott, author of *Little Women*. However, in 1944, Ruth and Leo separated, and Gloria and her mother temporarily resided in Amherst, Massachusetts, where Suzanne was attending Smith College. Eventually Steinem and her increasingly depressed mother moved to the dilapidated house in Toledo that Ruth had inherited from her parents. Steinem was often compelled to take on parental roles, including shopping, cooking, and cleaning the house. While attending public high school, she joined various student organizations, worked as a salesgirl, helped to form a sorority, and entered beauty contests. Due to Ruth's deteriorating emotional state, Gloria moved to the Georgetown district in Washington, DC, during her senior year, to live with her sister. Elected student council vice president at her new school, she was also voted Prettiest Girl by the senior class. In 1952, when the postwar cult of domesticity was flourishing, Steinem began attending Smith College.

Smith enabled Steinem to distance herself from her mother and the troubled financial circumstances back in Toledo. She related tales of her family to more affluent classmates, but at the time did not appear emotionally scarred by her childhood. Her expenses were covered by money received from her mother, a small scholarship, a student loan, and the pay and tips she earned as a waitress; Leo also sent funds, but seemingly never when the money was most needed. Steinem's lack of financial resources led to her characteristic attire of jeans and a gray sweatshirt, which contrasted markedly with the shorts and expensive sweaters worn by many classmates. Her Jewish background also set her at odds with the other Smith women, most of whom were Protestant.

After initial difficulties, Steinem excelled as a student at Smith, majoring in government and becoming temporarily attracted to Marxism. She spent her junior year in Europe, with a brief visit to Paris and Geneva before she enrolled in a summer program at St. Anthony's College in Oxford. Following her graduation magna cum laude and selection as class historian, Steinem took advantage of a Chester Bowles Fellowship to travel in India, where she remained for a year-and-a-half. While overseas, she broke off an early engagement shortly after undergoing an abortion in London, after a doctor indicated that her pregnancy constituted a "health risk." She recalled, "This was the first time I stopped passively accepting whatever happened to me and took responsibility." Legal abortions were then all but impossible to obtain in the United States.

After spending several weeks in London, Steinem traveled, via Paris, Geneva, and Athens, back to India, where she studied at the University of Delhi for three months. She covered her expenses by devising a guidebook, *The Thousand Indias*, for the Indian government's tourist bureau; and in Calcutta she darkened her brown hair, put on a sari, and appeared in advertisements for clothing, toothpaste, shampoo, and cold cream. In Madras, Steinem went to Gandhigram, where she met a number of Gandhi's followers.

Stopping in Burma, Hong Kong, and Japan along the way, Steinem returned to the United States in 1958, determined to write and engage in social advocacy. She sought work in New York City, but failed to garner a position with the India Committee of the Asia Society; or through Norman Cousins, editor of the *Saturday Review;* or with *The Ed Sullivan Show.* Unhappily moving to Cambridge, Massachusetts, Steinem became the director of the Independent Research Service, an educational foundation that helped young Americans participate in International Communist Youth festivals. In 1959, Steinem attended the Youth Festival, held in Vienna, which drew students from across the globe. Afterward, she condemned both "Western colonialism" and "Communist imperialism," concluding, "I suppose that this was my small world equivalent of going off to join the Spanish Revolution."

Soon returning to New York, Steinem sought to make a living as a freelance journalist. Through mutual friends, she was introduced to Clay Felker, then editor of *Esquire*, a literary men's magazine, who assigned her short articles. Although uncredited, she thus joined well-known writers like Gay Talese, Tom Wolfe, James Baldwin, and Gore Vidal as an *Esquire* contributor. She coauthored articles for *Esquire* with Robert Benton, all while the two carried on a love affair. Subsequently, Harold Hayes, another *Esquire* editor, recommended that Harvey Kurtzman, who had devised *Mad* magazine, hire her as an editorial assistant for his fledgling publication, *Help! For Tired Minds.* Kurtzman considered her "very talented" and admired her "chutzpah" and beauty. A wire-service article referred to "cool Miss Steinem," a tall "willowy beauty, 34–24–34," who was said to possess "so much I.Q. . . . way behind those big brown eyes."

In 1962, Steinem received an assignment from Felker to explore the impact of the birth control pill—then on the market for two years—on women attending institutions of higher learning. The article, appearing in *Esquire*'s September issue, was titled "The Moral Disarmament of Betty Coed." As Steinem's writing career developed, her relationship with Benton foundered, and she began dating Tom Guinzberg, a publisher at Viking Press, who had a home in Southampton, Long Island. Guinzberg later referred to her as "a very zesty lady; in no way inhibited; there was no one else like her." Art director Henry Wolf, who had left *Esquire* for *Show*, an arts and culture periodical, paid Steinem for a pair of articles on Hugh Hefner's Playboy Club. Operating undercover as a Playboy bunny waitress with "three-quarter-inch eyelashes, blue satin ears, and an overflowing bosom," Steinem crafted "A Bunny's Tale—an intended exposé about Hefner's operation in New York City and the sexual harassment she encountered. *Show* introduced her first article with the observation that she combined "the hidden qualities of a Phi Beta Kappa, *magna cum laude* graduate of Smith College with the more obvious ones of a dancer and beauty queen."

While worrying that her *Playboy* articles would stigmatize her, Steinem also wrote for *Glamour* magazine, producing essays on "Funny Ways to Find a Man on the Beach," "How the Single Girl *Really* Spends Her Money," and "How to (Put Up With/Put Down) a Difficult Man." *Glamour* featured a lengthy spread about Steinem, "one of the bold spirits," who had "beautiful legs on thin-heeled shoes" and would prefer to be "Audrey Hepburn in the CIA . . . with bosoms." In 1964, she wrote essays on author James Baldwin for *Vogue* and former first lady Jacqueline Kennedy for *Esquire*. The following year her article on the topless bathing suit designed by Rudy Gernreich appeared in the *New York Times Magazine*; she also wrote articles on actress Julie Andrews and author Saul Bellow for *Vogue*, "The Ins and Outs of Pop Culture" for *Life*, and "Why I Write" for *Harper's*.

Steinem shared an apartment with the artist Barbara Nessim, first on New York City's Upper East Side and then on West Fifty-sixth Street. For a short spell, she went out with the musician Paul Desmond, who performed with the Dave Brubeck Quartet; presidential assistant Theodore Sorensen, whom she visited at the White House; Herb Sargent, producer of the television program *That Was the Week That Was*, for which Steinem, like Buck Henry and Alan Alda, would write; and Mike Nichols, soon to become a foremost Broadway and Hollywood director. Steinem continued to write for *Glamour*, producing articles on Truman Capote and Barbra Streisand, as well as additional pieces for the *New York Times Magazine*. As she acquired a bit of fame, *Glamour* referred to her as "New York's Newest Young Wit"; *Newsday* offered an article about her, titled "The World's Most Beautiful Byline"; and *Newsweek* produced "News Girl," which referred to Steinem as "a striking brunette . . . as much a celebrity as a reporter . . . (who) often generates news in her own right." *Newsweek* quoted Nichols, who termed her "the smartest, funniest, and most serious person I know," and actress Julie Andrews, who stated, "I think I'd like to be her if I weren't me." Marilyn Bender, in *The Beautiful People*, wrote, "Miss Steinem swings with the new society despite the fact that she is what used to be called whistle-bait."

From time to time, Steinem also received assignments that placed her at the cutting edge of American politics during the 1960s. In mid-1965, she met with South Dakota senator George McGovern at the airport in Boston, as both prepared to head to a farm owned by Harvard economics professor John Kenneth Galbraith and his family, for the Galbraith family retreat. Sharing a car, Steinem and McGovern conversed about the war in Vietnam, North Vietnamese president Ho Chi Minh, and the stance of congressional doves. Sharing a ride with McGovern back from a weekend seminar in rural Vermont, Steinem recognized that he possessed courage, "anger and a sense of history," leading her to wonder "how this unpretentious, honest man became a politician." In September 1967, Steinem expressed regret that McGovern had declined Allard Lowenstein's suggestion that he run against President Johnson in the upcoming presidential primaries. Steinem wrote: "It would have been a brief flurry, but the country might have been made a little more aware of this man Robert Kennedy described as 'the only decent man in the Senate.'"

In 1968, Steinem began working regularly as writer and editor for Felker's *New York* magazine, which broke away from the faltering *New York Herald Tribune.* Her topics varied widely, from Ho Chi Minh to actor Paul Newman to New York City and national affairs, and she also produced a column, "The City Politic." Bitterly opposed to the Vietnam War, Steinem helped to draft a political advertisement, "Writers and Editors War Tax Protest," which conveyed the signatories' readiness to refuse to pay 10 percent of their federal income taxes as a statement condemning U.S. engagement in Vietnam. Driven by "desperation," she served as a speechwriter for Minnesota senator Eugene McCarthy, who ran as an antiwar candidate, but she became disenchanted with him, viewing him as too distant to have a real chance to be elected. Writing about the assassination of Martin Luther King Jr., Steinem quoted his line, "The patience of oppressed people cannot endure forever." Influenced by union organizer Cesar Chávez, she came to appreciate New York senator Robert F. Kennedy's "compassion, his peculiar ability to identify with the excluded and deprived"; after his murder, she expressed her sense that "there was nothing else to do, nothing *worth* doing." Steinem attended the disastrous Democratic National Convention in Chicago in August, where she supported a late bid by McGovern to deny Vice President Hubert Humphrey the presidential nomination; she helped put out buttons reading, "George McGovern: He's the *Real* McCarthy." During the protests, Steinem, who considered the police rampage to be "much worse" than even television coverage suggested, got roughed up by Mayor Richard Daley's security guards. The *Washington Post* contained a column that described her in Chicago as "the mini-skirted pin-up girl of the intelligentsia."

During the convention, Steinem met Rafer Johnson, the 1960 Olympics champion in the decathlon and a supporter of the recently assassinated Senator Kennedy; Steinem became romantically involved with Johnson and then with former NFL running back turned Hollywood actor Jim Brown, her first affairs with black men. She wrote about Brown in "The Black John Wayne," applauding his determination to be cast as "a Negro hero for Everyman." At the same time, she acknowledged that Brown was a "male chauvinist" who "has low standards for women." During this same period, Steinem became more conversant with feminism, as indicated by her review of Carolyn Bird's *Born Female* in the *New York Times*. Steinem acknowledged that she had long denied that being a professional writer was more difficult for a woman than for a man. She had regularly argued, "equal rights were won by our grandmothers in a necessary, but rather quaint revolution." Moreover, "it seemed unfeminine to complain." Now, she was more convinced about gender discrimination.

Steinem also became involved with Cesar Chávez's farm workers' movement after meeting Marion Moses, a union organizer who had traveled to New York City seeking support for the campaign. Steinem helped to convince the editors of *Time* to place Chávez on their cover, got the producers of the *Today* TV show to speak with him, and interviewed him for *Look*. Steinem and Moses helped set up a benefit for Chávez's movement at Carnegie Hall, with appearances by social comic Mort Sahl, actress Lauren Bacall, actor Eli Wallach, and George McGovern. In May 1969, Steinem garnered publicity for a march Chávez was undertaking in California, drawing in Senator Ted Kennedy, Congressman John Tunney, and former governor Pat Brown, among others.

In 1969, Steinem, along with Peter Maas, continued producing "The City Politic" column in *New York*, writing about "the New Marriage," Mayor John Lindsay, and women's liberation, while also providing support for McGovern's germinating presidential campaign. One biographer, Carolyn Heilbrun, indicates that Steinem failed to participate "in the radical women's movement" until that year, when she went to a gathering by the Redstockings, the militant women's group that had spun off from New York Radical Women. The latter group had been involved in the previous year's demonstration at the Miss America pageant, where feminists contended that beauty contests were inherently sexist. Slowly, Steinem was becoming more conscious of the gender divide that afflicted American womanhood. In March 1969, at a forum on abortion held by the Redstockings at the Washington Square Methodist Church in New York City, Steinem experienced, as Heilbrun suggests, "her conversion to feminism." Steinem later referred to this moment as "the great blinding lightbulb." As she recalled, "Suddenly, I was no longer learning intellectually what was wrong. I knew." In *New York* magazine, she predicted that radical women activists could help create "a long-lasting and important mass movement" if they acted to reshape the middle-class-oriented National Organization for Women (NOW) and linked up with less affluent women concerned about childcare and welfare.

As the 1960s approached an end, the women's movement had become a powerful social and political force, although already displaying the propensity for sectarianism that beset the New Left and civil rights campaigns. In 1963, President John Kennedy's Commission on the Status of Women had discussed "pervasive limitations" confronting working women, and Title VII of the 1964 Civil Right Act added to the ferment, prohibiting job discrimination related to race, creed, national origin, and sex. Betty Friedan's best-selling book *The Feminine Mystique* (1963) charged that American womanhood was ensnared by "a problem that has no name." Spurring the first wave of modern feminism, Friedan tellingly warned that the American woman was characterized simply as her "husband's wife, children's mother, server of physical needs of husband, children, home," not "by her own actions." Women in the civil rights, antiwar, and student movements, like female abolitionists before the Civil War, expressed their own concerns, condemning the gender-driven orientation of male compatriots. Eventually, young radical women joined consciousness-raising groups and formed organizations like New York Radical Women, WITCH (Women's International Terrorist Conspiracy from Hell), and Redstockings. In the meantime, a group of upper-middle-class women, like Friedan, established NOW, seeking to challenge gender discrimination in legislatures and the courts. By 1969, radical women were more alienated still and began defiantly demanding female empowerment, including abortion rights.

In September 1969, Steinem spoke at the Women's National Democratic Club in Washington, DC, on the women's liberation movement. Late that year, in a piece for *Look* titled "Why We Need a Woman President in 1976," Steinem stated, "Surely a woman in the White House is not an impossible feminist cause. It's only a small step in the feminist revolution." Increasingly, she began delivering speeches on behalf of the movement, often joined by Dorothy Pitman Hughes, a black woman who had established a leading childcare center on Manhattan's West Side, or Flo Kennedy, a militant African American attorney. They urged the legalization of abortion, equal pay for equal work, and adoption of an equal rights amendment to the U.S. Constitution. Writing in the *Washington Post* in June 1970, Steinem titled an article "Women's Liberation Aims to Free Men, Too." Harking back to her earliest entry on the national scene, she wrote an article for *McCall's* titled "What *Playboy* Doesn't Know About Women Could Fill a Book."

To the dismay of many women, Steinem began to receive attention as a symbol of the women's movement. A photograph of Steinem, taken despite her opposition, on the August 1970 cover of *Newsweek*, was paired with an essay, "The New Woman." The article highlighted her physical attractiveness and romantic involvements, along with her career. *Newsweek* termed her the "unlikely guru" of women's liberation, who was wrestling "against the handicaps of her own beauty, chic, celebrity and professional success." Her speaking partner, Flo Kennedy, was quoted as saying that Steinem's "principal value may be that she is so glamorous," given the fact that "we are a package-oriented society." The October 1971 edition of *Esquire* contained an article by Leonard Levitt, discussing this "enigmatic femme fatale" and contending, "No man who seems to know how the wind blows can afford to ignore Gloria, the intellectuals' pinup." The August 31, 1970, issue of *Time* included Steinem's article "What Would It Be Like If Women Win." She opened by acknowledging that "any change is fearful, especially one affecting both politics and sex roles." Then, she stated forthrightly, "Women don't want to exchange places with men," no matter what "male chauvinists" charged. On the other hand, women did seek to transform the system of American capitalism "to one more based on merit." "In Women's Lib Utopia," Steinem wrote, good jobs for women and "decent pay for the bad ones" performed by women would be available, the length of the workday would be reduced, and the nation's "*machismo* problems" would be sharply lessened. She went on to call for an end to unequal sexual partnerships; for child rearing focused on talent, not gender; and for an educationally based "break down" of "traditional sex roles." Parental responsibilities would be equalized, "blatantly sexist laws" eradicated, and "a more peaceful society" possibly forthcoming. Steinem concluded, "If women's lib wins, perhaps we all do."

In a period when media outlets and opponents of the women's movement attempted to denigrate feminists as unattractive, crazed man-haters, the seemingly unflappable Steinem obviously served to refute such notions. At the same time, she appeared at odds with more radical feminists, many of whom adopted anti-male perspectives, celebrated lesbianism (which Friedan decried), and condemned establishment politics. In the late 1970s, Steinem joined with Brenda Feigen Fasteau to found the Women's Action Alliance and explore the possibility of establishing a national women's newsletter. Rather than a newsletter, *Ms.* magazine soon appeared and immediately identified with the women's movement. The insert in the December 20, 1971, issue of *New York* contained articles titled "Raising Kids Without Sex Roles," "The Housewife's Moment of Truth," "Women Tell the Truth About Their Abortions," "I Want a Wife," and Steinem's "Sisterhood," among other selections.

The ideas propounded by the women's movement, Steinem wrote, proved "contagious and irresistible. They hit women like a revelation" and produced "this sea-change in women's view of ourselves" regardless of "age, economics, worldly experience, race, [or] culture." Women's "discovery" that gender differences fed "the economic and social profit of patriarchy males as a group" served to "give birth to sisterhood," producing "the exhilaration of growth and self-discovery." Now, Steinem asserted, a "lack of esteem that makes us put each other down" remained "the major enemy of sisterhood." Steinem believed that she could "sometimes deal with men as equals, and therefore . . . afford to like them as individual human beings"; she herself had begun to date Frank Thomas, another black man, who was then serving as director of the Bedford-Stuyvesant Development Corporation. Most important, Steinem wrote, "I no longer feel strange by myself, or with a group of women in public. I feel just fine. I am continually moved to discover I have sisters. I am beginning, just beginning, to find out who I am."

Her new magazine received a boost when David Frost allowed Steinem to expound at length on his television program regarding what *Ms.* represented. Nevertheless, *Ms.* encountered early difficulties, including fundamental disagreements between Steinem and cofounder Elizabeth Harris concerning the magazine's operations. To the dismay of Harris, who envisioned a more traditional workplace atmosphere, Steinem hoped to create a publication that was "writer-centered, nonhierarchical," as Amy Erdman Farrell records. Along with another cofounder, Patricia Carbine, Steinem sought to reshape the publishing and advertising industries to make them more democratic and less sexist. Nevertheless, radical feminists were displeased that "'respectable' feminists" filled staff positions. Still, thousands of women wrote impassioned letters to the editors of the magazine, pouring out heartfelt stories of personal anguish, faded dreams, battering, and rape.

Great hopes existed for Steinem and *Ms.* magazine, in the very period when the women's movement appeared to be making striking gains. *McCall's* named Steinem its 1972 Woman of the Year, terming her feminism's "most effective spokeswoman and symbol." In 1972, the U.S. Congress passed the equal rights amendment, while the Supreme Court ruled the following year in *Roe v. Wade* that abortion was generally legal within the first two trimesters of a woman's pregnancy. The Boston Women's Health Collective published *Our Bodies, Ourselves*, offering feminist perspectives on basic health care. More established organizations like the National Women's Political Caucus and NOW experienced expansion of their own. Women's studies programs cropped up on university campuses, while the number of women attending medical and law schools mounted. Rape crisis centers, shelters for battered women, and women's health clinics appeared in many American communities.

Supporting all these advances, Steinem and *Ms.* seemed to be at the forefront of the women's movement, which resulted in still greater celebrity for her but also sharp-edged criticism from both feminists and staunch opponents of feminism. While some feminists wanted *Ms.* to adopt an even stronger stance supporting women's rights, Phyllis Schlafly and other opponents of the movement and the ERA denounced the magazine as "anti-family, anti-children, and pro-abortion." At times, Steinem sought to adopt a lower profile, as when she expressed her new credo in late 1974 to *People* magazine, which placed her on its cover: "Don't do anything that another feminist could do instead." As she recognized, "It's the practice of the media to set up leaders and knock them down, which is damaging to movements. We need to have enough women in the public eye so that we can't all be knocked down." Fortunately for Steinem, the repeated blows she received were somewhat softened by a new, extended relationship she developed with Stan Pottinger, a younger man who headed the Justice Department's Civil Rights Division. *Ms.* had continued to adopt courageous stances supportive of women's rights and human rights in general, featuring covers that highlighted battered women, abused children, and sexual harassment. Such topics underscored a central premise of the women's movement, that "the personal is the political." Controversies swirled about the magazine and its editors as a result. In its own fashion, *Ms.* sought to encourage consciousness-raising among its readers and the general public, as it also emphasized the purportedly superior aspects of "the women's culture."

By the mid-1970s, nevertheless, both the magazine and Steinem suffered vilification at the hands of radical feminists, who produced a lengthy press release titled "Redstockings Discloses Gloria Steinem's CIA Cover-Up." They argued that Steinem had long been connected to the CIA and insisted that the publication she had founded and edited was "hurting the women's liberation movement." *Ms.* was said to be "blocking knowledge of the authentic activists and ideas" of the movement. The accusations stung Steinem noticeably, as she lost weight and appeared to be "on the verge of going to pieces." Steinem was reluctant to respond to the charges, although she had long ago acknowledged to *Ramparts*, the radical magazine, that twenty years earlier she had worked for the Independent Research Service, which had received CIA funding. Finally, however, she produced a six-page letter that was delivered to the feminist press, condemning the "breathtaking personal viciousness" of the Redstockings' press release. Hardly helping matters was the decision by Ellen Willis, a former leader of Redstockings, to resign from the *Ms.* staff, claiming that the magazine's editors failed to take to heart criticisms by radical feminists. Betty Friedan, an iconic figure inside the women's movement, took the opportunity to attack Steinem, by whom she frequently felt overshadowed. As the furor seemed about to dissipate, the *New York Times* presented a lengthy article on Steinem, highlighting the CIA accusation and discussing her mother's troubled history. The *Washington Post* offered its own harsh perspective regarding *Ms.* on October 5, 1975: "The *Ms.* myth is waning." Steinem was defended by Vivian Gornick, who worried about a revisiting of the Old Left's propensity to sectarianism and personal vilification.

Notwithstanding the withering attacks that came her way, Steinem continued to write and speak on behalf of the women's movement. She increasingly urged ratification of the ERA, which was suffering from a backlash of its own, led by Phyllis Schlafly, which eventually doomed it. In 1977, President Jimmy Carter appointed Steinem to the National Commission on the Observation of International Women's Year. In November 1977, the National Women's Conference held its convention in Houston, considered by Steinem "a landmark" because it highlighted "the economic rights of workers, including homemakers; a 'minority women's plank' . . . a 'sexual preference plank' . . . and 'a national health security program.'" Following the convention, Steinem received a Woodrow Wilson fellowship to explore "the long-term implications of feminism," but she spent most of her time on issues related to *Ms.* and the ERA, while also backing Bella Abzug's unsuccessful bid for New York City's mayoral post. Refuting arguments by Schlafly and other antifeminists, Steinem insisted that the ERA "has nothing to do with whether gays adopt children, does not increase the power of the Federal government, does not lead to unisex toilets," but would increase "the rights of women who work at home."

In the July 1978 issue of *Ms.*, Steinem analyzed the state of the women's movement, discussing "the second wave of feminism" and the backlash it had encountered. She continued working on *Ms.* and wrote a series of best sellers, many autobiographical but one focusing on the life and meaning of Marilyn Monroe. She maintained a high profile in the years ahead, through her opposition to pornography and violence against women, her involvement in social protest campaigns, and her well-publicized romances, including one with Mortimer Zuckerman, a wealthy Bostonian who owned *U.S. News & World Report* and the *New York Daily News*, among other publications. She also maintained her involvement with the Ms. Foundation for Women, which initiated Take Our Daughters to Work Day in 1992, and Voters for Choice, an organization designed to combat right-wing political action groups. In September 2000, the sixty-six-year-old Steinem married for the first time, wedding David Bale, a white South African entrepreneur, who suffered a fatal brain lymphoma three years later. She continued to be politically active, serving as president of Voters for Choice and as Founding President of the Ms. Foundation for Women, which sought to encourage grassroots efforts intended to empower both women and girls.

PHYLLIS SCHLAFLY
Counterrevolutionary on the Right

In 1923, Alice Paul, founder of the National Women's Party, urged passage of an equal rights amendment, designed to prevent gender-based discrimination. The amendment proved controversial, even among women activists, with some fearing the removal of legislation that protected working women. The 1963 *Presidential Report on American Women*, issued by the President's Commission on the Status of Women, acknowledged women's traditional roles as wives, housekeepers, and child-raisers, but also underscored the inequalities that female laborers encountered. Significantly, the work of the national commission led to the establishment of state commissions in all fifty states by 1967. In the meantime, Congress passed the Equal Pay Act (1963), which required equal pay for equal work, and the modern feminist movement arose, ranging from NOW, which largely served as a voice for professional women, to consciousness-raising groups, initially drawn from the New Left. In 1967, the eighty-two-year-old Alice Paul convinced NOW to endorse the ERA. The newest version of the ERA stated, "Equality of rights under the law shall not be denied or abridged by the United States or by any state on account of sex." The measure passed Congress in 1972, with the House voting approval by 354–23 and the Senate by 84–8. Democrats and Republicans, liberals and conservatives, including senators Ted Kennedy and Strom Thurmond, expressed support for the ERA. Within a month, fourteen states voted for its adoption and inside a year, thirty states had ratified the ERA, only eight fewer than required.

The ERA appeared headed for certain ratification, but a concerted campaign, orchestrated by Phyllis Schlafly, a right-wing Republican activist, prevented ratification, to the astonishment and dismay of feminists like Gloria Steinem. A believer in traditional values and an avowed opponent of government power, Schlafly was determined to halt the ERA. The amendment's initial clause requiring "equality of rights under the law," Schlafly feared, would demand sweeping transformations in private areas such as marriage, divorce, child custody, and adoption. The second section, empowering Congress "to enforce, by appropriate legislation, the provisions of this article," thereby delegating unprecedented powers to Washington, DC, troubled her even more. Initially, Schlafly had viewed the ERA as relatively innocuous. Another conservative, Shirley Spellerberg, attempted to convince Schlafly to oppose the measure while Congress debated it. As Spellerberg recalled, "Phyllis and I could have stopped ERA" at that point, but "I just couldn't get her to move." However, after a friend sent Schlafly additional information about the ERA, she determined to thwart its passage. She believed that state legislators would refuse to ratify the amendment if they "knew what ERA really meant." Schlafly moved to build a national mass movement in opposition to the ERA, declaring herself head of STOP ERA.

Schlafly was particularly upset that the version of the ERA that sailed through Congress excluded an earlier proposed clause declaring, "Nothing in the amendment will be construed to deprive persons of the female sex of any of the rights, benefits, and exemptions now conferred by law on persons of the female sex." She was equally disturbed that none of the nine amendments to the ERA proposed by Senator Sam J. Ervin of North Carolina had been accepted. Ervin insisted that the ERA should maintain preferential measures for women and provide that both the draft and military combat would remain male preserves. For her part, Schlafly was worried that the ERA would result in the discarding of state laws requiring husbands to support their wives. That would lead, she feared, to an inevitable weakening of the American family, which was already saddled with a rising divorce rate and the growing number of two-income households, many of which required both partners to work in order to maintain a certain standard of living. Schlafly especially worried about the fate of women's colleges, middle-aged homemakers who lacked occupational skills, and working-class women who were protected by special legislation.

Schlafly warned that the ERA would embolden homosexuals, who would undoubtedly demand the right to marry and to adopt children. The ERA, Schlafly noted, "bans discrimination on account of sex, and it is precisely on account of sex that a state now denies a marriage license to a man and a man." She also objected to the ERA's apparent encouragement of abortion, under the equal protection clause of the Fourteenth Amendment. But the issue of military service for women troubled her most of all, since the House Judiciary Committee had declared that under the ERA, if ratified, "not only would women, including mothers, be subject to the draft, but the military would be compelled to place them in combat units alongside of men." By contrast, she warned, the ERA would hardly result in equal pay for equal work, for the amendment failed to target individual behavior. Consequently, she dismissed the ERA as the "Men's Liberation Amendment," which would reduce long-standing protections for women without substituting new ones in their stead. Such provocative statements would soon make Phyllis Schlafly a prominent figure in the culture wars of the 1970s and beyond.

On August 15, 1924, Phyllis MacAlpin Stewart Schlafly was born in St. Louis, Missouri, the first child of twenty-eight-year-old Odile "Dadie" Dodge Stewart and forty-five-year-old John "Bruce" Stewart. Dadie's ancestors included General Henry Dodge, an Indian fighter, and François Valle, a Revolutionary War hero. The childhood of blonde, blue-eyed Phyllis proved comfortable and secure, although her father, a heavy-equipment sales engineer for Westinghouse, became unemployed during the Great Depression, shortly after the birth of a second child. Although Bruce lacked a pension, the family never went hungry or lacked housing, but the children went with Dadie to reside for a time with her uncle in Los Angeles; Bruce stayed in

St. Louis, fruitlessly searching for work. After her return from California, Dadie worked in a department store, taught English at a public elementary school, and became a librarian at the St. Louis Art Museum in 1937. Bruce finally found employment again, first with the War Production Board and later with the Reconstruction Finance Corporation. A staunch Republican, he disliked the welfare programs established under President Franklin D. Roosevelt, championing instead unfettered private enterprise.

Although Schlafly initially went to public schools, she attended a Catholic institution in the third grade and, beginning in the seventh grade, again received a parochial education at City House, an all-girls Sacred Heart school. She wore clothing hand-knitted by her grandmother, while Dadie insisted on exposing her daughters to "the finest things," including the theater and ballet. City House's regimen was rigorous, even rigid; the school day lasted eight full hours and the importance of adhering to moral values was underscored. Schlafly thrived at City House, acquiring a reputation as a disciplined, brilliant student and graduating as valedictorian in 1941. Hoping to enroll at Wellesley College, Schlafly was compelled, due to family circumstances, to accept a scholarship to attend another all-girls institution, Maryville College in St. Louis. After her freshman year, Schlafly transferred to Washington University. To keep expenses down, she resided at her parents' apartment, and she worked a demanding, forty-eight-hour-a-week nighttime shift at the St. Louis Ordnance Plant to pay her tuition. Schlafly continued on the assembly line for two full years, reveling in being "her own boss . . . delightfully free and important" and later referring to that period as "the most wonderful two years of my life—a unique experience." She graduated early with a major in political science, received honors, and became a member of Phi Beta Kappa. A year later, the twenty-year-old Schlafly, assisted by a scholarship and money earned from Todd Studios as a model, completed her master's degree at Radcliffe College, having taken her courses from Harvard faculty. Dating regularly, she attended theatrical performances, heard the Boston Symphony perform, and enjoyed various excursions outside Boston.

Heading for Washington, DC, Schlafly obtained a position with the American Enterprise Association (AEA), a congressional research organization that celebrated free enterprise. Already, she viewed with displeasure "bloated" bureaucracies that "overburdened" taxpayers. For the AEA, Schlafly analyzed prospective congressional legislation and drafted speeches for conservative congressional members. Following a year with the AEA, Schlafly determined that she had "had enough of the single woman's life in Washington," so she returned to her parents' home in St. Louis. Claude Bakewell, a conservative who was running for Congress against John Sullivan, a liberal, Democratic incumbent, hired her as his campaign manager. Bakewell was "impressed by her incredible knowledge of the most nitty-gritty details of St. Louis ward politics." As he recalled, "Here was this beautiful young girl sitting in my living room analyzing what I had to do to win, and she had so much plain good political sense, I had to keep looking at her to remind myself I wasn't talking to a fat, old cigar-chomping ward heeler." Schlafly, portraying Sullivan as enamored with foreign aid or what she called "foreign giveaways," accused him of favoring a policy of "spend and spend, tax and tax." She also insisted that during the Roosevelt and Truman administrations, communists "had wormed their way into positions of power," hoping to "disrupt a nation's economic foundation and destroy the people's confidence in their government." The "smooth, organized, tireless campaign" that Schlafly ran for Bakewell enabled him to win the race.

Schlafly next served as librarian and speechwriter for the First National Bank in St. Louis and as an assistant to the vice president of the St. Louis Union Trust Company, helping to put out its newsletter. the *St. Louis Union Trust Company Letter*, she noted, catered to "basically anti-New Deal" individuals who favored "personal integrity . . . freedom" and "responsibility," not "the all-powerful state." Greatly impressed with such an analysis, Fred Schlafly—a Harvard Law School graduate, successful practitioner of corporate law in Alton, and the son and grandson of wealthy businessmen—headed for St. Louis to meet the "man" he presumed to have crafted it. It proved to be "love at first sight," Schlafly remembered. Seven months later, on October 20, twenty-four-year-old Phyllis married thirty-nine-year-old Fred, who had considered himself a "confirmed bachelor"; she later quipped, "Fred rescued me from the life of a working girl." They shared a staunchly conservative philosophy, with Fred rhyming that a liberal was generous "with YOUR money and life, / He will even expropriate YOUR wife" and Phyllis claiming that liberals "lied and cheated the people," debasing "our language in line with the Red."

Later, Schlafly insisted that for the initial fifteen years of her marriage, she focused on her six children, whom she taught to read and write, and her husband, a devout Catholic and hard-line anticommunist who would be credited with helping to shape his wife's political outlook. Chief Justice Earl Warren angrily resigned from the American Bar Association following a series of scathing reports Fred produced for the association's Committee on Communist Tactics, Strategy, and Objectives. Fred often spoke at educational institutions connected with Dr. Fred Schwarz's Christian Anti-Communist Crusade. While attending to her growing family, Schlafly frequently wrote and conducted research in the late evening after her children had gone to bed. She became active in her community, serving as a leader of the YWCA's local chapter, the Community Chest drive, and the League of Women Voters and as a radio commentator for the National Conference of Christians and Jews. Deemed "one of Alton's most prominent civic leaders," she undertook her first run for a congressional seat in 1952, against incumbent congressman Melvyn Price. Schlafly seemed displeased at times with being called "the good-looking blond candidate" or "the power-puff candidate." She was quoted as blasting Secretary of State Dean Acheson, his "striped-pants diplomacy," and his friendship with accused spy Alger Hiss. Referring to the Korean conflict, she charged, "American boys feel their heroism is wasted in a war that the Truman-Acheson administration will not permit them to win." Calling for a balanced budget, Schlafly attacked Price as a supporter of "big government and big spending." Price, however, was reelected.

Schlafly remained politically active during the 1950s, delivering a series of speeches for the Daughters of the American Revolution, drafting a bibliography, *A Reading List for Americans* (1954), and becoming a delegate to the 1956 Republican National Convention. After meeting President Dwight D. Eisenhower at the White House, she agreed to serve as treasury secretary in his "Kitchen Kabinet," along with columnist Hedda Hopper; they helped highlight "GOP recipes on GOP accomplishments" through a monthly newsletter, *What's Cooking in Washington*. Displeased by the administration's failure to support the "freedom fighters" who challenged the communist dictatorship in Hungary, Schlafly linked up with the anticommunist Cardinal Mindszenty Foundation. She put out another bibliography, *Inside the Communist Conspiracy* (1959), presided over the Illinois Federation of Republican Women, and, in the midst of the Cuban missile crisis, initiated a radio program, *America, Wake Up!*, urging "victory over this godless menace." She condemned President Kennedy's support for a nuclear test ban treaty, terming it an "official confirmation of the . . . master plan . . . that we must not seek victory . . . over the Soviet Union or of capitalism over Communism."

Readying to serve as chair of the celebration of the twenty-fifth anniversary of the National Federation of Republican Women, a gathering held at the Palmer House in Chicago, Schlafly demanded that Barry Goldwater be invited to speak at the conference. Likening Goldwater to the Founding Fathers, she termed him a "defender of the American way of life" who "knows that the American military and nuclear power is [*sic*] the last best hope of the free world." By the time the Republicans met in San Francisco in 1964 to select their presidential candidate, Schlafly was something of a national figure, in part because of the recent release of her small volume, *A Choice Not an Echo*. That fast-selling book opened with "The Coming $100 Billion Robbery," Schlafly's blast against the seemingly ever-escalating national budget. She went on to ask "Who's Looney Now?" while listing a series of setbacks in international affairs, including Vietnam, which, she wrote, was "slipping fast into Communist clutches" and "embroiled in a bloody war" involving American soldiers, who were held back by administration policies. While President Johnson sent "American boys 9000 miles away" to battle against Vietnamese communists, Schlafly charged, he "won't do anything at all about the Communists only 90 miles away in Cuba."

During the 1964 presidential campaign, Rear Admiral Chester Ward telephoned Schlafly from Hawaii, asking her to coauthor a book with him on American military strategy. *The Gravediggers*, the first of five volumes they would collaborate on during the next fourteen years, sold 2 million copies almost immediately. Schlafly and Ward charged that "elite" figures—such as Secretary of Defense Robert McNamara and Henry Kissinger, later President Nixon's national security adviser and secretary of state—strove to unilaterally disarm their own country, notwithstanding the stockpiling of Soviet weapons. Only Goldwater, the authors insisted, "can give us PEACE WITHOUT SURRENDER."

In 1967, *Washington Post* columnist David Broder called Schlafly, then running for the presidency of the National Federation of Republican Women, "the heroine of the right wing." Fearing that Schlafly was too polarizing, figures associated with the Republican National Committee apparently backed another candidate. Schlafly noted, "The men in the Republican National Committee (the 'kingmakers' of this battle) know that they can't control me." She charged that a "purge" was threatened, but Barry Goldwater himself, while praising Schlafly, denied the charge. After her narrow defeat, Schlafly insisted the election had been "controlled and rigged," constituting "an election fraud," and threatened to create a "grass-roots organization . . . of just plain American women and mothers who believe in the cause of constitutional government and freedom."

Instead, she began putting out a monthly, four-page newsletter, *The Phyllis Schlafly Report*, and set up the Eagle Trust Fund to take in donations backing causes she espoused. She also began hosting "political-action leadership conferences," bringing together hundreds of supporters from across the United States to focus on political organizing at all levels. As Schlafly put it, the women attendees "are tired of doing all the menial work and being told they have to accept the candidate presented to them." Hoping to support Richard

Nixon's presidential run, Schlafly and Ward wrote *The Betrayers*, which had the Republicans promising to restore America's strength. On a less optimistic note, the book cried out, "On all sides we witness a spineless surrender to violence—to rioters, looters, arsonists, murderers, rapists, street mobs, university students carrying obscene signs, 'peace' demonstrators, pornographers, revolutionaries, and blackmailers." After Nixon's election, Schlafly supported his call for an antiballistic missile system to ward off a possible Soviet nuclear strike. She declared that the vote on the missile system would indicate "which senators believe in the defense of America against Communist aggression—and which senators are for appeasement of the Communists."

In 1970, Schlafly ran against the Democratic congressman George E. Shipley, who dismissed her as an "egghead" with "all her degrees and breeding and books." Attacking Shipley in turn for supporting "welfare giveaways," Schlafly insisted it was "not fair to tax the hard-working people in our small cities and rural areas to put large subsidies into fancy transportation systems and into the pockets of freeloaders who won't work." At one point, Shipley asked, "Who here thinks my Harvard-educated opponent ought to quit attacking my foreign-aid votes and stay home with her husband and six kids?" Schlafly responded by stating, "My opponent says a woman's place is in the home. But my husband replies that a woman's place is in the House—the U.S. House of Representatives." Ironically, a variation of that statement was adopted by feminists only a few short years later. Schlafly kept up the counterattack, condemning "campus rioters and police killers, bomb throwers, arsonists, and other terrorists" who were allegedly coddled by the same "politicians who do nothing about the criminals who stalk our streets but harass the law-abiding with 'gun control.'" As for race riots, she charged that to believe they were caused by "conditions such as rats and poor housing, is as silly as to believe that illegitimate babies are not caused by people but by conditions." In the end, she lost yet again, although the margin was much closer than in her previous congressional race, with only six percentage points separating the two candidates.

Returning to her book ventures, Schlafly joined with Ward to begin drafting *Kissinger on the Couch* (1975), a lengthy tome that condemned Nixon's top foreign policy adviser who proposed détente with the major communist powers. She also enrolled at Washington University Law School, in part to deflect attacks from critics who claimed that her lack of legal training resulted in a simplistic reading of complex statutory regulations. Beginning in 1972, Schlafly became involved in a concerted effort to prevent ratification of the equal rights amendment. During her recent bid for a congressional seat,

Schlafly had attacked the women's liberation movement, which she denounced as "destructive of family living." She emphatically declared, "Of all the classes of people who ever lived, the American woman is the most privileged. . . . We have the most rights and rewards and the fewest duties." Soon, Schlafly was heading the STOP ERA campaign, relying heavily on public relations. The ERA drive began to stall, with only five additional states ratifying it by 1977 and a handful of state legislatures seeking to rescind ratification.

More than any other figure, Schlafly was credited with—or damned for—preventing the ERA from becoming part of the U.S. Constitution. Constantly putting out her anti-ERA message through the national media, Schlafly helped shape a mass movement that sprang up around the country, acquiring dedicated followers determined to prevent the ERA's adoption. At one debate, feminist Betty Friedan shouted, "I'd like to burn you at the stake!" and later exclaimed, "I consider you a traitor to your sex. I consider you an Aunt Tom." Retaining her cool, Schlafly countered that she was pleased with Friedan's demonstration "that the intemperate, agitating proponents of ERA are so intolerant of the views of other people." *Ms.* magazine derisively tagged Schlafly with the label "The Sweetheart of the Silent Majority." However, conservative Republican congressman Henry Hyde of Illinois termed her "indispensable": "Individuals don't make that much difference anymore. I can think of only two in the last decade . . . [Howard] Jarvis [a California antitax activist] . . . and Phyllis Schlafly. Without her, I can say without a twinge of doubt, ERA would be part of the Constitution—unquestionably." Martha Shirk of the St. Louis *Post-Dispatch* declared, "Phyllis Schlafly *is* the STOP ERA movement." Schlafly relied heavily on her political-action leadership conferences to provide shock troops for the anti-ERA campaign. Women were instructed in debating techniques and primed on what colors and styles of clothing would show up best on television. Activists also turned to the *Phyllis Schlafly Report*, which early and persistently provided intellectual and emotional ammunition with which to attack the ERA. The *Eagle Forum Newsletter* offered more detailed tips on technical matters associated with public campaigning.

Schlafly produced a coalition of seemingly strange bedfellows, Carol Felsenthal reports, bringing together Catholics, fundamentalists, and Orthodox Jews. She attracted many with her warning, "If you like ERA, you'd better like congressmen and Washington bureaucrats and federal judges relieving you of what little power you have left over your own life." She dismissed feminists as a "bunch of anti-family radicals and lesbians and elitists," pointing to the apparent celebration of lesbianism at the International Women's Year conference in Houston in November 1977. Although Congress voted on

March 22, 1979, for a thirty-nine-month extension of the ERA's ratification process, Schlafly hosted a gathering celebrating the anticipated demise of the amendment. After terming the extension "wrong, crooked, and unfair," Schlafly asserted, "We are the most powerful, positive force in America today, because we have been able to give the bureaucrats and the politicians a stunning defeat." Her colleague Shirley Spellerberg noted, "Phyllis is a religious leader—perhaps the most powerful in the country today. Because it's women who keep the family's faith and it's women who support Phyllis. Make no mistake about this. This is a religious war. . . . ERA is a religious issue and that's why we're winning."

Supporting Ronald Reagan's bid for the 1980 Republican presidential nomination, Schlafly termed the expected defeat of the ERA "the finest statement of women's rights in history. It supports women's rights without taking away traditional rights such as exemption from the draft." She also condemned both school busing for purposes of racial balance and abortion, and she urged that the United States attain nuclear superiority, all positions backed by candidate Reagan and the New Right. Following Reagan's election, he appointed her to the Defense Policy Advisory Group. Schlafly was delighted that the nation's political orientation had altered course. She noted, "What we have been working for for twenty years has been established as the mainstream of American political thinking." When the period allowed for the ERA ratification process ended in mid-1982, with only thirty-five states having supported it, Schlafly gloatingly claimed "the most remarkable political victory of the twentieth century."

Relying on the Eagle Forum, her monthly newsletter, and a new publication, *Education Reporter*, which appeared in 1986, she continued supporting conservative causes. Schlafly also wrote a syndicated column that appeared in as many as a hundred newspapers, delivered regular radio commentaries heard on hundreds of stations, hosted a radio talk show focused on education, and regularly testified before state and congressional committees on various issues, ranging from the U.S. Constitution to the American family. She remained a prolific author, producing books on childcare in the United States, pornography, "feminist fantasies," and activist judges, among other subjects. She called for the impeachment of Justice Anthony Kennedy, viewing him as turncoat who had failed to uphold conservative values, as anticipated when President Reagan placed him on the U.S. Supreme Court. Schlafly also remained determined to prevent the passage of another version of the equal rights amendment.

Conclusion

The passionately held beliefs of Gloria Steinem and Phyllis Schlafly underscored the cultural divide in the United States during the 1960s and 1970s. Following the tradition of earlier feminists, Steinem challenged sex-based stereotypes that she believed relegated women to an inferior position in American life. In contrast, Schlafly favored the cult of domesticity long championed by antifeminists. Their own lives contained welters of contradictions. Steinem drew on her looks, along with her brains and ambition, to advance her career in journalism, long a male preserve; affairs with several influential men hardly narrowed the scope of her career opportunities. Schlafly trumpeted family values and virtues, including traditional domestic roles for women, while running for political office, becoming an important figure in the Republican Party, forming her own organizations, publishing books and newsletters, and returning to school to become an attorney. The two women and the institutions they were associated with, particularly *Ms.* magazine and the Eagle Forum, engaged in a running battle over the ERA, abortion rights, and sexual practices, among other matters. Similar clashes occurred within the ranks of the major political parties that Steinem and Schlafly became associated with, as both Democrats and Republicans became more ideological, further ensuring the demise of the liberal consensus. The impact of both Steinem and Schlafly proved enormous as they offered sharply contrasting role models for American women and helped to shape divergent public perceptions regarding fundamental social and cultural issues.

Study Questions

1. Given the conventional course of Gloria Steinem's early career, how did she come to adopt a feminist perspective?
2. Why did many Americans find Steinem and *Ms.* magazine so controversial?
3. Explain how Phyllis Schlafly became one of the iconic figures of the new conservatism of the 1970s and 1980s.
4. Describe Schlafly's role in the defeat of the equal rights amendment.
5. Compare and contrast the political philosophies of Steinem and Schlafly, as well as their ideas about the role of women in public affairs.

Selected Bibliography

Carroll, Peter N. *Famous in America: The Passion to Succeed.* New York: Dutton, 1985.

———. *It Seemed Like Nothing Happened: The Tragedy and Promise of America in the 1970s.* New York: Holt, Rinehart and Winston, 1982.

Cohen, Marcia. *The Sisterhood: The True Story of the Women Who Changed the World.* New York: Ballantine, 1988.

Critchlow, Donald T. *Phyllis Schlafly and Grassroots Conservatism: A Woman's Crusade.* Princeton: Princeton University Press, 2005.

Farrell, Amy Erdman. *Yours in Sisterhood:* Ms. *Magazine and the Promise of Popular Feminism.* Chapel Hill: University of North Carolina Press, 1998.

Felsenthal, Carol. *Phyllis Schlafly: The Sweetheart of the Silent Majority.* New York: Doubleday, 1981.

Heilbrun, Carolyn G. *The Education of a Woman: The Life of Gloria Steinem.* New York: Ballantine, 1995.

Kauffman, Linda. *American Feminist Thought at Century's End.* Cambridge, MA: Blackwell, 1993.

Martin, William. *With God on Our Side: The Rise of the Religious Right in America.* New York: Broadway, 1996.

Polsgrove, Carol. *It Wasn't Pretty, Folks, But Didn't We Have Fun?* Esquire *in the Sixties.* New York: W.W. Norton, 1995.

Rosen, Ruth. *The World Split Open: How the Modern Women's Movement Changed America.* New York: Penguin, 2000.

Schlafly, Phyllis. *A Choice Not an Echo.* Atlon, IL: Pere Marquette, 1964.

Schlafly, Phyllis, and Chester Ward. *The Betrayers.* Alton, IL: Pere Marquette, 1968.

———. *The Gravediggers.* Alton, IL: Pere Marquette, 1964.

Solinger, Rickie. *Abortion Wars: A Half Century of Struggle, 1950–2000.* Berkeley: University of California Press, 1998.

Steinem, Gloria. *Outrageous Acts and Everyday Rebellions.* New York: New American Library, 1983.

Stern, Sydney Ladensohn. *Gloria Steinem: Her Passions, Politics, and Mystique.* Secaucus, NJ: Carol Publishing Group, 1997.

Thom, Mary. *Inside* Ms.*: Twenty-Five Years of the Magazine and the Feminist Movement.* New York: H. Holt, 1997.

Part III

The Search for New Directions, 1980-Present

At the onset of the 1980s, the nation faced significant challenges. Inflation and unemployment wracked the economy, which had been staggered by the growing cost of energy throughout the previous decade. Abroad, America's influence and power appeared drastically weakened in the aftermath of the failed war in Vietnam, humiliations at the hands of Iranian Islamic radicals, and renewed Soviet adventurism in Afghanistan. A growing number of Americans associated these setbacks with Democratic liberalism and the seemingly failed presidency of Jimmy Carter. Some also saw the nation's myriad social problems and perceived moral decline as stemming from the liberal and radical enthusiasms of the 1960s. During the 1970s, the individuals and organizations composing the New Right had emerged to advocate conservative solutions to the nation's ills, and Ronald Reagan's presidential triumph in 1980 testified to the appeal of their message. "Government," the new president proclaimed, "is not the solution. Government is the problem." That terse utterance signaled the beginning of a political era that saw the broad repudiation of a cardinal point of the waning liberal creed.

In the early 1980s, many conservatives found reason to believe that a new national consensus, grounded in conservative principles, was in the making. Reagan's popularity, together with the growing influence of New Right constituencies like evangelical Christians, promised to make the Republican Party the vehicle for a potent new conservatism. In fact, much of the "new" conservatism derived from theories and policies extending at least as far back

271

as the 1920s—an era of laissez-faire government when "traditional values" and an unfettered marketplace took precedence over issues of social and economic justice. Indeed, more than one commentator noted the evident similarities between the two eras. Each was preceded by a period of busy, government-led reform and a foreign conflict that ended in disillusionment, sparking a conservative reaction. The 1980s, like the 1920s, brought new prominence for socially conservative evangelical Christians and saw a weakening of the regulatory state that encouraged astute entrepreneurs, bringing significant, if not always well distributed, prosperity. The "Reagan Revolution" seemed to come to an inconclusive end in 1989, however, when moderate Republican George H.W. Bush became president and pursued a less doctrinaire course than had his predecessor. Bush's pragmatic conservatism cost him the support of neoconservatives and evangelicals, allowing Democrat Bill Clinton to win the presidency in 1992. Having promised to steer his party away from the old, discredited liberalism of the past, Clinton sought through two terms to define his ideological "third way" between conservatism and liberalism, with no clear evidence of success.

These two last decades of the twentieth century did produce evidence of significant change in the lives of American minorities, as most made their way more fully into the mainstream of American life. With the era of mass movements apparently over, minority gains were achieved in much less dramatic fashion, but the consequences were nonetheless significant. By the end of the century, minorities had assumed powerful, prominent roles in American society, gaining access to all levels of government and industry. There were periodic reminders that the nation's racial problems were not fully resolved, as the 1992 Rodney King riots revealed. However, the broad acceptance of ethnic minorities as political representatives, business leaders, and celebrities suggested that many of the barriers that had existed a half century before had been largely dismantled.

Confident and prosperous as the millennium neared, Americans scarcely imagined the challenges that they would soon face. A bitterly disputed 2000 presidential election reinforced the political polarization that had been building through the 1990s. As George W. Bush pursued a strongly conservative agenda during his first months in office, national divisions intensified. The terrorist attacks of September 11, 2001, restored a temporary unity, but the subsequent debate over foreign policy and how the war on terror might best be waged brought new disagreements. Since the end of the Cold War, most Americans had paid little attention to the world, believing that the end of the great ideological clash had left American concepts of democracy and liberty supreme and unchallenged. A small group of neoconservative foreign policy analysts, however, had given considerable thought to America's role in a post–Cold War world. Since the 1970s, a few influential policy makers had pondered the shape of the "new world order," some concluding that the collapse of the Soviet empire afforded the United States an unparalleled opportunity to establish itself as the single, uncontested superpower. The new millennium might well become the real "American Century" as the United States established world hegemony because of democratic and capitalist principles. Advocates of this outlook played a significant role in the Bush administration's decisions to invade Iraq in 2003. Criticisms of this perspective were many, coming from the political opposition as well as independent intellectuals who had long been critical of American foreign policy. By 2007, as the American war in Iraq dragged on with only problematic success and no hint of resolution, the debate over America's war on terror, and the nation's role in the world, continued unabated. With a new century begun, the possibility of rebuilding a new national consensus seemed, at least in the short term, exceedingly remote. The American people remained deeply divided over fundamental issues of war and peace.

11

The Roaring Eighties

Piety and Profit

It is a great convenience to historians that, now and again, major transition points occur as new decades begin, and in subsequent years, clearly discernible patterns make it possible to assign specific characteristics to ten-year periods. The 1920s was such an era, its conservative, materialistic tone established with Warren Harding's election to the presidency in 1920 and decisively ending with the 1929 stock market crash and the repudiation of the era's business ethos. The 1980s were still young when numerous commentators began pointing out the apparent similarities with the decade of Harding, Calvin Coolidge, and Herbert Hoover. As in the 1920s, many Americans in the 1980s struggled to comprehend the impact of dramatic social changes that had transpired over the previous two decades. Americans in both decades were left disillusioned and uncertain after foreign interventions that were deemed failures. In the 1980s, the perceived excesses of liberalism, together with the psychological and political fallout from the failed effort in Vietnam, helped give rise to a potent new conservative movement.

As had been the case six decades earlier, one important dimension of this rapidly growing conservative impulse was evangelical Christianity. Many traditionally minded Christians feared that the cultural liberalism of the 1960s had seriously eroded conventional values and that a new relativism had crept into American institutions and habits. The Christian Right, or Religious Right, was composed of new, politically active evangelical groups intent upon restoring traditional social values in public and private life. The movement's potential for organizing like-minded evangelicals was immensely increased by the skillful use of television, to which new technologies had greatly increased access. "Congregations" were no longer limited to the physical confines of church buildings; broadcasts emanating from those churches reached untold thousands of viewers. "Almost without our recognizing it," sociologist Jeffrey K. Hadden observed at the time, "the communications revolution is reshaping American religion." The influence of these "televangelists," as Hadden termed the new electronic ministers, grew exporentially. "The rise of televangelists to a new position of power and influence, political as well as religious," wrote journalist and historian Haynes Johnson, "was one of the most widely reported stories of the Eighties."

Few could legitimately claim greater influence than the Reverend Jerry Falwell, who founded the Moral Majority in 1979 to promote biblical Christian principles in public life and combat what evangelicals saw as the scourge of secular humanism. Within a year, the organization played a central role in ending the political careers of several prominent liberal Democratic office-holders. Embraced by newly elected Republican president Ronald Reagan, Falwell, the Moral Majority, and other Christian Right organizations rapidly established themselves as an indispensable constituency of the Republican Party, which was quick to adopt their conservative social agenda. In 1984, Falwell was a featured speaker at the Republican National Convention, affirming the rising power of the movement. The fusion of political conservatism with fundamentalist Christianity created a new dynamic in national politics, playing an important role in the public debate over social policy in coming years.

Social conservatism was, however, only one dimension of the New Right of the 1980s. Like their predecessors in the 1920s, the adherents of the new conservatism also hailed the concept of laissez-faire and the unfettered marketplace. The enervation that conservatives perceived in the nation's moral fiber had been also evident in the economy during the 1970s. America's aging industrial infrastructure, growing competition from Japan, south Asia, and West Germany, and shifting consumer preferences had significantly eroded the nation's manufacturing sector Many conservatives proclaimed that economic renewal required freeing up capitalism's inherent dynamism. The "Reagan Revolution," as the conservative impulse of the 1980s was often deemed, brought with it an unprecedented fervor for deregulation, lessened government oversight of the private sector and tax reduction, especially for those in high-income categories. These policies were deemed indispensable to the fullest realization of capitalist prosperity and material abundance. In the heady early years of the Reagan era, wealth creation was embraced as a legitimate social value, and some commentators asserted that American capitalism even reflected Biblical principles. Theologian Michael Novak detected in the activities of corporate America "metaphors for grace, a kind of insight into God's ways in history." Falwell, who soon presided over a lucrative evangelical empire that included a massive church, a cable television network, and a university, reiterated the same idea more baldly when he declared, "The free enterprise system is clearly outlined in the Book of Proverbs." Any student of the America of the 1920s would have recognized these sentiments, which were ceaselessly proclaimed by businessmen and religionists alike during that decade. The justifications for the unrestrained capitalism of the Reagan years were accordingly varied, with references to both Adam Smith and Adam, but the result was a climate of opinion that encouraged ambitious and sometimes reckless business and investment activity. Some people who embraced the new opportunities proved, at the very least, irresponsible, and at worst unethical. Wall Street financier Ivan Boesky told a cheering audience at the University of California at Berkeley in 1985, "Greed is all right. . . . Everybody should be a little greedy. You shouldn't feel guilty." Together with Michael Milliken, the "junk bond king" who made millions manipulating often worthless stocks, Boesky personified the corporate buccaneering that disrupted the lives of countless white-collar workers and destabilized the nation's corporate structure, seeming to belie the idea that unregulated capitalism was innately benevolent.

Though the free market frenzy of the 1980s held the potential for such abuse, it nonetheless opened doors for legitimate entrepreneurs. Just like Henry Ford came to personify the mass production technology that revolutionized American life in the 1920s, Bill Gates emerged in the 1980s as the herald of a new economy exemplified by the high-technology fields of aerospace, electronics, and, above all, information processing. The public had yet to comprehend the full potential of personal computers, and those willing to take the risks that attended innovation could position themselves as the chief movers in an industry with tremendous future possibilities. One such visionary was Gates, a hyperambitious nineteen-year-old when he founded Microsoft Corporation in the summer of 1975. Brilliant and brash, Gates fit the contemporary definition of the nerd or technogeek, his obsession with computers matched only by his disregard for his personal appearance; even friends joked that he "never went anywhere without his dandruff." Evidently completely oblivious to the ideological clashes that marked the era, Gates focused instead on literally capitalizing on the new information technologies and their applications. Under his leadership, Microsoft set industry standards for crucial software as it continuously extended its market reach. Later, Gates's determination that Microsoft should dominate the Internet browser market initiated one of the great corporate conflicts of the late twentieth century, leading critics to denounce him as a "silicon bully," an amoral and ruthless corporate tyrant intent on destroying all competition. The absence of any relevant industry regulations, due both to the newness of the computer industry and the prevailing enthusiasm for the free market of the 1980s, allowed Gates to realize his professed ambition to become a millionaire before his twenty-fifth birthday. Under his leadership, Microsoft played a central role in making new information technologies broadly available to average Americans. It was one of the chief ironies of the 1980s, a decade in which social conservatives sought to reinvigorate traditional values and social institutions, that developments in the information technology industry began transforming private and public life in unprecedented ways. Computer and Internet technologies promised to enhance communication capabilities for any individual or group utilizing them, including both Christian evangelicals seeking supporters and pornographers seeking profit. Communication through the Internet brought both expanded horizons and individual isolation from the community. Ultimately, the 1980s combined the powerful appeal of tradition and the irresistible lure of unknown possibilities, an ambiguity of direction that was aptly captured in the title of one of the era's popular films, *Back to the Future*. Jerry Falwell and the Moral Majority offered Americans national salvation through "old-time religion." Bill Gates offered the public access to new technologies that would radically transform American life. Both men were integral to developments that defined the 1980s and, indeed, shaped American life well beyond the decade.

JERRY FALWELL
Standard-Bearer of the Christian Right

During the 1976 presidential campaign, evangelical Christians watched with fascination as one of their own, former Georgia governor Jimmy Carter, captured the Democratic Party nomination. Initially, many evangelicals, including some who had previously avoided political involvement, supported Carter's presidential bid and looked forward to morally based governance in Washington, DC. However, Carter's moderate-to-liberal positions on various social and cultural issues soon alienated a large number of conservative Christians and those who, like the president, professed to having been "born again." Few evangelicals were more disturbed by the direction they feared America was heading in than the Reverend Jerry Falwell, founder of Liberty University and host of his own radio program, *The Old Time Gospel Hour.* Indeed, before the 1976 election even occurred, Carter's admission in a *Playboy* interview that he had "lusted in his heart" after women other than his wife, Rosalyn, displeased Falwell. When Jody Powell, one of Carter's top aides, complained about Falwell's criticism, the minister recognized the impact evangelicals might have on political discourse.

Falwell joined ranks with the singer Anita Bryant, who was seeking to overturn a gay rights ordinance that supervisors in Dade County, Florida, had passed. On hearing of the murders of George Moscone, the mayor of San Francisco, and Supervisor Harvey Milk, a Moscone ally and one of the nation's few acknowledged gay public officials, Falwell suggested that the killings demonstrated God's judgment about the two men. The theologian and philosopher Francis Schaeffer sought to convince Falwell to use *The Old Time Gospel Hour* to encourage fellow evangelicals, historically prone to sectarianism, to become politically involved. Falwell believed that "Satan" sought "to destroy America by negating the Judeo-Christian ethic, secularizing our society and devaluating human life through the legalization of abortion and infanticide." Thus "the future of our nation," which had been selected by God "to share our spiritual and material wealth with the rest of the world," was at stake.

In May 1979, Falwell met with conservative leaders Paul Weyrich, Howard Phillips, Robert Billings, and Ed McAteer in Lynchburg, Virginia, to discuss how that goal might be accomplished. Weyrich stated that a "political and socially conservative" moral majority existed, which could reshape national politics. Within a month, Falwell established Moral Majority Incorporated, began political lobbying, and initiated the Moral Majority Foundation, which would sponsor newspapers, radio and television programs, and public addresses nationwide. Falwell and the other founders of the Moral Majority also moved to ensure that the Republican Party adopted a conservative platform at the 1980 national convention.

Jerry Falwell and his twin brother, Gene, were born in Lyncburg, Virgina, on August 11, 1933, to Carey and Helen Beasley Falwell, whose English ancestral roots dated to the early seventeenth century. Falwells had fought in the American Revolution, held slaves, and moved to Lynchburg, a prosperous tobacco center, before the Civil War. Helen Beasley was a devout Baptist who, in 1915, married Carey Falwell, who operated several service stations, stores, and restaurants near Lynchburg and established a hotel, the Power Oil Company, and a series of bus lines later called Trailways and Greyhound. Along with his younger brother Garland, Carey also engaged in bootlegging during Prohibition. Carey killed Garland during a family disturbance, although the investigation resulted in a finding of self-defense. Though melancholy enveloped the hard-drinking Carey, the Falwells soon welcomed twin sons, Jerry and Gene, to their country mansion just outside the city limits of Lynchburg. Carey increased his business operations, running a successful firewood and coal business and constructing the Merry Garden Dance Hall and Dining Room, which featured bands like Tommy Dorsey's and traveling circuses. World War II compelled Carey to close the Merry Garden and the Power Oil Company and sell the hotel and some of his several filling stations, while he held onto his restaurant and the firewood and coal business. Cirrhosis of the liver led to his death in 1948.

Jerry Falwell attended Brookville High School, where he served as editor of the school newspaper and, despite weighing less than 150 pounds, as captain of the football squad. On one occasion, Falwell attacked a teacher who had been humiliating students. He also engaged in a series of pranks directed at other teachers and joined the Wall Gang, which fought against another group of teenagers from Appomattox. He graduated as class valedictorian in 1949, although, after a theft of money from the school cafeteria, the principal refused to allow Falwell to deliver the valedictory address. He subsequently enrolled at Lynchburg College and later Virginia Polytechnic Institute, intending to study mechanical engineering.

By 1952, Falwell was listening frequently to a favorite radio program of his mother's, Charles Fuller's *Old Fashioned Revival Hour.* One evening, he went to the Park Avenue Baptist Church, along with a couple of other young men, where he heard the recording *Gospel Songs from the Old Fashioned Revival Hour* and met a young pastor, Paul F. Donnelson. Falwell later wrote, "That night . . . I accepted Christ as my Savior." He began attending nightly Bible study sessions and receiving instruction in how to "lead other people to Christ." One of the members of his Bible study group was a pretty eighteen-year-old, Macel Pate, whom he dated and later married. Falwell attended a large gathering of the Baptist Bible Fellowship in Cincinnati, excitedly now considering himself "part of a worldwide movement of God's spirit." He then enrolled in Bible and theology classes at Baptist Bible College in Springfield, Missouri, where he learned to consider "the Old Testament . . .

the historic record of God's attempts to rescue humanity from its sinfulness" and the New Testament "God's final attempts to rescue the world from sin and its consequence."

After two and a half years at Baptist Bible College, Falwell worked briefly at Park Avenue Baptist Church in Lynchburg, where he managed to convince several gang members to accept the faith. Returning to Springfield, he obtained his first full-time ministerial position, driving each Friday to the Kansas City Baptist Temple, and, in May 1956, completed his theological degree from Baptist Bible College, again graduating as class valedictorian. A schism at Park Avenue Baptist resulted in Falwell's heading a new church in Lynchburg, supported by thirty-five congregants, although the leadership of the Baptist Fellowship warned about the possibility of excommunication. Few witnessed his first sermons before the ramshackle Thomas Road Baptist Church, but Falwell began visiting residents in the surrounding neighborhoods, targeting a hundred homes daily. That fall, he spoke to the operator of a small radio station about the possibility of delivering a weekly radio program patterned after the *Old Fashioned Revival Hour.* The radio station owner urged Falwell to offer a daily program instead, indicating that it would cost "seven dollars a program." Each morning at 6:30, Falwell began his radio ministry. By December, he signed up for a half-hour weekly television show, *Thomas Road Baptist Church Presents*, which appeared early on Sunday evenings and cost $90 a program. Falwell's determination to spread the gospel led to a major building project for his church, where several hundred people were soon attending his Sunday morning services. In 1959, Falwell established Elim Home for Alcoholics and added a new radio station in Roanoke, Virginia; ten more soon became part of his radio ministry.

As the new decade opened, Falwell's ministerial work intensified, along with the number of congregants who attended Thomas Road Baptist Church or followed his radio and television programs. He regularly paid home or hospital visits to the infirmed, met with the men who stayed at Elim Home, helped to train volunteers, continued to push for his church's expansion, remained a media presence in the community, wrote sermons, devised Bible studies, led discussion and prayer sessions, held revival meetings outside Lynchburg, showed up for seminars by other ministers, and pored over the Bible. Later, Falwell helped to establish the Hope Aglow Halfway House for convicts. He also nurtured a growing family with Macel, whom he married in 1958, building a new ranch-style house on Grove Road that was completed two years later. Between 1962 and 1966, at intervals of two years, their three children—Jerry Jr., Jean Ann, and Jonathan—were born. Eventually, Falwell determined that Thomas Road required a new, larger church that soon offered classes at Lynchburg Christian Academy, which the Falwell children attended. The reach of Falwell's ministry continued to widen, and he repeatedly drove across the country to participate in pastoral conclaves and evangelical crusades. At the end of the 1960s, a local businessman donated a small Cessna 310 aircraft to Thomas Road Baptist Church, enabling Falwell to conduct his far-flung travels with less difficulty.

Eventually Falwell became conscious of the winds of change sweeping across the national landscape but failed to appreciate, as he acknowledged, "how black people had suffered. . . . We had closed our eyes or driven around their suffering for decades." In a sermon he delivered in 1958, "Segregation and Integration: Which?," he declared that integration was wrong and would bring about the demise of the white race. Falwell subsequently recognized that "the white Christian church" had been instrumental in sustaining the "destructive and dehumanizing" system of segregation. But at the time, Falwell wrote, "It didn't cross my mind that segregation and its consequences for the human family were evil." Indeed, after Martin Luther King Jr. led a march on Selma, Alabama, in support of voting rights for African Americans, Falwell delivered a widely distributed sermon, "Ministers and Marches," in which he insisted that "the Christian's citizenship is in heaven" and "Our only purpose on this earth is to know Christ and to make Him known." He continued, "I feel that we need to get off the streets and back into the pulpits and into the prayer rooms." In an interview, Falwell charged that civil rights legislation amounted to "a terrible violation of human and private property rights" and "should be considered civil wrongs rather than civil rights." To his chagrin, Falwell was damned as "a 'racist,' a 'Ku Klux Klan sympathizer,' a 'segregationist,' and 'a teacher of injustice, dissension and distrust.'" At that point, one scholar has noted, "Falwell was still a practicing segregationist," and it was "criticism from within his church, at least in part, [that] stopped Falwell from speaking out in favor of segregation."

Soon, however, Thomas Road Baptist Church experienced significant growth and change. The church accepted its first black members in 1968 and allowed the first African American student to attend Lynchburg Christian Academy the following year. The Sunday school became one of the nation's ten largest, serving more than 10,000 students regularly, while the Lynchburg Christian Academy offered classes from kindergarten through high school and dignitaries frequently spoke from the pulpit. The church's annual budget passed the million-dollar mark. By 1972, *Newsweek* referred to Thomas Road Baptist as "the fastest growing church in the nation." That year, Falwell and

Elmer Towns, who had joined the ministry in Lynchburg, founded Thomas Road Bible Institute with a two-year plan of study. This development was part of a program by evangelical Christians to construct "institutions of all kinds," historian Godfrey Hodgson suggests. At this point, evangelical and fundamentalist Christians remained "suspicious of the 'mainstream,'" instinctively choosing "to separate themselves from a secular culture" they deemed "not only wicked but also doomed to destruction."

However, in December 1972, the Securities and Exchange Commission (SEC) contacted Thomas Road Baptist to investigate whether church literature had proven misleading to potential bond purchasers; some $6.5 million worth of bonds had been sold to over 1,600 investors scattered across twenty-five states. The following July, the SEC charged the 13,000-member church with engaging in "fraud and deceit" in issuing the bonds and also declared the church to be insolvent. Falwell described this period as "the most difficult crisis I faced in all my years of ministry," for he was worried about the church's very survival. However, U.S. District Court judge James C. Turk found "no intentional wrongdoing" by Thomas Road Baptist Church, and Falwell established a special finance committee to place the church "on a sound financial footing."

During this same trying time, Falwell followed with "growing horror and disbelief" the Supreme Court ruling in *Roe v. Wade*, which generally permitted abortions during the first two trimesters of a woman's pregnancy. For Falwell, the High Court's decision "would legalize the killing of millions of unborn children." American leaders of the Catholic Church condemned the ruling, but Falwell was dismayed that Protestants, particularly evangelicals and fundamentalist ministers, "remained silent." Although he believed that "an avalanche of hatred and bile would achieve nothing," he began speaking out against "America's national sin," likening abortion to Hitler's destruction of European Jews. The Supreme Court, he charged, was unleashing a "biological holocaust" in the United States. Falwell had deliberately avoided becoming politically active in the past in recognition of the principle of separation of church and state. Now he came to believe that the doctrine had been established "to keep the government from interfering with the church," not "to keep the church out of politics." Indeed, he now reasoned that it was his "duty as a Christian to apply the truths of Scripture to every act of government." So he added a new mission to his regular tasks of ministering to the flock of 15,000 congregants who now attended Thomas Road Baptist, offering his radio and television sermons, writing, teaching, and delivering public addresses across the country.

His politically charged addresses condemning abortion, Falwell acknowledged, "shocked and surprised" even many committed Christians. Nevertheless, he was determined to take a "stand prophetically against the influence of Satan in our nation and through our nation to the world." Falwell urged Christians to back political candidates who represented "the renewal of morality and good sense in the land" and even to seek public office themselves. In 1976, Falwell joined with those who were putting on a musical, *I Love America*, around the country, in an effort "to mobilize Christians . . . for political action against abortion and the other social trends that menaced the nation's future." In Falwell's words, "We were calling America back to God." Thousands invariably showed up at "I Love America" rallies at state capitols to hear Falwell exhort the nation to repent. In 1976, leaders of the conservative movement, including Howard Phillips, Paul Weyrich, and Richard Viguerie, suggested that Falwell head an organization to convince fundamentalists and evangelicals to express themselves politically.

Although Falwell deflected that proposal, public affairs increasingly drew his attention. He denounced the National's Women Conference in Houston in 1977 as "anti-family, anti-God, and anti-America," referred to the proposed equal rights amendment as "a delusion," and attacked the feminist movement as "full of women who live in disobedience to God's laws." In 1978, Falwell's Liberty University sent a musical team across the country, offering a multimedia show, *America, You're Too Young to Die!* Falwell implored "the leaders of Christendom [to] stand up against immorality," castigated "liberal churches," and decried "abortion, pornography, the divorce rate, moral permissiveness, a soft attitude toward Marxism-Leninism, our nation's military unpreparedness, and the general breakdown of traditional family values." Urging massive voter registration efforts, he demanded that the religious "stand up and be counted." In May 1979, he helped to found the Moral Majority, which promised to counter the forces of secular humanism and "defend the free enterprise system, the family and Bible morality."

Demonstrating the growing potency of the religious Right, the Moral Majority mobilized Americans at the grassroots level to condemn pornography, abortion, gay rights, and the welfare state. At the same time, the Moral Majority advocated sharply increasing military spending to wage the Cold War fight against the Soviet Union, employing the death penalty as a deterrent against violent crime, and removing regulatory shackles from the nation's free enterprise system. Meanwhile, Falwell's radio program, *The Old Time Gospel Hour*, enjoyed an audience of 25 million, many new listeners drawn by his willingness to address politically charged issues. Despite this increased popularity, he received death threats and faced angry protests, purportedly compelling the Falwells to move to an old plantation house located just minutes from both Thomas Road Baptist and Lynchburgh Baptist College.

After the 1980 election, many media commentators credited the religious Right with helping to elect President Ronald Reagan and to defeat a dozen liberal members of the U.S. Senate, including George McGovern, Frank Church, and Birch Bayh; Falwell later referred to the election as "my finest hour." He also reported that during a subsequent conversation with Reagan, the president confided, "Jerry, I sometimes believe we're heading very fast for Armageddon right now." Falwell thrilled fundamentalist audiences with productions such as a lengthy audiovisual presentation containing "images of Charles Manson, Times Square 'adult' theaters, aborted fetuses in bloody hospital pans, nuclear explosions . . . and other offenses ostensibly charged to . . . communists, secular humanists, and, by implication, Democrats." Despite scathing criticism of such antics, the Moral Majority as of 1982 boasted "a $10 million dollar budget, 100,000 trained pastors, priests, and rabbis, and several millions volunteers." Increasingly, Falwell urged President Reagan to place social issues such as abortion and school prayer "on the front burner."

Before the 1984 Democratic and Republican national conventions in San Francisco and Dallas, Falwell organized Family Forum gatherings. The one in San Francisco proved highly controversial, thanks to condemnations of homosexuality and resulting protests by both gay and straight activists. Nonetheless, following the renomination of Ronald Reagan at the Republican Party convention, Falwell was chosen to offer the final benediction. That fall, Falwell's forces received credit for ensuring the reelection of Senator Jesse Helms, one of Congress's most right-wing members. Also in 1984, Falwell joined in the campaign to establish the Coalition for Religious Freedom, which received most of its initial funding from the Unification Church, headed by the Reverend Sun Myung Moon; questions about Moon's financial involvement led Falwell and other fundamentalists to withdraw support. Nevertheless, at a press conference in Washington, DC, in August 1985, Falwell backed Moon in his battles with the Internal Revenue Service. Falwell remained a controversial figure in his own right, as when he referred to AIDS as "the wrath of God upon homosexuals" and suggested quarantining AIDS victims in the manner of infected cattle, but acknowledged that was unlikely to occur because "homosexuals constitute a potent voting bloc and cows do not." Later, Falwell declared that "AIDS and syphilis and all the sexually transmitted diseases are God's judgment upon the total society for embracing what God has condemned: sex outside of marriage."

Falwell continued to make public appearances at colleges and universities across the United States, including unfriendly venues like Harvard University. There Falwell insisted that he had not established the Moral Majority "to enshrine into law any set of fundamentalist Christian doctrines." He opposed abortion, but would support legislation that allowed such a procedure for "victims of incest or rape or in pregnancies where the life of the mother is at stake." He did not oppose birth control, disapproved of denying civil rights to homosexuals, backed equal rights for women but not the equal rights amendment, supported prayer in schools but called for prayers to be "voluntary, nonsectarian," and believed that "no child should be intimidated or embarrassed for not participating." He believed "in a pluralistic, democratic society," did not favor "book burning or censorship of any kind," championed the free enterprise system, but condemned "the exploitation of workers, the misuse and abuse of power and wealth, the unequal and discriminatory distribution of profits."

By the 1980s, Falwell, as a leading representative of the New Christian Right, traveled "250,000 to 400,000 miles a year" and regularly appeared on television and radio programs. Falwell and Massachusetts senator Ted Kennedy reached across political and cultural divides to speak with each other and to deliver speeches in each other's backyards, Falwell at Harvard and Kennedy at Liberty University, which had grown out of Lynchburg Baptist College and enrolled 7,500 students. At the same time, Falwell and the Moral Majority, he believed, helped to further "the conservative consciousness of the nation." In 1986, Thomas Road Baptist Church purchased the Liberty Broadcasting Cable Network, enabling Falwell once again to expand his television ministry. The next year, Falwell resigned from the presidency of the Moral Majority—which had been renamed the Liberty Federation—to rededicate himself to Thomas Road Baptist, which now had 22,000 members, and Liberty University. He became more involved in Liberty Godparent Homes, which provided care for girls and women with unwanted pregnancies, and Elim Home for Alcoholics. Falwell also contended with recurrent concerns expressed by some of his own parishioners about the financial operations of Thomas Road Baptist, his other ministries, and Liberty University. Falwell's ministry amassed almost $100 million annually by the middle of the decade, placing it just below those associated with televangelists Pat Robertson, Jimmy Swaggart, and Jim and Tammy Faye Bakker. Following a sexual and financial scandal involving Bakker, head of the charismatic Praise the Lord (PTL) ministry, Falwell took over as chair of PTL in 1987. Attempting to garner financial support for the flagging PTL television network, he intensified his assault on homosexuality. Blasting the "gay-influenced" media and political figures for failing to unveil the "truth about AIDS," he insisted that gays deliberately donated blood because "they know they are going to die—and they are going to take as many people with them as they can." Soon, Falwell turned the PTL network over to the court that was wrestling with the organization's financial machinations. On February 24, 1988, the chambers of the U.S. Supreme Court served as the forum for the resolution of yet another controversial matter involving Falwell. The case, *Hustler Magazine, Inc., et al v. Jerry Falwell,* grew out of the pornographic periodical's publication of a parody of a Campari liquor advertisement that had Falwell confessing to incest with his mother in an outhouse. The outrageous advertisement was part of publisher Larry Flynt's ongoing campaign against Falwell, whom Flynt despised as a self-righteous hypocrite. The nation's highest tribunal ruled that Falwell was not entitled to recover damages for emotional distress.

Controversy again beset Falwell in the 1990s when he referred warmly to books by Reconstructionist theologians. These were writers who argued that the federal government should only deliver the mail and attend to national defense, that armed militias should protect county-level territories, that Social Security and most taxes should be terminated, and that the right to vote should be restricted to members of "biblically correct" churches. Falwell also put out a video, *New Clinton Chronicles*, which combined sensational gossip and innuendo to condemn President Bill Clinton and his wife, Hillary Rodham Clinton. Then, in 1999, Falwell's *National Liberty Journal* declared that Tinky Winky, a character in the children's television program *Teletubbies*, might represent homosexuality because he was purple, sported a triangular mark on his head, and carried a handbag. More controversial still, following the terrorist attacks on September 11, 2001, Falwell joined with Pat Robertson in suggesting that certain groups were responsible for bringing about the hor-rors that the country had endured. Falwell blamed the federal courts, pagans, abortionists, feminists, gays, lesbians, the American Civil Liberties Union, People for the American Way, and all who sought "to secularize America" for inviting the wrath of fundamentalist Islamic terrorists. "I point the finger in their face," he declared, "and say 'you helped this happen.'" After a public outcry, Falwell insisted in a CNN television interview, "I would never blame any human being except the terrorists, and if I left that impression with gays or lesbians or anyone else, I apologize." Still, he was adamant that seculariza-tion had "created an environment which possibly has caused God to lift the veil of protection which has allowed no one to attack America on our soil since 1812."

The election of Republican George W. Bush in 2000 placed in the White

House an individual who many evangelicals acknowledged as "one of us." Having made frequent public professions of his religious beliefs during the campaign, Bush set about realizing much of the Christian Right's agenda in public policy. Supported by a generally compliant Republican Congress, Bush urged the use of federal funds for "faith-based" social institutions, opposed U.S. funding for international health programs that promoted the use of condoms, and advocated passage of a constitutional amendment to prohibit homosexual marriage. As much of the social agenda of the religious Right was realized in legislation and policy, Falwell and other evangelical clergy warmly embraced the new president. The Bush administration's decision to invade Iraq in 2003 also brought broad support from evangelicals, many of whom saw in the unfolding of events in the Middle East the realization of biblical prophecies. As the 2004 presidential election approached, Falwell enthusiastically reported that evangelical Christians were now "by far the largest constituency" inside the Republican Party. Indicating his wholehearted support for President Bush, Falwell continued, "You cannot be a sincere, committed born-again believer who takes the Bible seriously and vote for a pro-choice, anti-family candidate." In the aftermath of the election, many political analysts concluded that Bush's victory was largely the result of get-out-the-vote efforts by evangelical Christians.

In the early years of the twenty-first century, Jerry Falwell, having weathered the controversies of more than two decades, could credibly claim that he had played a central role in making evangelical Christians the key constituency in the Republican coalition. It was an undeniably significant development, with major repercussions for conservative Christians, the Republican Party, and the nation. On May 17, 2007, Falwell collapsed in his office at Liberty University and died shortly afterward of heart failure. His death deprived the evangelical Christian movement of a voice that was as influential as it was controversial.

BILL GATES
Prophet of Techno-Times

Bill Gates had taken an enormous gamble, and he knew it. It was December 1974, and the nineteen-year-old Harvard student had just made an outrageous promise in a telephone conversation with Ed Roberts, owner of Model Instrumentation and Telemetry Systems (MITS)—a small electronics company in Albuquerque, New Mexico. MITS had just introduced the Altair 8080, heralded on the cover of the just-released January issue of *Popular Electronics* as the "World's First Microcomputer Kit to Rival Commercial Models." Gates's longtime friend and fellow computer enthusiast Paul Allen had chanced upon the magazine at a newsstand in Harvard Square and hurried back to the dormitory with a copy to break the news to Gates. The Altair computer was offered as a kit requiring assembly and was, by the standards of the 1990s, a machine of modest capabilities. Named after a planet mentioned in an episode of *Star Trek*, the Altair would not have looked incongruous on the bridge of the TV show's fictional starship *Enterprise*. A small, rectangular black box fronted with banks of flashing red lights and toggle switches for programming, the computer presented little outward evidence of its function; keyboards and monitor screens were still years in the future. In 1974, however, the Altair 8080 (so named because Intel, which had developed the microprocessor in 1971, provided the 8080 chip for it) was the vanguard of a new technology. Allen quickly convinced Gates that the new computer offered them an opportunity to develop software for what they both believed would be a burgeoning home computer market. Days later, Gates called Roberts and offered to provide a BASIC (Beginner's All-Purpose Symbolic Instruction Code) for the Altair 8080.

The problem was that Gates and Allen had not developed such a code, nor was it likely that they could produce one in the two to three weeks that Gates had promised. They did not have an Altair to work with, nor did they have an Intel 8080 chip. The software code had to be developed working with a PDP-10 minicomputer programmed to mimic the 8080 chip. Against all odds, however, Gates and Allen collaborated during the next several weeks to complete the promised software, doing much of the work at Harvard's Aiken Computer Center. In late February, Allen flew to Albuquerque to deliver and test the code, which was written on paper tape. At MITS, Allen loaded the BASIC into the Altair, a machine that he had never before touched. To the amazement of both Allen and Roberts, the code worked and the Altair came to life, even running some games the following day. Months later, in July, MITS signed an agreement with Micro-Soft (the hyphen was later deleted), the corporation that Gates and Allen had recently established, to purchase the rights to the BASIC that they had designed. The two young entrepreneurs received $3,000 on signing and a guarantee of future royalties up to $180,000 from their BASIC. Gates soon abandoned his studies at Harvard to devote all his energies to the company that would play a major role in America's high-tech revolution. He and his colleagues were the vanguard of a new generation of generally young entrepreneurs who would usher in "techno-times," an era in which information technology increasingly dominated the nation's economy and reshaped the way that Americans lived.

William Henry Gates III was born into a prominent Seattle family. His father, Bill Gates Jr., worked as an attorney and his mother, Mary Maxwell, as a teacher. The couple had married in 1952, and their first child, Kristi, was born in 1954. On October 28, 1955, the son that they called Trey joined the family. Young Bill was an active, even restless child, and early on his parents detected their son's precocity. In 1967, Bill was registered at Lakeside School, a private academy that offered the intellectual stimulation that he thrived on. The atmosphere of intense competition suited Gates's temperament perfectly and he easily adapted. A pivotal moment in his life came when his math teacher took the class to visit the school's computer room, where a teletype was connected to a PDP-10 minicomputer in downtown Seattle. The machine fascinated Gates and he was soon spending his spare time in the computer room, where he met upperclassman Paul Allen, destined to be one of the founders of Microsoft. Reading everything he could find about computers, Gates soon developed his first programs, including a tic-tac-toe game, a lunar landing game, and a computerized Monopoly game. While taking advanced math courses at the University of Washington, Gates helped to organize the Lakeside Programmers Group (LPG), a gathering of computer enthusiasts. A new school contract with Seattle's Computer Center Corporation, which sold computer time-sharing on its own PDP-10, presented Gates and his classmates with new opportunities for learning, and they were soon providing the company with a troubleshooting and debugging service. By age thirteen, Bill Gates had been transformed into what Joseph Weizenbaum, author of *Computer Power and Human Reason*, would call a "computer bum." The MIT professor described "bright young men of disheveled appearance," distinguished by their "sunken, glowing eyes . . . their rumpled clothes, their unwashed and unshaven faces, and their uncombed hair." In early 1971, Gates, Allen, and friend Keith Evans signed a contract with Information Sciences to write a payroll program, an agreement that compelled the LPG to become a formal partnership. Gates's father drew up the necessary papers for his fifteen-year-old son and the group quickly earned $10,000 worth of computer time. Allen had graduated and enrolled at the University of Washington by the time he and Gates went to work on Traf-O-Data, a program that analyzed traffic-counter tapes and earned the pair about $20,000.

Gates was a senior when his reputation as a computer whiz brought an opportunity to significantly develop his programming skills. The offer came from TRW, a major defense contractor, which needed help in debugging some crucial software programs that ran on a PDP-10. Gates and Allen traveled to Vancouver for interviews and, despite their obvious youth, were hired at a salary of $165 a week. Gates, who gained permission from Lakeside to be absent for part of his senior year, and Allen, who dropped out of the university, moved to Vancouver, where they shared an apartment. When Gates returned to Lakeside to graduate in June 1973 and was asked by a classmate what his plans were, he responded that he was going to Harvard and planned to make his first million by the time he was twenty-five.

Gates arrived on the Cambridge campus with no real idea of his purposes there. Though pre-law was his official major, he had no real inclination in that direction. He enrolled in the standard undergraduate prerequisites, but also signed up for advanced math, physics, and computer science courses that could be applied to a graduate degree. Associates remember Gates living at a frenetic pace, sleeping irregularly, eating poorly, and rarely dating. In 1974, Paul Allen joined Gates in Cambridge and that summer the two worked for Honeywell, one of the "Seven Dwarfs" that operated in the shadow of computer giant IBM. Both men were certain that the computer industry was on the verge of technological innovations that would mark the advent of a new high-tech era. Gates continued his haphazard approach to his studies at Harvard while devoting a great deal of time to nocturnal poker games at his residence in Currier House, where he met Steve Ballmer, also destined to play a major role in Microsoft. It was at this point, in late 1974, that Paul Allen came to Gates's room with the news about the Altair 8080.

Though the *Popular Electronics* piece on the Altair generated 4,000 orders for the minicomputer within several weeks, the market was still largely restricted to enthusiasts. Vague public awareness of computers had grown only slowly after World War II, during which IBM had financed the development of the Mark I, an electromechanical machine capable of performing relatively rudimentary calculations. In 1946, University of Pennsylvania scientists constructed ENIAC (Electronic Numerical Integrator and Calculator), a thirty-ton behemoth that filled a garage-size room. Though it had less capability than today's home computers, ENIAC was a major step forward in computing technology, which the invention of the transistor facilitated further in 1947. Used as semiconductors, transistors supplanted undependable vacuum tubes, permitting smaller and more reliable computers. In the late 1950s, the development of integrated circuits etched on silicon, known as chips, also proved crucial to the advance of computer technology. Through the 1970s, manufacturers such as IBM, which dominated the field, concentrated on marketing mainframe computers for commercial and government use. Public awareness of the existence of computers grew, and if depictions in popular culture were representative, Americans harbored significant anxieties about these high-technology marvels. In science fiction literature and film, computers were sometimes assigned benevolent roles, but more often were presented as potential threats to human existence. In Stanley Kubrick's film *Dr. Strangelove* (1964), a Soviet computer-linked "Doomsday Machine" unleashes a nuclear holocaust that devastates the planet. In *2001: A Space Odyssey* (1968), another Kubrick film, the psychotic computer HAL 9000 murders all but one of the crew of the spaceship *Discovery*. Computers that seek to either subjugate or destroy humanity were also featured in *Colossus: The Forbin Project* (1970), *WarGames* (1983), and the long-running *Terminator* series.

Few Americans gave much thought to owning a home computer at the time of Microsoft's founding in 1975. Bill Gates's genius was in his conviction that home computer ownership would become commonplace within a surprisingly short span of time. He was determined that Microsoft should remain the acknowledged leader in software technology so as to ensure that its products would set standards for the burgeoning high-tech industries. In the summer of 1975, Gates and Allen, who shared a room at a budget motel in Albuquerque, began assembling a team of young computer programmers, many of whom were former college classmates. Uniformly young, dedicated to the point of fanaticism, and partial to sloppy attire, long hair, and loud rock music in their workplace, they often drew puzzled looks from MITS employees. Late that year, Gates, who had returned to Harvard for the fall semester, flew to New Mexico to work with Allen to develop BASIC for a floppy disk that MITS was introducing. In the spring of 1976, Gates and Allen put together a staff of talented programmers, the "Microkids," in Albuquerque, where the company had moved into offices in a bank building. Gates, who dropped out of Harvard for the final time in January 1977, was devoting more of his energies to projects that anticipated future markets, such as the development of code for FORTRAN, the second most popular computer language. Late in 1976, even as Allen joined Microsoft as a full-time employee, the company won substantial accounts with National Cash Register and General Electric.

With the end of a successful first year, Gates turned to resolving a dilemma that threatened to limit Microsoft's future. The Altair 8080 was already dated, the Commodore and Tandy Corporations were preparing to introduce new microcomputers, and Steve Wozniak and Steve Jobs were on the verge of producing the Apple I, which would have a seminal effect on the industry.

With these new opportunities for software sales looming, Gates needed to terminate the agreement with MITS, a move that required that company's approval, before Microsoft could sell 8080 BASIC elsewhere. In April 1976, Microsoft notified MITS that their contract was being ended, and the subsequent court battle concluded with an arbitrator's decision in favor of Microsoft. The episode was a classic illustration of Gates's forward vision and the aggressive tactics he was willing to employ to secure his company's future. Later that year, Microsoft signed agreements with both Tandy and Apple to provide them with BASIC.

Gates moved the company to Seattle in 1978. Established in eighth-floor offices in the Old National Bank Building in the suburb of Bellevue, Microsoft continued its tradition as a casual workplace, its two-dozen jeans-clad and often barefoot employees maintaining flexible, if sometimes lengthy, work hours. Gates's personal eccentricities were a central part of the emerging corporate myth. Rarely attentive to his personal appearance, the five-foot-nine Gates was easily recognizable by his unruly hair, rumpled clothes, and oversize spectacles with hopelessly begrimed lenses. Obsessively committed to his company's success and intolerant of the perceived inadequacies of others, Gates was capable of cruel sarcasm when chastising employees, and his frequent emotional outbursts were legendary. In his drive to make Microsoft supreme, Gates did not spare himself. He worked long hours, went years without any vacation, and rarely indulged in personal enjoyments. Within five years of Microsoft's founding, the company was generating $7 million in annual sales revenue and was on the verge of securing a lucrative agreement with IBM, the titan of the computer industry.

Microsoft grew rapidly in the late 1970s, creating new opportunities that Gates seized on. In 1979, the company cut a deal with Intel to provide BASIC for the new 8086 chip, designed specifically for personal computers (PCs). Moving beyond producing computer languages, Microsoft established a consumer products division to facilitate its move into application programs, including word-processing, spreadsheets, and games. In February 1980, Microsoft expanded into operating systems, the low-level languages that drive a computer's basic functions. Moving into hardware, Microsoft engineers designed SoftCard, an expansion card that allowed the increasingly popular Apple computers to run Microsoft programs. An agreement with Xerox to provide BASIC for a personal computer that the Dallas company was developing signaled Microsoft's entrée into the big leagues. In July, a representative from IBM contacted Gates to propose a meeting that could result in a major contract and a potentially fruitful corporate relationship. The company known as Big Blue was in the initial stages of developing a personal computer, and corporate executives hoped to bring Microsoft into their Project Chess to provide the necessary software. In the course of several meetings, it was agreed that Microsoft would supply software development tools such as BASIC and a disk operating system (DOS) for the IBM machine. A contract was signed that November, marking the beginnings of a sometimes-tumultuous relationship between what was seen as a corporate odd couple.

Gates had shrewdly arranged for Microsoft to act as a licensing agent for Seattle Computer Product's disk operating system, sparing Microsoft the trouble of designing one for IBM's Acorn personal computer. Under Microsoft's name, MS-DOS became an industry standard. The new IBM contract permitted a rapid expansion of the Microsoft workforce, which had grown to seventy, among them Gates's longtime friend Steve Ballmer, who joined the company in 1980 to handle administrative duties. In August 1981, IBM introduced its much-heralded PC and indicated that it would offer future support only for MS-DOS. The association with IBM further established Microsoft's reputation, triggering a period of tremendous growth. Microsoft's annual revenues had doubled every year since 1975, reaching close to $16 million by 1981. That year, Gates and his employees shifted to new, larger offices as Microsoft underwent a necessary reorganization. Now a private corporation rather than a partnership, with Gates as chair of the board and Allen as director, Microsoft began offering its employees stock options to augment their relatively modest salaries. At about $1 per share, adroit investment in company stock assured that several employees would become instant millionaires when Microsoft shares went public several years later.

Emboldened by his achievements, Gates advocated an aggressive corporate strategy with the object of assuring Microsoft's dominance of the software industry. On several occasions that year, he declared his determination to crush competitors such as Digital Research, MicroPro, and Lotus. The initial success of the IBM PC provided a definite boost for Microsoft's software. Though the machines retailed for nearly $1,600, IBM sold 13,533 of them in the last five months of 1981, soon eclipsing sales of the Apple II computer. A Microsoft marketing goal that Gates and Ballmer had established the previous year, "A Computer on Every Desktop Running Microsoft Software," was on the way to being realized. The objective could be achieved more rapidly and comprehensively, however, if Microsoft directed its efforts to developing more applications software, a retail market that Gates began to consider more seriously in 1982. One of the strongest attributes of forthcoming Microsoft applications software was the incorporation of a graphical user interface (GUI), first used by Xerox researchers in the development of Smalltalk, an advanced language program. On Xerox's experimental Alto computer, Smalltalk allowed for on-screen menus and point-and-click mouse technology that obviated the need for keyboarding commands. When Xerox introduced its Star computer in 1981, which also utilized icons, Gates was quick to purchase one. The GUI technologies he found there and in Apple's upcoming Macintosh conformed to his own ideas as to what Microsoft's applications software should look like. Though Windows was still in the conceptual stage, both it and Microsoft's Word would reflect some of these innovations. Gates marketed newly developed applications software as Microsoft Word, Microsoft Plan, Microsoft Chart, and Microsoft File, with the intent of establishing the company's name as synonymous with the products.

In 1983, Gates turned to the most difficult and demanding project that Microsoft had undertaken to date—the development of Windows. Initially called Interface Manager, the program was intended to act as a facilitator between MS-DOS and applications, allowing all programs to be presented and operated almost identically. Windows was still not ready when Gates announced it in November 1983, but he hoped to preempt any competition prior to the scheduled unveiling of Apple's Macintosh in early 1984. At his direction, Microsoft moved quickly to develop application software that was compatible with the popular Macintosh, IBM's PC, and the growing number of PC clones. Microsoft's ability to outpace and best the competition was becoming legendary; Excel, Microsoft's spreadsheet application introduced in 1985, quickly overwhelmed Lotus's Jazz, once again establishing an industry standard. Windows was brought out the same year. As Gates celebrated his thirtieth birthday in October 1985, he was preparing to take the step that would make him and many of his associates instant multimillionaires—taking his company public. Months later, on March 13, 1986, Microsoft stock, of which Gates owned 11,220,000 shares, was traded on the New York Stock Exchange. Opening at $25.75 a share, the stock gained significantly in subsequent weeks. Gates earned $1.6 million from the shares he sold; those he retained were valued at $350 million.

By the time Microsoft went public, its workforce had grown to nearly 1,200, requiring a vastly expanded new headquarters complex of 260 acres. During Microsoft's rapid rise to prominence, the company had faced intermittent management problems, stemming partly from Gates's abrasive style. Wearied by the frenetic pace, Paul Allen had left in 1983. By the late 1980s, new challenges arose as past practices caught up with the company. In 1986, Seattle Computer Products sued Microsoft over rights to DOS and obtained an out-of-court settlement of $925,000. Two years later, Apple Computer filed a suit claiming that Microsoft had stolen some of the Macintosh's visual features for Windows, provoking a countersuit and a lengthy court battle that Apple lost. In 1987, a joint Microsoft-IBM project to develop OS/2, a new operating system, was announced, but Gates began to distance Microsoft from the project when he grew to doubt its profitability. The introduction of a much-improved Windows 3.0 in May 1990 was catastrophic for OS/2, further souring the relationship between Microsoft and Big Blue, and in early 1991, Microsoft announced that it was abandoning the project. At the end of that year, IBM announced net losses of $2.8 billion, while Microsoft reported a 55 percent rise in profits in only the last three months. Ironically, the Federal Trade Commission soon began an investigation into whether the two companies had been engaged in anticompetitive collusion.

Microsoft's profits soared in the 1990s, and although Gates was committing increasingly large amounts of money to philanthropic enterprises, negative publicity about the "silicon bully" proliferated. "Can Anyone Stop Bill Gates?" a *Newsweek* cover asked. *Business Month* featured a cover story titled "How Long Can Bill Gates Kick Sand in the Face of the Computer Industry?" Nonetheless, it was evident that no amount of criticism would deter Gates from his goal of establishing his company's dominance in a growing industry. Personal computer sales exploded from 4 million in 1990 to nearly 11 million in 1997, and the growth of the Internet presented new opportunities for Microsoft. The origins of the Internet go back to 1963, when J.C.R. Licklider, head of the U.S. Department of Defense's Advanced Research Projects Agency, initiated a program to link computers for the purpose of rapidly exchanging research information. By 1971, Arpanet, as it was then known, connected twenty-three computers. By 1984, the renamed Internet linked about 1,000 host computers; ten years later, some 6 million computers were wired into the system, and as of 2001, 130 million Americans were using the Internet. Gates's failure to grasp the future importance of the Internet was one of his few major missteps. Not until the introduction of Netscape's Internet browser in August 1995 did the Microsoft chief comprehend that the competition had outflanked him in a crucial area.

The subsequent browser war was the dominant industry topic of the late 1990s, as Gates battled Netscape's Marc Anderssen in a war of words, technologies, and marketing strategies. Marshaling its full corporate weight, Microsoft sought to crush its competitor by bundling its Internet Explorer browser with the popular Windows 95 operating system, essentially providing the browser to customers at no cost. As Netscape's market share declined precipitously,

Microsoft's grip tightened. The years of the browser war also saw Microsoft demonstrate its dominance elsewhere through the acquisition of forty-seven high-tech and entertainment companies, including Apple Computer, purchased in 1997. Microsoft's relentlessly predatory practices attracted the attention of the Justice Department, and the company was in court facing an antitrust suit relating to its browser bundling practices in October 1998. On November 5, 1999, a federal district judge ruled that Microsoft was a monopoly that stifled competition. Government officials subsequently won a court order compelling a breakup of Microsoft, but Gates's attorneys appealed to the U.S. Supreme Court, which referred the case to a lower court. In 2001, the new administration of George W. Bush, committed to a conservative, antiregulatory agenda, vacated the government's suit against Microsoft. In subsequent years, Gates's company faced additional lawsuits over its practices, including one filed by Novell, a software corporation specializing in network operating systems. In March 2003, the European Commission assessed Microsoft 497 million euros for anticompetitive behavior. Bill Gates could afford to accept the penalty with a shrug. At age 50 in 2007, he was still the richest man in the world, with an estimated net personal wealth of $50 billion. Since giving up his daily duties as corporation chair in June 2006, Gates has devoted much of his time to philanthropic activities. As early as 2003, Gates was acknowledged as the world's top charitable giver. The Bill and Melinda Gates Foundation, with an initial endowment of more than $28 billion dollars, has provided funds for global health organizations and learning opportunities. The Bill Gates Library Initiative was established to make computers and Internet access widely available in public libraries in low-income communities in the United States and Canada. In March 2005, Gates was knighted by Britain's Queen Elizabeth II for his contributions to private enterprise and his efforts to fight poverty.

Conclusion

Though Jerry Falwell and Bill Gates pursued radically different courses during the 1980s, they both represented key aspects of American life during that decade. Falwell, who founded the Moral Majority only a few years after a very young Gates incorporated Microsoft, was from an older generation that saw in the turmoil of the 1960s not progress, but social degeneration. Falwell represented a significant number of Americans who genuinely feared the consequences of an increasingly secular society and the erosion of traditional religious beliefs and values. This was not a new phenomenon in the nation's history. As Garry Wills noted in *Under God: Religion and American Politics*

(1991), religious fundamentalism has always been an element in American society; in some periods, however, when rapid change increased social anxieties, Christian fundamentalism assumed a greater prominence, offering an antidote to uncertainty through divinely ordained verities. In eras of unusually jarring change, like the 1920s and 1980s, Christian fundamentalism found a broad audience and achieved a prominent role in national life. What was unusual about the new Christian Right that Falwell represented was its enduring and increasingly influential role in national politics through the vehicle of the Republican Party. In recent years, that trend has provoked some Republicans, including analyst Kevin Phillips, to lament the disproportionate influence that evangelicals have within the party. In *American Theocracy* (2006), Phillips warns that the contemporary Republican Party, due largely to the influence of the Christian Right, has become America's "first religious party," a development that he views with considerable concern. In a pluralistic society, he argues, the successful resolution of important policy issues, in Congress and elsewhere, generally requires a flexibility that the politics of morality disallows. The growing polarization of American politics in the early twenty-first century stems in part from this phenomenon.

By contrast, the culture wars that took shape in the 1980s scarcely affected Bill Gates. Oblivious to the decade's shifting political currents, Gates turned his intellect and entrepreneurial talents to laying the foundation for the age of the personal computer. Before the decade was over, the phrase "get wired" would have significantly different connotations than it did in the 1960s, when it was broadly understood to refer to recreational drug use. Gates's adept corporate maneuverings ensured that Microsoft emerged as the unchallenged giant of the software industry, and the corporation's "user-friendly" products rapidly advanced the use of personal computers. In an era in which financial success was hailed as a measure of personal worth, Gates was unmatchable. Though he dominated the software industry as completely as John D. Rockefeller had dominated the petroleum industry of the nineteenth century, Gates never gained a reputation as one of the era's gurus of greed, as had corporate pirates Boesky and Milliken. Rather, Gates was a late twentieth-century version of the sort of individual that Americans had often admired throughout their history. Young, bright, and innovative, Gates realized his ambitions through his own initiative and resources and, at the same time, provided a commodity that significantly changed and in many ways improved American life. Likewise, high-tech industries, such as computer software, promised a new, prosperous direction for the nation's economy in the postindustrial era. Concerns about the permanence of the country's economic malaise seemed to lift in the 1980s, as the potential of the new high-tech industries became more obvious. By the 1990s, as the growth of the Internet brought even more opportunities for high-tech entrepreneurs like Gates, the outlines of a new breed of economy began to assume clearer definition. Based on the new technologies and promising greater stability than in the past, the New Economy, as some commentators called the heavily high-tech U.S. economy, brought unexpected prosperity through the 1990s. Led by the chic new dot-com companies, the New Economy would bring some surprises of its own before the new millennium.

Study Questions

1. To what factors did evangelical Christians like Jerry Falwell attribute America's perceived decline?
2. How did Falwell's Moral Majority and other Christian Right organizations gain political influence by the 1980s?
3. What solutions for America's problems did the Christian Right offer?
4. How did Bill Gates succeed in making Microsoft the giant of the software industry?
5. What changes characterized the American economy of the late twentieth century?

Selected Bibliography

Blumenthal, Sidney. *Our Long National Daydream: A Political Pageant of the Reagan Era.* New York: HarperCollins, 1988.

Brennan, Mary C. *Turning Right in the Sixties: The Conservative Capture of the GOP.* Chapel Hill: University of North Carolina Press, 1995.

Brown, Clayton D. *Globalization and America Since 1945.* Woodbridge, CT: Scholarly Resources, 2003.

Campbell-Kelly, Martin, and William Aspray. *Computer: A History of the Information Machine.* New York: HarperCollins, 1996.

Crawford, Alan. *Thunder on the Right: The "New Right" and the Politics of Resentment.* New York: Pantheon, 1980.

Diamond, Sara. *Spiritual Warfare: The Politics of the Christian Right.* Cambridge, MA: South End Press, 1989.

Falwell, Jerry. *Falwell: An Autobiography.* Lynchburg, VA: Liberty House, 1997.

Harding, Susan Friend. *The Book of Jerry Falwell: Fundamentalist Language on Politics.* Princeton: Princeton University Press, 2000.

Hodgson, Godfrey. *More Equal Than Others: America from Nixon to the New Century.* Princeton: Princeton University Press, 2006.

———. *The World Turned Right Side Up: A History of the Conservative Ascendancy in America.* New York: Houghton Mifflin, 1996.

Jenkins, Philip. *Decade of Nightmares: The End of the Sixties and the Making of Eighties America.* Oxford: Oxford University Press, 2006.

Johnson, Haynes. *The Best of Times: America in the Clinton Years.* New York: Harcourt, 2001.

———. *Sleepwalking Through History: America in the Reagan Years.* New York: W.W. Norton, 1992.

Leibovich, Mark. *The New Imperialists: How Five Restless Kids Grew Up to Virtually Rule Your World.* Upper Saddle River, NJ: Prentice Hall, 2002.

Manes, Stephen, and Paul Andrews. *Gates.* New York: Simon and Schuster, 1993.

Martin, William. *With God on Our Side: The Rise of the Religious Right in America.* New York: Broadway, 1996.

Phillips, Kevin. *American Theocracy.* New York: Viking, 2006.

Wills, Garry. *Reagan's America.* New York: Doubleday, 1984.

———. *Under God: Religion and American Politics.* New York: Simon and Schuster, 1991.

12

After the Revolution

New Horizons for Black Americans

By the opening stages of the twenty-first century, African Americans had achieved new horizons while still encountering racial stereotypes and discrimination. According to the 2005 census, 39.9 million African Americans resided in the United States, constituting nearly 14 percent of the total population. The Civil Rights Act of 1964 and the Voting Rights Act of 1965 effectively ended de jure segregation in the United States, and the number of black elected officials, middle-class families, and wealthy individuals continued to increase. Nevertheless, a large black underclass still existed, with a quarter of the African American populace situated below the poverty line and one-third of black men in their twenties behind bars, out on parole, or on probation. Single women headed a majority of black households. Racial stereotypes remained plentiful, including within the African American community.

Black role models ranged widely, from those associated with gangsta rap and the drug culture to figures of considerable note in such fields as education, journalism, politics, literature, entertainment, sports, and law. Princeton professor Cornel West, *New York Times* columnist Bob Herbert, U.S. senator Barack Obama, Nobel laureate Toni Morrison, actor Bill Cosby, talk show host Oprah Winfrey, golfer Tiger Woods, and Supreme Court justice Clarence Thomas were among the many African Americans at the top of their respective professions. Regardless of their varied backgrounds, all confronted obstacles along the way, ranging from Jim Crow practices to explicit, vicious barbs and perceived slights carelessly delivered. Recent allegations of efforts to limit the black vote in statewide and national elections demonstrate that even the old battles might have to be refought, all the while discriminatory realities beset African Americans and the nation as a whole.

In their own disparate fashions, Woods and Thomas serve as exemplars of black achievements, establishing new horizons for African Americans. An examination of Woods's standing as possibly the finest athlete of his era, whose stature promises to surpass his athletic feats, and Thomas's role in carving out a conservative judicial revolution affords an opportunity to explore the evolving nature of black America.

Notwithstanding the accomplishments of black athletes like heavyweight champions Jack Johnson and Joe Louis, Negro League architect Rube Foster, and Jesse Owens, the sprinter and broad jumper who won four gold medals at the Nazi-hosted Olympics in Berlin in 1936, the sporting world, like American society as a whole, remained plagued by discriminatory practices. The signing of Jackie Robinson to a contract with the Montreal franchise of the Brooklyn Dodgers in August 1945 and his subsequent stardom with the big league club shook racial barriers, although they hardly came down altogether. The National Football League soon featured the likes of Marion Motley and Jim Brown, while the National Basketball Association pitted Bill Russell against Wilt Chamberlain, and Elgin Baylor against Oscar Robertson, all African American superstars.

Hardly surprisingly, elite sports like tennis and golf took a bit longer to eliminate Jim Crow barricades. Initially, tennis proved more open, for, as the end of the 1950s approached, the finest female player in the world was Althea Gibson, the gifted African American star who won the French Open, Wimbledon, and U.S. Open titles. The Professional Golfers Association of America (PGA) sought to maintain racial divides, incorporating a "Caucasians only" clause in its constitution in 1943. Five years later, three black players—Theodore "Rags" Rhodes, Bill Spiller, and Madison Gunther—charged the PGA with violating their civil rights. Determined to retain its "Caucasian only" membership clause, the PGA subsequently required golfers to receive invitations to compete in sponsored events. Those who challenged these racially restrictive practices faced hostility, epithets, and even death threats. The PGA finally accepted its first black member, Charlie Sifford, the man Tiger Woods called the "honorary grandfather" of African American golfers, in 1962. Another thirteen years would pass before Lee Elder became the first African American to compete—instead of caddying or attending to the grounds—in the Masters Tournament, held at Augusta

National. Despite the accomplishments of Sifford, Elder, and other black golfers, various country clubs still refused to admit African Americans as members.

Nevertheless, racial stereotypes were losing their power, thanks to black celebrities like Bill Cosby, Oprah Winfrey, Michael Jordan, and Tiger Woods. The force of law, including federal enactments and rulings challenging Jim Crow, often assisted in that process. The Warren court (1953–1969) and various federal judges particularly helped to overturn segregation practices, but even the subsequent Burger and Rehnquist courts (1969–1986, 1986–2006) sustained much of the legal momentum initiated during the heyday of the civil rights movement. The Burger court upheld the practice of affirmative action, intended to overcome, at least in part, a long-standing history of discriminatory treatment. Affirmative action enabled any number of young black men and women first to enter elite schools and then to acquire prestigious jobs that might not otherwise have been attainable. One beneficiary of affirmative action was a highly ambitious young man from the small community of Pin Point, Georgia, who was admitted to Yale Law School. Clarence Thomas clearly benefited from collapsed racial shackles and heightened occupational opportunities. Resenting the perception that he had obtained preferential treatment, Thomas adopted a dogged commitment to succeed, as well as a growing aversion to the very practice of affirmative action that had aided him. Eventually, thanks to his unique stance as a black conservative, he was appointed to high-level government posts and the federal bench. Then, in 1991, President George H.W. Bush chose Thomas to replace Thurgood Marshall, a civil rights legend and the first black to sit on the U.S. Supreme Court.

TIGER WOODS
Golf's Great Black Hope

In early April 1997, twenty-one-year-old Tiger Woods competed in the Masters golf tournament at the pristine course in Augusta, Georgia, one of professional golf's four major competitions and the tournament most revered by many golfers. The founder of the Masters, Cliff Roberts, had stated years earlier, "As long as I'm alive, golfers will be white, and caddies black." Only months earlier, Woods had turned professional after winning the U.S. Amateur Championship for an unprecedented third straight time, a feat even the legendary Bobby Jones had been unable to accomplish. As an amateur, Woods had competed in a number of majors, including the previous two Masters, where he had finished tied for forty-first place and missed the cut. Having signed endorsements deals amounting to $60 million—a $40 million package with Nike and a $20 million contract with Titleist—Woods had won two of the eight professional tournaments he competed in during the fall of 1996, thus earning his tour card. He won the first tournament held in 1997, the Mercedes Championship, and finished tied for second at the Pebble Beach National Pro-Am tournament. Woods was hardly simply a golf prodigy, however. He also promised to become a racial pioneer, given professional golf's long history of segregation and his own racial threads, which included African American, Native American, Chinese, Thai, and Dutch ancestors.

During his first round at the Masters on Thursday, Woods opened inauspiciously, going out in a four-over-par 40 before carding a 30 on the final nine holes to finish at two under par, three-shots behind the leader. Woods took the thirty-six–hole lead on Friday and control of the tournament by firing the day's best round, a 66, placing him four shots in front of Constantino Rocca. A 65, again the day's low score, followed on Saturday, swelling his lead to nine shots ahead of Rocca. Leading the field in driving by averaging of 323.1 yards and delivering no dreaded three-putts throughout the entire tournament, Woods concluded his masterpiece by shooting a 69 on Sunday, producing an eighteen-under-par total of 270 and breaking the Masters record previously held by Jack Nicklaus and Raymond Floyd. Besting another Nicklaus mark, Woods won the tournament by twelve shots over second-place finisher Tom Kite. The victory, watched by CBS's largest television audience in its four-and-a-half-decade-long coverage of the Masters, enabled Woods, who shot twenty-two under in the final sixty-three holes, to become the third minority member of Augusta National.

The sporting world, soon caught up in the phenomenon of Tigermania, appeared stunned by the ease with which Woods mastered the famed golf course and lapped the greatest golfers gathered from across the globe. The overseers of Augusta National and other famed courses soon attempted to "Tigerproof" their eighteen-hole courses to withstand the onslaught of the sculpted athlete and improvements in golf technology. The obvious fact that a color barrier had been shattered in the process was recognized by many observers, including black pioneer Lee Elder, who greeted Woods as he concluded his practice session before the final round. Woods later remarked, "That meant a lot to me because he was the first; he was the one I looked up to. Because of what he did I was able to play on the PGA tour. When I turned pro when I was 20, I could live my dream." Reflecting on the racial divide that had long confronted black players, Woods acknowledged, "I wasn't the pioneer. Charlie Sifford, Lee Elder, Ted Rhodes, those are the guys who paved the way. All night I was thinking about them, what they've done for me and the game of golf. Coming up 18, I said a little prayer of thanks to those guys. Those guys are the ones who did it." South African golfer Gary Player, himself a three-time winner of the Masters, declared, "Tiger Woods has the opportunity to do something for the human race that no other golfer has before him. Imagine the black people in Africa—400 million watching Tiger Woods win the Masters." As for his triumph opening up doors to minority golfers, Woods stated, "We'll see. As time goes on, I think that young people who haven't normally pursued golf will." Participation by young minority golfers did nearly double from 1996 to 1997. With his athleticism, flair, and fierce competitiveness, Woods helped to make golf cool.

Washington Post sportswriter Michael Wilbon, reflecting on Woods's accomplishment in winning the Masters, was struck by the fact that Tiger's "brown-skinned father" had been respectfully escorted off a golf course by "southern state troopers at a country club where some members only 10 years ago would rather have died and gone to hell than see that man even walk the course, much less play it." A bridge, Wilbon noted, linked Jackie Robinson and Tiger Woods: "one ballplayer who endured unspeakable hatred in the name of progress" and "this young golfer who now has to negotiate unimaginable adulation." Wilbon wrote, "It certainly seems the baton has been passed once again, from Jesse Owens to Joe Louis, to Jackie Robinson to Muhammad Ali to Arthur Ashe and now to Tiger Woods." Interestingly, just as the great Negro Leaguers James "Cool Papa" Bell, Satchel Paige, and Josh Gibson had been heroes for Robinson—"the men who took all the earliest hits, who had doors slammed in their faces and roads blocked"—Sifford, Elder, and Rhodes were heroes for the young Tiger Woods.

Eldrick Tiger Woods was born in Cypress, California, on December 30, 1975, the son of Earl Woods, a retired U.S. Army lieutenant colonel and Green Beret with black, Chinese, and Native American ancestry, and his wife, Kultida Woods, a native of Thailand with Thai, Chinese, and Dutch relatives. As an infant, their son—named Tiger after a Vietnamese friend who had saved Earl's life during one of his two tours of duty in Vietnam—attempted to duplicate Earl's golf swing, and, at the age of two, he putted against entertainer Bob Hope on *The Mike Douglas Show*. Within a year, he shot 48 over a nine-hole stretch at the Navy Golf Club in his hometown. A few years later, Earl dropped Tiger off at the golf course one morning and picked him up in the early evening to find, to his chagrin, his son having won several dollars from considerably older, befuddled players. Tiger first appeared in *Golf Digest* in 1981, when he was five, and in 1984, he captured the first of a series of six Optimist International Junior Championships. In 1991, Woods became the youngest player ever to take the U.S. Junior Amateur Championship, triumphing again the next two years, on the last hole or in extra holes, in each instance. In his teens, he played alongside the legendary Sam Snead; entered (at the age of sixteen) his first PGA event, the Nissan Los Angeles Open, before which he received a death threat; and appeared in a series of other PGA tournaments while still in high school. In both 1991 and 1992, *Golf Digest* named him Amateur Player of the Year. In 1994, the eighteen-year-old Woods became the youngest and first black winner of the U.S. Amateur Championship, coming from six holes down, leading his father to proclaim, "Let the legend grow." Earl Woods noted, "This is the first black intuitive golfer ever raised in the United States." Tiger eventually became the first player to win that title three straight years, winning the final time by coming back after trailing late in the match. Tom Watson, the holder of eight major championships, called Woods "the most important young golfer in the last 50 years."

The March 27, 1995, issue of *Sports Illustrated* contained an article on Woods titled "Goodness Gracious, He's a Great Ball of Fire." The author, Rick Reilly, noted the determination of Earl and Kultida Woods "to raise the greatest golfer who ever lived." Describing the rigorous regimen that his son had been exposed to, in which he deliberately made a good deal of noise when Tiger addressed the ball, Earl explained, "I wanted to make sure he'd never run into anybody who was tougher mentally than he was." Referring to Woods as "the Great Black Hope," Reilly discussed Tiger's impending introduction to the Masters, which would make him the fourth African American, after Lee Elder, Calvin Peete, and Jim Thorpe, to compete in that revered tournament. Woods well recognized, Reilly reported, that "the Jackie Robinsons of golf" had opened the doors for him.

Following Tiger's second U.S. Amateur victory, Earl Woods predicted, "Before he's through, my son will win 14 major championships." Tiger himself envisioned shattering Jack Nicklaus's mark of twenty majors, counting both amateur and professional championships. The third U.S. Amateur title proved the most difficult, with Woods, who had been as far back as five holes down, still trailing by two holes with only three to play. Consecutive birdies on the sixteenth and seventeenth holes, topped off by a thirty-foot putt on the seventeenth green, evened the match, which resulted in a playoff, won by Woods on the second extra hole. Named a two-time All-American at Stanford, Woods competed in the 1995 Walker Cup matches in Wales and won the 1996 NCCA individual men's championship while a sophomore at Stanford University, when he was named College Player of the Year. As the most eagerly anticipated rookie since Jack Nicklaus, Woods entered the professional ranks in the fall of 1996, winning both the Las Vegas International in a playoff against Davis Love III and the Disney/Oldsmobile Classic by one shot over Payne Stewart. He earned nearly $800,000, garnering the twenty-fifth spot on the money chart and a spot on the PGA tour. He also demonstrated "that volcano of competitive fire," characteristic of his father, by breaking eight putters after failing to win the Texas Open. During that tournament, he remarked, "I never play for second. The idea is to win the damn thing."

At Stanford, Woods had taken a course in African American history and came to the following determination: "What I realized is that even though I'm mathematically Asian—if anything—if you have one drop of black blood in the United States, you're black. And how important it is for this country to talk about this subject." He understood that "golf has shied away from this for too long. Some clubs have brought in tokens, but nothing has really changed. I hope what I'm doing can change that." When questioned about racists, Woods, wielding a golf club, angrily responded, "It makes me want to stick it right up their asses. On the golf course." On September 12, 1996, the *Augusta Chronicle* noted, "TIGER WOODS—of mixed-race heritage—has marketers excited about the possibilities of attracting minorities to golf." Nike commented, "He wants to be an ambassador of change in golf. . . . His goal is to bring more minorities to the game." However, Earl Woods's aspirations for his son were clearly far greater. *Sports Illustrated*, naming Woods Sportsman of the Year for 1996, declared, "Tiger Woods was raised to believe that his destiny is not only to be the greatest golfer ever but also to change the world." Author Gary Smith referred to Earl's speech at the Fred Haskins Award dinner honoring Tiger as the year's top college golfer. Earl Woods, battle-hardened at sixty-four, choked up as he discussed his son: "He will transcend this game and bring to the world a humanitarianism which has never been known before. The world will be a better place to live in by virtue of his existence and his presence." Earl insisted that "Tiger will do more than any other man in history to change the course of humanity . . . he has a larger forum . . . he's qualified through his ethnicity to accomplish miracles. He's the bridge between the East and the West . . . he is the Chosen One."

In 1996, Tiger Woods took the first step in fulfilling his father's prophecy by establishing the Tiger Woods Foundation "to create positive opportunities for underprivileged youths and to emphasize the importance of parental involvement and responsibility in the lives of their children." Using "the platform golf provides," Woods strove to pass on the values his parents and teachers had transmitted to him—"tenacity, integrity, courage, self-esteem and drive for excellence"—by hosting clinics and exhibitions for 12,000 children in a half-dozen cities. Woods hoped to break through golf's racial barriers. "Golf has always been segregated," he remarked. "That's just the truth of it. I've always felt golf is a game everyone should enjoy. But our goal is not just to have kids play golf, but to have strong self-esteem, then to grow up to be solid individuals."

Altogether, Woods won four tournaments during his first full season, 1997, and established a record by winning $2,066,833, leading to his receipt of the PGA Player of the Year Award and recognition as the Associated Press (AP) Male Athlete of the Year. His agent, Hughes Norton of International Management Group, commented, "Tiger could be the first athlete to hit $1 billion in off-the-course earnings." The PGA itself benefited from golf's heightened popularity, signing a new television contract more than twice as lucrative as the previous one. Michael Jordan, predicting that Woods "will succeed and expand across all racial barriers," expressed admiration for Tiger's "establishing a new plateau, a higher ground. . . . I really do believe he was put here for a bigger reason than just to play golf. I don't think he is a god, but I do believe that he was sent by one." During an appearance on *The Oprah Winfrey Show*, the talk show host called Tiger "America's son" and asked, "What do you call yourself?" He replied, "Growing up, I came up with this name . . . Cablinasian," a term recognizing his white, black, Native American, and Asian ancestry. For her part, Winfrey asserted, "Tiger is exactly what our world needs right now."

Seeking to refine his powerful but sometimes erratic golf swing under the tutelage of Butch Harmon, Woods had something of an off-year in 1998, taking just one PGA tournament and ending up fourth on the money list, although he did win twice overseas. The swing alterations resulted in a big year in 1999, when he won eight PGA events, including his final four tournaments; a record $6,616,585 in earnings; and his second professional major when he nipped Sergio Garcia for the PGA Championship. He hosted the Target World Challenge, which brought together sixteen of the world's finest golfers at the Grayhawk Golf Club in Scottsdale, Arizona (the tournament soon moved to the Sherwood Country Club in Thousand Oaks, California). The tournament raised "money for the Tiger Woods Foundation and the charities that it supports, including the Tiger Woods Learning Center and the Start Something Program." Again, Woods was voted PGA Player of the Year by his peers and Male Athlete of the Year by the AP. The soaring earnings figure indicated his impact on the sport, with the PGA tour's prize money jumping from $61 million in 1995, the last pre-Tiger year, to $164 million by 2000 and to $252 million five years later.

Nevertheless, 1999 was merely a prelude to one of sports history's greatest seasons. Woods began 2000 with victories at both the Mercedes Championship and the AT&T Pebble Beach National Pro-Am, thus earning six wins in a row. His opening rounds of 75 and 72 at the Masters denied him much of a shot at a second green jacket, awarded to the tournament's winner, although he fired 68 and 69 on the weekend, leading to a fifth-place finish. Returning to Pebble Beach for the hundredth edition of the U.S. Open Championship, he led from start to finish in the most astonishing performance in majors history, even more impressive than his Masters showing three years earlier. Woods hit forty-one of fifty-six fairways and made greens in regulation fifty-one of seventy-two times. Firing a 65 on opening day, he followed up with rounds of 69, 71, and 67, leading to a twelve-under total of 272, fifteen shots better than his closest competitors, Miguel Angel Jimenez and Ernie Els. Woods's final mark tied the tournament record while his margin of victory was the largest ever achieved in a professional major. NBC analyst Johnny Miller, the 1973 U.S. Open champion, stated, "This is the greatest performance in golf history. Who knows? It might be the greatest in the history of sports." Two-time U.S. Open champion and Ryder Cup captain Curtis Strange asked one sportswriter, "Are you watching this guy? I'm telling you, he's the greatest player of all time." Television audiences seemed equally transfixed, with NBC reporting that this "was the most viewed U.S. Open in history." Sportswriter Ray Ratto suggested, "Tiger Woods could take us places we haven't been before, as a golfer and perhaps as a sporting figure. He could be the next Michael Jordan . . . the next Ali."

More superlatives came Woods's way following his eight-stroke victory in the British Open, the result of four straight rounds in the 60s and the largest margin in the history of a tournament that dated back to 1860. The triumph made the twenty-four-year-old Woods the youngest player and only the fifth man to win all of golf's professional majors—the Masters, the U.S. Open, the British Open, and the PGA Championship. Nick Faldo, a three-time British Open titlist, asserted, "This guy is simply in a different league," with Woods's fabled training regimen belying the stereotypes "that you can't physically train for golf, you can't be strong or you are going to lose your touch." George Diaz of the *Orlando Sentinel* wrote that Woods, "primed to supplant Muhammad Ali as the greatest athlete of our time," had the potential to "transcend social and cultural lines" and become "an icon on a worldwide stage," having already "established a significant cross-cultural impact in a sport that had a pathetic racial scorecard not so long ago."

The following month Woods equaled Ben Hogan's hitherto unmatched 1953 feat of winning three majors in one season. He did so by again taking the Wanamaker Trophy, having defeated Bob May in a playoff for the PGA Championship after the two golfers matched birdie for birdie in a scintillating finish. They tied in regulation at 270, giving Woods at least a share of the scoring record in each of the professional majors. Jack Nicklaus said, "He's playing a game I'm not familiar with," a comment that Bobby Jones had once made about him. Woods completed the 2000 season, which many commentators deemed the greatest in PGA history, with nine victories and almost $9.2 million in earnings, while breaking Byron Nelson's fifty-four-year-old record for the tour's best scoring average. Once more, Woods was named the PGA Player of the Year and AP Male Athlete of the Year, matching Michael Jordan as the only three-time recipients of the AP award. He also became the lone two-time winner of the *Sports Illustrated* Sportsman of the Year Award. The magazine indicated that Woods's performances to date had "changed golf. Because of him the game is more luminous in the galaxy of sport, a star of a different shape and magnitude." Comedian Chris Rock (some claim it was basketball star Charles Barkley) was heard to say, "You know the world is going crazy when the best rapper is a white guy [Eminem] and the best golfer is a black guy."

Firing rounds of 70, 66, 68, and 68 by hitting fifty-nine of seventy-two greens in regulation and leading the field in driving distance, Woods bested his nearest competitor and rival David Duval by two shots to win the 2001 Masters, garnering what many referred to as the Tiger slam—the simultaneous holding of all four professional majors, even though the wins had not all occurred in the same calendar year. Augusta National chair Hootie Johnson asserted, "We have witnessed the greatest golfing feat of our time." The 2001 season concluded with Woods having won five tournaments, including the prized Players Championship, nearly $6 million in earnings, and the Player of the Year Award. Woods gained a record $54 million in endorsements, far surpassing runner-up Michael Jordan, long the endorsement king. Some analysts suggested that Woods might be peaking in the arena of commercial appeal, but others predicted $100 million annual endorsements for the golfer.

The chance for a grand slam in one calendar year arose by mid-2002 when Woods won his second U.S. Open Championship, leading from start to finish at the lengthy public course, Bethpage Black, just outside New York City. This win followed his capture of a second straight Masters title in April, when he held off Retief Goosen. Woods looked to be in prime contention at the British Open in Muirfield, but even a closing round 65 failed to overcome a poor third-round shot during a blustery day, leaving him in twenty-fifth place, albeit a mere six shots from the lead. At the PGA Championship, held at the Hazeltine National Golf Course in Chaska, Minnesota, Woods put on a late charge to fall a shot behind the winner, unheralded Rich Beems. Nevertheless, 2002 had seen Woods win two more majors, six tournaments overall, his fourth consecutive money title, and his fourth consecutive Player of the Year Award, all while suffering from severe pain in his left knee.

The next two seasons proved less eventful, as Woods captured no majors, temporarily lost his five-year-old hold on the Official World Golf Ranking, picked up only one more Player of the Year Award, and took five tournaments in 2003 but only one the next year. On the other hand, Tiger's celebrity was such that David Brooks, former presidential speechwriter to President George W. Bush, exclaimed, following Barack Obama's riveting speech at the 2004 Democratic Party national convention, "It was like watching Tiger Woods play golf." In October 2004, Tiger married Elin Nordegren, a Swede who had served as nanny for golfer Jespar Parnevik's children. The ceremony took place on the island of Barbados and cost a reputed $1.5 million; in 2007, they had their first child. All the while, Woods continued to dominate his sport, as a top CBS programmer recognized. "He's crucial to the sport. He transcends it, like Muhammad Ali in boxing and Michael Jordan in basketball." Having again retooled his golf swing and now working with Hank Haney, Woods bounced back in 2005, coming very close to capturing a single-season grand slam. In April, he opened the Masters with a 74, which included a putt on the thirteenth green that landed in the creek and left him in danger of missing the cut. He fired consecutive rounds of 65 and 66 to take a three-shot lead into the final round, but golf's greatest frontrunner was caught by journeyman golfer Chris DeMarco, who shot a 68 to Woods's 71 to end regulation play in a tie. Woods missed the green on the par-three sixteenth hole, but made a miraculous chip that resulted in a birdie. His lead evaporated with bogeys on the final two holes before the playoff began, which was decided by Woods's fifteen-foot birdie on the first extra hole.

The year's second major, the U.S. Open, played at the famed Pinehurst course in North Carolina, ended with Woods as runner-up to New Zealand's Michael Campbell, who matched Tiger (and two others) for low round of the final day. Woods played brilliantly from tee to green over the course of the tournament, but his putting failed him, leaving him two shots short. His all-around game returned for the British Open, held at St. Andrews, where he led from start to finish, ending five shots ahead of Scotland's Colin Montgomerie. Thanks to this win at the British Open, Woods joined Nicklaus as the only golfers to have captured all the professional majors at least twice. With his ten professional majors, Woods now trailed only Nicklaus and Walter Hagen;

adding his three U.S. Amateur titles, he had won thirteen majors altogether, equaling the number won by Bobby Jones. This was the third season Woods had won at least two majors, tying Ben Hogan and again lagging behind only Nicklaus, who had accomplished that feat five times. Woods hit 73.4 percent of the fairways, while leading the field in driving with a 341.5 average and tying for the lead in putting. Nicklaus noted, "I have to say, that is the best I have seen Tiger swing. . . . It was a pretty awesome performance." While Woods came in fourth at the PGA Championship, two shots behind winner Phil Mickelson, he ended 2005 with six victories, another money title, and his seventh Player of the Year Award. He ran his consecutive cuts streak to 142, obliterating the whole mark held by Byron Nelson, before missing a cut for the first time in over seven years.

As Woods neared thirty, sportswriter Gary van Sickle contended that Tiger "has already had more impact on the game than any other golfer." One reason was the interconnected nature of the modern world, thanks to the never-ending cycle of news, the Internet, and satellite-transmitted radio messages. For many people around the globe, van Sickle continued, Woods represented golf. Furthermore, because of his charisma and multiethnic background, his appeal was "cross-cultural." Tiger had transformed his own sport, sparking a fitness craze and strengthening interest in junior golf. As *Golf World*'s Ron Sirak noted, "Tiger made it cool to be a golfer," although certainly the muscular, pants-pulling, telegenic Arnold Palmer had boasted his famed "Arnie's Army" three and a half decades earlier.

The new year saw the dedication of the 35,000-square-foot Tiger Woods Learning Center, located on fourteen acres in Anaheim, California, which sought "to get students thinking about the role education plays in their future." As the Learning Center board members said, "We want to show them how to relate what they learn in school to their future careers" by presenting "exciting courses that revolve around careers in math, science, technology and language arts. . . . We hope to show students how their personal interests can develop into an exciting career." The Learning Center featured a day program for elementary students and an after-school session for junior high and high school students, in addition to summer camps. Woods put up $5 million of his own toward the $25 million project, which also received considerable support from Nike and Target, among other corporate sponsors. Orange County donated the land, located next to a golf course Woods had frequented during his high school years. The Learning Center was dedicated on February 10, 2006, at a ceremony featuring speeches by local dignitaries; Maria Shriver, the wife of California governor Arnold Schwarzenegger; and former President

Bill Clinton, who declared, "I'm impressed that Tiger Woods decided to do this when he was 30 instead of when he was 60." Woods reflected, "This is by far the greatest thing that's ever happened to me, to come back and create a learning center for these kids. It's near and dear to my heart."

The 2006 season opened well for Woods, with a playoff victory overseas against Ernie Els and two early PGA victories, upping his career total to forty-eight, the seventh-highest total of all time. His bid for a fifth Masters came up short when he finished third, three strokes back of Phil Mickelson. Woods's usual laser-like concentration appeared somewhat lacking, perhaps understandable given the condition of his father, mentor, and best friend, Earl Woods, who was suffering a recurrence of cancer. That summer witnessed Earl's death and Tiger's withdrawal from the PGA tour, which ended with an aborted run at another U.S. Open Championship. For the first time as a professional, Woods missed the cut in a major, ending his streak at thirty-nine overall, a record shared with Nicklaus. In mid-July, however, at the Royal Lytham & St. Annes Golf Club outside Liverpool, Woods won his third British Open and eleventh professional major. After taking the Buick Open, Woods captured his third PGA Championship and his fifteen major altogether by five shots, leaving him just five shy of Nicklaus's once seemingly insurmountable mark. ESPN.com's Gene Wojciechowski deemed Woods "the greatest individual athlete ever." *Sports Illustrated* and SI.com recently announced that Woods, having earned $97.6 million during the past year, more than doubled the mark associated with the next sports figure, his longtime rival, golfer Phil Mickelson.

In the first several months of the 2007 PGA campaign, Woods again performed brilliantly, winning his initial time out, giving him wins in his last seven PGA tournaments. He went on to amass six more victories, giving him sixty-one altogether, and capturing his thirteenth professional major, the PGA championship. It appeared certain that Woods would win the money title for the eighth time and be named Player of the Year for the ninth time during his career.

Having completed eleven years on the PGA tour, Woods possessed an athletic record already among the greatest in the history of American sport. More important, whether considered an African American or a "Cablinasian," he exemplified golf's increased openness to all players, reflecting the multiracial nature of twenty-first-century America. His relationships with white women and subsequent marriage to Elin Nordegren piqued no controversy, in marked contrast to the indignities suffered by black entertainer Sammy Davis Jr. in the 1960s when he too wedded a blonde Swede. Rather, Woods's commercial appeal only counted to mount, along with conjecture about a potential political future, following the conclusion of his playing days.

CLARENCE THOMAS
Black Conservative in Judicial Robes

Television's klieg lights and sound system augmented the intensity of the moment. The U.S. Senate Judiciary Committee was holding confirmation hearings on the nomination of federal judge Clarence Thomas by President George H.W. Bush to the Supreme Court. For three days, in often charged testimony, the short, stocky, dark-hued Thomas battled with Democratic senators regarding accusations of sexual harassment by Professor Anita Hill of the University of Oklahoma—a young black woman who had worked for the judge when he served as an assistant secretary of education and when he headed the Equal Employment Opportunity Commission (EEOC). Thomas's confirmation appeared to be uncertain, along with President Bush's effort to replace Thurgood Marshall, the first African American to sit on the nation's top judicial bench, with a black conservative. Although once a champion of black power and a beneficiary of affirmative action, Thomas had adopted a hard-line conservative stance, causing liberal, feminist, and civil rights organizations to view his nomination with disdain.

On October 11, 1991, the forty-three-year-old Thomas, a member of the U.S. Court of Appeals in Washington, DC, angrily testified at the hearing. Sporting close-cropped hair, horn-rimmed glasses, and an immaculately tailored suit, Thomas denied the allegations of sexual harassment that threatened to doom his nomination. Two and a half weeks earlier, he reported, an FBI agent had informed him of Professor Hill's charge. "I was shocked, surprised, hurt, and enormously saddened," Thomas stated at the outset of his speech before the Senate committee. "I have not been the same since that day." Indeed, Thomas indicated, he had led efforts, for nearly a decade, to protect the "victims of sexual harassment." Moreover, no such charge had ever been leveled at him, in any capacity. Consequently, Hill's accusations, which he had "categorically denied" to the FBI operative, befuddled him. Thomas's relationship with Hill, he testified, had always been "both cordial and professional," and she sought his "advice and counsel," as did most of his staff members. He insisted, "I have not said or done the things that Anita Hill has alleged. God has gotten me through the days since September 25 and He is my judge."

Thomas harked back to late June, when he proudly stood side by side with President Bush at the presidential compound in Kennebunkport, Maine, as the press received word about his nomination to the High Court. "That honor has been crushed," he said. From the onset of the confirmation process, charges were thrown at him involving "drug abuse, anti-Semitism, wife-beating . . . that I was a quota appointment . . . and much, much more, and now, this." He had acted in good faith, producing tens of thousands of pages of documents and testifying "for five full days under oath." Various "reporters and interest groups" had delved into his "divorce papers, looking for dirt," while "unnamed people" started "preposterous and damaging rumors." Thomas declared, "This is not American. This is Kafka-esque. It has got to stop. It must stop for the benefit of future nominees, and our country. Enough is enough." Over the course of his life, he had managed "to defy poverty, avoid prison, overcome segregation, bigotry, racism," and acquire an exceptional education. "But I have not been able to overcome this process. This is worse than any obstacle or anything that I have ever faced." As he wrapped up his testimony, Thomas bristled: "I will not provide the rope for my own lynching or for further humiliation."

During additional testimony, Thomas again emphatically denied all Hill's allegations: "This today is a travesty. I think that it is disgusting . . . this hearing should never occur in America." Even an appointment to the Supreme Court, Thomas declared, "is not worth it. No job is worth it." But he felt compelled to speak "for my name, my family, my life, and my integrity." Thomas's final words captured headlines nationwide:

> This is a circus. It is a national disgrace. And from my standpoint, as a black American, as far as I am concerned, it is a high-tech lynching for uppity blacks

who in any way deign to think for themselves, to do for themselves, to have different ideas, and it is a message that, unless you kow-tow to an old order this is what will happen to you, you will be lynched, destroyed, caricatured by a committee of the U.S. Senate, rather than hung from a tree.

In one of the closest confirmation votes ever, the Senate split 52–48 in favor of Thomas's nomination. He immediately positioned himself on the right side of the Supreme Court, seemingly patterning his judicial renderings after Justice Antonin Scalia.

Clarence Thomas was born outside Savannah, in Pin Point, Georgia, on June 23, 1948, the child of M.C. Thomas, a maintenance man, and Leola Williams, who suffered an impoverished, racially segregated childhood of her own. When Clarence was but a year old, his father abandoned his family. Leola and her three children endured hard times in the poor, Jim Crow–afflicted community of Pin Point; she toiled as a maid and received charity from her church. After she remarried and the family house burned down, Leola sent seven-year-old Clarence and his brother to live with their grandfather, Myers Anderson, who opened a fuel oil business in Savannah. The children now enjoyed steady meals and indoor plumbing, while Anderson extolled the importance of education. After school, they helped their grandfather, a stern taskmaster, make fuel deliveries. Encouraged by Anderson, who had converted to Catholicism, Clarence considered becoming a priest and attended the otherwise all-white boarding school St. John Vianney Minor Seminary, located on the campus of the University of St. Thomas in St. Paul, Minnesota. There he endured racial insults, such as being referred to as "ABC—America's Blackest Child." Later he attended Conception Seminary College in Missouri, but faced considerable racism there too. Eventually, Thomas enrolled at the College of the Holy Cross, situated in Worcester, Massachusetts, where he helped to establish the Black Student Union and identified with the Black Muslims, Malcolm X, and the Black Panther Party during the period he later referred to as his "days of rage." Reading Richard Wright's *Native Son* and *Black Boy*, Thomas recalled, "really woke me up." Registered as a Democrat, Thomas received a draft deferment, due to curvature of the spine, as the Vietnam War raged. In 1971, he graduated from Holy Cross with a bachelor of arts cum laude and married Kathy Ambush, the daughter of a black man and a Japanese American woman, with whom he eventually had a son, Jamal. Meanwhile, Thomas attended Yale University Law School, thanks to its affirmative action program and a financial aid package, graduating in 1974.

Declining a job with a Savannah firm where he had clerked and unable to obtain a preferred position with an elite law firm during an era when such institutions hired few African American lawyers, Thomas went to work as assistant attorney general for John Danforth—a patrician, Yale Law School graduate and attorney general of the state of Missouri. Perhaps because he had been "hired for reasons of diversity," Thomas sought to demonstrate "that his value had nothing to do with the color of his skin," his biographers Jane Mayer and Jill Abramson suggest. He also switched his voter registration to the Republican Party and adopted a conservative posture, expounding about the debilitating effects of welfare. After Danforth was elected to the U.S. Senate, Thomas took a job with the pesticide and agriculture division of the Monsanto Company, where his salary doubled. In 1979, he joined Danforth in Washington as a legislative aide, focusing on issues related to the environment and energy. Thomas became increasingly influenced by another black conservative, Thomas Sowell of the Hoover Institute, who propounded the gospel of laissez-faire and attacked civil rights leaders for their purported elitism. At the Fairmont Conference in San Francisco in 1980, black conservatives gathered and Thomas spoke: "If I ever went to work for the EEOC or did anything directly connected with blacks, my career would be irreparably ruined. The monkey would be on my back to prove that I didn't have the job because I'm black."

In 1981, President Ronald Reagan named Thomas assistant secretary of education for the Office of Civil Rights in the Department of Education. Thomas accepted, despite being "insulted" by the appointment. The following year, Reagan appointed the young lawyer chair of the Equal Employment Opportunity Commission, which involved, among other matters, exploring instances of racial discrimination and sexual harassment. In line with the Reagan administration, Thomas downplayed class action suits and viewed affirmative action, which had enabled him to attend Yale and obtain his initial position with Senator Danforth, as a "crutch" that was injurious to African Americans. He now faced a number of attacks by black leaders, who dismissed Thomas as an "Uncle Tom." Meanwhile, his marriage unraveled, leading to a divorce in 1984. During that same period, another Yale Law School graduate, Anita Hill, began working for Thomas and soon had to contend with unwarranted sexual advances from her boss, or so she later claimed. In May 1987, Thomas married Virginia "Ginni" Lamp, a deeply conservative white attorney from Nebraska, whom he had met months earlier. He also joined Ginni's church, Truro Episcopal, a stronghold of antiabortion activists.

Thomas's conservative tilt, along with his depiction of a hardscrabble background, became more pronounced during his years with the EEOC. In a commencement address at Savannah State College on June 9, 1985, he referred to himself as "a child of those marshes, a son of this soil," who endured "the segregated, hate-filled city of my youth" thanks to the love of his relatives and neighbors. He learned "you can survive, but first, you must endure . . . the indignities." Thomas told the graduating class that a world awaited them where illegitimate black children were the norm and black teenage unemployment remained sky-high. He castigated the readiness to procreate readily and then avoid responsibility for "the babies we produce," and he insisted on the need to own up to "our own destiny." Blacks sought out the wrong kinds of role models, disregarding "the reality of positive values." While "not blind to our history," Thomas acknowledged his "outrage at what has happened to Black Americans . . . what we let happen and what we do to ourselves." Although he recognized the continued presence of discrimination, racism, and bigotry, he insisted that African Americans could not "roll over and give up" and denounced the recent propensity "to wallow in excuses." Speaking at the Heritage Foundation on June 18, 1987, Thomas decried other stereotypes, including the notion that blacks must necessarily subscribe to "leftist ideas and Democratic politics." He charged, "Any black who deviated from the ideological litany of requisites was an oddity . . . to be cut from the herd and attacked." The media would "smirk" at black conservatives, reasoning that they lacked genuine political or economic support. However, fellow members of the Reagan administration, who happened to be white, hardly viewed individuals like himself any more respectfully. "To be accepted within the conservative ranks," Thomas asserted, "to be treated with some degree of acceptance, a black was required to become a caricature of sorts, providing sideshows of anti-black quips and attacks." As for "race-conscious remedies," Thomas dismissed them as "dangerous" and stated, "We were raised to survive in spite of government-sanctioned bigotry."

Continuing to station himself on the right side of the political spectrum, Thomas, in a speech before the Pacific Research Institute in August 1987, called for "an activist Supreme Court" to "strike down laws restricting property rights," including environmental codes and minimum wage laws. He referred to the latter as an "outright denial of economic liberty." Instead, he celebrated "natural law" and supported "the liberation of commerce" rather than government regulation. He also declared that the "leftist exploitation of poor black people . . . is simply a means to advance the principle that the rights and freedoms of all should be cast aside." Redistributive policies, Thomas insisted, amounted to "the very definition of slavery" for they disregarded "hard work, intelligence, and purposefulness."

Juan Williams, writing in the *Atlantic*, described Thomas as "something of a black nationalist, as well as a sad, lonely, troubled, and deeply pessimistic public servant." The avowedly libertarian magazine *Reason* said that Thomas had been transformed from "an angry black militant" to "a leading critic of civil rights orthodoxy." In an interview with assistant editor Bill Kauffman, Thomas indicated that the EEOC existed "for political reasons or whatever," which required the enforcement of laws precluding discrimination "or at least there was a perceived need to do that." Then Thomas suggested that "you don't really need" the Departments of Agriculture and Labor, among others. He admitted that "if properly run," the EEOC possessed "much more legitimacy." Still, he warned that "authority can be abused": "When EEOC or any organization starts dictating to people, I think they go far beyond anything that should be tolerated in this society." Challenging liberal platitudes, Thomas blasted quotas; however, he indicated such government assistance, if it existed, should be afforded the underclass. He warned, "Don't shuttle them off into public housing, which in some instances amounts to concentration camps." When asked if "the civil rights establishment" was accomplishing anything productive, Thomas replied, "No," claiming that it had treated him with "malice." He worried about "the erosion of freedoms," which he deemed "incredible," and about the ability of the American people "to mind our own business. . . . To live our lives, raise our families." Speaking at the Cato Institute, Thomas agreed with former treasury secretary William Simon's observation that the United States was rapidly heading "toward collectivism . . . toward a statist, dictatorial system and away from a nation in which individual liberty is sacred."

On July 11, 1989, President Bush nominated Thomas to the Circuit Court of Appeals in Washington, DC, an appointment that Thomas viewed as "a stepping stone to the Supreme Court." Before this announcement, several Democratic members of the House of Representatives criticized Thomas's performance at the EEOC, contending that he had undermined civil rights legislation and demonstrated "an overall disdain for the rule of law." After his swearing-in the following March, Thomas joined a court that was sharply divided into liberal and conservative camps, headed by Abner Mikva, Ruth Bader Ginsburg, and Patricia Wald, on the one hand, and Kenneth Starr and Laurence Silberman, on the other. Following the retirement of William Brennan from the U.S. Supreme Court, speculation arose that Thomas, Silberman, Edith Jones, and David Souter were being seriously considered by Bush to replace the liberal jurist. Bush selected Souter, but conservatives apparently were assured by the administration that a conservative would occupy the next available seat on the Court. That opportunity arose more quickly than anticipated when, a year later, eighty-two-year-old Thurgood Marshall announced that he too was leaving the Supreme Court. This time President Bush nominated Clarence Thomas to the vacancy. The *International Herald Tribune*'s Paul F. Horvitz noted that Thomas's appointment might strengthen the Court's conservative majority into the indefinite future, although "the full range" of the nominee's views was "not known."

Denying that race was involved in the selection process, Bush insisted that Thomas was "the best qualified at this time," a claim that many analysts found impossible to believe. At a news conference, Thomas stated, "Only in America could this have been possible." Conservatives responded enthusiastically to the nomination: Senator Orrin G. Hatch of Utah, the leading Republican on the Senate Judiciary Committee, suggested that Thomas "could go down in time as one of the all-time great justices," while the Christian Right dismissed his foes as "anti-Christ." Liberal Democrats who opposed Thomas's placement on the Supreme Court confronted a dilemma because of the issue of race. Labor unions and women's groups such as the National Organization for Women and the National Abortion Rights Action League opposed Thomas's nomination, promising "to Bork him." (Liberal groups and senators had earlier blocked federal judge Robert Bork's appointment to the Supreme Court, disturbed by his right-wing views that they characterized as extremist.) Eventually, the National Association for the Advancement of Colored People (NAACP), with its board voting 49–1 to contest the nomination, condemned Thomas's "reactionary philosophical approach" to issues like affirmative action. NAACP chair William Gibson acknowledged Thomas's impoverished background, but blasted "his insensitivity to giving those who may not have any bootstraps the opportunity to pull them up." The American Bar Association's Standing Committee on the Federal Judiciary gave Thomas only a "qualified" rating, the lowest for a Supreme Court nominee since the organization began its review of nominees thirty-five years earlier.

In the meantime, the candidate himself adopted a twinfold strategy. On the one hand, he attempted to mute criticism through his declarations of a hardscrabble upbringing. On the other hand, he operated as recent nominees Anthony Kennedy and David Souter had, offering as little information about his judicial philosophy as possible. During the hearings before the Senate Judiciary Committee, Thomas repeatedly denied having expressed his opinions regarding *Roe v. Wade*—the controversial 1973 Supreme Court ruling that effectively authorized abortions during the first two trimesters of a woman's pregnancy. Conservatives viewed that decision with outrage, demanding its reversal, while liberals considered support for *Roe* a litmus test for judicial nominees. Thomas stated that he did not believe ideological considerations should influence justices: "I think it is important for us . . . to eliminate agendas, to eliminate ideologies. And when one becomes a judge . . . that's precisely what you start doing. You start putting the speeches away. You start putting the policy statements away. You begin to decline forming opinions in areas that could come before your court because you want to be stripped down like a runner. So I have no agenda."

Deadlocked after nearly two weeks of sessions, the Judiciary Committee voted to allow the full Senate to vote on the matter. At that point, allegations arose regarding incidents of sexual harassment involving Anita Hill, as reported by *Newsday* and by Nina Totenberg on National Public Radio. Writing in the *Washington Post*, Juan Williams defended Thomas: "Here is indiscriminate, mean-spirited mudslinging supported by the so-called champions of fairness: liberal politicians, unions, civil rights groups, and women's organizations." Their treatment of Thomas, Williams declared, amounted to "gutter politics. . . . In the pursuit of abuses by a conservative president the liberals have become abusive monsters." Nevertheless, from October 11 to October 13, the Senate Judiciary Committee conducted nationally televised hearings to address the accusations of sexual harassment. Many Americans were transfixed as the proceedings unfolded. Hill reported that while working for Thomas at the Department of Education, he repeatedly asked her to go out and "began to use work situations to discuss sex." On a number of occasions, Hill claimed, Thomas's language was quite suggestive, and he seemed particularly enamored with pornography and oral sex. Hill recalled that at one point, Thomas, referring to his can of soft drink, asked, "Who has put pubic hair on my Coke?" As a consequence, Hill claimed to have experienced "severe stress on the job." Thomas vehemently denied Hill's accusations, which threatened to derail his nomination. The press categorized the conflict as amounting to a "he said, she said" conundrum, such as occurred during cases involving accusations of rape and resulting defense arguments claiming consensual sex. Thomas's champions vilified Hill, questioning her motivation, truthfulness, and sanity. Goaded by Utah senator Orrin Hatch, Thomas's own charged testimony proved effective, at least effective enough for the fifty-two senators, including eleven Democrats, who voted to place him on the Supreme Court. Thomas soothed the trauma of his confirmation hearing by listening to the "rants" of right-wing radio host Rush Limbaugh, which "gave voice to his own anger." Still, the battle over his confirmation scarred Thomas. Even years later, he would indicate, "I've been called names, I've been accused of things that didn't happen. Fine, but I'm still here."

Within a year of his swearing-in, the public attitude regarding the veracity of Clarence Thomas and his accuser had dramatically shifted. In October 1991, by a margin of 47–24, those polled considered Thomas more credible. Fourteen months later, by a 53–37 count, the public expressed greater confidence in Hill.

Thomas's actual service on the Supreme Court justified both the concerns of his critics and the hopes of his most fervent supporters. He proved to be one of the most conservative figures ever to sit on the Court, often lining up with Chief Justice William Rehnquist and Justice Antonin Scalia. Despite promises to the contrary, Thomas seemed to be ideologically driven, adopting a position almost wholly supportive of corporate interests and government in the areas of criminal procedure and national security, respectively. His professed belief in a strict reading of the Constitution proved highly flexible in such instances, in contrast to those cases involving personal liberties and privacy considerations, including abortion decisions. During his first term on the Court, Thomas, along with Rehnquist and Justice Byron White, joined the dissent by Scalia in the case of *Planned Parenthood v. Casey*, which contended, "Roe was wrongly decided." He also dismissed affirmative action as "racial paternalism" and opposed a Court ruling, *Lawrence v. Texas*, overturning sodomy legislation passed by the Texas state legislature. His analysis of the Constitution guided Thomas's decisions and centered on his belief in originalism, which he ascribed to the Founders, and natural law, purportedly derived from basic moral principles. Proponents of originalism believe that interpretations of the Constitution should replicate those that existed at its origin. In public addresses, Thomas indicated that the framers of the Constitution championed natural law.

In a series of speeches and rulings, Thomas reinforced his allegiance to conservative tenets, while indicating the price for doing so. Speaking at Mercer University in Macon, Georgia, in May 1993, he referred to the dismissive manner in which an African American who challenged "the New Orthodoxy" was treated. Such an individual was viewed as "a traitor to your race . . . not a 'real black,'" condemned for "ideological trespass" and often suffering "character assassination," which Thomas likened to "old public floggings." Thomas charged that this "New Intolerance" was "just the same old things we've seen before, just as invidious and perhaps more pervasive" than the earlier "incivility" African Americans faced. At a conference of black conservatives held in Washington, DC, in 1998, Thomas admitted, "It's hard to be disliked. It is hard to walk into a room and know you're going to always be beaten up."

During his first decade and a half on the Supreme Court, Thomas helped to strengthen both the conservative majority and the conservative judicial activism spearheaded by William Rehnquist. Along with Rehnquist, Scalia, Sandra Day O'Connor, and Kennedy—the other four justices who effectively handed the presidency to George W. Bush in 2000—Thomas participated in rulings that whittled away at protective shields involving civil rights, civil liberties, and criminal procedure established by earlier Courts, particularly the one led by Earl Warren. Rehnquist, Scalia, and Thomas in particular maintained the conservative position consistently, while O'Connor and Kennedy sometimes served as swing votes, as they did in cases involving abortion rights. The conservative jurists supported school vouchers, but split regarding the issue of the establishment clause, with O'Connor and Kennedy accepting a more liberal analysis. For their part, Scalia and Thomas called for interpreting the Fourteenth Amendment as demanding a stringently color-blind approach, not one supporting affirmative action, with Thomas opposing statutorily drawn mandates requiring "egalitarian reforms" of schools and prisons. The most conservative members of the Court also backed a "federalism revolution," challenging congressional statutes of a welfare or regulatory variety that supposedly violated state authority. Legal analysts began referring to a conservative constitutional revolution, which was undoubtedly heightened with the retirement of Justice O'Connor and her replacement by Samuel Alito.

The aggressive nature of that revolution, at least as represented by Thomas's jurisprudence, was noted in a new biography by Ken Foskett, *Judging Thomas*. Foskett quoted Scalia as stating that Thomas "doesn't believe in *stare decisis*, period," referring to the policy of following judicial precedents. Scalia explained, "If a constitutional line of authority is wrong, he would say let's get it right"—an analysis Scalia himself opposed. Foskett referred to Thomas as "perhaps the Court's boldest conservative" in his disregard of rulings dating back to the Great Depression concerning congressional authority to regulate interstate commerce. The new biography revisited the controversies involving Anita Hill, with Foskett supporting Thomas's denial regarding her accusations of sexual harassment.

Conclusion

In their own distinct ways, Tiger Woods and Clarence Thomas pushed aside racial boundaries while serving as iconic figures for African Americans. Far more popular and better known than Thomas, Woods stands as the embodiment of unparalleled athletic preeminence, establishing new marks and promising to obliterate other, long-standing records held by his sport's greatest stars while tossing aside racial barriers that continue to beset the game of golf. At the same time, thanks to his father's schooling, Woods promises to reach far beyond the athletic realm, to make his mark in the fields of business, popular culture, and education. Another kind of pathfinder, Thomas broke racial barriers too, becoming first a top government official and then the second African American to sit on the U.S. Supreme Court. What makes Thomas so distinctive is his contesting of the civil rights establishment and his fierce adherence to conservative principles, thus shattering the stereotype of the ideologically liberal stance of black Americans. A beneficiary of affirmative action, Thomas challenges that very practice, along with other shibboleths associated with the civil rights movement. Like Woods, Thomas's reach is likely to become larger still, as he seeks to transform American jurisprudence by countering the legal reasoning associated with the federal courts since the Great Depression. That attitude makes the tightly wound Thomas a far more controversial figure than Woods, whose multiracial background, poised presence, good looks, and athletic prowess enable him to transcend racial boundaries of many types. In contrast to basketball great Michael Jordan, who refused to involve himself in racial matters, particularly those of a political cast, Woods possesses the potential to become an actor on a larger stage in the fields of both politics and philanthropy. That potential reflects the broader horizons that African Americans, albeit those of a select, elite group, faced by the opening decade of the twenty-first century.

Study Questions

1. Early in his career, Tiger Woods was described as "golf's great black hope." Explore the role that sports have played in transforming American race relations since 1945.
2. Woods refers to himself as "Cablinasian." Discuss how Woods is representative of an increasingly multiracial American society in the early twenty-first century.
3. What significance did the issue of race have in the Clarence Thomas nomination hearing?
4. Analyze the ideas that shaped Thomas's decidedly conservative judicial perspective.
5. In their own sharply contrasting manners, Woods and Thomas offer remarkable success stories. How do they differ as role models for black Americans?

Selected Bibliography

Brock, David. *The Real Anita Hill: The Untold Story*. New York: Free Press, 1993.

Comiskey, Michael. *Seeking Justices: The Judging of Supreme Court Nominees*. Lawrence: University Press of Kansas, 2004.

Feinstein, John. *The First Coming: Tiger Woods, Master or Martyr*. New York: Ballantine, 1998.

————. *The Majors: In Pursuit of Golf's Holy Grail*. Boston: Little, Brown, 1999.

————. *Open: Inside the Ropes at Bethpage Black*. Boston: Little, Brown, 2003.

Foskett, Ken. *Judging Thomas: The Life and Times of Clarence Thomas*. New York: William Morrow, 2004.

Keck, Thomas M. *The Most Activist Supreme Court in History: The Road to Modern Judicial Conservatism*. Chicago: University of Chicago Press, 2004.

Londino, Lawrence. *Tiger Woods: A Biography*. Westport, CT: Greenwood, 2005.

Mayer, Jane, and Jill Abramson. *Strange Justice: The Selling of Clarence Thomas*. New York: Houghton Mifflin, 1994.

Merida, Kevin, and Michael Fletcher. *Supreme Discomfort: The Divided Soul of Clarence Thomas*. New York: Doubleday, 2007.

Miller, Anita, ed. *The Complete Transcripts of the Clarence Thomas–Anita Hill Hearings, October 11, 12, 13, 1991*. Chicago: Academy Chicago, 1994.

O'Brien, David M. *Storm Center: The Supreme Court in American Politics*. New York: W.W. Norton, 1996.

Sailes, Garry A., ed. *African Americans in Sport*. New Brunswick, NJ: Transaction, 1998.

Thomas, Clarence. *Confronting the Future: Selections from the Senate Confirmation Hearings and Prior Speeches*. Washington, DC: Regnery Gateway, 1992.

————. *My Grandfather's Son: A Memoir*. New York: Harper, 2007.

Toobin, Jeffrey. *The Nine: Inside the Secret World of the Supreme Court*. New York: Doubleday, 2007.

Tushnet, Mark. *A Court Divided: The Rehnquist Court and the Future of Constitutional Law*. New York: W.W. Norton, 2005.

Wiggins, David, and Patrick B. Miller. *The Unlevel Playing Field: A Documentary History of the African American Experience in Sport*. Urbana: University of Illinois Press, 2003.

Woods, Tiger. *How I Play Golf*. New York: Warner, 2001.

Yalof, David Alistair. *Pursuit of Justices: Presidential Politics and the Selection of Supreme Court Nominees*. Chicago: University of Chicago Press, 1999.

Yu, Henry. "Tiger Woods at the Center of History: Looking Back at the Twentieth Century Through the Lenses of Race, Sports, and Mass Communications." In *Sports Matters: Race, Recreation, and Culture*, ed. John Bloom and Michael Nevin Willard. New York: New York University Press, 2002.

13

America and the New World Order

To the relief of many Americans, the year 2000 opened quietly. In previous months, alarmists had aroused considerable anxiety by conjecturing that the advent of the new century would cause massive, global computer malfunctions and worldwide chaos. Some experts had warned that computers would erroneously reset their internal clocks to the year 1900, causing disastrous problems for a vast number of institutions. That "Y2K" (year 2000) scenario proved a fantasy, but Americans found themselves facing an unprecedented political crisis by year's end. The 2000 presidential election, which pitted Democratic Vice President Al Gore against the Republican governor of Texas, George W. Bush, was a bitterly fought campaign. Polls showed the electorate evenly split between the two contenders, and the election in November confirmed those figures. Though Gore drew about 500,000 more popular votes than Bush, the outcome depended on the Electoral College vote and ultimately on the voting results in Florida. With both candidates claiming victory there, the dispute continued into mid-December, when a 5–4 U.S. Supreme Court decision to halt the ballot recount in Florida handed Bush the presidency.

The resolution of the electoral impasse caused much bitterness among Democrats and threatened to deepen preexisting partisan animosities. Speculation that Bush might seek to heal national divisions by governing from the ideological center quickly proved wrong. Though he had campaigned as a "compassionate conservative," an ambiguous label that vaguely promised moderation, Bush soon demonstrated that he would pursue a strongly conservative domestic agenda. It became evident in the early months of 2001 that Bush's goal was to reduce government regulation of the workplace, the environment, and corporations; fiscal policy would center on massive tax cuts that disproportionately favored the very wealthy. The new administration also endorsed much of the agenda of social conservatives, including measures aimed at restricting abortion, providing federal funding to "faith-based" institutions, and opposing what many on the Christian Right denounced as the "homosexual agenda." Though these positions appealed to the Republican Party's important conservative base, they found no broad national support, as was evident in Bush's mediocre public approval ratings through the summer.

Another source of controversy was the Bush administration's foreign policy. During the presidential campaign, Bush, whom critics chided for his lack of knowledge about international affairs, had generally taken uncontroversial positions, declaring his support for a militarily strengthened nation, but also conceding that the United States should be "humble" in world affairs and avoid futile adventures in "nation building." In the October debates, candidate Bush had denounced Gore as a believer in such follies, declaring, "I would be very careful about using our troops as nation builders. . . . I believe we're overextended in too many places." Bush's vice presidential running mate, Richard "Dick" Cheney, a former secretary of defense, echoed these sentiments, giving no indication that he favored any radical departures in foreign policy. Cheney defended the decision not to seize Baghdad during the 1991 Gulf War and, in a televised interview, asserted that the United States should not behave as if "we were an imperialist power, willy-nilly moving into capitals in that part of the world, taking down governments."

Less publicly, Cheney had been advocating a more aggressive foreign policy since the early 1990s, believing that in the wake of the Cold War, the United States should establish itself as the sole, uncontested superpower. During his years out of government, Cheney grew more dismissive of the United Nations, multinational agreements, and the long-standing concept of containing aggressors. The new secretary of defense, Donald Rumsfeld, a blunt and sometimes prickly man, likewise supported the idea of U.S. world hegemony. It was, however, Rumsfeld's deputy secretary, Paul Wolfowitz, whose ideas most accurately prefigured the administration's radical, post–9/11 foreign policy innovations. With a doctorate in international relations, Wolfowitz worked variously in academe and government beginning in the 1970s, participating in and shaping some of the most consequential foreign policy debates of the next decades. During the 1980s, Wolfowitz embraced neoconservatism, rejecting the idea of détente with the communist powers and advocating a muscular U.S. foreign policy to advance world democracy. Following the collapse of the Soviet Union in 1991, Wolfowitz, then an undersecretary of defense for policy, continually asserted the need to maintain U.S. strength and influence around the world and warned of the crucial importance of a stable Middle East. In testimony before the Senate Armed Services Committee in early 2001, the soft-spoken intellectual with the professorial manner again turned to problems in that region. "Regime change" in Iraq should be a top U.S. priority, Wolfowitz asserted. "I think there's no question that the whole region would be a safer place, Iraq would be a much more successful country, and the American national interest would benefit," he told the senators, "if there was a change of regime in Iraq." Wolfowitz's neoconservative perspective remained a minority viewpoint within the administration until the horrors of September 11, 2001.

In subsequent months, Wolfowitz, as a prominent member of an influential policy-making group known as the Vulcans, left an indelible imprint on the Bush administration's rapidly evolving foreign policy. The Vulcans were a group of highly experienced international affairs experts who were brought together in 1999 by Condoleezza Rice, soon to be Bush's national security adviser. The intent was to provide the Texas governor, who had no experience in and little knowledge of foreign affairs, with an able advisory group. Taking their name from the statue of the Roman god of fire that overlooked Rice's hometown of Birmingham, Alabama, the Vulcans included Richard Perle, Richard Armitage, Stephen Hadley, and Robert Blackwell. Some had served previous administrations, but what all held in common was a commitment to neoconservative ideology, which held that in the post–Cold War world, the U.S. should strive to maintain its exclusive claim to superpower status, employing whatever diplomatic, economic and military means were necessary to do so. In the aftermath of the September 11 attacks, Wolfowitz and the Vulcans embraced the concept of preemptive war and took U.S. forces into the longest, costliest, and most controversial conflict since the Vietnam War. *Time* magazine identified the always neatly attired scholar as "the intellectual godfather of the war." Wolfowitz was a tireless advocate of the idea that the United States could easily oust Saddam Hussein's brutal regime in Iraq and democratize the country with minimal cost in lives and resources. Success in Iraq, he insisted, would mark the beginning of a "march of freedom" across the region, toppling unstable, autocratic regimes and establishing productive, stable democracies. The root causes of radical Islamic terrorism would be eliminated, thus ensuring U.S. national security and stability in a crucial, energy-rich region. This ambitious endeavor was to be, however, only one aspect of a new American mission of promoting worldwide democracy. Foreign policy scholar Andrew Bacevich acknowledged the extent of Wolfowitz's influence on Bush administration policy in a 2005 article in *American Conservative*. "More than any other dramatis personae in contemporary Washington," wrote Bacevich, "Wolfowitz embodies the central convictions to which the United States in the age of Bush subscribes." Foremost was "an extraordinary certainty in the righteousness of American actions married to an extraordinary confidence in the efficacy of American arms."

The Bush administration's radical departures in foreign policy provoked significant debate, and as the conflict in Iraq continued with little discernible progress, criticism of the administration's miscalculations grew, both among political pundits and the public. But few early critics went beyond complaints about the inept manner in which the U.S. occupation of Iraq was managed. Few mainstream voices were willing to challenge the fundamental assumptions that had led to the invasion, much less the issue of whether the United States had the right or authority to overthrow the governments of sovereign nations. Nor did many Americans seem disposed to question the means by which the United States sought to achieve its objectives in Iraq or in the broader "war on terror." Concern about domestic surveillance, the treatment of suspected terrorist detainees at Guantanamo Bay, Cuba, and the Abu Ghraib prison abuses, though sometimes voiced, brought little serious examination of either the means or objectives of American policies. During the 2004 presidential campaign, Bush's Democratic rival, Massachusetts senator John Kerry, never challenged the wisdom of the U.S. invasion, but insisted instead that, under his leadership, the egregious errors that followed the defeat of Saddam's military would have been avoided. Kerry lost the race by a small margin, having never successfully articulated what distinguished his foreign policy positions from those of his opponent.

One individual willing to question the assumptions that underlay U.S. foreign policy for many decades was Noam Chomsky, an MIT linguistics professor and self-described "libertarian socialist." Despite his voluminous writings, which included more than seventy books and a thousand articles, Chomsky remained largely unknown to the American public. Though renowned in the academic world for his contributions to linguistics theory and widely hailed by leftist intellectuals and activists for his analytical acuity, Chomsky was rarely granted a forum in any mass-circulation print media and was almost never seen among the crowd of "talking heads" that regularly provided political analysis on television. Nevertheless, since the 1960s, when he had first gained prominence as an incisive critic of U.S. foreign policy, he had consistently drawn plaudits from those familiar with his analyses. In 1979, a *New York Times* writer concluded, "Judged in terms of the power, range, novelty and influence of his thought, Noam Chomsky is arguably the most important intellectual alive." The explanation for Chomsky's low public visibility was self-evident to those familiar with his work. James Peck, who has edited some of Chomsky's writings, put it most succinctly: "In all American history, no one's writings are more unsettling than Noam Chomsky's. He is our greatest dissenter."

Chomsky's writings are "unsettling" because he insists that his readers examine public policy issues through a "consistent application of reason," a methodology that often challenges fundamental assumptions about the rectitude of American foreign policy and the nature of America's democratic society. In the 1960s, Chomsky shocked many Americans with his unsparing indictments of the U.S. intervention in Vietnam. The American "invasion" of South Vietnam, Chomsky asserted, was being undertaken not to protect democracy there, but to defend U.S. interests that were no more idealistic than those of any other nation. The means that the United States used to achieve those ends, he concluded, bespoke the hypocrisy in U.S. foreign policy. During the next four decades, Chomsky directed his analytical talents to a broad range of international issues, including the Cold War, the Middle East, and Central America. The issue of terrorism had been of interest to Chomsky since the 1960s, and he ruffled many feathers with his assertion that, according to the definition offered in a U.S. Army manual, the United States qualified as a major source of terrorism.

Chomsky did not hesitate to address the implications of the September 11 attacks and the consequences of the Bush administration's new directions in foreign policy. In his best-selling book *9-11* (2001), he was, as always, provocative. "Nothing can justify crimes such as those of September 11," Chomsky remarked, "but we can think of the United States as an 'innocent victim' only if we adopt the conventional path of ignoring the record of its actions." Chomsky warned that the Bush administration would use the attacks to realize a radically right-wing agenda: a space-based missile defense system, assaults on social programs and the environment, and a massive transfer of wealth "to the very few." He cautioned, "There are hawkish elements who want to use the occasion to strike out at their enemies, with extreme violence, no matter how many innocent people may suffer." An outspoken critic of the "Bush Doctrine" of preemption, the U.S. invasion of Iraq, and the Bush administration's proclaimed mission of promoting world democracy, Chomsky was especially critical of Paul Wolfowitz. Responding to the *Washington Post* editor David Ignatius's characterization of Wolfowitz as "the idealist in chief," Chomsky retorted that "Paul Wolfowitz . . . has probably the most extreme record of passionate hatred of democracy of anybody in the administration." A review of Wolfowitz's career in government service, Chomsky observed, would confirm that he was a defender of "friendly" dictators and an advocate of human rights and democracy only when it suited American international interests.

Not surprisingly, when Chomsky asks that Americans divest themselves of their presumptions, apply a steely logic to public policy issues, and be willing to accept the most discomfiting conclusions, he has frequently met resistance, most often manifest in efforts to marginalize his opinions. Paul Berman, in *Terror and Liberalism* (2003), claims that most media ignore Chomsky "because of his reputation as a crank." Chomsky, however, has long argued that established public intellectuals, wedded to and dependent on the establishment, create a limited framework within which all legitimate public discourse must be held, and any who take the discussion beyond those boundaries are deemed "radical" and thus illegitimate. Some Chomsky critics have gone beyond efforts to marginalize the MIT professor. Chomsky has been the target of repeated death threats and was on the target list compiled by Ted Kaczynski, the Unabomber, a serial killer who murdered several prominent individuals with mail bombs. David Horowitz, a New Left radical turned right-wing activist, has mounted a virtual crusade against Chomsky, denouncing him as the "ayatollah of anti-American hate" and "the most treacherous intellect in America." Chomsky featured prominently in Horowitz's 2006 work *The Professors*, which promised to expose the "101 most dangerous academics in America." Often misrepresented as an anti-American Marxist, Chomsky, who advocates no specific ideology, describes himself as a libertarian socialist who rejects Leninist dogma and as a defender of the classical liberal view of free speech, one of the aspects of American life that he values most.

There are interesting similarities between Paul Wolfowitz and Noam Chomsky. Though separated in age by twenty years, both came from East Coast immigrant Jewish families that placed considerable stress on education and intellectual achievement. As adolescents, both were immersed in the cultural milieu of Zionism. Both found their way into academia, though Wolfowitz was intermittently drawn into government service. Both turned their intellectual talents to policy analysis, but with strikingly different results. Drawn into politics in the tumultuous 1960s, Chomsky discovered much in American foreign policy that failed to hold up to his rigorous standards of rational inquiry. Professed American idealism, he concluded, often only masked blatant self-interest. Wolfowitz never questioned American ideals or rectitude, but rather was concerned primarily with how U.S. strategic interests and national security might be served. Ultimately, Wolfowitz was chief among those who argued that American security could be assured through promoting American-style democracy, which he identified as a universal value. Chomsky disagreed, contending that democracy was far from realized even in the United States and that the greatest threat to international stability came not from terrorists, but from the blunderings of the world's sole remaining superpower as it pursued an ill-considered "war on terror" and an improbable crusade for world democracy. Both offered, from very different perspectives, radical views of America's role in the world.

PAUL WOLFOWITZ
Democratic Imperialist

For committed idealists like Deputy Secretary of Defense Paul Wolfowitz, events during the early months of the administration of George W. Bush seemed to offer little opportunity for defining new directions in foreign policy. The new president had not been disposed to dedicate much time to foreign policy issues during the recent campaign, preferring to focus instead on the faltering economy and the need to "restore dignity" to the White House in the aftermath of the Clinton scandals. In February 2001, U.S. forces carried out air strikes against five Iraqi antiaircraft sites so as to enforce the no-fly zone established at the end of the 1991 Gulf War. However, it was, in the president's words, only "a routine mission," a continuation of the policy of "containing" Saddam Hussein's regime. The greater concern was that the strikes had been necessitated because China supplied the Iraqis with updated radar technology. Growing tensions between China and the United States climaxed in May when a Chinese interceptor collided with a U.S. intelligence-gathering aircraft near the island of Hainan. The subsequent crisis was resolved diplomatically, and the only role Wolfowitz played was to issue an order for the destruction of 600,000 Chinese-made berets that had been purchased for U.S. troops, an apparent demonstration of U.S. resolve in the face of Chinese perfidy. Iraq, meanwhile, remained a low priority, with Secretary of State Colin Powell confirming that sanctions had effectively defanged Saddam's regime. "He had not developed any significant capability with respect to weapons of mass destruction," Powell concluded. Indeed, Wolfowitz's expressed support for overthrowing Saddam during his nomination hearings seemed in stark contrast to the policies that his superior publicly endorsed. Wolfowitz was virtually the lone Iraq hawk at the Pentagon, and no one, save Lewis "Scooter" Libby, Cheney's chief of staff, seemed to offer any support. Powell's views, it was clear, had prevailed at the top levels in the administration. Then, on September 11, a whole new universe of options opened up.

Wolfowitz interpreted the events of that day as having meaning beyond seeking out the perpetrators. He saw the attacks as a "wake-up call," adding, "If we say our only problem was to respond to 9/11, and we wait until somebody hits us with nuclear weapons, we will have made a very big mistake." The day after the attacks, Wolfowitz pressed his case against Iraq at a National Security Council meeting, where Rumsfeld introduced the issue, asking "Why shouldn't we go against Iraq, not just al-Qaeda?" The deputy secretary was quick to add that Iraq was "a brittle, oppressive regime that might break easily." Despite Wolfowitz's insistence that toppling Saddam was "doable," the Iraq option was rejected. Four days later, at another security council meeting at Camp David, Maryland, Rumsfeld presented a list of three proposed targets in the new war on terrorism: al-Qaeda, the Islamic terrorist organization created by Osama bin Laden; the Taliban, the Muslim fighters who had imposed a radically fundamentalist Islamic regime in Afghanistan; and Saddam Hussein's Iraq, which had remained a continuing concern for U.S. policy makers since the 1990–91 Gulf War. Again, Wolfowitz was alone in advocating priority for and an attack on Iraq. Nevertheless, in memos to Rumsfeld later that month, Wolfowitz continued to press for an attack on Saddam's regime. Over the next several months, Wolfowitz, Rumsfeld, and other key Vulcans succeeded in marginalizing the much more cautious Powell and establishing their neoconservative vision as the dominant perspective in the administration. The degree of their success was clear in the president's January 2002 State of the Union address. Bush identified Iraq, Iran, and North Korea as "an axis of evil, arming to threaten the peace of the world." "I will not wait on events while danger gathers," the president proclaimed. "I will not stand by as peril draws closer and closer. The United States will not permit the world's most dangerous regimes to threaten us with the world's most destructive weapons." The focus seemed already to have shifted from the Taliban and al-Qaeda to "rogue states" supposedly possessing weapons of mass destruction (WMDs). Two years later, Wolfowitz explained the rationale for the war against Iraq to a *Vanity Fair* interviewer: "We settled on the one issue that everyone could agree on, which was weapons of mass destruction, as the core reason." In March 2003, U.S. forces, supported by a small "coalition of the willing," invaded Iraq, inaugurating the new, aggressive foreign policy that neoconservatives like Wolfowitz had advocated for decades.

Paul Wolfowitz was born in 1943, the second child of Jacob and Lillian Wolfowitz. At the age of ten, Jacob and his parents had left Warsaw to come to New York City, where he eventually attended City College of New York before completing a doctorate in mathematics at New York University. Subsequently, he taught at Columbia and Cornell, becoming a well-regarded theoretician in the field of statistics. An ardent Zionist, Jacob had lost numerous relatives in the Holocaust, a catastrophe that greatly shaped his son Paul's formative political perspectives. The younger Wolfowitz always carried with him the lesson that aggression appeased was aggression rewarded, inevitably paving the way for horrors like the Holocaust, the Nazis' attempt to eradicate Europe's Jewish population. In 1961, Wolfowitz won a full scholarship to Cornell, where he majored in mathematics and chemistry. The undergraduate joined the Telluride Association, established by wealthy businessmen to cover living expenses for gifted students. At Cornell, philosophy professor Allan Bloom, a strong believer in classical studies and traditional values, greatly influenced Wolfowitz's intellectual development. Bloom was a protégé of émigré German political philosopher Leo Strauss, whose works stressed "the crisis of liberalism" resulting from its alleged "relativistic" foundation. Strauss had argued that freedom's survival would depend upon "an elite group of advisers" who would emphasis the importance of "virtue and . . . strong moral judgments about good and evil." While at Cornell, Wolfowitz met his future wife, Clare Seigin. Married in 1968, the couple had three children before divorcing in 2001.

Completing a bachelor's degree in mathematics in 1965, Wolfowitz decided to pursue graduate studies in international relations and politics at the University of Chicago, where Leo Strauss was on the faculty. Though he studied under Strauss, Wolfowitz was increasingly drawn to Albert Wohlstetter, an acknowledged expert on nuclear strategies and an advocate of American military supremacy. Through Wohlstetter, Wolfowitz met and worked with some of the country's chief architects of foreign policy, including Dean Acheson, Paul Nitze, and Richard Perle. In 1972, while teaching at Yale, Wolfowitz completed his doctorate with a dissertation focusing on the dangers posed by nuclear proliferation in the Middle East and the undependability of weapons inspection programs. The next year, he left academia to work with Fred Ikle at the Arms Control and Disarmament Agency. Through much of the decade, Wolfowitz participated in intellectual battles both inside the government and within the major political parties, but particularly among Republican ranks. Many debates involved Cold War strategies, and Wolfowitz was among those who were sharply critical of the policy of détente. In 1976, Central Intelligence Agency (CIA) director George H.W. Bush selected a group of experts, identified as Team B, to produce a report on Soviet designs. Richard Pipes, professor of Russian history at Harvard, headed the project, while Wolfowitz served as one of the ten members. Their report asserted that the Soviet Union was busily constructing horrific new WMDs, a finding comprehensively challenged in later years.

When the new Carter administration took office in 1977, Wolfowitz became deputy assistant secretary of defense for regional programs, where one of his responsibilities was envisioning possible military challenges. The new secretary of defense, Harold Brown, instructed Wolfowitz to focus on third-world scenarios that could involve the American military. In light of the recent Arab oil embargo, Wolfowitz focused on the Persian Gulf region, with its vast natural resources and volatile political makeup, stressing the problems that might arise if Saudi Arabian oil fields were targeted for attack by Islamic radicals. To address these concerns, Wolfowitz guided the Limited Contingency Study, which involved the Defense Department's first detailed analysis of the American need to safeguard the Persian Gulf. The report highlighted issues involving both oil and Arab-Israeli hostilities. Wolfowitz warned of the possibility of Soviet incursions in the region, but also warned that a Middle Eastern state, such as Iraq, could move against Kuwait or Saudi Arabia. Some of Wolfowitz's analyses of Middle Eastern contingencies thus proved prescient, but at the time it was produced, the Limited Contingency Study had little influence on U.S. policy making. The study assumed a new significance in 1979, however, in the aftermath of a revolution in Iran that toppled the shah and brought to power the radical Islamic cleric Ayatollah Ruhollah Khomeini. The seizure of the U.S. embassy and sixty-six hostages in Tehran provoked a crisis that focused national attention on the Middle East as never before. President Carter responded by ordering the Pentagon to establish a rapid deployment force, announced that any move "by an outside force" into the region would be considered hostile to the United States, and began setting up American bases in Oman, Kenya, and Somalia. But the Carter administration seemed impotent in the face of Iranian taunts, its ineptness affirmed when a planned rescue mission failed in April 1980.

Appalled at the decline in U.S. prestige under Carter, many formerly liberal intellectuals, together with some well-known Democrats, endorsed Ronald Reagan's 1980 presidential bid, giving considerable new dynamism to the neoconservative movement that had been taking shape in previous years. The older neocons, as they were known, included individuals like Irving Kristol and Norman Podhoretz—Jews from lower- and middle-income families who had been drawn to Franklin D. Roosevelt's New Deal. They, and younger neocons like Wolfowitz and Richard Perle, were distressed with the Democrats' apparent shift leftward during the Vietnam era. Firm believers in a strong U.S. foreign policy, the neocons gravitated toward the Reagan camp as the 1980 election approached. Hoping for a job in the new administration, Wolfowitz resigned from his post at the Pentagon in early 1980, joining the faculty of the Johns Hopkins University School of Advanced International Studies.

Wolfowitz's time at Johns Hopkins proved brief as Reagan national security adviser Richard Allen invited him to join the new administration as director of policy planning at the State Department. Wolfowitz hired his own staffers, including Lewis Libby, Francis Fukuyama, Alan Keyes, and James Roche, all prominent neoconservatives. Almost immediately, the new director demonstrated a readiness to challenge Cold War assumptions and the theories of influential fellow neocon Jeane Kirkpatrick, the U.S. ambassador to the United Nations. She had been critical of the Carter administration's policy of withholding U.S. support from authoritarian allies who refused to democratize. Such idealism was naive, Kirkpatrick argued, as it undercut important allies such as Iranian shah Mohammed Reza Pahlavi and Nicaragua's Anastasio So-moza. Both dictators had been dependable, long-term allies, but were ousted by anti-American revolutions. It was unrealistic, she insisted, to insist that every U.S. ally adopt democracy. "Decades, if not centuries, are normally required for people to acquire the necessary disciplines and habits" that democracy re-quired, Kirkpatrick argued. It was an idea that Wolfowitz challenged; his belief in the universal feasibility of democracy led him to break ranks with his own administration over Iraq's Saddam Hussein, whose regime the Reagan admin-istration supported as a counterbalance to Iranian Shiite radicalism. After two years as head of policy planning at State, Wolfowitz became assistant secretary of state for East Asian and Pacific affairs, overseeing American diplomatic dealings with more than twenty nations. During his three-and-a-half-year stint in that post, he helped to improve U.S. relations with China and Japan, while pressuring various Asian leaders to adopt more democratic practices. During these years, he was central to the effort to shore up the faltering dictatorship of Philippine president Ferdinand Marcos through democratic reforms, but the corrupt regime was finally overthrown by a "people power" revolution in 1986. That same year, Wolfowitz was named U.S. ambassador to Indonesia. His effectiveness there as a proponent of democracy and human rights is in dispute, with critics arguing that the ambassador never confronted the strong-man Suharto about human rights abuses. Still, the Reagan administration's championing of democracy in the Philippines, Indonesia, and South Korea represented something of a sea change for American conservatives, including the neocons. In previous decades, it had been liberal Democrats, rather than conservative Republicans, who were most supportive of a foreign policy based on promoting democracy abroad.

Following the election of George H.W. Bush to the presidency in 1988, Wolfowitz became undersecretary of defense for policy under Cheney. With dramatic transformations occurring in the Soviet Union under Mikhail Gor-bachev, Wolfowitz headed a policy staff that helped shape presidential initia-tives leading to the destruction of tens of thousands of weapons from American and Soviet nuclear stockpiles. Discussion of America's role in the new world order that was bound to emerge in the aftermath of the USSR's decline was superseded in 1990 by a new crisis in the Persian Gulf region, where Saddam's army had invaded and seized oil-rich Kuwait. In top-level administration discussions regarding the U.S. response, Wolfowitz persistently advocated the need to act forcefully, but was wary about an all-out invasion. He argued instead for Operation Scorpion, which called for setting up an American desert base to the west of Baghdad, from which Saddam could be intimidated into stepping down. The head of the U.S. Central Command, General H. Norman Schwarzkopf, dismissed the idea, instead organizing Operation Desert Storm, an invasion by U.S.-led coalition forces that stepped off in early 1991. Desert Storm proved to be a smashing victory, but the troops stopped well short of Baghdad, enabling Saddam to remain in power. Wolfowitz hoped that rebelling Kurds and Shiites might topple the dictator from power, and President Bush's public remarks suggested that the United States would support an internal rebellion. But Saddam's Republican Guard, which remained largely intact, savagely suppressed the uprisings as the United States stood by. Wolfowitz was unwilling to endorse more ambitious schemes at the time, and several years later, he explained his thinking. Writing in the *National Interest* in the spring of 1994, he acknowledged, "Nothing could have insured Saddam Hussein's removal from power short of a full-scale occupation of Iraq. . . . Even if easy initially, it is unclear how or when it would have ended." Three years later, in another article, Wolfowitz concluded, "A new regime would have become the United States' responsibility. Conceivably, this could have led the United States into a more or less permanent occupation of a country that could not govern itself, but where the rule of a foreign occupier would be increasingly resented." A decade later, Wolfowitz's perspective would be radically different.

The final collapse of the USSR in late 1991 offered Wolfowitz the opportunity to help redefine U.S. foreign policy along lines amenable to the neoconservative viewpoint. Underlying his advocacy of sustained U.S. military strength was his belief that the Western democracies, including the United States, had abrogated their responsibilities after the end of both world wars and that such dereliction must not be repeated. Aided by his assistants, Wolfowitz revised the *Defense Planning,* a set of periodically revised military guidelines, in a manner that some interpreted as "a blueprint for U.S. hegemony." Two chief points of the document, which stressed the importance of maintaining American predominance in the world, were the policies of preemption and unilateralism, both of which were destined to become key components of what would be called the Bush Doctrine a decade later. "In the Middle East and Southwest Asia," the document stated, "our overall objective is to remain the predominant outside power and preserve U.S. and Western access to the region's oil." The implementation of this grand vision was deferred when George H.W. Bush lost his 1992 bid for reelection. The new Clinton administration hewed to conventional policies such as containment of Saddam while promoting the benefits of globalization, free trade, and internationalism. Returning to academia as dean of the Johns Hopkins School of Advanced International Studies, Wolfowitz continued to promote a neoconservative foreign policy. During the 1996 presidential campaign, Wolfowitz worked with Donald Rumsfeld to provide foreign policy guidance to Republican nominee Robert Dole. Increasingly, however, Wolfowitz returned to the subject of Iraq, insisting that the United States had blundered in not ousting Saddam Hussein after the Gulf War. As Clinton's second term began, Wolfowitz sharpened his critique, urging in an article in the *Weekly Standard* that Saddam be removed from power. In various forums, Wolfowitz called for the United States to back Iraqi opposition figures, indict Saddam as a war criminal, and set up a liberated zone in the southern portion of Iraq. In 1998, the Project for the New American Century, a neocon policy institute founded by Rumsfeld and Cheney, drafted a letter to President Clinton urging "regime change" in Iraq. Wolfowitz was among the signers of the document that stated, "Iraq is ripe for a broad-based insurrection" and insisted that ending Saddam's rule "needs to become the aim of American foreign policy." Bowing to the political winds, Clinton signed the Iraq Liberation Act, which offered support to Iraqi dissidents but disallowed U.S. military action beyond the current containment policies.

As the decade ended, Wolfowitz continued to challenge the "drift" in U.S. foreign policy. In early 2000, writing in the *National Interest*, he declared that one of the Cold War's most enduring lessons was "demonstrating that your friends will be protected and taken care of, that your enemies will be punished, and that those who refuse to support you will live to regret it." George W. Bush, the successful Republican presidential candidate in 2000, uttered strikingly similar phrases within several years. Bush began putting together a foreign policy team in 1999, including Rice, Wolfowitz, Richard Armitage, Richard Perle, Cheney, and Rumsfeld. As deputy secretary of defense, Wolfowitz undoubtedly detected the strong influence of unilateralism in the new administration, which rejected the Kyoto Treaty, expressed its disapproval of the 1972 Anti-Ballistic Missile Treaty, and generally indicated its disdain for international agreements. Yet there was little indication that Wolfowitz might sell his ideas about the imminence of the Iraqi threat to the inner circle of policy makers. In April 2001, in the midst of a meeting with deputy secretaries, Richard Clark—the national coordinator for security, infrastructure protection and counterterrorism—sought to convince those in attendance that al-Qaeda and its head, Saudi Arabian exile Osama bin Laden, should be a priority concern. Angrily, Wolfowitz blurted out, "Well, I just don't understand why we are beginning by talking about this man bin Laden." The discussion, Clarke responded, centered about al-Qaeda, "because it and it alone poses an immediate and serious threat to the United States." Undeterred, Wolfowitz replied, "Well, there are others that do as well, at least as much—Iraqi terrorism for example." Clarke replied that he was "unaware of any Iraqi-sponsored terrorism directed at the United States . . . since 1993," an evaluation shared by the FBI and the CIA. An exasperated Wolfowitz finally told Clarke, "You give bin Laden too much credit. He could not do all these things like the 1993 attack on New York, not without a state sponsor. Just because FBI and CIA have failed to find the linkages does not mean they don't exist." Clearly, despite all available evidence, Wolfowitz stubbornly clung to Iraq's centrality to the terrorist threat. At the end of May, deputy secretaries began meeting to carve out a policy on Iraq. Journalist Bob Woodward identified Wolfowitz as "the intellectual godfather and fiercest advocate for toppling Saddam" at this point, noting that the deputy secretary felt "it was necessary and . . . would be relatively easy." The U.S. military, Wolfowitz contended, would quickly take control of Iraq's oil fields in the south, creating an enclave from which support could be provided to those who sought to depose Saddam. Secretary of State Powell considered the idea "lunacy." In June, Wolfowitz spoke at West Point, noting that the "surprise attack" by Japan on Pearl Harbor in 1941 had been "preceded by an astonishing number of unheeded warnings and missed signals." But the administration evidently accorded little significance to a similar contemporary warning. A President's Daily Briefing memo on August 6 warned that bin Laden's al-Qaeda operatives were planning an attack on the United States, possibly with hijacked airplanes. National Security Adviser Rice dismissed the warning as "a historical memo" of no immediate consequence, and the president continued his vacation in Texas.

Shortly after the September 11 attacks, the Vulcans determined that the United States had to respond in an unprecedented fashion. In the tense atmosphere, these aggressive neocons at the Pentagon gained much greater influence and the group pushed hard for moving against Saddam as part of a strategy of acting preemptively to fight terrorism. As strongly as any member of that group, Wolfowitz—later called by *Time* magazine "the administration's most influential strategist" and "Washington's most menacing hawk"— considered it essential to wage a broad war that would bring down both the Taliban in Afghanistan and Saddam in Iraq. The deputy secretary even asserted that there existed "a 10 to 50 percent chance" that Saddam Hussein was connected with the September 11 attacks. Despite pressure from Wolfowitz, Cheney, Libby, and others, the Bush administration initially gave priority to an invasion of Afghanistan to oust the Taliban and destroy al-Qaeda. Operation Enduring Freedom was launched on October 7, and in subsequent weeks a U.S.-led coalition effectively ended the Taliban's grip on the central Asian nation, driving the remnants into barren mountains and deserts. Victory was declared in March 2002, and the focus shifted to making Afghanistan a test case for democracy in the Muslim world. Wolfowitz's attention, however, remained firmly fixed on Iraq.

Following the removal of the Taliban regime in Afghanistan, the Vulcans cast their net wider, insisting on the need to reshape Cold War national security policies. In December 2001, President Bush declared that the United States would abandon the Anti-Ballistic Missile Treaty, renounced as a "relic of the Cold War." By early 2002, the influence of Wolfowitz's worldview was clearly discernible in Bush's "axis of evil" State of the Union address, which Democratic Congressman Ike Skelton interpreted as "a declaration of war." A writer for the *Economist* noted, "It was Mr. Wolfowitz's fingerprints, not Colin Powell's, that were all over the state-of-the-union speech" with "its commitment to tackling explosively unpredictable dictatorships . . . its unabashed enthusiasm for asserting American power, its insistence that this involves a desperate race against time." The British publication stated that Wolfowitz's "influence seems to grow by the day," and one alarmed European diplomat was quoted as observing that the conventional term "hawk" did not adequately convey the deputy secretary's aggressiveness. "What about velociraptor?" he suggested, referring to a dinosaur species renowned for its reputed pugnacity. Clearly, the publication concluded, President Bush had chosen Wolfowitz "to speak for the Defense Department" and it seemed that "history has moved in his direction." Dramatically underestimating the hubris of the Vulcans, the *Economist* ventured that the United States could hardly wage "a multi-pronged war on terrorism" without allies.

By early 2002, as political commentator Kevin Phillips observed, one could distinctly "hear the war drums beating." At the Pentagon, Rumsfeld and Wolfowitz produced the Nuclear Posture Review, urging the building of a new generation of small tactical nuclear weapons. Meanwhile, the next phase of the war on terror came into sharper focus after the defeat of the Taliban. Wolfowitz and the Vulcans interpreted the apparent coalition victory in Afghanistan as proof that their grand scheme for ousting hostile Middle Eastern regimes and introducing democracy and free market capitalism into the region was feasible. A free Iraq, Wolfowitz was convinced, would serve as a model and a stepping-off point for future U.S. operations in the region. In June, Bush's enthusiasm for the preemption doctrine was evident in a speech to West Point cadets. "We must take the battle to the enemy, disrupt his plans and confront the worst threats before they emerge," the president declared. "If we wait for threats to fully materialize, we will have waited too long." To convince the public and skeptical foreign policy figures of the necessity for an attack on Iraq, the administration undertook two initiatives. At the Pentagon, Rumsfeld and Wolfowitz set up the Office of Special Plans (OSP), which was charged with collecting evidence that Saddam possessed WMDs. Much of the information that the OSP collated was provided by dubious sources, notably Ahmad Chalabi—a leader of the exiled Iraqi National Congress, who had his own agenda. Publicly, administration officials began a steady chorus of alarming warnings in September. In a CNN interview, Rice warned that, while there "will always be some uncertainty" about Iraqi WMDs, "we don't want the smoking gun to be a mushroom cloud." Bush, addressing the United Nations General Assembly, declared Iraq "a grave and gathering danger." The next day, the administration issued the National Security Strategy statement that formalized the preemption doctrine. Throughout the fall, as a compliant Congress, with little debate, approved a resolution authorizing the presidential use of armed force against Iraq, administration representatives continued to warn of dire consequences unless the Iraq danger were addressed. Prominent foreign policy experts, former diplomats, and military officials who voiced doubts about the administration's conclusions and course were dismissed as timid and ill informed.

The triumph of the Vulcans was evident in February 2003, when Secretary of State Colin Powell, a persistent skeptic about the necessity and wisdom of war with Iraq, presented the administration's case for Iraqi WMDs before the United Nations General Assembly. Much of the intelligence that Powell's allegations were based on was, as a Senate Select Committee later concluded, "overstated, misleading or incorrect." Nevertheless, having seemingly established the existence of a clear and present danger, the administration presented its plan for a short, conclusive war against Saddam's regime to be followed by the creation of a new, democratic Iraq. Testifying before a Senate committee in February 2003, Wolfowitz laid out the Vulcans' scenario. Dismissing the U.S. Army Chief of Staff's conclusion that an occupation would require more than a quarter million troops as "wildly off the mark," the deputy secretary likewise brushed off concerns about a postinvasion war between ethnic militias. He was also certain that the Iraqis "will greet us as liberators" and that Iraqi oil revenue would cover much of the cost of the venture. "There is a lot of money there," he assured the committee. "The country can finance its own reconstruction." One year later, these predictions returned to haunt him.

Begun on March 21, the military campaign to oust Saddam, like the earlier Gulf War, proved remarkably brief, and the president declared major military operations ended as of May 1. However, in this second war against Saddam

Hussein, the United States had entered the conflict without the military support of its major Western allies, supported instead only by a considerably reduced "coalition of the willing." The administration's bellicose unilateralism, evident in Bush's assertion before Congress on September 20, 2001, that "you are either with us, or you are with the terrorists," deprived the United States of potentially crucial international support. In addition, the Iraqis generally did not enthusiastically welcome coalition forces, and it quickly became evident that U.S. administration officials, having anticipated an easy transition to stability and democracy in Iraq, had made virtually no specific plans for an extended occupation. By midsummer Iraq was a killing ground as opposition to the occupation mounted and a dimly understood insurgency targeted U.S. troops and Iraqis with increasing violence. Worse, the chief rationale for the invasion came into question as searches turned up no weapons of mass destruction. With each passing month, Iraqi realities seemed to contravene the optimistic scenario that the Vulcans had been so successful in promoting.

In late June 2003, *Newsweek* noted that the mounting obstacles in Iraq had left Wolfowitz and his fellow neoconservatives in a difficult position. "Fairly or not," the magazine observed, "Paul Wolfowitz has become a lightning rod for much of this criticism, and to 'cry Wolfowitz' has already become a catchphrase for the pressing questions about U.S. credibility." The deputy secretary's credibility was clearly in dispute when he testified before the Senate again in 2004. Senator Hillary Clinton leveled a blistering attack noting, "You have made numerous predictions, time and time again, that have turned out to be untrue and were based on faulty assumptions." Wolfowitz dismissed her characterizations, especially regarding his low estimates of troop requirements, claiming that he had only been echoing General Thomas Franks. At House hearings in June, Wolfowitz confronted equally skeptical representatives. "I see two Iraqs," Congressman Skelton observed. "One is the optimistic Iraq that you describe . . . and the other Iraq is the one I see every morning, with the violence, the deaths of soldiers and Marines. I must tell you, it breaks my heart a little more each day." Again, Wolfowitz refused to concede that he had erred. Instead, he spoke of the brutality of the Baathist regime, comparing Saddam's secret police to Nazis, then accused the media of refusing to report the "good news" from Iraq. An article in the November 1, 2004 issue of the *New Yorker* offered an explanation for Wolfowitz's stubborn commitment to the Vulcan scenario for Iraq, regardless of actual events in that increasingly chaotic nation: the deputy secretary believed that the lengthy effort to contain Iraq was comparable to events in the late 1930s, when the civilized world failed to respond adequately to Hitler's encroachments on Austria and

Czechoslovakia. Wolfowitz, the writer noted, employed language "almost indistinguishable" from that of President Bush when referring to Iraq. "It is the stark tone of evangelical conviction: evil versus good, the 'worship of death' and 'philosophy of despair' versus our 'love of life and democracy.'" "Alongside Bush himself," the article concluded, "Wolfowitz is, even now, among the last of the true believers."

President Bush, reelected in 2004, continually issued public assurances that he was determined to "stay the course" in Iraq, despite an increasingly violent insurgency and warnings by numerous intelligence analysts that the U.S. presence there was actually winning new recruits for Islamic terrorist groups. When the search for WMDs was called off in 2004 and the Iraq Survey Group concluded that Saddam had not possessed any since 1991, the Bush administration's rationale for the war shifted to the contention that "the world was safer" because of Saddam's ouster in 2003, that Iraq was now "the central front in the war on terror," and that it was "better to fight them there than here at home." By 2005, as Iraq descended into a condition approaching anarchy, despite the establishment of a sovereign Iraqi government, the American public grew increasingly skeptical of both the rationale for the war and the likelihood of success in establishing a stable, democratic Iraq. That June, Wolfowitz left the Defense Department to accept the presidency of the World Bank. For those with a long historical memory, it was an ominous replay of history: in 1968, Secretary of Defense Robert McNamara, a chief architect of the U.S. war in Vietnam, had resigned his post as the public turned against the conflict and accepted the presidency of the World Bank. Wolfowitz, in an interview shortly after his resignation, continued to voice optimism about the outcome in Iraq, though he offered little in the way of evidence for his view. "Three years is a very short time into this," he declared. "War is a tough business. This has been a tough war." Such platitudes confirmed his detractors in their belief that Wolfowitz, together with the chief officials of the Bush administration, were dangerously obtuse, convinced of their own rectitude despite compelling contrary evidence. A significant but dwindling number of Americans, however, remained confident of U.S. success in Iraq and the realization of the Vulcans' vision of a transformed Middle East.

Paul Wolfowitz's influence on American foreign policy during the Bush presidency was immense, and its full consequences may not be knowable for years. Advocate of a controversial departure in U.S. international policy, he remains a controversial individual, hailed by some as a courageous visionary who laid the foundations for American hegemony in the twenty-first century. Even his detractors concede his intelligence and sincerity. One Washington insider who worked with him observed, "He isn't a hack. He's deeply misguided, he's impervious to evidence—and he's a serious, thoughtful guy." It was Wolfowitz's thoughtful, authoritative demeanor that made him such an effective proponent of the Iraq war, and many critics place blame for the debacle squarely on him. Historian Thomas Ricks quotes Iraq war veteran Paul Arcangeli as remarking, "I was actually surprised to find, the first time I met him, that he was pretty likeable, which surprised me, because I hate him. I blame him for all this shit in Iraq. Even more than Rumsfeld, I blame him." The embittered officer summed up the deputy secretary as "dangerously idealistic. And crack-smoking stupid." Author Tom Clancy came away from a Pentagon briefing with similar concerns. "Is he really on our side?" Clancy asked himself.

The inflamed rhetoric about Wolfowitz reflected the deep domestic divisions over the war in Iraq and the ambitious, idealistic, and controversial foreign policy that he and the other Vulcans implemented during the Bush presidency. The broader consequences of both could only be guessed at when Wolfowitz moved to the World Bank in 2005. During 2006, the violence in Iraq rose to near-apocalyptic proportions, with monthly civilian death tolls over 3,000 becoming commonplace in the last half of the year. The American public's rapidly growing disillusionment with the war was demonstrated in that November's congressional elections, which gave the Democrats a majority in both houses for the first time since 1994. Faced with broad electoral opposition to his policy of "staying the course" in Iraq, President Bush accepted the resignation of Defense Secretary Donald Rumsfeld, a chief architect of that conflict. The departure of Wolfowitz's former mentor did not, however, signal a repudiation of the foreign policy direction that the Vulcans had set in previous years. President Bush, rejecting the advice of the bipartisan Iraq Study Group in late 2006, settled on a policy of "surging" more U.S. troops into Baghdad with the objective of establishing a secure environment for sectarian reconciliation within the unstable Iraqi government. The success or failure of the strategy, both advocates and critics agreed, would not be ascertainable in the immediate future. As of fall 2007, the war in Iraq had cost more than 3,800 American lives, brought about an estimated 180,000 Iraqi deaths, and cost more than $500 billion. Wolfowitz, who had maintained a low profile after leaving the Defense Department, became embroiled in several controversies at the World Bank during this period. Determined to impose stringent conditions on World Bank funds granted to historically corrupt African nations, Wolfowitz provoked criticism from some members of the bank's board when he refused to write off the substantial debts of the Republic of the Congo. Others sup-

348

ported the director's stand, however, arguing that developing nations had to accept responsibility for the conduct of their governments. Simultaneously, serious ethical issues arose when it was revealed that Wolfowitz had used his position to ensure that Shaha Riza, his girlfriend who worked at the World Bank, was transferred to a lucrative post at the U.S. State Department with guarantees of retaining her salary and benefits at the World Bank. The former Vulcan claimed that the controversies were generated by those who hoped to discredit him as one of the chief architects of the Iraq war. On May 18, 2007, after weeks of controversy, Wolfowitz resigned as the World Bank's director. President Bush "reluctantly" acknowledged the resignation of one of the most ardent of the Vulcans. Though Cheney and Rice continued to serve the Bush administration, the policies that they and Wolfowitz had set in motion seemed less credible with each passing month, as conditions in Iraq deteriorated and instability threatened the entire Middle East. The reign of the Vulcans, it appeared, was coming to an inglorious end.

NOAM CHOMSKY
Radical Gadfly

In the days following the 9/11 attacks, President George W. Bush presented stunned Americans with a Manichean perspective on the unfolding struggle with terrorism, which he depicted in stark terms devoid of subtleties and nuance. His public rhetoric consistently affirmed America's innate goodness, evident in the nation's historical commitment to freedom and democracy, and contrasted it with the evil designs that motivated the terrorists. America's enemies were "evil-doers," the president asserted, who attacked because "they hate our freedoms." While such sentiments reached a receptive audience in the tense aftermath of 9/11, they did little, in the estimation of left-wing intellectual Noam Chomsky, to accurately explain the character of the challenge that Americans now faced. Yet Chomsky was not to be seen among the hundreds of commentators espousing their analyses on television in the weeks after the attack. CNN's Jeff Greenfield was unusually honest about why the man described by the *Dictionary of Modern American Philosophers* as "one of the most influential left-wing critics of American foreign policy" was rarely asked to appear on the air. Guests needed to "say things between two commercials," Greenfield stated, and Chomsky's observations rarely comported with the television medium's requirement for "concision." Long aware that these media constraints ensured that "you can only repeat conventional thoughts," Chomsky had most often turned to print to express his thoughts.

Thus, in a series of newspaper interviews in the weeks after the attacks, Chomsky presented his evaluation of recent events. His were not words of comfort and reassurance, but were instead calculated to compel thinking Americans to confront some very unpleasant realities, past and present. As to the motivations of the terrorists, Chomsky was blunt. The bespectacled, silver-haired professor noted the *New York Times'* assertion that "the perpetrators acted out of hatred for the values cherished in the West, such as freedom, tolerance, prosperity, religious pluralism and universal suffrage." "This is a comforting picture," he rejoined. "It happens to be completely at variance with everything we know, but has all the merits of self-adulation and uncritical support for power." To proceed based on of this flawed assumption, Chomsky warned, "contributes significantly to the likelihood of further atrocities, including atrocities directed against us, even more horrendous ones than those of 9/11." "It is much easier," he continued, "to personalize the enemy, identified as the symbol of ultimate evil, than to seek to understand what lies behind major atrocities. And there are, naturally, very strong tendencies to ignore one's own role." Chomsky also found much to criticize in the unilateralist policy of the Bush administration, characterizing the president's September 20 speech as "virtually a declaration of war against much of the world." The administration's vaunted war on terror was likewise challenged. "To call it a 'war against terrorism,'" he observed, "... is simply more propaganda, unless the 'war' really does target terrorism. But that is plainly not contemplated because Western powers could never abide by their own official definitions of the term, as in the U.S. Code or Army manuals. To do so would reveal that the U.S. is a leading terrorist state, as are its clients."

Such comments were extremely provocative in the aftermath of 9/11, but among the failings that Chomsky refused to countenance were intellectual sloth and hypocrisy. A rational, clear-headed examination of the nation's past, Chomsky had often argued, inevitably brought the inquirer to the inescapable conclusion that the United States had often acted in contravention of the standards that its leaders professed to embrace, provoking considerable ill-will around the world. He saw the same dynamics at work in the twenty-first century: "If we choose, we can live in a world of comforting illusions. Or we can look at recent history, at the institutional structures that remain essentially unchanged, at the plans that are being announced—and answer questions accordingly. I know of no reason to suppose that there has been a sudden change in long-standing motivations or policy goals, apart from tactical adjustments to changing circumstances. . . . The literature on this is voluminous. There is no reason, beyond choice, to remain unaware of the facts." This was vintage Chomsky—a clearly articulated, radically unorthodox perspective, often strikingly provocative, that virtually compelled the listener to respond. What was so maddening about Chomsky was that he insisted that Americans be willing to question their most closely held assumptions about themselves and their nation and to hold themselves to the standards that they set for others.

Noam Chomsky was literally born into a dissenting tradition. The child who entered the world in Philadelphia, Pennsylvania, on December 28, 1928, was the son of Dr. William Chomsky—a Jewish Russian émigré who had come to the United States in 1913 to avoid service in the czar's army. The doctor was a school principal, Hebrew scholar, committed Zionist, and member of the Industrial Workers of the World, arguably the most radical organization in the country. Noam's mother Elsie, also from Russia, was said to hold even more extreme left-wing views. As Chomsky's biographer has written, "One can only imagine the dinner-table conversations in such a household." Both parents encouraged Noam and his brother David to be independently minded and to strive to make the world a better place. Noam proved a precocious child, attending an experimental Deweyite school where free-ranging inquiry was encouraged. At age ten, Chomsky, writing for the school's newspaper, authored his first article, which dealt with the complex politics of the Spanish Civil War. Many of the themes that he first explored in that piece, such as the feasibility of popular mass uprisings against authority, reappeared in his adult writings. Developing empathy for underdogs at an early age, Chomsky remembered, "I was always on the side of the losers." The intellectual freedom that he enjoyed at Oak Lane was absent from Philadelphia's Central High School, where Chomsky first detected and resisted institutional regimentation and indoctrination. He experienced a major epiphany there, remembering that he suddenly asked himself, "Why am I cheering for my high school football team? I don't know any of those people. They don't know me. I don't care about them. I hate the high school." While in others this sentiment might have been interpreted as little more than typical adolescent rebellion, in Chomsky it signaled the beginning of a lifelong willingness to challenge convention and question behavior.

During his school years, Chomsky began to draw together the elements that would compose his eclectic adult political creed. Well versed in modern political theory, he drifted away from traditional Marxism in favor of a left-libertarian socialism or anarchism, which he saw as best meeting the needs of individuals and society. The writings of George Orwell, especially *Homage to Catalonia*, had a tremendous influence on Chomsky. In addition to praising libertarian socialism, the English author also insisted that "bourgeois" democracy and fascism were simply two different names for capitalism and that a free society could be achieved only through "workers' control." This somewhat simplified analysis had a lasting impact on the young Chomsky, who ever afterward questioned the fundamental American assumption that democracy and capitalism were equivalents. The lesson that Chomsky drew from Orwell and the Spanish Civil War was that both the United States and the Soviet Union acted to crush the liberation movement in Spain, the former by refusing to provide support for the anti-Franco forces and the latter by supporting Stalinist communist militias. Chomsky's growing disdain for orthodox Marxism, whether Leninist or Stalinist, led him away from the self-deceiving path that many leftist intellectuals trod in the years before World War II. He remained, intellectually, his own man, disciple of no specific creed. The Spanish conflict also first woke Chomsky to the difference between how events were depicted in the mainstream press and in the left-wing press. The vast disparity suggested to him that the mainstream media inevitably sought to define reality for the masses and maintain the status quo.

During the 1940s, Chomsky's intellectual odyssey continued as he was drawn to the writings of Dwight MacDonald, publisher of *Politics*, an influential leftist journal. MacDonald, a libertarian, renounced Marxism in 1946 and turned to troubling questions emanating from the recent war. Taking a provocative stance in a series of essays, MacDonald addressed the question of war guilt, not only the guilt of the German and Japanese people for atrocities their governments had committed, but also the responsibility of Americans and Britons for tragedies such as the massive civilian deaths caused by strategic bombing campaigns in Europe and Asia. It was not a direction of inquiry that many Americans were willing to pursue then or later, but Chomsky came to believe, as had MacDonald, that "the policies of governments should be judged by their effects and not by the reasons advanced to justify them." This principle underlay much of Chomsky's later critical evaluation of American foreign policy. In 1945, the sixteen-year-old Chomsky enrolled at the University of Pennsylvania, where he hoped to pursue a broad range of liberal studies. Soon disillusioned by the regimented curriculum, he gave some thought to dropping out and going to Palestine. He stayed at Penn, however, to study under Zellig S. Harris, who was renowned for his work in structural linguistics and discourse analysis. Harris encouraged Chomsky to study philosophy, math, and psychoanalysis. This eclectic curriculum earned Chomsky a bachelor's degree in linguistics, philosophy, and logic, all of which honed his analytical abilities. That same year, 1949, he married linguist Carol Doris Schatz; the couple eventually had three children.

During the next several years, Chomsky sought to balance his graduate education at Penn with his growing interest in the newly independent Israeli state. He had long supported the idea of a binational Palestine and could not endorse the idea of Israel as a Jewish state. Rather, he favored Arab-Jewish cooperation in a socialist society. Chomsky's later criticism of some Israeli policies, which led detractors to attack him as anti-Semitic, stemmed from this perspective. In 1953, the Chomskys joined a kibbutz in Israel for six weeks. Though he considered emigrating there, he never returned after this visit. Chomsky completed his PhD at Penn in 1955, producing a dissertation that was published in 1975 as *The Logical Structure of Linguistic Theory*. Here Chomsky built his foundational theories on the hypothesis that all children have an innate knowledge of basic grammatical structure common to all languages—a universal grammar. Over the next several decades, Chomsky dedicated much research and writing to implications that might be drawn from this theory, contending that the grammatical principles underlying language are innate and fixed and that the "productivity" of language was to be found in syntax, or generative grammar. He built an international reputation in the field of linguistics, though his theories did not always gain immediate acceptance. Nevertheless, one reviewer of *Logical Structure* acknowledged the scope of Chomsky's intellectual ambition by describing the study as "one of the first serious attempts on the part of a linguist to construct within the tradition of scientific theory-construction a comprehensive theory of language which may be understood in the same sense that a chemical, biological theory is ordinarily understood in those fields."

As a newly minted PhD, Chomsky found a faculty position at the Massachusetts Institute of Technology (MIT), where he taught language and philosophy and did research in linguistics. The young professor gained considerable attention in 1959 when he challenged B.F. Skinner's behaviorist theory in a review of the psychologist's *Verbal Behavior*. Chomsky argued against Skinner's theory that human behavior could be explained and controlled by the same external processes that control animal behavior. This perspective, Chomsky argued, failed to allow for human creativity. During these same years, Chomsky's commitment to intellectual inquiry based on rationality deepened, and he determined to apply the most stringent standards of what he called "Cartesian common sense" to the issues that he addressed. He also embraced the idea that discourse was most productive when the language used was clear and simple; verbosity was little more than obfuscation. This commitment to clarity and directness became evident as Chomsky entered the arena of public debate in the mid-1960s.

Events in the early 1960s compelled Chomsky to develop the rudiments of his perspective on American foreign policy. Alarmed at the effects of U.S. actions in Vietnam and Latin America, he made a commitment to the ideals that his parents had instilled in him and decided to begin working toward creating the "good society." "I knew that signing petitions, sending money, and showing up now and then at a meeting was not enough," he remembered. "I thought it was critically necessary to take a more active role." That meant a lifetime dedicated to persistent, thoughtful questioning of government policies. He viewed the upheavals on campuses and the "politics of the street" as unproductive, since history suggested that they would not bring about the necessary changes. Though Chomsky did participate in a few protests, such as the 1967 march on the Pentagon, his energies were directed toward urging Americans to ponder what their government did and why. The MIT professor did not immediately find a large audience. His first talks about the Vietnam War, he remembered, were often in churches "with maybe four people: the organizer, some drunk who walked in, the minister, and some guy who wanted to kill me." Chomsky's forthright criticism of U.S. policy in Vietnam found a broader audience with the 1966 essay "The Responsibility of the Intellectuals," which appeared in the *New York Review of Books*. The article introduced a number of themes that pervade much of Chomsky's writing. "The deceit and distortion surrounding the American invasion of Vietnam are by now so familiar that they have lost the power to shock," Chomsky declared, arguing that misleading government rationales offered for the escalation had an immediate historical antecedent in the U.S. intervention to overthrow Guatemala's government in 1954. If objectively examined, Chomsky reasoned, patterns of history often revealed the motive forces and objectives that governments sought to obscure, and objective analysis quickly revealed that American policies were not always as altruistic as many believed. Chomsky derided historian Arthur Schlesinger's assertion that the U.S. policy in Vietnam was "part of our general program of international goodwill." "Unless intended as irony," Chomsky wrote, "this remark shows either a colossal cynicism or an inability, on a scale that defies comment, to comprehend elementary phenomena of contemporary history."

Unlike many critics of the Vietnam War, Chomsky did not see the conflict as a terrible error or an anomaly in the pattern of U.S. international behavior. Vietnam was, he insisted, another episode in a lengthy history of self-serving policies that the United States, just like any other major power, routinely pursued. The United States was, in other words, no better or worse than other countries. This challenge to the deeply rooted concept of American exceptionalism, which held that a selfless and righteous United States was unique among nations, was one of the most "unsettling" contentions of Chomsky's writings. The essay also included a challenge to intellectuals, who bore "the responsibility to speak the truth and to expose lies." Too many intellectuals who "have already achieved power and affluence, or who sense that they can achieve them by 'accepting society' as it is and promoting the values that are 'being honored' in this society," he declared, had surrendered their intellectual independence. In 1969, in *American Power and the New Mandarins*, the increasingly prominent dissident denounced "the mentality of the colonial civil servant," which he perceived in those intellectuals who provided the rationale for America's imperial policies. As the violence in Vietnam escalated in the late 1960s, Chomsky was unsparing in his assaults on the deceit and deception that cloaked the reality of U.S. policy. In "After 'Pinkville'"—a 1969 essay titled in reference to a U.S. atrocity in South Vietnam—Chomsky wrote, "It is important to understand that the massacre of the rural population of Vietnam and their forced evacuation is not an accidental by-product of the war. Rather it is the very essence of American strategy." He wondered if "our history of extermination and racism is reaching its climax in Vietnam today." Later essays, such as "The Mentality of the Backroom Boys" (1973), criticized the policy makers who coldly approved policies that would mean misery, death, and destruction for untold numbers, inevitably claiming that the ends justified the means. Chomsky concluded with a painfully accurate summation of the course of U.S. policy in Vietnam: "Since the United States never succeeded in 'saturating the minds of the people' with a sufficiently attractive ideology, it turned to the easier task of saturating the country with troops and bomb and defoliants." No doubt it was comments like these that earned him a place on President Richard Nixon's "enemies list."

Chomsky's dissent against U.S policy in Vietnam was part of a broader criticism of Cold War policies, which the increasingly renowned professor challenged in writings that would span a quarter of a century. American Cold War policy, Chomsky argued, was driven less by anti-Soviet fears than by "the twin goals of reinforcing the private interests that largely control the state, and maintaining an international environment in which they can prosper." U.S. policies targeting states such as Vietnam, Laos, Cuba, Guatemala, and Nicaragua, he argued, stemmed from the determination to prevent the establishment of "a good example" of any state-economy model that might offer a serious alternative to capitalism. Chomsky argued that business interests were central in shaping foreign policy, seeking to ensure the dominance of American capitalism. Successful indoctrination, he argued, allowed these fundamental realities to go unchallenged by the general public. In the 1984 essay "The Manufacture of Consent," Chomsky discussed how an "official" perspective on affairs was created and sustained so as to secure the existing order against any substantive criticism. In democratic societies, where "the state lacks the capacity to ensure obedience by force," he wrote, "it is necessary to control not only what people do, but what they think." Core groups of public intellectuals were always willing to provide credibility to the official vision because "to achieve respectability, to be admitted to the debate, they must accept without question or inquiry the fundamental doctrine that the state is benevolent, governed by the loftiest intentions." These docile intellectuals would "establish a framework for possible thought that is constrained within the principles of the state religion" and "divert attention from the sources of our own conduct, so that elite groups can act without popular constraint to achieve their goals—which are called 'the national interest' in academic theology." Working from these analytical foundations, Chomsky, though less often in the public eye after the Vietnam War, continued to comment regularly on American foreign policy through the Carter, Reagan, Bush, and Clinton years.

Though Americans would not develop a significant interest in the issue of terrorism until the events of 9/11, it was an issue that Chomsky confronted in the 1960s, when some American leftists hailed the terrorist tactics of the

Vietcong in South Vietnam. Chomsky denounced Vietcong terrorism as unjustified, but maintained that there were circumstances in which terrorism could be justified—depending on the consequences "of using terror or not using terror." If terrorism could free a people from unendurable, inhumane conditions, then it might be justified. Its use boiled down, he maintained, to "questions of comparable cost, ugly as that may sound." Chomsky also challenged conventional thinking about terrorism when he asserted, "terrorism works. It doesn't fail. It works. Violence usually works. That's world history." He also argued that terror was not exclusively the weapon of the weak. As evidence, he cited the successful Nazi use of terror to suppress resistance in occupied Europe. Even more controversial was his frequent assertion that the United States was, according to definitions in its own official publications, a terrorist state. The U.S. Army manual, he noted, defines terrorism as "the calculated use of violence or the threat of violence to inculcate fear; intended to coerce or to intimidate governments or societies in the pursuit of goals that are generally political, religious or ideological." Throughout the final two decades of the century, Chomsky identified numerous U.S. actions and policies that met some aspect of that definition. To critics of this position he responded, as he often has, that the profession of idealistic goals does not justify the use of questionable means.

Ten years after the dissolution of the Soviet Union and at the end of a decade in which both the "new world order" and U.S. foreign policy seemed to defy precise definition, the horrors of 9/11 compelled Americans to address substantive foreign policy issues. Now an emeritus professor at MIT and senior scholar with the Institute for Policy Studies, Chomsky quickly demonstrated his readiness to speak to the myriad issues subsequent to the attack. His immediate thoughts, expressed in interviews collected in *9/11*, suggested that his analytical framework remained unchanged. Chomsky denounced the attacks, noting that he "condemned all terrorist actions, not only those that are called 'terrorist' for propaganda purposes." "We should recognize," he told one interviewer, "that in much of the world, the U.S. is regarded as a leading terrorist state, and with good reason." The 9/11 attacks, he stated, "are a gift to the harshest and most oppressive elements on all sides, and are sure to be exploited." He refused to characterize the emerging confrontation as between the civilized, democratic West and backward, fanatical Muslim fundamentalists, noting that the chief U.S. ally in the Middle East was the repressive Wahhabist Saudi regime. He also noted that "the U.S. is one of the most extreme religious fundamentalist cultures in the world," given the pervasiveness of religion in American culture and the political influence of evangelical Christians. Chomsky advised that the best course was to analyze and address the grievances that spawned terrorism while taking action against the perpetrators "within the rule of law." Unfortunately, he cautioned, "there has been, so far, a steady drumbeat of calls for violent reaction." By the time of the U.S. invasion of Iraq in March 2003, the intentions of the Bush administration were, in Chomsky's estimation, all too clear. That year, in *Hegemony and Survival*, Chomsky revealed his concern about the self-inflicted difficulties that the United States faced, which led him to new skepticism about humanity's survival. Reflecting on biologist Ernst Mayr's contention that the human form of intellectual organization might work in contravention of natural selection, Chomsky wrote, "We are entering a period of human history that may provide an answer to the question of whether it is better [for the survival of the species] to be smart than stupid. The most hopeful prospect is that the question will *not* be answered." The answer, he feared, would be that humans were a "biological error" and had, in their 100,000 years of existence, only worked toward their own destruction.

Behind Chomsky's grim perspective was the Bush foreign policy, which had taken clear shape within a year of the 9/11 attacks. "High on the global agenda by fall 2002," Chomsky wrote, "was the declared intention of the most powerful state in history to maintain its hegemony through the threat or use of military force, the dimension of power in which it reigns supreme." The Bush administration had unveiled an "imperial grand strategy," at the heart of which was the right of the United States to undertake preventive war. "Preventive, not preemptive," Chomsky emphasized. "Preemptive war might fall within the framework of international law. . . . Preventive war falls within a category of war crimes." Underlying this new strategy was "the guiding principle of Wilsonian idealism"—that Americans "are good, even noble. Hence our interventions are necessarily righteous in intent, if occasionally clumsy in execution." The proclaimed mission of transforming the world through democracy and capitalism was intended chiefly, however, to ensure the global dominance of the United States. The domestic component of this strategy was a radical transformation of American society, which would see the reversal of a century of progressive reforms and the rule of corporate interests secured. However, Chomsky maintained, Bush policies were already producing a dangerous global backlash, fueling anti-American sentiments even among peoples who had expressed sympathy with the United States in the aftermath of 9/11. "For Osama bin Laden," Chomsky concluded, "it is a victory probably beyond his wildest dreams." The "forward-leaning" policies of the neocons, he noted, had not served U.S. strategic interests. Though Saddam had been ousted, the likelihood of a stable, democratic Iraq was little more than a fantasy; the U.S. occupation there was "an astonishing failure." And, Chomsky observed, the Bush administration "was teaching an ugly lesson to the world: if you want to defend yourself from us, you had better mimic North Korea and pose a credible military threat."

Increasingly popular on the lecture circuit, where he was often booked for months in advance, Chomsky continued his comprehensive criticism of U.S. policy in 2004. In several interviews, he elaborated on central issues such as the Bush Doctrine, a policy that former Secretary of State Henry Kissinger had endorsed. Chomsky observed that Kissinger had unconsciously revealed the innate arrogance in the doctrine by noting that preemptive war could not be "a universal principle available to every nation." As for the doctrine's assertion that nations harboring terrorists were as guilty as the terrorists, Chomsky noted that the U.S government had in the past sheltered a variety of terrorists, most notably anti-Castro Cubans who carried out raids on that nation. Iraq was an issue of continuing interest, and as public opinion about the war began to turn, Chomsky noted that what criticism there was echoed that voiced against the Vietnam War—that the United States was doing the right thing but doing it badly. "The critics of the war point out that Bush didn't tell us the truth about weapons of mass destruction," he told a questioner. "Suppose he had told us the truth. Would it change anything? Or suppose he had found them. Would that change anything?" As always, Chomsky insisted that Americans should challenge their fundamental assumptions about the innate rectitude and soundness of U.S. policy, such as President Bush's claim that his administration was bringing democracy to Iraq. "It takes a minute's thought to see that there is no possible way that the United States and Britain would permit a sovereign, democratic Iraq," he declared, for, eventually, Iraqi Shiites would dominate the government and, together with their religious brethren in Iran, control "the core of the world's energy resources." Such developments would not bode well for U.S. interests.

Though foreign affairs remained of primary concern to Chomsky, he often turned his analytical talents toward domestic issues, arguing that the Bush administration's rightward path was a conscious effort to "benefit the superrich and corporations and to harm the general population." While the disparity between rich and poor grew, average Americans faced declining real incomes, longer working hours, and the consequences of government efforts to dismantle the social welfare system. The state of health care, Chomsky often declared, was an embarrassment for a modern, industrial democracy, and it had deteriorated during the Bush years. He summed up the crisis in a sardonic remark to a Harvard audience. The United States did have a form of universal health care, he observed—"They're called emergency rooms." Though he often challenged the efficacy of electoral politics, Chomsky urged Americans to participate in the 2004 elections, suggesting that where Green Party candidates were not running, Democrats were preferable to Republicans. The mild-mannered professor endorsed Green Party presidential candidate Paul Lachelier. After Bush's reelection, Chomsky noted that the president had triumphed with the support of only about 30 percent of the qualified electorate. "Not much of a mandate," Chomsky proclaimed, despite Bush's public claims to the contrary.

As Bush took the presidential oath for the second time in January 2005, many of Chomsky's early concerns about the direction of events in Iraq seemed to be borne out. Elections and the establishing of a new national government in Iraq did nothing to stem the spread of increasingly deadly sectarian and insurgent violence. Significant reconstruction languished because of the violence, and Iraqi oil production was never effectively restarted. To a growing number of Americans, the war in Iraq seemed a hopeless stalemate, draining billions of American dollars and wounding and killing tens of thousands. It was becoming clear that the United States had handed the radical Shiite regime in Iran, which had been unable to defeat Saddam's Iraq in a bloody eight-year war in the 1980s, a tremendous gift—the dismantling of Saddam's regime. With Iraq's future as a united nation increasingly in doubt, Iran stood poised as the new arbiter of regional power. The apparent failure of the new "imperial grand strategy" in Iraq had momentous consequences for U.S. policy worldwide, especially given the dearth of dependable allies. With North Korea and Iran threatening to pursue nuclear weapons, the United States seemed to face unprecedented challenges, and with frighteningly few options.

Chomsky addressed the nation's predicament in his 2006 book *Failed States*, in which he posited that imperial overreach abroad and a "deficit of democracy" at home seriously threatened the republic's future. It was the neoconservatives who had first pointed out the threat posed by "failed states" like Iraq in order to justify the invasion of that country. Deftly turning the phrase, Chomsky argued that, according to accepted criteria, the United States had become a failed state. These are nations, Chomsky observed, that are unwilling or unable to protect their citizens from violence, that regard themselves as beyond the reach of domestic or international law and hence free to carry out aggression, and that lack truly democratic institutions. The United States, he declared, had become such an "outlaw state," rejecting the authority of international bodies even as it endorsed torture and engaged in war crimes in the effort to stamp out the Iraqi insurgency. These policies, which had cost the United States the support of traditional allies and earned the intensifying hatred of much of the world, could be laid at the feet of neoconservatives such as Paul Wolfowitz, who had convinced Bush of the feasibility of their grand scheme for world democracy. Instead, Chomsky wrote, given the increasingly volatile circumstances in the Middle East, the likely spread of nuclear weapons, and the dangers posed by global warming, the world faced the prospect of "Apocalypse Soon."

While he attributed many of these difficulties to the obtuseness and ideological rigidity of the Bush administration, Chomsky also warned that the more fundamental problem lay in the structure and practice of American politics. The existing system perpetuated the powerful and affluent in office and insulated them from the public. Few congressional seats were actually competitive, and expensive campaigns, often funded by special interest lobbies, precluded the electoral aspirations of all but the wealthy, influential few. No real public discourse on significant issues ever occurred; instead, corporate-owned media focused on superficial concerns such as a candidate's likability. Wedge and hot-button issues were used to distract voter attention away from important issues and toward trivial concerns such as flag-burning and gay marriage. Consequently, many voters either succumbed to alienation and disengagement, or, beguiled by "values" politics, ended up consistently voting against their own economic interests. The elite who manipulated the electoral machinery were "reactionary statists" whose "policies serve the substantial people—in fact, an unusually narrow sector of them—and disregard or harm the underlying population and future generations." Ultimately, Chomsky discerned serious problems in almost every area of American life: the political system, the schools, the penal system, the social welfare system, and the national government. The new imperial strategy, he declared, was the inevitable adjunct of these developments. "No one familiar with history," he wrote, "should be surprised that the growing democratic deficit in the United States is accompanied by declaration of messianic missions to bring democracy to a suffering world." The need for action was urgent. "Reforms will not suffice," Chomsky counseled. "Fundamental social change is necessary to bring meaningful democracy."

Noam Chomsky's analysis of America's condition was distinctly at odds with the perspectives of the neoconservatives, and as the latter held the reins of power, there seemed little reason for optimism about achieving the degree of change that Chomsky called for. As of 2007, Chomsky was still excluded from the American mainstream media's spotlight, though his admirers have grown in number and include a number of rock stars. U2's Bono hailed Chomsky as "a rebel without a pause, the Elvis of academia," a characterization that the MIT professor would probably dispute. Both Rage Against the Machine and Pearl Jam have made known their affinity for his work, and R.E.M. once requested that he accompany them on tour. As public disaffection with the course of American foreign policy grew after 2001, Chomsky's dissident perspective retained its relevance, as did his prescription for reform:

> If you want to make changes in the world, you're going to have to be there day after day, doing the boring straightforward work of getting a couple of people interested in an issue, building a slightly bigger organization, carrying out the next move, experiencing frustration, and finally getting somewhere. That's how the world changes, that's how you get rid of slavery, that's how you get women's rights, that's how you get the vote, that's how you get protection for working people. Every gain you can point to came from that kind of effort.

Such declarations affirm the evaluation of biographer Robert Barsky, who observed that the quiet-spoken professor was not a Che Guevara, a Lenin, or a Mao. "He was," wrote Barsky, "a scientist who had rational ideas that made him famous in his field, and a social conscience that gave him the courage and the confidence to recognize that rationality could be employed to a greater end: encouraging people to think for, and believe in, themselves."

Conclusion

The radically divergent perspectives of Paul Wolfowitz and Noam Chomsky mirror the debate over America's role in the world that began unfolding as the earliest English colonists arrived in New England in the seventeenth century. John Winthrop, Puritan governor of Massachusetts Bay, famously proclaimed that the nascent settlement would be as "a city upon a hill," a model for the world to take note of and emulate. That conception of America's role was reiterated by many of the Founders, some of whom interpreted the French Revolution as evidence that the American model had been embraced abroad. Radical democrat Thomas Paine, renowned for his declaration that "the cause of America is in great measure the cause of all mankind," hailed the liberating mission of the United States: "The true idea of a great nation, is that which promotes and extends the principles of universal society." But Paine believed that the universal principle of liberty would be advanced not by war, but through "commerce, letters, and science." Thomas Jefferson's assertion that the United States would be an "empire for liberty" seemed to prefigure the emergence of a potentially more militant conception of America's mission. There were some who believed that America's destiny involved more than being a model for democracy and that the country should actively seek to spread the ideal. During an era of expansion in the 1840s, the concept of manifest destiny captured both the idealistic quality and crusading element of American democracy, as many justified the conquest of Mexican territory as expanding the area of freedom. Similar rationales emerged in the late nineteenth and early twentieth centuries, when the imperial urge took Americans beyond their continental borders and into distant lands where again it was argued that the United States was bringing the benefits of democracy to benighted peoples. The logic of democratic imperialism seemed to crest during the presidency of Woodrow Wilson, who authorized interventions in Haiti, Santo Domingo, Mexico, and finally Europe. However, by the 1920s, a cynical public sneered at Wilson's failed mission of "making the world safe for democracy," and the nation retreated into relative isolation. The signal change came in the aftermath of World War II—a conflict that the United States joined only after an attack on American soil—despite the obvious threat that the fascist powers, especially Nazi Germany, posed to democratic societies. The global conflict left the United States in a new position of international preeminence and in possession of unprecedented economic and military power, which could be turned to the realizing of the nation's historical mission, however policy makers chose to define it. During the half century of the Cold War, democracy was seen as a weapon in an essentially ideological struggle, and Americans were divided as to how it might be most effectively employed. Some continued to argue that the cause of democracy could best be served by extending and strengthening democracy at home; others retorted that the democratic model could be superimposed abroad, thus preempting the spread of communism. The debacle in Vietnam not only seemed to demonstrate that democracy could not be easily transplanted abroad, but created circumstances in which democracy at home came under assault by a government determined to limit dissent and suppress civil unrest. It was only after the collapse of the Soviet Union in 1991, however, that the proponents of imperial democracy encountered circumstances in which their theory could be adequately tested. With the collapse of the USSR, there existed no effective counterbalance to U.S. power. The events of 9/11 provided the pretext for the implementation of the "imperial grand strategy." What remains to be fully discerned are the consequences. Paul Wolfowitz and the Vulcans, heirs to the tradition of manifest destiny and Wilsonian idealism, theorized that democracy was a universal value and that the United States could ensure its security by maintaining hegemony over a democratized globe. Noam Chomsky, on the other hand, seemed to have more in common with those Founders who stressed the full realization of democracy in America. Since the 1960s, Chomsky has argued that American democracy is best nurtured and preserved through rational, objective analysis and the restoration of democracy at home. As of 2007, it remained to be seen which vision of America's future, if either, would be borne out by events.

Study Questions

1. What were the chief elements of the neoconservative foreign policy that took shape in the 1990s?
2. Discuss the major components of the Bush Doctrine and explain why it is controversial.
3. What events and ideas influenced Noam Chomsky's political beliefs?
4. Why are Chomsky's ideas about U.S. foreign policy "unsettling" to many Americans?
5. Discuss the strengths and weaknesses of the foreign policy perspectives of the neoconservatives and Chomsky.

Selected Bibliography

Ackerman, Spencer, and Franklin Foer. "The Radical." *New Republic*, December 1, 2003.

Barsky, Robert F. *Noam Chomsky: A Life of Dissent*. Cambridge: MIT Press, 1997.

Boyer, Peter J. "The Believer." *New Yorker*, November 1, 2004.

Chomsky, Noam. *Failed States: The Abuse of Power and the Assault on Democracy*. New York: Metropolitan, 2006.

———. *Hegemony or Survival: America's Quest for Global Dominance*. New York: Owl, 2003.

———. *Imperial Ambitions: Conversations on the Post–9/11 World*. New York: Metro, 2005.

———. *Middle East Illusions*. New York: Rowman and Littlefield, 2003.

———. *9-11*. New York: Seven Stories, 2001.

Clarke, Richard A. *Against All Enemies: Inside America's War on Terror*. New York: Free Press, 2004.

Galbraith, Peter W. *The End of Iraq: How American Incompetence Created a War Without End*. New York: Simon and Schuster, 2006.

Gordon, Michael. *Cobra II: The Inside Story of the Invasion and Occupation of Iraq*. New York: Pantheon, 2006.

Halper, Stefan, and Jonathan Clarke. *America Alone: The Neo-Conservatives and the Global Order*. Cambridge, UK: Cambridge University Press, 2004.

Hersh, Seymour M. *Chain of Command: The Road from 9/11 to Abu Ghraib*. New York: HarperCollins, 2004.

Hirsh, Michael. "Neocons on the Line Welcome to the Real World." *Newsweek*, June 23, 2003.

Kinzer, Stephen. *Overthrow: America's Century of Regime Change from Hawaii to Iraq*. New York: Times Books, 2006.

Mann, James. *Rise of the Vulcans: The History of Bush's War Cabinet*. New York: Viking, 2004.

Olmstead, Paul. "Fixin' for a Fight." *U.S. News & World Report*, October 25, 2004.

Packer, George. *The Assassin's Gate: America in Iraq*. New York: Farrar, Straus and Giroux, 2005.

"Paul Wolfowitz, Velociraptor." *Economist,* February 9, 2002.

Peck, James, ed. *The Chomsky Reader*. New York: Pantheon, 1987.

Pollack, Kenneth. *The Threatening Storm: The Case for Invading Iraq*. New York: Random House, 2002.

Ratenesar, Romesh, James Carney, and Mark Thompson. "Bush's Brainiest Hawk." *Time*, January 27, 2003.

Ricks, Thomas E. *Fiasco: The American Military Adventure in Iraq*. New York: Penguin, 2006.

Suskind, Ron. *The One Percent Doctrine*. New York: Simon and Schuster, 2006.

Thompson, Mark. "The Godfather of the Iraq War." *Time*, December 29, 2004.

Wolfowitz, Paul. "The United States and Iraq." In *The Future of Iraq*, ed. John Calabrese. Washington, DC: Middle East Institute, 1997.

———. "Victory Came Too Easily." *National Interest* 35, Spring 1994.

Woodward, Bob. *Bush at War*. New York: Simon and Schuster, 2002.

———. *The Commanders*. New York: Simon and Schuster, 1991.

———. *Plan of Attack*. New York: Simon and Schuster, 2004.

———. *State of Denial*. New York: Simon and Schuster, 2006.

Wright, Lawrence. *The Looming Tower: Al-Qaeda and the Road to 9/11*. New York: Alfred A. Knopf, 2006.

About the Authors

Blaine T. Browne completed a PhD in American history at the University of Oklahoma. Having taught at several universities and community colleges, he is currently a senior professor of history at Broward Community College, where he has been on the faculty since 1988. He was awarded the Children's Opportunity Group Endowed Teaching Chair in 2007. He has served twice as president of the Florida Conference of Historians, and is the author of numerous articles and several textbooks.

Robert C. Cottrell is a professor of history and American studies at California State University, Chico. He is the author of numerous works, including *Izzy: A Biography of I.F. Stone; Roger Nash Baldwin and the American Civil Liberties Union; The Best Pitcher in Baseball: The Life of Rube Foster, Negro League Giant;* and *Uncertain Order: The World in the Twentieth Century.* He is the recipient of several awards, including the system-wide (twenty-three campuses) Wang Award for Social & Behavioral Sciences & Public Services.